THE
CEREMONIAL
ANIMAL

D0813644

'Reminiscing Cushing' by the late Zuni artist Phil Hughte. Drawn in the early 1990s, this is one of a series of cartoons portraying the life of Frank Cushing, ethnographer from the Smithsonian Institution, who carried out research in Zuni Pueblo mainly during the years 1879–84. Hughte's original caption reads: 'An elderly Zuni is reminiscing about Cushing and some of the funny things he did. He is talking about the time Cushing dressed as a Plains Indian and had his photo taken.' From *A Zuni Artist Looks at Frank Hamilton Cushing: Cartoons by Phil Hughte* (Zuni, N. Mex.: Pueblo of Zuni Arts & Crafts, A:shiwi A:wan Museum and Heritage Center, 1994), 102–3. Photo: Adrian Arbib.

THE CEREMONIAL ANIMAL

A New Portrait of Anthropology

WENDY JAMES

WITH A FOREWORD BY

MICHAEL LAMBEK

OXFORD
UNIVERSITY PRESS

OXFORD

UNIVERSITY PRESS

Great Clarendon Street, Oxford OX2 6DP

Oxford University Press is a department of the University of Oxford.
It furthers the University's objective of excellence in research, scholarship,
and education by publishing worldwide in

Oxford New York

Auckland Bangkok Buenos Aires Cape Town Chennai
Dar es Salaam Delhi Hong Kong Istanbul Karachi Kolkata
Kuala Lumpur Madrid Melbourne Mexico City Mumbai Nairobi
São Paulo Shanghai Taipei Tokyo Toronto

Oxford is a registered trade mark of Oxford University Press
in the UK and in certain other countries

Published in the United States
by Oxford University Press Inc., New York

© Wendy James 2003

Foreword © Michael Lambek 2003

The moral rights of the author have been asserted

Database right Oxford University Press (maker)

First published 2003
First published in paperback 2005

All rights reserved. No part of this publication may be reproduced,
stored in a retrieval system, or transmitted, in any form or by any means,
without the prior permission in writing of Oxford University Press,
or as expressly permitted by law, or under terms agreed with the appropriate
reprographics rights organization. Enquiries concerning reproduction
outside the scope of the above should be sent to the Rights Department,
Oxford University Press, at the address above

You must not circulate this book in any other binding or cover
and you must impose this same condition on any acquirer

British Library Cataloguing in Publication Data

Data available

Library of Congress Cataloging in Publication Data

Data available

ISBN 0–19–926333–7
ISBN 0–19–926334–5 (Pbk.)

1 3 5 7 9 10 8 6 4 2

Typeset by Graphicraft Limited, Hong Kong
Printed in Great Britain
on acid-free paper by
T.J. International Ltd.
Padstow, Cornwall
and bound by
Biddles Ltd.,
King's Lynn, Norfolk

IN MEMORY OF
GODFREY AND PETER LIENHARDT

Preface

IT was first suggested to me by Henry Hardy, many years ago, that I should write an introductory book about social anthropology. At that time, the discipline was spreading out in many directions, and it was not easy to see how to go beyond the scope of existing texts to include a range of questions across the anthropological field, without losing the thread of any continuing argument. I wanted to write within the tradition I had been brought up in, and not vainly attempt an encyclopaedic overview of what is known in North America as the 'four fields' approach to anthropology—including archaeology, linguistics, biological, and cultural anthropology. Partly because of my daily efforts at teaching, and learning from, undergraduate students doing interdisciplinary courses reaching into the biological sciences and archaeology, as well as postgraduate students doing research in social anthropology, material culture, art and museum studies, and on topics in overseas development, I gradually began to see how some threads might be drawn together, and the present text is the result. I offer it as a new synthesis of the field, its roots firmly in the social science tradition but its branches reaching out to touch all these neighbouring fields. Important issues are arising across the anthropological spectrum, and some of these are indicated in the book.

I am indebted to all those students with whom I have discussed anthropology and sometimes argued issues in tutorials and classes over the years: students in the Sudan, in Scandinavia, and in Oxford particularly. Over time my colleagues have patiently clarified their special insights into large areas of common concern for my benefit; I am particularly conscious of learning a great deal in this way from conversations with Paul Dresch and Nick Allen. I was one of the last generation of doctoral students to be formally under the supervision of Professor Sir Edward Evans-Pritchard, whose writings had captivated me at an early stage when I was still an undergraduate studying geography; but I picked up most of the anthropological tricks of thought that I know from the late, and much missed, Godfrey and Peter Lienhardt.

A wide range of other people have unwittingly helped in the gestation of the ideas in this book: including Tim Allen, Dave Anderson, Shirley Ardener,

Talal Asad, Marcus Banks, Karin Barber, Fredrik Barth, Gerd Baumann, Janice Boddy, David Boucher, Hilary Callan, Tony Cohen, Elisabeth Colson, Ian Cunnison, John Davis, Alex de Waal, Don Donham, Mark Duffield, Richard Fardon, Ruth Finnegan, Kirsten Hastrup, Elisabeth Hsu, Eisei Kurimoto, Michael Lambek, David Parkin, Terry Ranger, John Ryle, Philip Smallwood, Marilyn Strathern, David Turton, and David Zeitlyn. I owe much also to late colleagues like Edwin Ardener, Abner Cohen, and Maurice Freedman; and to the late Okot p'Bitek, who first taught me not to take the conceits of Western social science too seriously. Several people have been good enough to read through and comment on earlier drafts of this text: Nick Allen, Hilary Callan, Philippe de Lara, Clare Harris, David Mills, Knut Myhre, Hélène Neveu-Kringelbach, Julia Powles, Jonathan Skinner, Richard Vokes, and Chris Wingfield. My husband, Douglas H. Johnson, has been a rock of support and good sense throughout the endless queries and vague ideas I have tried out first on him. He and our children Fiona and Roger have not only made some of the sharpest observations about my initial insights but have allowed me the periods of space and time I needed to bring this book towards completion, along with material and moral support for which I am deeply thankful.

I have concentrated here mainly on work in English-language anthropology, or on writings which are easily accessible in English translation. I hope readers will find a reasonable balance between older works from which we can still learn, and accounts of current research questions and findings. The illustrations may not all look conventionally 'anthropological', but then that is deliberate. The book is presented not only to students in the various subfields of anthropology, but to their friends who wonder what they are enaged in; to people in neighbouring disciplines—whether sciences or humanities; and indeed to all who may share a sense of wonder and curiosity about the nature and history of our imaginative, sometimes fierce but always vulnerable, species.

W.J.

Institute of Social & Cultural Anthropology
Oxford

Acknowledgements

I AM most grateful to Carlton Jamon, Director of the A:shiwi A:wan Museum and Heritage Center, Zuni, New Mexico, and to Tom Kennedy, Director of Tourism in Zuni, for helping arrange permission to use the Phil Hughte cartoon (frontispiece); to Gary Avey and Keith Kintigh for putting me in touch with the photographer Adriel Heisey (Fig. 2); to Elizabeth Edwards and Claire Freeman of the Pitt Rivers Museum in Oxford for arranging my use of Evans-Pritchard's photograph (Fig. 4); to the Oxford Playhouse and Leigh Colombick for putting me in contact with the *SeZaR* photographer Ruphin Coudyzer (Fig. 7); to Larry Wild for emailing his picture of *Shakespeare's R & J* (Fig. 8); to Janice Boddy for providing one of her images of the *zar* (Fig. 13) and to Karin Barber and Paulo Farias for supplying me with pictures of *oriki* performances (Figs. 16 and 17); to Arthur L. Olivas of the Photo Archives of the Palace of the Governors in Sante Fe for locating and sending pictures of the *fiesta* (Figs. 26 and 27); to Arkadiusz Bentowski for arranging access to and use of the photographic collection of the Royal Anthropological Institute (Fig. 28); and to the invariably helpful staff of the various commercial photo libraries I have used. Detailed acknowledgements are given with the figure captions.

Certain passages in the book draw upon textual material already published, and I would like to make the following acknowledgements. Chapter 2, section 2, includes some passages originally published in 'Illusions of freedom: a comment on Barth's individuals', *Journal of the Anthropological Society of Oxford*, 4 (1973), 155–67; the discussion of Evans-Pritchard's work in section 4 of the same chapter includes some revised versions of passages in my piece 'Evans-Pritchard, Sir Edward E. (1902–1973)', *International Encyclopedia of the Social and Behavioral Sciences* (Kidlington, Oxford: Elsevier Science Ltd.), 4937–41; the passage in Chapter 4, section 1, dealing with the history of the circular dance, includes material which appeared in 'Reforming the circle: fragments of the social history of a vernacular African dance form', *Journal of African Cultural Studies* 13 (2000), 140–52; in Chapter 8, section 2, the passage dealing with conception, pregnancy, birth, and the beginning of personhood draws in part on 'Placing the unborn: on the social recognition of new life', *Anthropology and Medicine*, 7 (2000), 169–89.

Contents

List of Illustrations xiv

Abbreviations xv

Foreword by Michael Lambek xvii

I. THE QUEST FOR PATTERN

1. Key Questions in Anthropology 3

2. Dialogues with Grand Theory 18

   1. The Search for Nature's Reasons 20

   2. Problems for the Anthropologist with 'Rational Choice Theory' 33

   3. Culture, 'Cultures', and Ethnography as an Art 36

   4. The Idea of a Social Science: And its Variants in Anthropology 40

II. SHAPE AND RHYTHM IN SOCIAL FORMS

3. Species, Space, and Time 53

4. Life in Motion: Daughters of the Dance 74

   1. Dance and Social Form: Ethnographies 75

   2. Dance and Social Form: Prototypes 84

   3. Melodies of the Air 92

   4. From 'Ways of Seeing' to the Production of Art 95

5. Ritual, Memory, and Religion 100

   1. Social Form as Drama: Memory, Expectation, and the Tendency of Words to Fail 100

   2. Major Themes in the Anthropology of Religion 118

CONTENTS

III. LANGUAGE AND THE MAKING OF PERSONS

6. Speech and Social Engagement   139
   1. *Approaches to Language*   142
   2. *Language within the 'Dance' of Social Life: Barber on* Oriki   149

7. The Dialectics of Gender and Generation   156
   1. *'Marrying out': Language and Logic of the Reproductive Game*   159
   2. *'Marrying in': Modern Kinds of Belonging*   167
   3. *An African Perspective: From Colonial to Post-Colonial Themes*   170

8. Human Bodies, Social Persons, and Conscious Selves   181
   1. *Mauss's Triangle: The Organic, the Psychological, and the Social*   182
   2. *The Beginnings and Endings of Persons*   196
   3. *Social Shaping of the Private Self: Ethnographic Cases*   202

IV. PRACTICE, PRODUCTION, AND POLITICS IN THE CEREMONIAL ARENA

9. The 'Home-Made' Patterns of Livelihood   213
   1. *Place, Home, and* Habitus   213
   2. *Work, Wealth, and Exchange*   226

10. Towards Large-Scale Modern Forms   237
    1. *The New Spaces: Communications, Cities, and Popular Culture*   238
    2. *The Modern Person and 'The Market'*   258

11. From Local to Global Peace and War   269
    1. *Theatres of Order and of Violence—and the Need for History*   269
    2. *States, 'Nations', and the Struggles of the People*   282

V. CONCLUDING ESSAY

12. Anthropology as a Human Science: Conversations with History and Religion   297

CONTENTS

Notes   307

Select Bibliography   346

Index   355

List of Illustrations

Frontispiece   'Reminiscing Cushing' by the late Zuni artist Phil Hughte   ii

1. Palaeolithic rock painting, Tanzania   32
2. View over Acoma Pueblo, New Mexico   60
3. Stonehenge: an ancient and special place   66
4. Preparing for the dance: Zande drums   76
5. *Pas de deux*: Fonteyn and Nureyev in rehearsal   89
6. The dancer 'sees the world': Fonteyn   90
7. *SeZaR*: an African 'Julius Caesar'   104
8. *R & J*: minimal form   104
9. Romeo and Juliet: classic style   105
10. *West Side Story*: George and Rita   105
11. Baal dancers: May Day, Northumberland, *c.*1910   113
12. The shape of expectation: the Baal fire ready for lighting   113
13. The *zar* spirit rises   114
14. Shia Muslims on the road to Karbala, April 2003   134
15. Sign Language   140
16. The bride's lament: Okuku, Nigeria   150
17. Sangowemi: *oriki* expert   152
18. Fonteyn: with mask   187
19. Building on each other's work: Makonde carving   227
20. Rhythms of industrial life (weekday): *Coming from the Mill*,
     L. S. Lowry   240
21. Rhythms of industrial life (weekend): *The Bandstand*, L. S. Lowry   241
22. Choreography of a late imperial afternoon: The Sudan Club, 1952   242
23. Nationalism embodied: Prague, *c.*1935   242
24. Camel racing for Elizabeth II and Philip   244
25. New traffic in old streets: Bath, 2000   247
26. Fiesta parade, Santa Fe   250
27. Zozobra burning, Santa Fe   255

28. Symbols through and through: a Seattle store   260
29. War's glory: *The Battle of Adowa, 1896*   275
30. Still hopeful: Sudanese guerrillas, 1971   291

Jacket illustration   *L'Arlecchino (The Harlequin)* by Gianfranco Missiaja,
© Schola San Zaccaria. This image must not be reproduced in whole or
in part without permission from the artist at Studio Schola San Zaccaria,
Castello, 4967, 30122 Venezia, Italy: www.schola-sanzaccaria.com;
www.scholasanzaccaria.it; e-mail info@schola-sanzaccaria.com; tel.
+39.041.5234343, +39.041.5221209; telefax +39.041.5228912
    Gianfranco Missiaja was born in Venice where he still lives and works.
He received a degree in architecture, having specialized in stage design
at the Venice Fine Arts Academy. He spent 21 years teaching design at
art institutes in Rome, Trento, Civitavecchia, and Venice. A member of
the Artists' and Architects' International Association, he has received
numerous prizes and international acclaim for his work and has exhibited
widely in Italy and abroad including the USA.

Abbreviations

ASA   Association of Social Anthropologists
JASO   *Journal of the Anthropological Society of Oxford*
JRAI   *Journal of the Royal Anthropological Institute*
SAR   School of American Research, Santa Fe

Foreword

by Michael Lambek

IN writing this book Wendy James rekindles a tradition. In the 1960s a series of eminent British social anthropologists—David Pocock, John Beattie, and Godfrey Lienhardt—wrote introductions to their discipline. Following the mode already established at Oxford by Evans-Pritchard, these were sketches of the scope and significance of anthropology as their authors saw it developing at the time. These books were distinct from the introductory classroom texts we are familiar with today, especially as they have developed in the USA since the time when Kroeber's classic text prevailed in North America.[1] They presumed a certain level of intellectual maturity and thoughtfulness in their readers, and they were essayistic rather than encyclopaedic in style. They exhibited the fact that central to anthropology is a set of ongoing arguments about how to understand social life and the human condition, and they offered not a lowest common denominator consensus nor an inventory of facts, but serious attempts to think through basic assumptions. Wendy James, Professor of Social Anthropology at the University of Oxford, has produced a book of this kind, happily reflecting with her more original title the wider horizons of today's anthropology. Like its predecessors, this 'new portrait of anthropology' will engage readers at all levels of acquaintance with the subject.

Wendy James stands in a distinguished lineage. Following geographically in the footsteps of her teachers, Edward Evans-Pritchard and Godfrey Lienhardt, she conducted extensive fieldwork in North-East Africa, in her case mainly among the Uduk and other minority cultural groups living on one side or the other of the Sudan–Ethiopian frontier. Like her teachers, she produced superb and original ethnographic monographs: *'Kwanim pa: The Making of the Uduk People: An Ethnographic Study of Survival in the Sudan-Ethiopian Borderlands* (1979) and the pathbreaking *The Listening Ebony: Moral Knowledge, Religion, and Power among the Uduk of Sudan* (1988). She also spent several years teaching at the University of Khartoum before returning to

Oxford, where she has made her mark, among many other ways, by conducting an ongoing seminar on North-East Africa and by her extensive contributions to a very rich series of books on Methodology and History in Anthropology (under the general editorship of her colleague David Parkin). She has also edited *The Pursuit of Certainty: Religious and Cultural Formulations* (1995), one of the first serious attempts to address the rise in 'fundamentalisms' of various sorts that emerged into anthropological discussion from the 1993 decennial meeting of the Association of Social Anthropologists, and she has co-edited lively collections in honour of each of her teachers, as well as three books on Ethiopia. Like many of her generation, Wendy James has had to wrestle not only with a changing academic scene but with the forces of politics and history and their impact on her research subjects. She has lived to witness the Uduk overrun by the civil war in the Sudan and dispersed into refugee camps. She has documented their disaster and resilience and has worked hard, together with her husband, historian Douglas Johnson, to seek solutions to the broader conflict.

Wendy James's latest book is much more than an introduction. It is a remarkably comprehensive, confident, and generous account of contemporary anthropology, a *tour de horizon* that covers much ground yet affirms a central intellectual core and a sure sense of direction.

Some features of James's portrait stand out. First, it is a rather crowded canvas. It does not swoop from 'great thinker' to 'great thinker,' painted in bold strokes, but is rather more pointillist in style, building its images as the sum of a remarkable number of detailed studies it comprehends and appreciates. If Collingwood or Evans-Pritchard stand somewhat larger than others, the overall effect is strikingly egalitarian; James portrays with equal interest the work of younger and lesser known scholars alongside that of more established figures. The author assumes that anthropology is a craft and she rests her case implicitly on the high quality of the craftsmanship.

Second, despite the size of the crowd, it is still recognizably a family portrait. While definitively beyond the divide that once separated 'social' anthropology in the UK from its 'cultural' counterpart in the US, James naturally draws most extensively on illustrations from the work of British scholars. Readers will note an underlying though muted Durkheimianism. The key intellectual figure here is less the uncle than the nephew, Marcel Mauss. Among the attractions are the attention to social classification, to social wholes and persons, and to the *techniques du corps*. Conspicuous by his relative absence is Radcliffe-Brown. Hence what this book represents is not the first, positivist wave of British Durkheimianism but a much more nuanced and mature one, filtered through successive readings of Mauss (and other figures of the *Année Sociologique*) and happily mediated by strains of French structuralism and Marxism, American culturalism, and of course, the British empirical tradition of superb ethnography.

Marx and Foucault are reasonably integrated, but no symbolic capital is drawn by invoking the constructors of grand theory, continental-style, nor from the deconstructors. It is important not to be misled by this; flamboyance and name-dropping are no substitute for the intellectual seriousness and honesty of the work and the tradition it represents. James is seeking precisely that which she describes as the aim of contemporary ethnography, namely 'psychological and philosophical depth' (p. 10).

Wendy James's striking title, *The Ceremonial Animal*, is of course borrowed from Wittgenstein. The full citation reads 'One could almost say that man is a ceremonial animal. This is, no doubt, partly wrong and partly nonsensical, but there is also something right about it.'[2] James shows us precisely what is right about it, going well beyond Wittgenstein's aphorisms to produce an elaborate picture of the ceremonial forms or patterns anthropology discovers in human life, while attending carefully to his reservations concerning general explanation. Wittgenstein suggests that much human activity is the expression of imagination, and yet he does not wish to reduce this to psychology. James grasps that the attribution 'ceremonial animal' is not as mentalistic as calling humanity the 'cultural animal' (or, for that matter, *homo sapiens*) as it has often been taken (e.g. by structuralists). 'Ceremony' assumes sociality in a way that 'culture' sometimes does not.

Hence James refuses to start with the single biological or psychological individual. In Durkheimian fashion, she is very interested in the concept of the 'person' as a social or moral category and in how persons are socially formed in the series of rituals and attention directed at them from conception, birth, and naming onwards. For James, the very notion of the individual—not to mention the advocacy of methodological individualism that often accompanies it—is itself a social product, the outcome of specific historical contingencies. And so she rejects both utilitarianism and biological essentialism and sees their critique, correctly in my view, as one of the ongoing intellectual tasks of anthropology. At the same time, James's approach is not one of naive social constructionism. 'Culture', she says, in a phrase that echoes Geertz, 'is not an add-on extra . . . It is built in . . . to our very capacity for sociality' (p. 5). Wittgenstein would have concurred.

The main point in all this is the firm commitment to avoid reductionism that stands as anthropology's hallmark. Thus 'ceremony', in James's usage, is not a sign or a symptom, neither a reflection of something more solid nor an effect of something deeper. Nor is ceremony performed necessarily or entirely as a means to some other end, but is an end in itself, or at least a means internal to a given end.[3] Although James does not move in such a direction, this could be compared to an Aristotelian account of virtue.

Note that she does not say the 'ritual animal'. This is wise, as 'ritual' has developed connotations, both outside anthropology and, somewhat differently, within it, that would have been unwanted. Specifically, James is at pains to avoid what she calls the 'aura of incense' (p. 124) that accompanies the term 'ritual', that is, the general religiosity that stems from its origins in Western Christianity. Whatever its applicability in the specific case of Aboriginal Australia, Durkheim's general distinction between absolute spheres of 'sacred' and 'profane' is dismissed for similar reasons. James would also demur from the way some Durkheimians have interpreted ritual in either functionalist or reflectionist terms. For James, ceremony cannot reflect (or represent) 'society' because it is intrinsic to what we mean by society. 'Ceremonial' is thus a somewhat freer term than 'ritual', connoting, in my mind, at least, a kind of bodily gracefulness that James picks up in her image of the dance. Indeed, James's inspired metaphor of choreography brilliantly captures the idea of form in motion, hence bridging insights of both the 'structure' and 'embodiment' schools of theory. James understands the patterns and rhythms of embodied action to be apparent in the way humans make and respond to music and dance, but also as implicit in all forms of activity, as 'primary phenomena of human life' (p. 92).

Conversely, James is wary of giving pride of place to the human capacity for language. Or rather, she is mistrustful of looking to language as an abstract, decontextualized, unchoreographed phenomenon. Like Wittgenstein, who wrote that, 'Philosophy is a battle against the bewitchment of our intelligence by means of language', James does not find 'explanation' in words a necessarily superior way to grasp the existence of ritual performance.[4] Like Bakhtin and linguistic pragmatists, she attends to the sociality of language, to the fact that language is instanced in the situation of speech. Like Durkheim and Mauss, she is interested in exploring the categories of understanding, such as space, time, and causality, that must underpin language and society and that, as James suggests, 'encompass cultural variation' and the differences between specific languages (p. 54). Language thus is not an autonomous tool which individuals can apply in order to reason 'freely' so much as always already socially situated. We can certainly use language to reflect on our sociality, but we cannot look to language as a means of transcending it or as an independent model for it.

A somewhat unusual and admirable feature of this book is that James does not draw back from her assumptions when confronting the human capacity for violence. Aggression, she argues, is neither more nor less human than any of the other practices she has described. This is certainly not to naturalize or condone it. Just as she extends her emphasis on the ceremonial to politics, the city, and the economy, and sees ceremoniousness as possibly a more profound characteristic of humanity than rationality itself, so she entertains the 'deeply ceremonial' quality of human acts of war and violence as well as of peace. This is not a complacent picture; at the same time, she is careful to specify the historical contexts—especially the modern state—in which particular acts, representations, and fantasies of violence emerge and are supported.

This contemporary portrait of anthropology is especially welcome for its comfortable forthrightness. James does not spend too much time in post-modern ontological hand-wringing about whether our subject still exists or whether it ever did, nor in epistemological quandaries about what we can know, nor yet in ethical anxiety about our rights to know or to conduct and report on research. Nor does she worry unduly about boundary problems, about what distinguishes anthropology from neighbouring fields like sociology or history. Indeed, she appreciates the overlap.

Although Wendy James is quietly assertive rather than defensive, I will resort briefly to the latter, weaker stance, the better to mark the importance of her achievement. In North America in recent years cultural anthropology has had trouble defining itself. It is confronted by a fragmentation into sub-disciplines (such as medical anthropology) and a variety of special interest groups each clamouring for equal recognition and representation as auto-nomous fields of inquiry in a fashion that seems to violate both Maussian and Boasian understandings of holism even while it expresses the very ration-alizing, fragmenting, and competitive tendencies of modernity that the field has subjected to critique. Anthropology has also had to come to terms with a changed world in which its traditional subjects have seemed to dis-appear—whether through incorporation, transformation, or objectification, and whether through the sheer erosion of meaning, autonomy, value, and purpose produced by the combined onslaught of colonialism, capitalism,

Christianity, and commodified consumption or by their creative reappro-priation in multiple novel refractions of 'modernity'. Since its onset, but sadly exacerbated in recent years, anthropology has been witness to immense tragedy, injustice, and horror, ranging from increasing impoverization and exploitation, to outbreaks of violence and torture (whether occasioned by states or by their dissolution), to the deep insecurities produced by continuous 'low level' warfare or the fluctuations of capital. Despite the evident urgency of understanding and reporting on such matters, anthropology's relevance in the academy has been challenged by fields with stronger funding sources and more 'flexible' or ostensibly 'muscular' methodologies and research agendas that fit better with the current hegemony. Anthropology does not attract wealthy philanthropists and would shun corporate partners. Much as it dis-misses utilitarian explanations, as James describes in this book, so it is not itself immediately useful to government or industry, and hence not the recipi-ent of the attention that, in the present political and economic ('neoliberal') climate, appears to be necessary for success within the academy. To top it off, many of anthropology's assumptions and discoveries get rediscovered (or anachronistically critiqued) by some of the very disciplines that are expand-ing at its expense. In sum (and in some exaggeration), anthropology has risked losing its confidence, centre, institutional position, and sense of balance.

Here lies the significance of this book. In Wendy James's hands anthropo-logy remains an essential (i.e. critical) and distinctive tradition of debate and inquiry from which to grasp the human condition in its universal, existential purity and in all its historical messiness. Anthropology provides both a substantiation of philosophy and a philosophy of human substantiality—of embodied persons mating, caring, fighting, reasoning, creating, exercising judgement, producing livelihoods, engaging in politics, celebrating, and all the surprising and diverse ways these are integrated. 'Philosophy', as James paraphrases Collingwood, 'should not be founded on pure metaphysical speculation transcending any particular starting point but should operate critically from the present upon the whole range of ways in which we can dis-cover that humanity has thought' (p. 55). As against much philosophy, she rightly insists that those who take 'the abstract individual, and his or her exercise of reason, or of choice, or creative talent as the locus of human nature, have missed the key point that human life is irreducibly shared' (p. 8). Sociality, relatedness, being and action in cognized time and in space are fundamental. Our ceremoniousness, the manifestation of mindful bodies and embodied minds located in social communities, is not to be reduced to biology, economics, or psychology, nor to the contemporary reigning paradigms of these fields—which, from an anthropological vantage, are largely the rationalizations of wider and more powerful social forces.

No two portraits of any subject will be identical and, like anyone else, anthropologists look with a critical eye at portraits of themselves. But readers will find much to celebrate in this distinctive and lively canvas. James's portrait is congenial to me because it is serious, thought-provoking, thorough, engaged with substantive ethnographic material, and philosophically attuned. It sustains the difficult path 'beyond objectivism and relativism' that so well distinguishes the best anthropology from Mauss through Evans-Pritchard and Geertz to the present.[5] The centre of balance is located firmly within the anthropological tradition and the scholarly activities of contemporary field-workers. In this book anthropology retains its voice as an active, exciting, deeply intellectual, and yes, ceremonial discipline. I welcome you to a magnificent overview of the subject.

3 March 2003

NOTES

[1] E. E. Evans-Pritchard, *Social Anthropology* (London: Allen & Unwin, 1951), *Social Anthropology and Other Essays* (New York: The Free Press, 1962); D. F. Pocock, *Social Anthropology* (London & New York: Sheed & Ward, 1961); J. H. M. Beattie, *Other Cultures* (New York: The Free Press, 1964); and R. G. Lienhardt, *Social Anthropology* (London, New York, & Toronto: Oxford University Press, 1964). Cf. A. L. Kroeber, *Anthropology* (New York: Harcourt Brace, 1923, 1948).

[2] L. Wittgenstein, 'Remarks on Frazer's Golden Bough', in James Klagge and Alfred Nordmann (eds.), *Philosophical Occasions 1912–1951* (Indianapolis & Cambridge: Hackett, 1993), from an original dictation *c.*1931. An abridged version from an earlier translation is readily available in M. Lambek, *A Reader in the Anthropology of Religion* (Malden, Mass.: Blackwell, 2002). Wittgenstein no doubt meant 'man' in the generic sense of 'humankind'.

[3] I refer here to the discussion by MacIntyre who calls a means 'internal to a given end' when the end 'cannot be adequately characterized independently of a characterization of the means'. A. MacIntyre, *After Virtue* (Notre Dame, Ind.: University of Notre Dame Press, 1984), 184.

[4] L. Wittgenstein (1953), *Philosophical Investigations*, trans. G. E. M. Anscombe (New York: Macmillan, 1953), section 109.

[5] Cf. R. J. Bernstein, *Beyond Objectivism and Relativism* (Philadelphia: University of Pennsylvania Press, 1988).

PART I

The Quest for Pattern

CHAPTER ONE

Key Questions in Anthropology

THE questions we ask about the past and the present, not to mention the future, are mostly attempts to divine some kind of *fitting shape* in the material world, in events, and in people's actions—partly because we have to respond to all these, especially the latter. From where do we get our feeling that there must be significant design and reason behind the appearance of things? Do we re-theorize the world and what other people are up to each time we leave our front doors? Sometimes, perhaps, we do. But most of the time, we operate with patterns of expectation we have learned through sharing our language, ideas, and life with others since we were born. Our sense of intellectual and personal being does not exist in a vacuum—we are engaged in continual games of give-and-take with the acts and thoughts of others, as we work, play and fight, grow up, grow old, and reproduce our families, our languages, even the wider forms of our political economy. It is not easy to find universal rules of psychology, social need, or evolutionary advantage which account for the very elaborate forms in which we conspire, sometimes very close to home, in the project of creating, maintaining, and drawing others into sharing the patterns we make in the way we live our lives together. Anthropologists, however, have always specialized in describing and trying to interpret these forms, drawing both on science and on the literary imagination in doing so. This book is an account of these efforts. It is a polemical one in that it repeatedly points to the shortcomings of reductionist explanations and champions, by contrast, the capacity of the anthropological imagination to empathize with, reconstruct intellectually, and analyse comparatively the way in which human beings collude in the making and transmission of the shapes of social life.

The biological scientist and well-known writer Matt Ridley recently re-posed an old question: 'What is society but a collection of individuals?'[1] It is a deceptively easy question. What makes a set of individuals a society is not necessarily obvious; it may be silent, or implicit, because people often relate to each other through unspoken memories and expectations. These shared, if tacit, understandings of how to engage with others in appropriate (or even significantly inappropriate) ways make it possible for us to sense that there are depths to the *forms* of social life. These are not easy to observe and compare. What we need is a way of first conceptualizing their underlying coherence, and then analysing their relation to the material world and its workings. Nick Allen, an anthropologist who has done fieldwork in Nepal and India, and who has a particular interest in long-term aspects of human history, especially in the Indo-European world, has offered a helpful formu-lation here. Social anthropology's task aims 'to come to terms intellectually with the whole range of socio-cultural forms about which we can know'. He explains further that 'although encyclopaedic knowledge is by no means to be despised, the highest aim of a discipline cannot be to maximise the number of known facts within its remit, but rather to know what to make of them. . . . Sometimes one needs not so much to understand the facts as to understand what sorts of question have been asked of them and with what success.'[2]

While general comment on the social life around us is easy, and indeed an everyday pastime we all indulge in, serious description-cum-'explanation' (because the two *are* linked)—or even framing the right sort of questions—has proved to be extremely difficult. Think for a moment how you would describe-and-'explain' to different kinds of visitors the opening of Parliament in London, or American Thanksgiving, or the role of a peacekeeping army in a war zone, or the game of chess anywhere, even a nod, a handshake, a wink between friends. A dozen accounts could be offered, some mutually con-tradictory; there is so much else going on in life besides language. How you accounted for such events would depend in part on what questions you asked, who you were talking to, and what you assumed were their own con-cerns. Most accounts would be angled and might seem to miss the wholeness, what we might call, evoking Marcel Mauss, the *morphology* of these occasions as social phenomena.[3] For human behaviour is not a category of data one can easily dissect for observation. Edwin Ardener pointed out how the very notion of 'behaviour' is deceptive as a neutral observer's term. 'To behave' once meant to comport oneself, to behave well, or badly in a moral sense (we could ask whether 'behaviour' includes what people say about their actions). Ardener also suggested that the attempt to document the minutiae of social life as though they were explicable without reference to an encompassing social context was a waste of time: puzzling data about micro-movements of chairs scraping on a floor over a week could be suddenly illuminated by the realization 'this is a dining room . . . except on Thursdays when it is a dance hall'.[4] The recognizable whole here has an overall choreography, which changes on one day of the week. We shall return at various points in this book to the imagery of 'choreography' as a shorthand for grasping the idea of social form in movement, its deeply ceremonial character, the place of language and feeling within and perhaps against it, and its organic implication in the history of those structures of wealth, authority, and power, within which we all live. Existing uses of 'society' and 'culture' seem too fixed.

Difficult though it is, the ambition to 'explain' at one level or another has driven the discipline of anthropology since its beginnings. The current waves of uncertainty in the social sciences about the very possibility of general explanation, or even systematic comparison, leaves us in the field of anthropology with something of a dilemma. It is sometimes supposed that we are content to celebrate cultural diversity and interpret singularities for their own sake, as we have always, notoriously, taken an interest in the widest spectrum of human pecularities—witchcraft, cannibalism, and so forth. It is sometimes thought even by students that anthropology explores and catalogues cultural difference for its own sake, delighting in its rare and specific forms, and that the job of attempting 'explanation' lies with genetics, or economics, or psychology. But the nobler aim of anthropology has always been to relate the diversities of cultural expression to the basic material conditions of bodily and social life—for example, the meeting of the sexes, child care, the provision of food and shelter, and the drive to survival of a demographically viable group, even at the expense of other groups. Culture is not an add-on extra to the maintenance and reproduction of our organic life, nor to the investment of labour in productive activity, nor to our capacity for political aggrandizement. It is built in to these activities and to our very capacity for sociality—that is, of relating in mutually intelligible ways to others, including our 'nastier' warlike capacity for making enemies. The deeply encultured way we pursue these activities often has an unthinking momentum of its own, though the particular gift of language makes it possible for us to reflect intellectually upon what we do, and even to perceive the ways in which we act as historical phenomena in themselves.

How are we to maintain the goal of explanation or even improved general understanding of the compulsive pressures behind the phenomena of social action? Is it possible to focus on the character of those encoded patterns we live by, their relation to the 'reason' we associate with language, and their recursive connectedness over history? The philosopher Ludwig Wittgenstein, well known for his dissatisfaction with the explicit levels of language as the only locus of thought and communicable experience, made some pertinent observations for the anthropologist in the course of his commentary on the famous work of James Frazer, *The Golden Bough*. This was a massive, multi-volume work of the early twentieth century on the roots of religion, surveying an extraordinarily rich range of myth and ritual from all over the world. Wittgenstein noted how some phenomena as experienced, such as fire, come to make a direct impression on the human mind, leaving verbal 'explanations' redundant, whether those of the native or of the anthropologist. He seemed to identify as more 'basic' the kind of actions commonly distinguished as 'ritual'. He suggested, for example, 'One could begin a book on anthropology by saying: When one examines the life and behaviour of humankind throughout the world, one sees that, except for what might be called animal activities, such as ingestion, etc., etc., etc., human beings also perform actions which bear a characteristic peculiar to themselves, and these could be called ritualistic actions.'[5] We might be a little careful, however, about accepting any hard and fast line between everyday activities and 'ritualistic' actions. This would be a falsely sharp distinction to make across the board; taking food certainly, and probably any other humdrum biologically necessary activity of human beings, is surely always different in quality from the activities of 'other animals'. If we open our eyes to the coded way in which all aspects of our lives are led, we can endorse more fully, and for anthropological purposes of comparison and explanation more usefully, Wittgenstein's comment that we could view the human species as 'the ceremonial animal'.[6] He does not in this context use the phrase 'forms of life', though recent commentators have often chosen to point to it as a particularly clarifying phrase in his later writings, capturing the presence of a lived reality behind language. This idea lends itself very suggestively to my line of argument in the present book, that we should try to *see* as clearly as we can, for what they are, the lived-in ceremonial forms in which we pass our days. As Rodney Needham puts it, ritual is 'a kind of activity—like speech or dancing—that man as a "ceremonial animal" happens naturally to perform'.[7]

Ritual, symbol, and ceremony are not simply present or absent in the things we do; they are built in to human action. Examples of human action free of them are impossible to find, because all human action relates in some way to arenas of culturally specified significance we participate in with others. The technical and the ritual do not form distinct classes in nature or in life. They participate in one another in different degrees. The Oxford philosophy don R. G. Collingwood, active in the 1920s–1930s and like Wittgenstein and many other writers of the time an eager reader of *The Golden Bough*, has provided a range of suggestions we can draw on here. Collingwood was not only a teacher of ancient civilization and philosophy but a practising archaeologist throughout his life, specializing in Roman Britain. Many of his philosophical writings bear directly on questions of how we understand ourselves, not in relation to abstract metaphysical truths as such, but in relation to history and the historically rooted kinds of understanding we have inherited from the past. He proposed that concepts of the kind we often tend to contrast and oppose within a broader field did not necessarily exclude each other in essence. They can be looked at as related terms in a series, in which classes overlap. There may be as many aspects of connection as of distinction in such a series, for example as between steam, water, and ice. This model of a 'scale of forms' would lend itself very effectively to the shades of ceremonial colouring we always find in the range of human actions, however distinguished as work or play, utility or ritual.[8] To assume there must be 'pure' forms of this kind, as polar opposites, is an academic conceit. Actions, however plain, tend to carry something of the ambivalent about them, to refer implicitly to other actions and actors off-stage, and thus to resist reduction to plain singular meaning. Through action, as well as speech, we can represent and re-represent things, we can call one thing by the name of another, we can cover up alternative interpretations innocently or deliberately. We can produce art, irony, jokes, and challenge the authority of official representations. We can play upon the emotions of our fellow participants or audience, evoking in them joy, or fear. Our way of behaving commonly lends itself to multiple readings. This is why simple description by an observer (or 'ethnography') is always incomplete and often deceptive. This is why a focus on the 'ceremonial' character of human life is my key motif in the present book, as an image of the human condition against which other broad and sometimes ambitious explanatory schemes within the human sciences can be set, and found wanting.

The scholar often seems to operate in a self-referential space. Silent reading no doubt encourages this feeling, and reading philosophy positively cultivates it. But we do not exist alone, and arguably do not think, feel, or imagine the world independently. Those philosophies and social sciences which have taken the abstract individual, and his or her exercise of reason, or of choice, or creative talent as the locus of human nature, have missed the key point that human life is irreducibly shared. We live our lives, as children, women, men, even as scholars, in shaped spaces of connection to others, and to larger schemes of which we are (and can only be) partially aware. It is these patterns of relatedness, and the universal human sense of participating at one level or another, with greater or lesser effectiveness, in a locally 'formatted' social space, that anthropologists focus on.

There has been a long tradition of debate in social and cultural anthropology about the relation between the life of the individual and the persistence of wider forms within which this life finds significance. Many reductive arguments have been put forward, have played a recurring role in anthropological debate, and in several cases are still with us. In the next chapter I point to some of the problems they run into, and argue that the human sciences must accept our individual dependence on historical forms of sociality and a capacity for complex cultural learning as integral to our condition. We require a new way of speaking about the formation and re-formation of social life. In Part II, I invoke and develop the image of the choreographed quality of sociality in general: from the shapes and rhythms of our way of handling space, time, and of knowing nature; through the dance-like character of our lives in action, in work as well as play, in the ubiquitous nature of music and art; to the power of religious and ritual forms in the making of memory. I then consider, in Part III, how language as a shared medium of life enhances the individual person as a conscious locus of experience and agency; but how, at the same time, the very reproduction of ourselves as organic beings who bear this consciousness is achievable only through complex—and yes, 'ceremonial'—structures of reciprocity in the making of kinship, marriage, and family life. Part IV moves on to consider more aspects of the collective choreography of social form: of the patterned nature of geographical settings, of production and exchange, wealth and power; and of the theatrical aspects of political process, traditional and modern. Cities are considered as showplaces; large-scale, as well as small-scale, economic activities are shown to be as much arenas for cultural and personal display as for the operations of rationality; and the question is raised as to how far our sense of reason, employing mere language, can exert any influence over the spectacular clashes of states and clamour of nations.

What anthropologists do today

Anthropology used to be a specialist and arcane discipline, a hobby for a few, and a profession for even fewer. Today, especially perhaps in the anglophone world, but also in continental and eastern Europe, Asia, Africa, and Latin America, it is enjoying tremendous expansion as an academic subject, through its own diversification and in its combination with other subjects. Varieties of anthropology have also engaged the public imagination and stimulated a great deal of popular writing, photography, film, and programme-making for the media. The current range of research in anthropology and its inter-disciplinary combinations is extraordinary, and only a small proportion would fit the earlier stereotype of the lone ethnographer documenting unknown tribes, as a natural scientist might seek to discover flora and fauna. Consider, for example, Georgina Born's exploration of the way in which powerful institutions of modern culture and the media, such as IRCAM, the world-class Paris music research centre, or the BBC, operate as symbolically and ceremonially dense human communities directing the stream of sophis-ticated technical outpourings which influence us all; Mukulika Banerjee on the historical memories of a 'pacifist' anti-colonial movement among Muslims on the Afghan/Pakistan border, valued memories now very much at odds with today's images of the region's endemic social violence; Sarah Franklin on the question of how far we are culturally shaping, rather than being passively shaped by, scientific advance in the medical, agricultural, and reproductive fields.[9]

Only a small part of the work of anthropologists is now directly to do with recording the ways of life of 'traditional' communities. A recent collection of essays by distinguished anthropologists entitled *Exotic No More: Anthropology on the Front Lines* brilliantly argues the relevance of the discipline for the world of affairs (including inner-city poverty, organ-stealing rumours, hunger, refugees, aid and the politics of global power, socialism, race and gender, chil-dren's rights, media, music, art and tourism, religious fundamentalism, and more).[10] The expansion of anthropological activity signalled here is impor-tant and vital, and the book makes excellent reading for anyone needing persuasion on this point; at the same time, in my view, the older questions and curiosities about comparative cultural history and the range of human experience remain valid. They remain specific to our field of study and there-fore of high priority. There are still unrecorded languages and 'unknown' communities in the world: we should not apologize for our continuing disciplinary commitment to primary, open-ended ethnographic research among them. This is not just a matter of recording facts, but of seeking to extend as far as we can our qualitative understanding. Ethnography in 'tribal' communities today aims at psychological and philosophical depth. For example, Steven Feld and Alfred Gell have written striking studies of the culturally organized perception of sound among the Kaluli and the Umeda peoples of New Guinea, opening up a new agenda for 'aural' anthropology (discussed further in Chapters 4 and 9).[11] Akira Okazaki's exploration of dreaming as a social as well as private phenomenon among the Gamk of the Sudan (earlier known as Ingessana) fully rewards the effort of reading primary ethnography and at the same time, through a parallel drawn with pre-Freudian European ideas about dreaming, helps contextualize modern self-understanding.[12] Laura Rival's work among the Huaorani of the lowland forests of Ecuador strikes at the heart of issues concerning gender, sexuality, and birth, providing a point from which we have to seriously reconsider our conventional notions of parenthood and the beginnings of 'personhood' (this example is elaborated in Chapter 8).[13] In classic style, these ethnographers did not define their topics in a cut-and-dried way from the start; they developed a number of specific foci of interest in the course of prolonged and language-intensive fieldwork. The quality of the results justifies the importance that anthropology has traditionally claimed for the method.

Recent 'exotic' studies of this kind have benefited from the newly sensitive and often inter-subjective approaches to social life and experience which have been developed 'close to home', especially in studies of western European and North American communities. Here, one is obliged to admit historicality, self-reflexive understandings, plurality and multiplicity of perspectives, different and competing registers of meaning, individual agency, political power, and the give-and-take of cultural exchange at many levels across regions. Instead of seeking the holistic comparison of one exotic society (or 'culture') with another, the most interesting anthropology now seeks to transpose the scholar's own experience of social life and his or her own historical circumstances to the context of life among others whose experience is not so much radically, as subtly, different. Eileen Barker was a professional actor before she gravitated into sociology, and found that research by participant observation among the Moonies was rather like taking on one more part in a play; both the actor and the social researcher, she suggested, are able to bring out different parts of themselves according to context. Kirsten Hastrup has recently offered an anthropological study of play-acting, with special reference to Shakespeare, as an example of social action in general.[14] This developing alertness of the 'fieldworker' in familiar scenes at home has in turn helped to make for much greater sophistication in approaching what used to be dubbed 'simple' or 'primitive' societies.

Given the expansion and variety of current work in anthropology and its convergence with much that is being done in neighbouring fields, it is reasonable to ask whether the subject still has its own coherence, and a distinctive approach. Is there any continuity with anthropology's past which should be held on to, or should we proclaim once again (as has been claimed several times since the end of the colonial era) that the subject is dead and has no future? Should the field now be left to cultural studies, on the one hand, and to the more technical human sciences, such as genetics, economics, archaeology, and experimental psychology, on the other? You will have guessed already that my answer is no, and that anthropology's distinctiveness can still be justified on the basis that in our pursuit of the study of humanity, however fragmented our particular gaze, we are always dealing with 'social' phenomena which can potentially be grasped in a holistic and comparative way.

There are many illuminating studies of the history and transformations of anthropology, since its formation in the century of industrial and scientific expansion, imperial rule and European nationalism from the late nineteenth to the late twentieth century.[15] I have written this book as an introduction to the subject as it exists today, as we enter the twenty-first century, rather than as a history of the discipline, but it inevitably views the present in the light of the past. My perspective is that of a British-trained anthropologist whose original studies were in geography and whose field research has been in Africa. I write as a one-time student of Sir Edward Evans-Pritchard, more than half a century after the publication of his classic works on Africa which helped establish the character of 'British social anthropology'.[16] However, this field itself has metamorphosed since the 1960s. There has been a real convergence between 'social' and 'cultural' anthropology, or the field of social organization versus that of material culture, literature, and art; a rapprochement with history and archaeology; and new links are being worked out with the biological and medical fields. Many of these developments in Britain have been stimulated by the quickening pace of contacts with North American anthropology, where the inclusive 'four fields' approach has long been established as the scope of anthropology (linguistics, archaeology, culture, and human biology) and there are now new ambitions towards greater coherence in theory and collaboration in research. In the chapters which follow I develop the argument that there are ideas and questions from anthropology's past which have sufficiently deep roots to have outlived colonialism, and sufficient modern appeal to explain something of the discipline's current success. Against the claims of reductionist grand theory, these ideas and questions include a respect for individual voices and experience, but also a recognition that there are patterns to social life which are in themselves part of our 'heritage' whether we celebrate that fact or try to escape it.

Older questions: imagining the 'peoples of the world'

We have long asked the questions of where we have come from, what were our beginnings as distinctively human beings. What was life like for the person living in remote times? Scholarship, and literature, in the West have typically concerned themselves with the major question, as it was perceived, of the sources of civilization; what were the early forms, and what gave them their historical momentum? These questions arose very understandably from within archaeology, or classical, biblical, philological, or oriental studies. The anthropology of the nineteenth century introduced further perspectives from the developing sciences of the physical and biological world, working within a paradigm of the evolution of modern human life from a context of what was understood as a relatively 'natural' form of existence, closer to the rest of organic life. Anthropology tended to specialize in what were commonly understood as the less developed forms, though often on very slender evidence.

We now know more about the human colonization of the globe and the subsequent marvellous complexity of our history. A clear story has emerged of successive periods of emigration of ancestral stock out of Africa, most recently of the spread of our species out of that continent only some one hundred thousand years ago, first to the Near East and thence to Europe, Asia, Australia, and eventually the Americas. Anatomically modern humans (*Homo sapiens sapiens* or 'Modern Humans' for short) displaced various kinds of Early Humans in different parts of the Old World, for example, at a surprisingly late date, the Neanderthals in Europe.[17] Africa is now well established as the biological home of humanity. Archaeologists and palaeoanthropologists alike see the African continent as a place of origin and emergence, and recent research has strengthened this focus.[18] However, within the tradition of social and cultural anthropology, scholars have sought the traces of primeval times rather in the regions of Australia, the Pacific, and the Americas, where technically simple modes of life seemed to have been least disturbed (until very recent times). Australia offered the greatest hope of a glimpse into our own human past, because the aboriginal peoples 'discovered' there in the eighteenth century were exclusively hunters and gatherers by subsistence, substantial in numbers, diverse in language and groupings, and evidently had developed more or less in isolation from other continents for many thousands of years. They were therefore seen as the very best representatives of what was imagined to have been a very widespread form of human life at an earlier stage of social evolution. Unlike hunter-gatherers in most other parts of the world they had not been faced with competition from the spread of herding and farming communities. It cannot be denied that for the last 40,000–60,000 years, without major disruption as far as we know right up to modern times, they were able to elaborate internal cultural specialization—famously in intricate patternings of kinship and rich cosmology—upon a materially simple base.[19]

Among those scholars on whom Australia exerted a special pull was Émile Durkheim, a French pioneer of the methods of sociology at the turn of the twentieth century. His writings exercised imagination and empathy, seeing depths in the raw ethnographic reports which helped him draw the Australians into direct relation with the concerns of 'higher' civilization in the fields of language, symbol, intellectual thought, and religious experience. His classic work of 1912, *The Elementary Forms of Religious Life*, has recently been translated afresh into modern English by Karen Fields, with a helpful introduction pointing to his concern with the sources of what we take to be *real* in our experience. Through his explorations of Australian ethnography, Durkheim demonstrates for us 'the distinctively human means of knowing', that is through sociability. 'Society is the form in which nature produced humankind, and religion is reason's first harbor . . . In those very processes of abstraction that enabled the Australian to imagine who he was by imagining his relations with other Australians and with the natural world, we meet the beginning of abstract thought.' Fields explains that the case study of the Australians is the point of departure for 'his investigation into distinctive traits of humankind: reason, identity, and community'—subjects not often treated under the same heading, nor always linked with 'religion', today.[20] Her translation is accessible and sympathetic, allowing today's student to bypass the heavy literature of secondary commentary on Durkheim and to appreciate directly the fine-tuning of much of his argument. For Durkheim, we might suggest, the difference between the Australians and the world of his readers lay not in any essence, but simply in the way that the conventional elements of language, religious representation, and ceremonial action were configured in the regular practices of social life, thus providing the locally available material for personal and intellectual reflection. We could say that anthropology still owes a prime debt to Durkheim's view of the core aspects of what we would today call sociality.

In the standard study of civilizations, the presence of writing and written testimony has long been assumed the chief criterion of, and evidence for, the self-consciousness of a period; it was often suggested that before writing, there was no real self-awareness or self-expression in history, and thus no moral or religious sensibility in the modern sense. Durkheim's great achievement, in part, was his productive effort to relate together elements of spoken language and of ritual action among various Australian peoples, as reported in the ethnography, and to analyse their meaning in terms precisely of experience, awareness, religion, and reason, an effort which brought these peoples into the same moral fold as the civilized, though still representing an archaic form of organization. Partly because of the power of his analysis, and the related writings of his collaborators in the French journal *l'Année Sociologique* in the early years of the twentieth century, a vision of the elements of human society was established which drew heavily on Australia and the Pacific, though also the Americas to some extent, and this vision has helped shape anglophone social anthropology ever since.[21] It is primarily anthropology's effort to treat the 'symbolic' aspects of action and language seriously, and to see society as an arena of living interaction, that came to distinguish it from the disciplines of classical, biblical, oriental, and historical studies, founded as they are upon faith in written texts as the authoritative respository of knowledge. As I argue in the chapters that follow, this respect for communicative actions, including language, *as they take place between people* still helps to mark anthropology's distinctiveness as a 'human science'.

Why a new overview is needed

Are there not anthropology books aplenty; what is the purpose of a fresh attempt at synthesis? The problem is that the subject expanded so greatly in the late twentieth century that it has become difficult to keep up, to 'see the wood for the trees', whether for the student, or the teacher; or perhaps especially for the researcher, always seeking grants and permissions, trying to meet the priorities of funders and gatekeepers in an increasingly political and business-oriented world which has little patience with blue-skies research in faraway places.

By contrast with archaeology, which has long enjoyed a special popularity as revealing visible evidence about 'our own' past and the wonders of civilization, anthropology was little heard of until fairly recently. It was rarely regarded anyway as the study of 'ourselves' in quite the same obvious way as archaeology; it seemed to deal with ancestors so remote they were presumed sometimes not to have used language or in any other way been recognizably 'human'; or to do with such remote peoples of today in the far-flung corners of Euro-American Empire that they could scarcely be understood as our 'kin'. Thanks partly to the end of formal Empire all this has changed. Anthropology was widely slated in the 1960s because of its seeming nostalgia for an anti-quarian past, and lack of enthusiasm for 'change' and modernization. To some, especially from the perspective of newly independent countries, it seemed tied up with colonial interests, concerned not with progress but only with tribes and moribund customs and therefore bound to die out. But surprisingly perhaps, from the perspective of half a century later, it has returned to some of its older catholicity, and wholeness of vision, and it has survived. The expansion has been the result of several factors: for example, the spread of concern in the developed world for the conservation of forests, 'traditional communities', and wild life through the ecological movement. There are also new forms of political consciousness, raising questions about human rights at home and abroad, in relation for example to gender and minority rights. The injustices of underdevelopment, hunger, war, and the sufferings of displaced people across the world have engaged the passions and devoted labours of a new generation of anthropology students looking to put their lives to good use.

The 1960s were a great watershed for British and American anthropology. The political self-critique within the discipline began, and alternatives were sought to what came to be labelled as the conservative functionalism of the colonial era. Some of these represented experiments in general and analytical theory, and opened up great new vistas: for example, the universal human vision of Lévi-Strauss's structuralism, and also a reinvigorated Marxist tradition, both initially launched from France to be enthusiastically embraced in Britain and increasingly in influential American anthropology.[22] Other efforts sought to make anthropology more relevant to current events and pragmatic concerns. In the first decades after the independence of many countries it attempted, moderately successfully, to link itself with questions of economic development and social change. Many practitioners moved with vigour into 'applied' questions concerning economic development in the former colonies, into European rural studies, and into towns and urbanization. The nationalism of former colonies was echoed in the civil rights movement in the United States, to be closely followed in anthropological sympathy by the women's movement.

From the early 1970s on, anthropology in common with all the humanities and social sciences (not to mention even some of the 'harder' sciences) was re-oriented by the rising tide of gender consciousness and the political and theoretical critique from feminism. Notions of automatic tradition, of community consensus and institutional authority were turned upside down. No family, let alone society, could escape the point now being made that there were not only different interests, but different perspectives, continually negotiated within any social world. One of the results is that the older key field of anthropological study concerning kinship and marriage, whether based on 'jural/legal' or cognitively structural principles, is now being revitalized. Sociology itself loosened up its methods and its concerns, embracing qualitative notions of social differentiation, subjectivity, and culturally shaped viewpoints in a fresh way. Feminist scholarship opened up new ways of distinguishing and analysing other pluralities of perspective within society, and because of its 'cross-cultural' agenda anthropology played an important role in this development.[23]

For similar reasons, gender difference, local 'culture', and human diversity have come to be celebrated widely by politicians, media planners, and educators in a way which has no doubt added to the popularity of anthropology as an academic subject. Ethnographic and other museums, always given a central place in continental European and American anthropology, have also grown in the public consciousness and modernized their offerings to meet the new interest. In Britain, the efforts of social anthropology to ally itself with sociology and the political and economic sciences from the 1920s to the 1960s meant a temporary distancing from what was represented as the antiquarian stuffiness of museums, but this has been overcome with a shift back to the humanities and a warmer embrace of history, language, religion, material culture, art, and music. Museums are moving again into a vital role in the teaching and research agendas of British anthropology, and at the same time modernizing their popular appeal in line with best practice in North America and elsewhere.[24]

There are, however, some problems arising from the way in which popular discourse about 'culture' has taken up and run with the language of anthropology. The massive sense of 'civilization' has gone, to be replaced by a profusion of home-grown 'cultures' and groups proclaiming their own 'identity' and 'ethnicity' in every town and district. 'Culture' and 'ethnicity' have been reduced in scale, sometimes down to a personal attribute or essence of individuals. A restatement of the prime focus of our discipline as the comparative study of the phenomena of *social form* is timely, because we need to recognize that such a view of the 'possessive individual' is itself an aspect of social form, and one which itself has a history.[25] Anthropology does more than seek out differences of culture and identity between groups or individuals: it seeks to locate the sources of those perceived differences, how and why they are given the significance they are, and how they are transmitted, reproduced, and transformed over time. The way that human difference is marked out and made relevant is always a matter of 'ceremonial action', including the use of discriminative language; this is as true in industrial, class-based national or international contexts as it is in traditional tribal ones. Such processes are inherently political, including specifically the formation, representation, and artful deployment of the means of power, at domestic and higher levels (including the military domain); and the understandable ways in which these strategies may provoke resistance. In this book, I present a range of work in older and in contemporary anthropology in the light of our need to 're-cognize' the collectively structured nature of our lives, upon which the justification of a sociological approach to the human sciences has always rested.

CHAPTER TWO

Dialogues with Grand Theory

MODERN efforts (since, say, the late eighteenth century) to make systematic, scientific investigations into the foundations of human life have been driven by a search for relatively simple explanatory principles lying beneath immediate appearances, and behind what people might actually say are the reasons for their actions. Anthropologists have played a role in developing various branches of this search, but just as often they have sought to use the enormous archive of ethnographic evidence to criticize, qualify, and contradict the generalizing theorists. It is in fact not difficult to do this, to find some group of people somewhere who do not fit a given theory.

Today the social sciences are faced with a double challenge: on the one hand, from the new biology and its claims that the roots of both social behaviour and individuality are to be found in our genes—a position which is plausibly compatible both with the economists' agenda and with 'rational choice' theories in sociology. On the other hand, a more sophisticated challenge to the social sciences has been mounted by postmodern criticism from the humanities side, giving pride of place to subjective impression and reflexive personal empathy on the part of the observer, and raising doubts about the possibility of 'ethnographic' or other knowledge about the world outside oneself. The best anthropology tries to find a way between these extreme positions; and in engaging with either, defends not only fieldwork but also the validity of written, visual, and artefactual records of human activity (in the way that a historian might). The evidence of field research in anthropology has been used effectively in the past to mount criticism of the claims of more than one Western 'grand theory', and this is a continuing role the discipline should play.

A well-known case of the anthropologist as critic of Western theory is that of Bronislaw Malinowski. His early twentieth-century study of the people of the Trobriand Islands in Melanesia was presented in part as a critique of the classical economists' assumptions about the basic maximizing drive built into human nature. He emphasized the role of gift-giving and mutual co-operation among the islanders, and in their overseas relations with other islands, thus providing one of the major ethnographic accounts of a pre-modern economy.[1] In a second work on the Trobriands, Malinowski developed a critique of psychological, especially Freudian, assumptions about the deep sexual drives in human nature. He argued, provocatively, that if, like these islanders, you assume continuity of humankind through the line from a mother to her children, and see the father's role as that of a benevolent outsider, you are not likely to share the Oedipus complex so celebrated at least in popular versions of Freudian theory.[2] E. E. Evans-Pritchard's 1937 ethnographic analysis of reasoning among the Azande of central Africa was even more explicitly a challenge, in this case directed against Western scholarly and lay assumptions about the non-rational nature of 'primitive' or un-tutored thought.[3] In his later books on the dispersed herding communities of the Nuer of the southern Sudan he undermined existing political philosophy by showing how these peoples could achieve orderly relations among themselves without the benefit of the framework of state institutions and sovereignty; and by provocatively using the language of the Old Testament for describing 'pagan' Nuer beliefs and practices, he succeeded in upsetting some of the comfortable assumptions made by churchgoers, lay commentators, and theologians alike about what might seriously constitute 'religion' (this work is referred to more fully in the last part of this chapter).

In the following sections, I start by reviewing some of the important features of our debate with the generalizing sciences of human behaviour. First, I consider some of our links and exchanges with biology and the new evolutionary studies. I then offer a critical discussion of the continuing debate with economics and the uses that are still made of models based on 'rational choice' drawn from classical economics and widely applied to the study of social life. In the third section I review the continuing tradition of 'cultural' anthropology as it developed in America, and this is followed by a brief survey of the appeal of phenomenological approaches in anthropology, and the siren calls of the new romantics. I then conclude the chapter with a defence of the 'socio-centric' perspective as it has developed in anthropology, especially in France and Britain.

I. THE SEARCH FOR NATURE'S REASONS

There are several modern varieties of sociobiology, which claim to account for human social behaviour, at least in large part, in terms of organically inherited tendencies of the same kind as shape the behaviour of other species.[4] Initial views of the evolution of behaviour tended to focus on the idea of the struggle for survival and reproduction through sexual selection of whole animals and whole groups, whereas the focus today is on the idea of an internal mechanism driving genes as such to survive and replicate. This idea was popularized very effectively by Richard Dawkins in his book *The Selfish Gene*, where we find ourselves like the other creatures mere vehicles, and disposable ones at that, 'blindly programmed to preserve the selfish molecules known as genes'.[5] Our supposedly moral behaviour in looking after our children first, our nieces and nephews next, and strange orphans last is entirely in the interest of the genes we carry, maximizing their chance of surviving in the future. Even a stranger 'altruistically' helped by us may one day assist our survival in return, and in this way we can account for almost any kind of human act. Even the occasional suicide can plausibly be explained, in this vein, as being in the interests of close kin.

This sort of explanation refreshes older ideas which are clearly simplistic, for example in accounting for the existence of matriliny. It used to be said that a man was naturally disposed to care for his sister's children ahead of his own, for *he knew* they were his own physical kin (and he could not be sure about his own wife's children). Now, the assumption has shifted—a man's own opinion is neither here nor there, for he is *unconsciously guided* by his genes and their interest in their own immortality. It has even been argued that limitations on the birth of children can be an evolutionary strategy for the reproductive success of one's genes, because proportionately more attention will be devoted to bringing up each child in a small family and therefore they themselves will be successful parents in the future.[6] Anthropomorphic 'intelligent' genes with an eye on the welfare of the *generation after next* do take a bit of a leap of faith. In his original book on the theme Dawkins admits that his argument is designed to appeal to the imagination, though he insists it is science rather than science fiction.[7]

The new sociobiological studies are heirs to an older kind of 'ethology', that is the empirical study of behaviour without discrimination between animal and human cases. There are traps for the unwary, however. A study by Hilary

Callan in 1970 revealed how easily the idioms of human sociality can slip over into the apparently more objective world of animal behaviour. We speak too glibly of birds having rituals, swans getting married, or bees having royalty and political structure, and the elision becomes quite bewitching when we watch and talk about our 'closest relatives' (a cosy domestic metaphor in itself) among the primates.[8] We sometimes speak today as though genes had motivation; Callan's critique pre-dated the 'selfish gene' theories, but we can still usefully apply the lessons of her work to these more microscopic anthropomorphs. At all levels, from the horde to the individual animal organism, to the gene to the DNA 'fingerprint', we are faced with the difficulty of distinguishing the fact of survival (for anything that did not survive or leave a fossil trace we can scarcely study) from the *intention* or otherwise *programmed drive* to survive. Are there such future orientations in the organic world?

Primary questions about human nature are certainly raised by the new genetics. Students in interdisciplinary anthropology courses tend to make the point in argument that everything is the result of genes; without them, we wouldn't be here at all. The same, however, is true of water or oxygen, since these too are necessary as supports for life, but nobody would regard them as sufficient. A related difficulty over accepting simple genetic 'determinism' of human capacities then follows when we ask: So, where is the big difference between ourselves and other animals? We share more than 98 per cent of our genes with chimpanzees, so why should we not accept our profound 'kinship' with them? The old question of what makes us the creatures we are, our biological or our learned inheritance, is as fresh as ever in science, literature, and even theology. The serious debates once framed in terms of a simple opposition of nature versus nurture are in modern terms transposed to a question of genes (carried in the body) versus culture ('all in the mind'). The arguments to and fro are, however, wearing a little thin, and it is becoming clearer on both sides that we should be very wary of taking such an opposition for granted. The collectivity of our genetic inheritance may well dispose us to be inventive, communicative, and to make and remake language and culture; at the same time it is becoming very clear that we have the beginnings of a sobering capacity to modify, deliberately, the patterns of our own genetic make-up and its transmission. Our 'cultural' actions have long impinged on biological patterns of reproduction and associated human genetic history (think of birth control and medical advances in managing child survival for a start), but it is only very recently that we have discovered ways of 'interfering' in the genetic composition of living organisms, and indeed in the very combination and recombination of the reproductive elements. A simple dualism of nature/culture, or even analogies between them (as with Dawkins's invention of 'memes' as elements of culture which replicate themselves like genes and survive through natural selection),[9] is quite inappropriate as a starting point for any modern anthropology and is not the perspective taken in this book.

At the same time, while accepting our common organic ancestry with much of the rest of the animal world, we should not underestimate the qualitative complexity of our lives by comparison with those of our non-human kin. While today's biological sciences are strongly tempted to focus down on the simplest possible level of organized life-stuff, seeing the dog or the turkey essentially as epiphenomena of self-directed genes, the integrity of the animal as an organized and conscious whole resists easy deconstruction. And above the level of the whole animal is the more intricate organization of its co-operative communication with others. In the human case, it is here that we begin to speak of language, imagination, and culture. Now no one could deny that you require genes before you can organize a philosophy seminar, but it would be difficult to identify those precisely responsible. To adapt an idea from the classic sociological tradition, we are faced here with sophisticated arrangements made at quite another level.

Pure genes: traps for the unwary

Accounts of human evolution and early history tend to have a bold narrative form around the latest-discovered fossil as hero, as Misia Landau has pointed out, and we can easily understand the temptation of even the most sober scientific writers to use pungent scenarios of drama, even soap opera, to make our species' history come alive for us.[10] A popular example is Bryan Sykes's fulsome addition of imagination to the evidence of pure genes in his book *The Seven Daughters of Eve*. Here he sets out startling evidence of the direct physical connection between individual living people and various examples of ancient individuals through the matching up of samples of mitochondrial DNA.[11] This form of DNA is found in the outer part of human cells (including ova), not in the nucleus. It is not recombined at fertilization, but transmitted intact to offspring of the female (unless there is a mutation, as happens very rarely). Physical matrilines can therefore be traced, and the relative time-depth of their branches estimated by comparing the number of mutations which have occurred. In this way, Sykes has found evidence that 95 per cent of Europe's local population falls into seven categories based on shared maternal ancestry. He calls these categories 'clans', tracing each back to an individual woman for whom he invents a name. The earliest is Ursula, who lived in very cold times 45,000 years ago, moving according to the seasons between the mountain caves and coastline of Greece.[12] After her band's various encounters with shy Neanderthals and fierce animals, Ursula manages to bring up two daughters (themselves to become progenitors of diverging branches of the matriline) before she is left behind in a cave in winter only to be eaten by a bear. She and the other 'Seven Daughters of Eve' are each given a chapter of imaginative life history, in which Sykes reconstructs what he can of conditions at the time.

The underlying problem with this way of doing prehistory is that the line of transmission identified by his use of 'clan' is a purely biological trace, and a partial one at that, not necessarily congruent with any kind of continuing social group. The method gives possibly arbitrary prominence to Ursula while omitting a large number of people in her band who may have contributed to its survival without leaving a genetic trace through a line of daughters (they might have died off, or been incorporated elsewhere). Sykes himself makes this point by including in a later chapter the motif of adoption by a foreign band of an identical twin borne by another 'daughter of Eve'. At the same time we could ask what aspects of behaviour or cultural capacity are transmitted anyway in the extra-nuclear mitochondrial DNA. Recent research is concentrating, however, on the Y chromosome, which is transmitted at each nuclear recombination down the male line, and scientists are beginning to find exciting results.[13] Sykes's discoveries are amazing, and undoubtedly constitute very important evidence about ancient human migrations. Their appeal to the general public is, notwithstanding, greatly enhanced by literary fictions about persons, social life, and 'clan' continuity, which add to popular expectations about the potential of the new genetic sciences.

It is very tempting to put forward explanations even of today's human activities in terms of pure genes. There are many competing suggestions to explain the evolutionary causes of specific—and usually problematic or criminal—aspects of behaviour. Such theories seem to project back onto earlier times images taken from modern assumptions about how 'civilization' is a thin veneer over a former unrestrained, 'wild' animality in which the essence of individual 'human nature' lies. Hence, justifications of male domination, sexual violence, even racism can be put forward on the basis of what is 'only natural' to our species. There have been passionate rejections of this whole thrust that lies behind much writing in sociobiology, as well as sustained criticism of the slippery slope into distortion and prejudice.[14] I will comment briefly on one example of the no-nonsense type of dogmatic evolutionary psychology now promoting the Darwinian ideas 'that are setting today's intellectual agenda': on this view, according to Martin Daly and Margo Wilson, the 'truth' about Cinderella is that parents love only their genetic offspring. As a stepchild, it follows naturally that the poor girl was abused.[15] Losing a genetic parent or parents is a risk factor not only for human offspring, but for all kinds of animals too. The well-known case of lions is mentioned, for example, in which a coalition of new males takes over a pride of matrilineally related adults and kills off their existing cubs before fathering new ones. Both males and females of every species are engaged in competitive reproduction, according to modern evolutionary theory, and 'since the human animal has evolved by the same Darwinian processes as other animals, there is no apparent reason why the same principles should not apply'.[16]

However, there are some problems in the Cinderella case, quite apart from the fact that in the end, adversity is overcome and she marries her prince. The main problem facing both Cinderella's genetic father and 'unrelated' stepmother alike is to find suitable marriages for all the girls. The European story has many parallels in India, where there is a similar concern. Both regions offer highly stratified social systems where dowry is normally trans-mitted with the bride at marriage, and girls of poor families are somewhat stranded as a result. We should recall Mrs Bennet in Jane Austen's *Pride and Prejudice*, with no property to speak of and the problem of marrying off five daughters. The rivalry between female siblings, whether full or step, becomes very clear in a dowry system, where resources are divided between them. However, social circumstances may differ elsewhere. For example, in the polygynous systems characteristic of Africa, where bridewealth is transferred at marriage from the groom's to the bride's family, girls of a family do not find themselves rivals in the same way.[17] Daughters are seen as a source of future prosperity, not a drain. Stepdaughters are unlikely to be left unmarried at the bottom of the status system, and exploited Cinderella style. So the position of stepchild is not a human constant; it varies from one kind of social system to another, and the question of cruelty and persecution (which I am not deny-ing takes place in certain circumstances) cannot be compared directly with the way in which rival animals may destroy each other's offspring. In the case of Britain and North America, where disturbing levels of child abuse by stepparents are detailed by Daly and Wilson, we have to recall the context of the modern nuclear family, and the moral expectations of closeness we have to some extent imposed upon it, along with quasi-'ownership' attitudes of parents towards children which our modern economy has encouraged (see further discussion in Chapter 10).

We are living in times which are essentializing the notion of genetic identity as the most real thing about ourselves and our connections with others, but we should not forget that biological essentialism has had some treacherous variations in the past and we should be wary of new and dazzling claims by some of the neo-Darwinists anxious to leap ahead. The question of human essentials, and human beginnings, is moreover a field in which careful biologists are being joined by archaeologists, psychologists, linguists, and social anthropologists. Against the denials of any difference, on the one hand, and stark formulations of the animal/human divide as a presence or absence of culture, on the other, current debate seeks to allow the claim that there are things which make us human, and set us apart from the other animals, but—to show how complex and plural the question has become—it is no longer helpful to think of a simple watershed. Recent research with the other higher primates, for example, has been of such quality that we are obliged to consider seriously the fascinating problem of whether they have the capacity for symbolic behaviour and language as 'we' understand these things. Those like Jane Goodall and Vernon Reynolds who have worked with chimpanzees in the wild have shown them to be just as astonishingly 'clever' there as in captivity.[18] Of course our findings in this field depend very largely on how 'we' decide to define symbolic behaviour, intention, memory, language, and so on, and a number of very interesting books have been appearing by scholars in different fields which attempt to place these philosophical problems in the context of new understandings of human evolution—I introduce a sample below. While inevitably offering somewhat mythical scenarios, these studies all emphasize partial and fragmentary, regional and localized developments of skill among a variety of competing primate and hominid groups, rather than a heroic tale of general upward progress.

Genetic capacities for sociality and culture

The tremendous recent advances in genetic science, its medical applications, and the mapping of the whole human genome have reinforced the claims of the biological approach, and yet at the same time are beginning to modify the more rigid views of genetic determinism. A very persuasive and readable book is Matthew Ridley's *Genome*, for example. He uses the image of language for the 'four letters' or *bases* of DNA, which are combined in varying ways into 'words', and these into the 'paragraphs' constituting genes; these instructions are translated (by a primeval 'messenger' or catalyst called RNA) into proteins which enable and control life. In extraordinarily detailed ways, our genes control the production of proteins which affect our behaviour, moods, and actions. Little bits of the catalyst RNA 'survive' in our bodies from very ancient evolutionary times, from the beginnings of life itself. The human genome as a whole is like a book, a store of memories, and on the basis of this image Ridley distances himself from the old determinism versus free will arguments. His book is certainly a corrective to the spreading popular conception of genes and DNA as little packets of essential traits guaranteeing identity. He concentrates more subtly on the immense importance of the environment of nurture, the social environment, and learning upon the actual outcome of genetically based potential.[19] This clearly allows scope for kinds of variation over time, especially in the case of human history.

Even in physical terms, the various characteristics of human beings have developed in a less systematic way than was once thought. Bipedalism, large brains, tool-using, prolonged infancy, sexual dimorphism, and other traits, have been developed through evolutionary patterns in different places and at different times, as Robert Foley has explained, according to very local combinations of factors. There has been no sharp watershed between the various branches of the hominid lineage and the emergence of a unique species, no single point at which it can be said that Modern Humans suddenly appeared in full glory.[20] Looking back to the sources of our human heritage (rather than teleologically tracing it forward) we can say that the hominid brain reached a weight of about 1,000 grams about 300,000 years ago, and that this development is likely to have entailed a life-history strategy among Early Humans, including a pattern of infant care, close to our own. It also coincides with a greater diversity of technological activity. While language may not yet have developed, it is possible that there was a great increase in pre-linguistic communicative activity including the practice of imagining the intentions and actions of others. Human brains are six times larger in relation to body size than they are in the average primate, and evolutionary psychologists see this as a key research problem. Theories as to why there was a great increase in brain size among our ancestors used to focus on utilitarian needs and stimuli, such as the need to develop hunting skills and tools, but a most interesting set of new theories emphasizes how the increasing scale and complexity of group living itself has been a key factor in stimulating (and *selecting for*) intelligence. Evidence has now been found of the remarkable abilities even of other primates to guess at others' motivations, and to manipulate them—dubbed 'Machiavellian' intelligence. There can be no doubt that in Early Human communities an increasingly sharp perception of self and others within a changing, fast-moving group, and the advantage to individuals of a capacity for complex levels of communication with them, would have been a crucial stimulant towards the development of language—'from grooming to gossip', as it has been put by Robin Dunbar. The 'social brain' hypothesis, while obviously very attractive to the imagination of social and cultural anthropology, is receiving intense attention at present from the kind of researchers, like Dunbar, who demand rigorous evidence from the fossil record. His key arguments move from the organic evidence of individual intelligence to careful speculation about the socially negotiated nature of collective life and the sustained intra-communal interactions which themselves may be the sharpest mental stimulant to individuals.[21] Here, the contribution of the archaeologists and philosophically minded psychologists is also lively, and beginning to enrich new syntheses—for example, W. G. Runciman's *The Social Animal*.[22] The anatomy of Modern Humans, including the large brain, has an antiquity of at least 100,000 years according to Foley, but much had led up to the early period in human history that deserves reflection, and the careful kind of imaginative recreation that historians have always exercised upon the past.

What did 'we', as a small population still apparently based in Africa (though earlier hominid groups had already dispersed), have to build on at this point? What if anything made this a definitive watershed in socio-cultural as distinct from genetic history, and what has followed on from there? My first example of a sustained effort to tell a story about the human past is by the archaeologist Stephen Mithen, and reaches far back beyond the beginning of our modern species. He does seek evidence for internal features of mind, intention, skill, and so on, and tries to evaluate the evidence for ways in which these have changed over long periods. He also makes use of dramatic scenarios, evoking our whole history as a long-drawn-out play upon a stage. According to Mithen, the brain structure of Early Humans remained for some time essentially one of separate compartments, harbouring specific kinds of intelligences which worked very well in their own context. The domains of natural history, technical, and social intelligence, for example, developed separately from each other, for plausible reasons of evolutionary advantage in these dedicated skills. In the core area of this imagined brain architecture there was an unspecialized 'general intelligence' but it was not very effective. Nor was there much communication between the separate zones. The brain was like a Swiss army knife, in having specialized tools for particular tasks.[23]

Mithen argues that those chimpanzees who have been encouraged to learn manual skills and language-like signalling behaviour are applying their general intelligence, but have neither a dedicated area of the brain specializing in linguistic intelligence nor the 'cognitive fluidity' necessary for the development of 'real' language. Technical intelligence allowed Early Humans, including Neanderthals, to develop quite impressive tool-making skills, but these never seemed to lead to innovation. Natural history intelligence enabled them to become expert hunters and gatherers. Social intelligence was also present, that is the ability to respond to the behaviour and intentions of others, and to have a sense of self-presentation to those others—even through deceptive actions. Mithen argues that environmental, bodily, and demographic changes, along with increased overall brain size and the need for better nourishment and prolonged child care, may have triggered a crucial increase in this kind of 'dedicated' social intelligence. It was probably in this context (and brain area) that language began to be generated. A breakthrough finally occurred and was genetically transmitted in brain architecture, in that the barriers separating the compartments were breached, and with the help of general intelligence, fluid connections could be made for the first time between the different dedicated intelligences. Language suddenly acquired new levels of reference, the world of animals and the environment could be thought about in the kinds of ways we had previously only thought about human beings. Human beings could begin to perceive each other as manipulable, like animals, or even objects or tools; and they could begin to formulate art and religious ideas.[24]

My second example of a major survey of the roots of our cultural capacity, which also seeks to place it firmly in a broadly evolutionary framework, is the work of the psychologist Merlin Donald. Like Mithen, he has turned himself into something of a philosopher. While concerned with the life of the mind and personal experience, he emphasizes very strongly their dependence on the external sources of those shared symbolic codes by which we come to know things and to take action. His vision of the communicative and thus *collective* nature of culture, as explored in his books *Origins of the Modern Mind* and especially *A Mind So Rare*, converges very closely with the anthropological themes of my present argument.[25] In his second book he focuses on human consciousness as the distinguishing mark of our species. Essentially aware of itself in the context of others, the conscious brain is actively directed towards the assimilation and processing of information received through networks of social communication from infancy onwards. Out of 'a felt need to extend the reach of human consciousness' have emerged languages, symbolic culture, and many social institutions including organized religion. Donald uses literature and art as well as psychological research to illustrate the complexity of self-consciousness, and its anchorage in ongoing social life.[26] Human consciousness is more than sensory awareness, but is about 'building and sustaining mental models of reality'; the 'engine of the symbolic mind . . . is much larger and more powerful than language, which is after all its own (generally inadequate) invention. . . . [It] is an active and causative element in cognition and a regulator and arbitrator of action.'[27]

Donald distinguishes three levels of consciousness present in our social life today, and regards these as evolutionary stages. The deepest, and oldest, is the way in which we remember events and experiences in whole scenarios or significantly coherent 'episodes'; many animals must do this too, as a dog remembers a fight with a particular rival in a particular place. Episodic knowledge requires a good deal of sorting and shaping of fragmentary sensations by the working memory, which among chimpanzees, for example, will include a lot of details relevant to social relations which have to be updated constantly—of dominance and hierarchy, grooming and so forth.[28] Here lies the 'cognitive heart' of culture, which itself was the crucible in which consciousness generated 'the almost inconceivable complexity and beauty of language'. For Donald, language is not an isolated phenomenon but embedded in a wider set of 'instincts for culture'. Before it emerged, he diagnoses a second level in the development of consciousness (probably found among early hominids), again corresponding to a layer of our modern existence, characterizing it as the 'mimetic' stage. Here he suggests the presence of 'action metaphor', of imitation, mime, and implicitly 'grammatical' gesture, which eventually yield mythic frameworks of a narrative kind and the beginnings of language.[29] 'The great divide in human evolution was not language but the formation of cognitive communities in the first place. . . . Human ancestors could not have evolved an ability to generate language unless they had already connected with one another somehow in simple communities of mind. . . . we could not even begin to think our most private thoughts without satisfying our brain's cultural habits first.'[30] The family is a small 'theatre-in-the-round', children easily playing out roles, acting father, mother, or even the dog or the family car, long before they can verbally describe what they are doing. The way in which infants begin to acquire language is now seen as a product of shared attention and participation in social interaction; those individuals who are deprived of this in early life never do develop communicative capacity, while those who have the misfortune to become deaf and blind after the first year or two of normal life are sometimes able to recapitulate the process of language-like learning and conscious expression. Donald points also to the importance of non-verbal mimetic aspects of adult life too. Even NASA, for example, could not operate efficiently without mimetic consensus; as part of 'the group theatrical production that we call social life'.[31] Mimesis once stood as a self-sufficient cultural adaptation which did not need language, and 'its vestiges persist today, as the unspoken foundation of all cultures'.[32] Following the emergence of language in the 'mythic-oral' stage where narrative stories became an explicit way of creating virtual realities (we might use opera as a modern analogy), Donald's scheme arrives at the third transition, completed by Modern Humans during the course of the last hundred thousand years or slightly more. This period saw the establishment of theoretic and institutional culture, the production of external depositories of cultural memory through symbolic technology in forms of art and eventually writing. Modern culture is multi-layered, modern consciousness multi-stranded and always 'boxing and weaving' with received patterns of knowledge.

Neither Dunbar, Mithen, Donald, nor other important pioneers of the 'social' vision of early human development, tackle the topic of kinship as a symbolically loaded, ceremonially structured, and linguistically influenced way of organizing sexuality and the raising of children within and between groups. Analyses of kin relationships do have a place in the work of biologists and evolutionary psychologists working on modern populations, but these are less concerned with cultural principle than with the pragmatic outcomes of childbearing.[33] This is a contact zone between branches of the human sciences, and there are potentially some live debates to come. My final example of an evolutionary story, however, does tackle sexuality and kinship in a deeply structural and 'symbolic' way. Chris Knight has offered a vivid model of the way that cultural rules about social relations may have been consciously created in early human history. He starts with the assumption of a basic tension between the sexes, in which females begin to control their own sexuality over the menstrual-lunar cycle and use it as a way of bargaining with males over their success in bringing home meat from the hunt—also dependent on the phases of the moon. It is not so much a simple matter of all against all, but rather the formation of defensive coalitions of women and their close male kin around young girls, against the interest of non-kin males in the promise of new sexuality and fertility. Using a range of modern ethnography as a guide, Knight seeks the beginnings of ritual, specifically initiation ritual, in the richly symbolic performances of such coalitions, which enact a 'No!' to philandering potential partners by using red cosmetic body paint as a defiant cover to advertise their solidarity, and to conceal just who is menstruating and therefore imminently fertile, by presenting themselves symbolically as animals and even as males. Such rituals, at least their modern analogies, embody basic metaphoric associations such as between rain and fertility of the kind which we can see permeating 'art' and 'religion', and also construct social time in that they invest the seasons and the lunar cycle with tremendous significance. In this scenario of the periodic enactment of a counter-reality Knight sees the beginnings of symbolic culture and the political power of ritual, quite different from the low-key individual exchanges of ordinary speech which he argues would have developed more informally within ritually defined coalitions. This basic model has been taken further and elaborated by others, especially on the basis of comparative mythology from southern Africa. Archaeological evidence for the extreme antiquity of red ochre use has been adduced from the same region, and plausible arguments made for long continuities in the essentially symbolic ways it has been deployed.[34] Knight's whole approach is essentially a bold guess, couched in an ambitious effort to explain the transition from animal to human society in directly Darwinian terms which not everyone would accept. Nevertheless he and his collaborators have seriously tackled the question of identifying what we might mean by organized social form and linked it crucially, as few others have, with the beginnings of art, ritual, language, and conscious direction in human affairs, including the logic of kinship and gender.

What we can accept, in any of these evolutionary scenarios, is that you or I would find ourselves in principle 'at home' in the social environment of those Modern Humans who first developed physically in Africa, and then left to colonize the rest of the world. They were the first of any human populations to move into Australia and the Americas, and they eventually displaced, possibly interbred with, or otherwise obliterated traces of previous Early Human populations in Europe, Asia, and Africa itself. We cannot deny that aspects of Wittgenstein's observation about the prevalence of ritualistic activities might well have applied to aspects of the lives of Early Humans, including for example the Neanderthals who went on surviving in Europe until 30,000 years

FIG. 1. Palaeolithic rock painting from the Sandawe region of Tanzania. Once interpreted as an abduction, more recently as a shamanistic trance dance; possibly both compatible with a Stone Age version of the drama of Romeo and Juliet? Tanzania National Museum, Dar es Salaam. Werner Forman Archive.

ago. But there is little doubt that this vision can be appropriately applied to the history of Modern Humans since the flourishing of art from about 60,000 years ago or possibly more. By 40,000–30,000 years ago, we find people in distant parts of the world similarly sketching pictures of themselves dancing, probably singing; probably painting themselves, wearing beads and masks, enacting dramas, and representing themselves as animals (see Fig. 1 for an example). Language, as Foley says, 'changes all the rules',[35] but language-as-speech is interwoven with (sometimes embroidered upon) many other coded shapes of significant and structured sociality, which we have to regard as foundational. What is crucial about the transition, whenever it took place, is that it was from a world in which a zoologist can sum up a set of observed tendencies among co-operating and reproducing animals as their living in 'matrilineal' groups, as most of the monkey species do, or as having developed signs of 'male bonding', as the chimpanzees have; and a world in which such representations are given weight in ritual, art, or language by the participants themselves, forming a virtual or ideal schema which may have its own moral compulsion.

There used to be two main myths about the driving force behind ancestral human development: either language-capable and individually imaginative because of an increase in brain capacity—Man the Speechmaker; or technical, rational, and productive—Man the Toolmaker. A range of writers from various research backgrounds in archaeology, genetics, animal behaviour, and psychology have recently been converging on a rather different conception: of the pre-linguistic social and cultural capacities of human beings, and the deep roots of shared 'symbolic' consciousness. It is in the context of this convergence that we can perhaps agree upon a vision of the human species as at heart the 'ceremonial animal'. And further, we can argue that this conception applies to us still, and that attempts to reduce the symbolic complexity of present human action to models of individual rationality, or to examine items of culture and language outside their connection with social form, are bound to fall short.

2. PROBLEMS FOR THE ANTHROPOLOGIST WITH 'RATIONAL CHOICE THEORY'

We have considered the 'explanatory mechanisms' sought by the sociobiologists, supposedly lying deep within the self-directed genes of the individual. This view corresponds, on a micro-scale, to models of explanation in the social sciences which assume the rational, self-interested nature of all interaction. Society is no less, and no more, than the sum of these interactions. The most powerful theories that have been elaborated upon this motif are those of classical economics, where the great systems of production and trade are the outcome of rational self-interest at every level. Moreover, the operation of this principle in theory works for the general good: what benefits the individual also benefits society. This equation, upon which policy can ideally be based in order to maximize the greatest good for the greatest number, is the 'principle of utility', underlying 'utilitarian' philosophy and social science.[36] There has recently been a revival of this general line of approach in sociology under the rubric of 'rational choice theory', and while this tradition has never dominated anthropology, analogous arguments and models have regularly been put forward.

One of the most skilful and persuasive advocates of this rationalistic style of analysis in modern anthropology is Fredrik Barth, whose fieldwork has spanned regions from the Middle East to New Guinea, and who has tackled topics across the spectrum of anthropology, from pastoral modes of production, through politics, ethnicity, and development studies, to ritual and cognition.[37] His analytical stance, while ultimately in the tradition of seeing society as the abstract sum of rational individual action, has been elegantly applied to the ethnographic details of the lives of farmers and herders and ritual specialists in absolutely concrete and complex circumstances. Barth rejects the analytical value of such holistic concepts as norms, institutions, chiefly structures, traditions, or religion. He points out that such things do not explain themselves; they exist because people have set them up, and continue to uphold them, for very good reasons of their own; and the same people may change their minds in their own self-interest at any time. Priority must be given to the ebb and flow of politics and social processes before one can see where formal organization and cultural values have come from. Barth applied the economists' 'theory of games' to the patterns of political rivalry and alliance among the Pathans of the Swat valley in northern Pakistan, contrasting the way that they formed strategic coalitions always cross-cutting groups of kin, by contrast with the model of moral solidarity based on descent that Evans-Pritchard had provided for the Nuer.[38] The individual is represented as a free agent, exercising choice of action and allegiance, and innovating in the entrepreneurial sense when he (and this individual really does seem to be thought of as a 'he') sees an opportunity. In the case of the Swat Pathans, Barth argued that no one is simply born into a social position; 'persons find their place in the political order through a series of choices', and while self-interest and group interest may coincide, for instance where the group offers protection to the individual, they may also be at odds with each other, the individual pursuing private advantage and a personal political career. Barth himself comments that in this case 'the political life of Swat resembles that of Western societies'.[39]

There is little place for 'power' in this analysis; and none for the structural understandings of class or the historical inertia of social forms. Culture, with all that it might entail in the way of language and inscribed patterns of life, or even historically derived intellectual and moral ideas about social relations as such, is reduced to the variable 'values' which are held by individuals. Once the anthropologist can specify what these values are, on this account even strange behaviour becomes intelligible, because it can be seen as rational in the light of those values. We may study the processes whereby these values are learned by the growing child, a theme Barth has pursued in the context of childhood initiation rites among the Baktaman of New Guinea. But there is no 'symbolic structure' as a whole lying outside the immediate understanding of individuals. Barth admitted, interestingly, in one of his most influential works, that 'the behaviour of any one particular person [cannot] be firmly predicted—such human conditions as inattentiveness, stupidity or contrariness will, for the anthropologist's purposes, be unpredictably distributed in the population'; this is absolutely in line with the economist's view of the human imperfections in the way the market works.[40] Complete rationality, attention, and intelligence thus, by implication, lead to 'predictable' behaviour, and therefore questions arise about the sort of 'freedom' allowed to human agency in a social world modelled on 'rational choice'.[41] Social theory in this field rarely notices the way in which people in real life are dependent on and connected with each other. Any differences of gender or age, for a start, are resources like any others to be used in the pursuit of self-interest.

Classical utilitarian thought rests on a few clear assumptions: that human beings are governed by the idea of seeking pleasure and avoiding pain, that our system of ethics must therefore endorse the goodness of actions which produce pleasure and condemn those which produce misery, and our politics must seek to secure conditions in which the general happiness can flourish. Social duty and self-interest therefore coincide. John Stuart Mill recognized the provocative character of these arguments, which he himself helped articulate, in relation to other more conservative positions in the nineteenth century; and his comment that 'In all ages of philosophy, one of its schools has been utilitarian' remains true today.[42] It applies also to the social sciences; for just as the ethical scheme rests upon the equation of individual happiness with the social good, so the corresponding sociology equates the 'nature of the human being' with the forms of society. Mill struggled with the dilemma of specifying where personal liberty and morality might lie within a scheme of general utility, and we might ask the same of 'rational choice' behavioural theory today. It is represented in some very sophisticated work by, for example, Diego Gambetta, who has investigated the way that 'trust' operates within organizations like the Mafia.[43] Today's outstanding parallel to the figure of John Stuart Mill is perhaps Anthony Giddens, given the way in which he has attempted to reconcile concepts of what we term today structure and agency, and his practical work as a policy adviser to Britain's 'New Labour' party.[44] The practical usefulness of a broadly utilitarian rule of thumb in planning social improvements, particularly in the development field, has been recognized by anthropologists, who have often found Barth's models a good guide here. Outcomes are another matter (see my discussion in Chapter II). The academic argument continues, and we might note that Mary Douglas has endorsed Steven Lukes's view of utilitarianism as the 'old enemy' of anthropology.[45]

In concluding this section, it is worth noting that there are commentators who have openly recommended a direct link between genetic sociobiology and rational choice in sociology as a complete human science package. The scope of such a package could arguably include a limited place for consciousness, culture, and co-operation between individuals. However, it would not reflect the compulsive quality of our actual experience of these very things: of lifetime commitments to other persons and to abstract projects, of personal consciousness and its shared extensions in memory, or hope; or the meaning of dreams, or the making of art for art's sake, or in the fear of kings and priests; and such a package would therefore fail to see the historical character of the social worlds in which we live.

3. CULTURE, 'CULTURES', AND ETHNOGRAPHY AS AN ART

If we accept that sociobiology and 'rational choice' theory alike leave 'culture' with very little weight—an epiphenomenon—can we therefore turn to the central ideas of what has been known (mainly in America) as 'cultural anthropology' to correct our view?

Writers of the nineteenth and early twentieth centuries treated the idea of 'culture' as a very tangible thing, observable in the material record of human activity and creative expression. It was a notion of culture derived from the archaeologists as much as anywhere else; in North America it was extensively developed in relation to the arts and practices of living native American groups. In Britain E. B. Tylor (curator of the Pitt Rivers Museum in Oxford) elaborated an approach to historical development which sought to penetrate beneath the material expressions of art and manufacture to the operations of thought and imagination behind them. What these approaches shared was a view of history which saw the invention, spread, sharing, and blending of cultural traits, combined in different ways as one moved from one region of the world to another. M. J. Herskovits developed the archaeologists' idea of 'complexes' of culture traits as they typified one region or one period as against another, and applied this to the living ethnographic scene in Africa. Thus, in identifying the 'cattle complex' of the plateaux of eastern and southern Africa, he drew attention to the characteristic clustering of elements of cultural practice and symbolic values relating to the rearing of cattle in those regions. He was not intending to suggest a regional 'psychological complex' or individual mental hang-up concerning cattle, though this meaning was attributed to him by some later commentators. Moreover, his concept of culture did not correspond to a closed system. His culture areas did not have sharp boundaries on the ground, and he emphasized continuities and connections of practices and styles within and between them.[46]

Franz Boas had established the tradition of detailed, intensive fieldwork in American anthropology, working mainly in northern latitudes from the late nineteenth century on. The work of two of his students in the 1920s–1930s, Ruth Benedict and Margaret Mead, was to move cultural anthropology in exciting new directions. They both sought the nature of subjectivity in deliberately contrasted cultural contexts. Benedict's book *Patterns of Culture* formulated a systematic conception of the 'holistic' nature of culture, and the way in which individual personality and character were honed within it. She contrasted 'types' of culture on the basis of the characteristic psychological attitudes they fostered. Her most famous contrast drew on Nietzsche's distinction of styles in Greek tragedy. She characterized the Zuñi (to use the older spelling) of the American South-West, with their patient agriculture and slow-moving rain rituals, as 'Apollonian' or peaceful and collaborative in their style of culture-and-personality. The more aggressive, agonistic style of the Plains Indians with their mobile, hunting life and individualistic vision-seeking spirituality was linked with the 'Dionysian' style.[47] Essential to the analysis was the identification of typical individual subjectivity and inner purpose with a cultural milieu that promoted such characteristics. Mead compared Polynesian Samoa with modern American society, and also with the more puritan world of the Manus people of New Guinea. She drew particular attention to the young girl's experience of growing up in such different circumstances, presenting sex and sexuality (today we would include 'gender') as culturally shaped.[48] What can certainly be said about Mead and Benedict is that they introduced a new sensitivity to women's lives and experiences in the work of anthropology. These issues began to be recognized in American anthropology long before the women's movement and feminism really launched their broadside from the 1970s. We would now see in their work, however, a very conservative attitude to 'gender', and a certain cultural over-determination of the 'position of women' within patterns of family and marriage.

The new concept of psychologically embedded culture also, arguably, facilitated a new kind of relativism, emphasizing holistic images of difference between one population and another. The notion of culture tended to become reified as a 'thing in itself', as against the specific trajectories of language, religion, techniques, and art, not to mention the ecological, political, or historical processes of which they are a part. Cultural generalization meant that intellectual comment, along with the idea of dialogue, difference of view, or structural contradiction, was difficult to find. The mature developments of American cultural anthropology are much more sophisticated than the work of the pioneers. Clifford Geertz is rightly regarded as a leading exponent; and his work has been influential in reshaping anthropology across the world. He has always sought to know individuals and to recognize the complexity of cultural meaning through their eyes in his ethnographies, though it is not always easy to get an analytical grip on his diffuse vision of culture as a 'web of values', or to incorporate his harmonious idea of 'religion as a cultural system' into the often harsh politics and eventful history of the world religions.[49] He has written about a range of widely separated communities, many but not all located in dominantly Muslim countries across the world, from Morocco to Indonesia. Like Barth, Geertz has always rejected over-formalized concepts of the collective, in favour of richly detailed ethnography of 'real people in real situations'; but whereas Barth always seeks reasons for action, Geertz's portrayals have been guided by a kind of creative empathy, a communion of feeling. Both men gave memorable, and very accessible, masterly lectures on their life's work at the centennial meetings of the American Anthropological Association in New Orleans, November 2002.

It was the notion of culture as a generalized 'thing in itself' that called forth images and analogies to try and pin down what it really consisted of; the most influential idea, itself partly promoted by Geertz, has been that we should think of 'culture as text'. The book edited by James Clifford and George Marcus under the title *Writing Culture* became a famous critique of this very idea.[50] Do the writings of anthropology themselves simply consist of 'text' in this vague sense of 'cultural expression' too? Do anthropologists deceive themselves as to their project of really acquiring valid knowledge of the world and of those who live in it? Are their ethnographies anything more than one more variant of conventional travellers' tales, or yet more stereotyping of the oriental, or the tribal world? Supposedly scientific ethnographic writing does often resemble or overlap with personal creative writing, or even pure fiction, to a remarkable degree, so how can we differentiate between them? The undeniably subjective aspects of the field research process came under fresh scrutiny in the 1980s, along with the collective Western cultural habit of writing in clichés about imagined 'others'. This new self-conscious doubt about representing culture was only reinforced by the wide acclaim given Edward Said's impassioned critique of Western 'Orientalism', and related political doubt about the right of any particular person to represent the views—or culture—'belonging to' someone else.[51] This debate over the 'crisis of representation' was joined by several voices pointing to the complexity of issues involved in the history of anthropological writing about various different parts of the world, which all had different historical relations to the Western academic tradition; and by several critics who defended the generalizing, comparative ambitions of anthropology as a social science.[52] The debate has helped to create fruitful exchanges between what used to be seen as the distinctive traditions of British social, and American cultural, anthropology. The former is now more generously disposed to incorporating 'culture' into the very conception of the social, and the latter is tending to proclaim the need for historical depth and the need for a more 'political' view of cultural phenomena and events (see, for example, the new collection edited by George Marcus on *Critical Anthropology Now*).[53]

Research has a life outside the written text as such, often a multiple one; and it is nearly always more than a simple description of 'my experience of the strange so-and-sos'. Anthropologists may also write in other genres; several have produced ironical fictional accounts of 'the field' or set in the field—an early example was Laura Bohannan's *Return to Laughter*, written under the pseudonym Elenore Bowen. Nigel Barley has published several recent semi-fictional accounts really poking fun at the researcher and the absurdities of the field situation, starting with *The Innocent Anthropologist*. In a more serious vein, but still fascinating to a wide readership, are the novels of Amitav Ghosh, starting with *In An Antique Land* which followed his doctoral research as an anthropologist in Egypt.[54] Anthropologists themselves seem to appeal to other people's sense of the absurd, including the people they study—as in the frontispiece to this book, a satirical cartoon by the Zuni artist Phil Hughte of the way they remember the weird ways of their classic ethnographer, Frank Cushing. Anthropologists often appear as eccentrics in various novels written by their friends and acquaintances, usually under feigned names but totally recognizable. Barbara Pym, well placed as Secretary of the International African Institute to observe the foibles of the anthropologists of the colonial era, mixed and matched them in her novels. The weird things anthropologists study easily lend an edge to satire—on the English character in particular—as in the entertaining book *Krippendorf's Tribe* by Frank Parkin, or the more delicate satire *Brides of Price* offered by Dan Davin, well placed as a very sociable academic publisher to capture in 'fictional ethnography' some of the goings-on of his day among Oxford's anthropologists.[55]

Anthropology can scarcely be separated from the culture of writing and publishing, academic and other. However, it is more than the mere production of writing: even the transmission of an academic tradition involves face-to-face teaching, formal and informal; it has a complicated relationship to other practices such as those of the visual media; of the development agencies; the medical profession; business and the workings of finance; politics, and more notoriously, intelligence and even the military.[56] Anthropologists as individuals are mixed up in all sorts of projects in the world, and may promote or hinder their interests and those of the communities they target. What anthropologists do and how they live are often just as important, or just as irrelevant, as what they write. Their writing in any case has to be directed to the 'real world' of publishers, the book-buying public, teaching courses, jobs, and potential research funds. Here, an understanding of the way that society works, rather than simply the way that 'culture' is written, is a great advantage for the practitioner.

4. THE IDEA OF A SOCIAL SCIENCE: AND ITS VARIANTS IN ANTHROPOLOGY

I have taken the title of this section from a short but influential book published by Peter Winch in 1958.[57] His argument, in outline, was that the social studies, still in their infancy, should not be tempted to emulate the natural sciences, but in so far as they dealt with human beings, recognize rather their affinity with philosophy. Winch's formulation was offered to the whole field of social science, and drew many ideas from Wittgenstein. His argument took its bearings from the idea of language as 'a form of life' in which we share an understanding of reality. At the same time it had an anthropological and historical cast, making good use of reference to Collingwood. Winch emphasized how making things intelligible in the social studies was different from making things intelligible in the natural sciences in that the former involved making human beings themselves intelligible, that is, communicating with them. There was always an 'internality' to such understanding, as was characteristic of social relations in general. Historical explanation (and he is here following Collingwood) is not the application of general theories to particular instances; 'it is the tracing of internal relations. It is like applying one's knowledge of a language in order to understand a conversation rather than like applying one's knowledge of the laws of mechanics to understand the workings of a watch.' Winch's book was welcomed by younger anthropologists, and while it has sometimes received a rather 'relativist' reading, it is a convincing presentation which has lasted well.[58]

Generalizing about the social sciences beyond Winch's formulation, we could usefully underscore the principle that with respect to the phenomena of human life, at some level 'the whole' involves relational connections between the constituent elements. Thus, for example, it is not enough simply to add up economic, political, cultural, and religious facts; they are constituted in relation to each other, and the real challenge is to understand the interrelation. Nor is it enough to think of social life as merely the sum of the interactions, intentions, and experiences of individual persons or even the agreements they may make with each other: again, there are senses in which we must recognize encompassing pattern and structure in social form behind the particular circumstances of individual life, even to some degree behind the sense of personal will, intention, and experience. The 'internalities' invoked by Winch are not those of separate individual consciousnesses; they are those of shared codes of mutual understanding. They are not fixed or closed but open-ended and accessible to new participants. To see an 'objectivity' in these patterns does not deny them elasticity and openness.

Winch's 'idea of a social science' helps us pinpoint something of the distinctive character of what became 'British social anthropology' in the mid-twentieth century, a tradition which is still active in shaping modern anthropology as a whole. In the rest of this section, I try to provide a sort of genealogy for this tradition in the light of Winch's conception, starting with the debt to the Durkheimian school and moving on towards the work of Evans-Pritchard, which retains its exemplary status even today in the post-colonial world.

The French school and the formation of 'British social anthropology'

Durkheim famously referred to 'social facts' and their 'objective' existence, a formulation which has often been criticized for its rigidity. But we can find a more sympathetic rendering of the French 'fait social' as 'social phenomenon', that is a phenomenon of human life *irreducibly social* in the sense that Winch later pinpointed. There is a particular reason why Durkheim, out of the whole range of writers on sociology, politics, and economics of the nineteenth and early twentieth century has been firmly appropriated as a founder of theoretical anthropology, and that is because he, and his followers who contributed from 1898 onwards to the journal *l'Année Sociologique*, treated ethnographic reports from across the lesser-known parts of the world as serious sociological information. In fact there was no split in the Durkheim school between anthropology and sociology; they were one field of study, and ethnographic textual or artistic fragments from remote areas were treated with as much scholarly care as details from classical or European civilizations. Marx and Weber, by contrast, made only passing reference to tribal societies, and then in order mainly to highlight organizational distinctions between pre-modern and modern social forms by drawing on the historically known parts of Asia.[59] Other major figures in the founding of the social sciences, such as John Stuart Mill in the utilitarian tradition, scarcely acknowledged the importance of non-Western traditions. The devotion of Durkheim and his followers to the detailed understanding and analysis of the widest possible range of social forms through a scrutiny of the ethnographic record was not matched anywhere, and while the circumstances of the First World War in the event largely ruled out their plans to engage in field research, their work became a very important foundation for much later developments in the theoretical and analytical ideas of social anthropology. In recent decades, as anthropology's horizons have widened from the 'tribal fringe' to mainstream world civilizations and global social processes, there has been increasingly fertile use of the other major social theorists.

It is generally accepted that two anthropologists who became productive in the inter-war years laid the ground plans for social anthropology in Britain: Bronislaw Malinowski and A. R. Radcliffe-Brown. We have to remember that their programme was to break out of the context of the ethnographic museums and the long-established association of anthropology with archaeology and ancient history. In the effort to revitalize what they saw as the lifeless antiquarianism of folklore studies and museum work, they both emphasized first-hand, empirical field research as the proper method for anthropology, and the relevance of anthropological investigations to practical questions of colonial administration (especially those of native welfare). For guidance on theory in their project of what eventually was labelled a kind of comparative sociology, they looked to the Durkheimian school for inspiration. In Malinowski's case, this inspiration was fairly vague and open-ended; he wrote and taught a lot about the need to place customs and beliefs and practices in their context, to see their function in completing the whole, a cultural whole which satisfied the needs of individuals in every way. His approach, which does not have much of an explanatory edge, became known as 'functionalism'.[60] Malinowski became more effectively famous as a passionate advocate of what was to become a distinguishing feature of the subject, that is the period of many months or years in which the student is immersed in a local community, learning the language and studying everything that goes on. He was the person who really institutionalized the importance of prolonged field research for anthropologists in Britain (already well established in the United States by Franz Boas). His near contemporary, Radcliffe-Brown, approached anthropology with a more systematic and comparative curiosity, seeking the local 'jural' or customary legal framework of rules and regulations within which authority operated, groups were constituted, and resources were held. He used the idea of 'structure' very comfortably, but unlike the images of structure as an underlying grammar of principle which is implicit in Durkheim and Mauss and which Lévi-Strauss was later to develop, Radcliffe-Brown pointed to closed, mechanical or biological analogies. The structure of a society was like a house with an internal framework of beams, or like a clock, or like an organism, or a patterned shell on the sea shore which one could take home and classify in one's collection. Social anthropology for him was a comparative sociology, focusing on the total set of links between individuals and enduring groups in society, and should try harder to model itself on the natural sciences.[61] His style of analysis came to be known as 'structural-functionalism', and suffered, like Malinowski's, from a failure to take historical connections into account.

However, much more than the idea of social function lay behind the early twentieth-century body of French-language writing on anthropology. Their ideas of pattern, even structure, were richer than any conception of the 'sum' of links between individuals. Moreover, writers in French aimed at diagnosing the principles of religious, symbolic, and ritual life, even systems of thought in themselves. Though not a collaborator in Durkheim's group, the Belgian anthropologist Arnold van Gennep published his study *The Rites of Passage* in 1909, a book which illustrates this point well, and has come to have a profound impact on modern anthropology.[62] Van Gennep noticed the cross-cultural, world-wide similarity of form between those ceremonies which mark the movement of persons through the various stages of life, the birth rites, Christenings or namings, initiations, weddings, funerals, and commemorations; and he included in his comparison ceremonies which mark the geographical passage from one space to another or the seasonal passage of time. He also included the very dramatic rites marking the transition between the reigns of kings. He articulated a systematic model by which such ceremonies mark the leaving of one stage, a 'liminal' passage through a kind of limbo, and incorporation into the next. What we can see is a broadly 'structural' pattern involving every aspect of individual and social life, replicated and marked by ritual detail in surprisingly characteristic ways across the world (regardless of what might today be distinguished as 'local culture'). Van Gennep's analysis retains its power, and has been elaborated and further worked out by anthropologists ever since (the name of Victor Turner is central here), though today we would expect to find more of a historical and political dynamic to accounts of such rites. There are examples in the chapters which follow.

Another major anthropologist with a philosophical bent and interest in the broad comparison of essentially *social* phenomena was the French writer Lucien Lévy-Bruhl, who like van Gennep worked independently of the Durkheim group. He published extensively in the inter-war period in French on topics such as 'primitive mentality' and ideas of the soul, combing the ethnographic record for the kind of detail which would illuminate the nature of the sources from which there would eventually develop modern scientific rationality and modern religious thought about the person. Because his work was based on a broad division between 'them and us', that is the world of the primitive and the modern, it was dismissed as reactionary by many in British anthropology, and only a few took up the deeper significance of Lévy-Bruhl's engagement with the emotional, poetic, and intuitive aspects of human life, which even he recognized had persisted in the face of scientific rationality and was part of the modern world too. Among those who did engage with his ideas, however, and helped to ensure that anthropology remained open to questions of the sociology of feeling, cognition, and poetic resonance, were Evans-Pritchard and Rodney Needham.[63]

From within the Durkheimian tradition, we should briefly recall the importance of a series of essays which again presented analysis of the form of 'collective representations' and their intimate relation to the morphology of social life, as organized and enacted in a literal sense. Several from the early period most significantly provided a continuing agenda for anthropology: Durkheim and Mauss's *Primitive Classification*, Robert Hertz's two essays on death rituals and on the pre-eminence of the right hand, both treated as general social phenomena; of less fame, but comparable importance for British anthropology, were Mauss and Beuchat's essay on the contrastive morphology of summer and winter settlement patterns among the Arctic hunters (mentioned earlier), and Hubert and Mauss's analysis of the ritual 'grammar' of sacrifice. A late essay by Mauss on 'the gift' or rather the nature of exchange in pre-monetary society, where things were passed on and circulated on the basis of 'donation', became a key text.[64]

Inherent in the mainstream idea of a social science is the theme of communication: of codes, of language, and of the exchange of shared signs, even the possibility of translation between codes and languages themselves. This broad view of what society is like underlay much of the Durkheimian school and was made explicit in a fresh way by the 'structural analysis' of Claude Lévi-Strauss, who had been a pupil of Mauss.[65] He worked out new principles behind the way that social relations were constructed and reconstructed by the exchanges carried out through the making of marriages (discussed further in Chapter 7) and, using models from structural linguistics, showed how there were surprising depths of order and syntax in the storyline of myths. Transmitted over thousands of miles and over the millennia, myths certainly varied in their surface detail, but their underlying structure of oppositional contrast at different levels could be revealed as a series of mirror images, analogies, and nesting thematic patterns which signified not only inter-translatable operations of the human mind everywhere, but a much wider community of contact and circulation than standard literary or historical comparison could reveal (further discussed in Chapter 5).

Lévi-Strauss's work profoundly transformed the way that anthropologists have since approached kinship and marriage, the materials of verbal narrative and especially myth, and also the transmission of style and structure in the visual arts. He himself often used the motif of musical form as a metaphor for the kind of patterning he divined in culture generally, a patterning of a deeper order than is immediately apparent and which was itself the vehicle for long-term and long-distance transmission and the production of many variants. Edmund Leach was one of the key figures in British anthropology to import the ideas of Lévi-Strauss, and he used the motifs of communication, codes, and systematic variation to criticize the standard 'structural-functionalism' of the 1950s. Leach famously described the comparison of whole social structures as like collecting butterflies, and classifying them according to colour. He did not want, he said, to know about blue butterflies as such, he wanted to know how their bodies worked so they could fly. It was necessary to recapture a view of the *relational* qualities of social life, including the way that social relations might change over time.[66]

The idea of an anthropology linked with social process, history, and the humanities

Edward Evans-Pritchard, appointed in 1946 to the Chair of Social Anthropology in Oxford, in succession to Radcliffe-Brown, was able to bring several elements from the pre-war British and French traditions together in an effective way. These included the method of fieldwork by local immersion, the insights of Radcliffe-Brown as applied to the structure of local jural and political systems, and the older and deeper understandings of Durkheim and Mauss about the patterns of underlying communication and shared significance in a social world. Like Lévi-Strauss he harboured a deep interest in language, though we could say on the 'literary' rather than the 'grammatical' or analytical side. Evans-Pritchard's intellectual ambitions for anthropology sprang from an interest in the rich role of spoken understandings in the formation of social relations, in widening the scope of history to include those who rarely appear in its textbooks, and in the challenge of writing ethnography good enough to provoke the attention of colleagues in neighbouring fields. He introduced his students to the writings of R. G. Collingwood, whose work on Roman Britain he had himself reviewed with admiration in the early 1930s.[67]

Evans-Pritchard's 1937 analysis of the place of witchcraft, oracles, and magic in the world of the central African Azande struck immediate chords.[68] The book became widely influential in the debate opening up within philosophy over the socially and historically placed foundations of what could be understood as knowledge (it is referred to for example by Winch, discussed above). It also resonated with the more flexible approaches being taken by historians towards the social context of 'witchcraft' phenomena in the European and American past. Because of its pace and well-constructed storyline, the book easily moved into teaching syllabuses and has always been popular with students. The Azande and their doggedly 'rational' and clever way of monitoring and justifying the operation of their oracles (still quite surprising to many readers) have helped to define what modern anthropology is about. They have certainly entered the majority of textbooks on the subject published over the last half-century. Ironically, however, the appeal of the Azande has more recently converged with new and easy forms of cultural relativism which lead students to ask, 'Why *shouldn't* the Azande believe in witchcraft, if it suits their way of life, and who am I to criticize them?' This is not Evans-Pritchard's line; on the contrary, he shows how most ordinary Azande themselves are not at all comfortable with the presence of witchcraft. It is those in powerful and privileged positions who focus on the idea, as the source of suffering and death, and turn their accusations on the relatively helpless. The oracles are ultimately controlled by (sometimes cruel) kings and princes. Even at the household level only senior men have access to them, while women constitute a large proportion of the accused. Evans-Pritchard's analysis is set explicitly in a political and historical context which offers a more nuanced reading than that of simple relativism, and ultimately, we could say that this extra depth is what gives the text its lasting qualities.

The Nuer of the southern Sudan, as a people, and *The Nuer* as Evans-Pritchard's first book on them, entered the life and language of academic anthropology in 1940.[69] This was the first time that 'œcology' had explicitly been selected for analysis in a field monograph, though Evans-Pritchard acknowledged his debt to Mauss and Beuchat's essay on the seasonal variation of 'social morphology' among the Arctic peoples.[70] It was also the first analytical field study of the political principles behind regularly recurring patterns of hostility and alliance between apparently unrelated groups of mobile herders, here cast in a strong idiom of moral obligation invoked through the situational rhetoric of paternal descent. Structured conceptions of spatial and temporal relations were shown to lie behind the way in which groups identified each other and entered into political games of reciprocal action and counter-action that an observer could learn to 'read'. The book offered quite a different vision of 'social structure' from the empiricism of Radcliffe-Brown, and, significantly, has since been interpreted as an analogue, even a forerunner of the abstract 'structuralism' associated especially with Lévi-Strauss. Louis Dumont even claimed that it had not been properly appreciated by English-speaking anthropologists.[71] *The Nuer* nevertheless served as model and inspiration to a wide range of field studies of 'segmentary' political systems both in Africa and elsewhere. Along with the collection on *African Political Systems* co-edited with Meyer Fortes which appeared in the same year, it marked the birth of the subdiscipline of field-based political anthropology and a new dialogue with the growing subject of political science. With its successor *Kinship and Marriage among the Nuer* it provoked a considerable industry of re-analysis, criticism, and comment.[72]

The final volume in Evans-Pritchard's trilogy also helped create a subdiscipline, in this case the field-based anthropology of religion, and also established a new baseline for conversations with a neighbouring discipline. *Nuer Religion* was written quite provocatively as a challenge to academic theology, requiring its specialists as well as a wider readership in religious studies to take tribal systems of belief and practice seriously. Evans-Pritchard's presentation of Nuer trust in *kwoth*, the Spirit of the above, has the schematic character of a creed, but at the same time a lived and shared reality. He portrays for us in almost biblical tone an elemental confrontation between God and Man, demanding recognition across the gulf between the historical religions and their sacred texts, on the one hand, and, on the other, the worlds they often denigrate as erring paganism or blind custom. The work is presented as social analysis, emphasizing how diversity of perception and representation reflects the relativity of points of view within Nuer society established in his first book, though it draws the line (explicitly) at entering the subjectivity of religious experience. A turn towards this very subjectivity, however, has been at the heart of more recent work in the anthropology of religion (as I shall discuss in Chapter 5).

Evans-Pritchard made explicit his lifelong sympathy for the historian's perspective and his ambition to establish social anthropology as 'a kind of historiography', a comparative study of the forms of social life which did not caricature those forms as mere empirical data but recognized their moral character and their participation in the same historical world as that of the observer. It has sometimes been suggested that Evans-Pritchard's style of anthropology could be glossed as 'the translation of culture', and indeed this was adopted as the title of one of the main volumes of essays offered to him on his retirement in 1970. However, as a gloss on his overall repositioning of anthropology this phrase sits a little uncomfortably, deriving more from late twentieth-century ideas of 'culture' difference than from the disciplined comparison of social forms towards which Evans-Pritchard strove. His identification of similar political principles among the Nuer and the Bedouin of Cyrenaica is clearly about more than the 'translation of culture'.[73]

Evans-Pritchard was certainly concerned with translation, but essentially as a craftsman in handling the subtleties of language as such, as for example in his elegant paper on *sanza*, the way in which Azande employ proverbs in double-talk, or in his treatments of poetry and oral literature. A project he undertook with colleagues in the 1960s was the launching of the Oxford Library of African Literature, a series which flourished over the following two decades, and had considerable influence in developing anthropology's openness to art, performance, narrative, and the uses of textual material generally.

A generation of anthropologists born long after Evans-Pritchard's era have naturally sought to refashion and refresh the subject in the fast-changing world of the late twentieth century, and various lines of criticism have been directed towards his work. Along with his contemporaries, he has been taken to task for not keeping more of an intellectual distance from the colonial situation in which anthropology had such a privileged position. He has been criticized for being too impressionistic in his ethnographic portrayals, for using a patronizing tone and perpetuating character stereotypes; and on the question of religion, of presenting Nuer beliefs as too biblical and the people as too pious. He has also had his fair share of accusations over 'male bias'. With hindsight, and the turn of another century, however, we can see that Evans-Pritchard's work remains a source of inspiration. He put very vividly those paradoxes of multiple belonging or 'positionality' which the modern student ponders, focusing in a still helpful way on the relativities of 'self and other' in the making of personal and group identities, as we might rephrase segmentary theory today. He placed 'dialogue' both between the Azande themselves and between himself and his informants firmly at the heart of the analysis of knowledge and belief which he carried out among them. He also respected, explicitly, the privacy and inner religious consciousness of the Nuer whose world became in so many other ways public property through his work. It is clearly true that in many respects Evans-Pritchard failed to take 'colonialism' into account in his analyses, but then again, looking back, he is foremost among those who worked to re-orient anthropology towards history.

The colonial period abounded in its own well-intentioned practitioners who sought to use their professional skills to improve the lot of native peoples. There was a distinctively liberal, even radical, streak in the anthropology of the British colonial period, as there had been in the devoted work of mission-aries and scholars in North America from the mid-nineteenth century. In the drive to reveal the *realities of social process* on the ground, Max Gluckman was a leading figure, and found useful tools to hand in the works of mainstream sociological writers, including Marx and Weber. What are the dynamics behind social action, which on a small scale create chains of linked significance in events over time in a particular place, and on a larger scale feed into history? Gluckman's formulation of the 'extended case method' in Manchester led to a series of field studies in central Africa that are now gaining fresh attention for their insights into issues of community political action and the pursuit of rights and claims.[74] With the end of the colonial period, in particular, this investigative style of inquiry led a new generation of anthropologists to criticize the whole power imbalances of imperial rule, and in doing so they began to draw creatively on Marx. Their commitment to revealing injustice and to finding a proper basis for political action in the world was combined with the aim of understanding social processes over time, and a newly acute consciousness of history.

Today many students across the world take up anthropology with a view to a career in the development field, or in the international agencies, or in charitable and welfare work with the underprivileged. The 'idea of a social science' has again and again been implicated in the quest not only for understanding as an end in itself, but for understanding as a basis for correcting wrongs. This promise of seeing into the machinations of power more clearly, both at the level of gender and family affairs and at the national or international level of political policy and élites, is the most powerful source of momentum in today's anthropology and its theoretical potential is still to be fully developed. In my view anthropology has always had a capacity for social criticism, even subversion.[75] In discussing 'globalization' and human rights (see Chapter 11) today's anthropologists are following their predecessors in trying to use their discipline to gain a 'usable' kind of understanding of what is happening in the real world. Anthropology's dialogues with grand theory will continue: and so will its moral impetus.

PART II

Shape and Rhythm in Social Forms

CHAPTER THREE

Species, Space, and Time

A NTHROPOLOGISTS often talk of basic categories of conceptual organiza- tion or understanding. In doing this, they sometimes seek to follow the philosophers in looking for the foundational aspects of categorical thinking in such domains as space, or time, or ideas of the material and non-material, species of the human and non-human, self and other. While philosophers focus on the formal specification of such primary conditions of thought, and the way they facilitate access to the world as it is, anthropologists tend to focus on their content and their historical variation, with a focus on the coherence of a cultural tradition and its arbitrary relation to reality. The term 'category' is commonly used in both contexts, highlighting form and con- tent respectively, and these uses can often slide into one another and help to make this a confusing area to understand. Nick Allen, whose interests in world-wide comparison and the span of world history have been mentioned, has clarified many of these issues.[1] In the Aristotelian and indeed Kantian sense, a 'category' refers to some common dimension of human understand- ing which makes it possible for us to articulate conceptual and experiential knowledge. Aristotle listed ten such categories: substance (or essence), quantity, quality, relation, space, time, position (or posture), possession (or condition), activity, passivity. Many of these were closely linked to the kinds of question one could ask of the world in the ancient Greek language, and we can immediately see that such a list might look different in Zuñi or Chinese (though we would have to educate ourselves, in each case, to see exactly how and why). Modern commentators have played around with the list, for example the nineteenth-century philosopher Renouvier who strongly influenced Durkheim. Renouvier offered as his list: relation (a category which penetrated all the others), number, position, succession, quality; and then becoming, causality, finality, personality. Allen has argued that the Durkheimian school were essentially tracing the contextual and historical expression of such foundational categories of understanding, and that Mauss in particular was working out the fundamental implications of the idea of 'relation' in his study of 'exchange'. 'Relation' carries with it the idea of *movement*, as in the Greek question 'towards or against what?' It provides a way of theorizing the connections between things and becomes, as Allen's discussion clearly suggests (though this point is not put so bluntly), a beautiful tool for the sociologist, because 'society' is undeniably a thing of flux, and flow, and of people actively engaging in that flow.

It could be argued that a very basic apprehension of space, time, matter, movement, and so on was part of animal consciousness and individual learning as the organism manages its life in the world, and not exclusive to human beings. But the idea of a *relation*, and especially of a set of schematically linked relations, is a way of apprehending the world in the kind of way that symbolic language-and-action makes possible and is not found (as far as we know) in the wider animal world. And further, it is only upon the basis of the idea of *relationship* that nested 'classifications' of the world and its contents, of the kind that fascinate anthropologists, can be constructed. It is at this level that we speak of the way that colours or animal species or even human occupations are classified, or of how such 'categories' of similarity and difference on several planes are culturally constructed. Here is the ethnographic evidence for extending the philosopher's questions about basic forms of understanding. As scholars we can translate between classifications, as ordinary people who travel from home and literally or figuratively 'know more than one language' have always done. The fact that such translation can be done, however provisionally and partially, means that as human beings we must be operating in terms of foundational categorical understandings which encompass cultural variation as they do specific language differences.

This situation, philosophically difficult but an everyday experience, presents us with a problem lying at the heart of anthropology. We find it difficult to entertain two seemingly contradictory ideas about 'human understanding' at the same time. Most of us think that there is some reality out there which the scientists are getting to know better and better through the specialist deployment of a kind of reason we ourselves share; but we also know that it is hard to specify what kind of reality we can discover for which we have not already found a name, or already prefigured conceptually, out of our own subjective capacities. We also know that even the most abstract of the philosopher's categories, such as space and time, have themselves undergone conceptual revolutions in the course of history; for today's scientists, not even these most basic categories are constant. Time/space relativity in modern physics, and the dissolution of the solidity of 'matter', have upended previous understandings. While ordinary people, and scientists in their everyday lives, still operate on the basis of the older square and solid understandings, there is a widespread popular appetite for the latest scientific formulations, however apprehended as a purely imagined world, a kind of poetry.[2] We can live with different kinds of knowledge today, we are conscious of their comings and goings, and probably have had this capacity too throughout history.

In seeking, as Durkheim and Mauss did in their essay *Primitive Classification*, to uncover the basic categories of understanding which governed archaic or 'primitive' civilizations, anthropologists are not necessarily trying to separate the past from the present, or one cultural system from another.[3] They are trying, primarily, to trace connections; and to work out the ways in which one set of understandings can lead to, or displace, another. If the key ambition of Mauss, and the *Année Sociologique* writers generally, was to explore the *history* of the classic philosophical categories, their project was very close to that of R. G. Collingwood, who saw the proper task of the philosopher as revealing the underlying presuppositions, ultimately the absolute presuppositions, of those systems of thought-and-action (whether explicit scientific creations or the implicit underlying orientations of an age, a civilization) *which have actually existed* as historical phenomena.[4] That is, philosophy should not be founded on pure metaphysical speculation transcending any particular starting point but should operate critically from the present upon the whole range of ways in which we can discover that humanity has thought.

Thus, for example, it might be thought that 'nature' constituted a common-sense empirical baseline and one could directly compare what one or another scientist or philosopher said about it. But the concept of 'nature' itself has taken different shapes, traced by Collingwood from the time of the ancient Greeks, as human beings have measured and reassessed themselves against it.[5] As perhaps with time, and space, we cannot seriously ditch the whole notion of nature, and in that sense it remains a general predicate of human understanding. However, what we do with it or within it is not simply a matter of arbitrary variation; it is more a matter of human history, as one set of ideas and practices comes to impinge on another. To understand nature better, and our place in relation to it, we need to understand, critically, our own and others' images of it and how they have been formed over history. This is not the same as cultural relativism. In the interest of clarity, in what follows I shall reserve the term 'category' for the classic philosopher's 'mode of apprehending and making linguistic statements about the world' or its analogue in the world's vernacular philosophies. I shall reserve the terms 'class' and 'classification' for the domains and species distinguished and positioned relative to each other within such a mode or even overlapping modes of understanding, that is, within the context of human life in practice. Maintaining an analytical distinction of this kind is useful because the really striking things about ritual and religion, art and science, start to happen when the human imagination begins to mix and match across domains and boundaries, even to make active transformations between them.

Natural kinds

Let me explain this point with reference to some recent work by Maurice Bloch, who combines an interest in cognition with what we could still call structural and historical approaches in social anthropology. His arguments, often drawing on his research in Madagascar, will help refresh our perception of the themes which have concerned anthropological writers in the Durkheimian tradition on categories and classifications. Bloch insists on a distinction between 'culture', and cognition; and also between the particular representations of explicit knowledge, of the kind which an ethnographer might encounter because they are verbalized, and those implicit 'categories of understanding' with which the philosophers have concerned themselves for centuries. He equates the latter with Durkheim's 'collective representations', the 'very foundation of all knowledge'. He criticizes anthropology's tendency to highlight the odd or strange content of verbalized or ritualized cultural expression, while neglecting the kind of everyday knowledge which is implicit and 'enmeshed in action'.[6] It is in the latter that we can find the proper basis for coherent comparison of human understanding. At this level, there are 'classificatory' concepts which are learned and transmitted as complex clusters of elements, through practice and an ability to grasp patterns and wholes rather than through analytical language. Cognitive psychologists speak of 'scripts' or 'schemata', prototypes or exemplars or 'chunked' networks of understandings which enable us (perhaps especially as young children) to appreciate, for example, what is involved in 'a house' without prescribing roof, walls, etc., or to know as a whole the cluster of activities involved in 'getting the breakfast ready'. Such concepts, as wholes, can be non- or pre-linguistic, and undergo a definite transformation when rendered into language as explicit, sequential discourse. This view helps us see how non-verbal learning, through participation and 'apprenticeship', may apply much more widely than simply in acquiring the skills of weaving or cooking.[7] It also provides a way of thinking about memory, and of the transformations involved in moving between linguistic and non-linguistic domains, or 'putting knowledge into words'. Such transmutation between domains, employing analogy and substitution, is a source of potential innovation and creativity. By putting an account of knowledge into writing, ethnography itself involves a transmutation of this kind, and ethnographers must beware of relying simply on what people say to them as adequate evidence of culture or knowledge. Here is the real justification for learning by 'participant' observation. Classifications, in other words, are not merely linguistic or intellectual; they are 'lived-in' models of the world.[8]

A further line of cognitive research which Bloch has found illuminating relates to the idea that there are distinctive ways of apprehending specific domains in the world which are common to humanity. One of these concerns the domain of 'living kinds', of moving animals in particular, and the difference between this domain and that of artefacts, that is, things made by people for their own use (compare Mithen's ideas about the evolution of mental processes, discussed in the previous chapter). It is suggested that this recognition of specific domain difference could be compared with, for example, the inborn capacity of children to learn languages, whatever those languages might be, or to recognize faces. A tiger which has lost its stripes and even three of its legs will still be a tiger, even to a very young child and in the 'metaphorical' play-form of a stuffed toy. Now some 'living kinds' are transformed by human beings into artefacts; food and building timber are obvious examples. Tomatoes are unambiguously classified as fruits in the 'living' domain, only to become a puzzle when brought into the kitchen and used 'as vegetables'. This distinction is not, however, devised by the botanist but by the cook for purposes of processing ingredients into dishes, which have their own classification and structure. The linking up of domains involved here is very significant for anthropologists, for much rich symbolic effect and religious profundity arises from the transformations which result when things are moved, we might say translated, from one domain to another. Animal sacrifice, as among the Nuer, is offered by Bloch as an example of such transformations, where the ox is at first a metaphorical parallel for the person on whose behalf the sacrifice takes place; the ox becomes a substitute for that person, and then in being killed is transformed into an 'artefact', of meat. It is suggested that dialectical transformations, or transmutations, between such domains, represented in more or less paradoxical forms, can be found at the heart of religious symbolism across the world.[9]

Now let us go back in scholarly time to consider the foundational works of the Durkheimian school on categories and classification, and some of their successors in anglophone anthropology. Considered here are some defining frameworks of natural, cosmological, and social reality, presumed archaic but already predicated on the idea of cross-reference, transformation, substitutability, and connectivity. In considering Durkheim and Mauss's *Primitive Classification*, Nick Allen finds it useful to employ the structural linguists' contrast between the relations holding between, on the one hand, elements that are co-present in a single sentence and, on the other, the relations, such as contrast or association, that link these elements to others which are not part of the sentence.[10] Thus, the well-known fourfold list of the purported physical elements, air, fire, water, and earth, which dominated science through the Middle Ages, is analogous to such a sentence: each element was put in correspondence to specific cosmological bodies (Jupiter, Mars, Moon, and Saturn), to human dispositions (sanguine, choleric, phlegmatic, and melancholy), and sometimes also to colours. Associations and influences were strong between the respective elements linked across these domains, as is still reflected in popular astrology. In *Primitive Classification* three main kinds of such encompassing structure were explored, and presented as a historical sequence.[11] In the native Australian cases selected, it is argued that the classification of things reproduces that of people; the divisions of the world into which things are distributed are modelled on nesting sets of distinctions within a tribe, its sections, and its clans, and the patterns of reciprocity in kinship and intermarriage which partly define them. There are strong associations (whether of metaphor or substitutability) between the people classed together at any particular level, and the animals, and things, also classed at that level. They may be represented in some way as in a mutually life-sustaining relation to each other, and in a life-giving relation to those other parties in the classification with whom there are patterns of organized intermarriage. We should not forget that the pragmatic context of these classifications is one of human mobility, and a foraging, hunting way of life, of seasonal movements and both remembered and expected encounters.

Allen reminds us that all classifications of this holistic kind are 'lived in'—and in this they are not exactly comparable with the speculative constructions of specialized scientists or philosophers.

A second mode of 'primitive classification' or the abstract organization of reality is then offered in Durkheim and Mauss's essay, taking its bearings from ideas of relative space and orientation rather than from the formal organization of society through kinship categories and marriage exchange. The world of the Zuñi pueblo-dwellers of New Mexico is given as an example. Like other 'pueblo' peoples of the American South-West, themselves classed as a 'type' by the Spanish term for their distinctive clustered villages, typically on a hilltop or excavated into its cliffs and surrounded by cultivated fields, the Zuñi take their bearings from a very prominent concept of 'the centre'. Here, the elements of the cosmos, and people themselves, are distributed conceptually according to their relation to that centre, not only in a directly subjective way as though one were always looking out from that centre, but also in an 'objective' conceptual sense (the centre itself is a division in the classification). There are hence seven regions distinguished spatially; the four cardinal points, the zenith, the nadir, and the centre. Seasons and elements are distributed according to the first four; species, social functions, and colours according to all seven, priests according to the first six. Three clans are distributed to each of the first six directions, and one to the centre. This schema is applied in many other domains, and still underlies the cultural vitality of Zuñi art and crafts. When I had the opportunity to visit it, the old cathedral at Zuñi was being redecorated by local artists for the Millennium celebrations, with a continuous frieze around the walls of scenes from myth set out according to the rhythm and direction of the seasons. Zuñi is sited on elevated ground, like the other Pueblo settlements—some of which, like Acoma, are on spectacular, cliff-sided *mesas*. Each settlement thus has a distinctive 'outlook', a centre from which the directions are vividly signalled by the topography itself. They remind us how 'cosmology' is not independent of the land and the way we live upon it; without naively assuming a naturalistic fit between the spaces of the human imagination and the physical setting, we have to accept that they are linked, and shaped partly by reference to each other. Like the Australian systems, the Zuñi and other American cases mentioned incorporate the divisions of the people, and their structured interrelation, into the very categories of 'existential' reality. Durkheim and Mauss were keen to suggest that certain ethnographic cases of classificatory systems indicate historical development. For example, in the Zuñi case,

FIG. 2. Acoma Pueblo, New Mexico. Known as Sky City, this settlement is reputed to be one of the oldest continuously inhabited towns on the continent. Perched atop a 365-foot high *mesa* it is the year-round home of 12 families who keep it in good repair for cerremonial events The San Estoban Rey adobe mission, at top centre, was built in the seventeenth century. Photo Adriel Heisey (NM18-487–02).

notwithstanding the prominence of the idea of the centre, much mythology recalls a fourfold pattern, as in a creation story referring to two pairs of eggs, which they treat as possible evidence of a prior form. Today we have much more evidence on the long time-span and complexity of cultural history, and we need not place much weight on simple evolutionary schemas. Today we would expect multiplicity in any classification, however apparently archaic.

The third main mode of classification identified in the essay, of which Chinese cosmology is discussed as an example, does not entail (or has historically become separated from) the encompassing of social relations within the cosmic scheme. Nevertheless, as is well known, a powerful system of associations encompassing regions of space, periods of time, animals, colours, powers, the contents of the world and so on has influenced the science, philosophy, medicine, and other practices of this major world civilization over millennia. Here, suggest our authors, lies a key to understanding where 'modern science' and other systematic thought has its roots, in Chinese and in other civilizations alike. The disentanglement, however, of the purely intellectual forms of logic from those which formerly commanded the affective commitment of human beings, and sometimes governed their lives within a system of the division of labour or of systematic intermarriage, has not had a simple history. Allen's view is that in the long term, there has been a gradual 'unravelling' or flattening out of the cohesion of those human worlds Durkheim and Mauss distinguished as examples of 'primitive classification', a separation of the domains they embraced together, and the proliferation of many more restricted and specific kinds of classification in these particular domains. He has applied his argument in a comprehensive way to the foundations of Indo-European ideology, tracing a basic fourfold, or arguably fivefold, articulation of the world at its roots.[12] At the heart of the old systems, perhaps we could guess, metaphor (the association of elements from different domains in one class together) was so strong that it was reality; we now see reality in a more piecemeal way, but then, as a direct consequence, horizons are opened up for the conscious use of all kinds of 'new' metaphor.

This vision is shared by Robert Hertz in his still exciting and relevant essay of 1907 on the pre-eminence of the right hand.[13] Whatever the organic basis or predisposition to right-handedness in human beings, it does not explain the enormous weight so many cultural traditions have placed upon the symbolic aspects of right as pure, good, and true, and sometimes male, while the left is weak, even evil, subordinate, and sometimes female. The image of balanced complementary opposition offers a holistic model of the world divided into cleaving halves or 'moieties'. This 'dualism' was regarded as ancient by Lévi-Strauss, who identified its living traces in aspects of social organization in South America, for example, where it is still elaborately reflected in art and myth.[14] Right/left oppositions are also characteristic of the asymmetrical or lopsided relations which pervade hierarchically organized societies, for example the caste system of Hindu India.[15] However, we do not need to imagine ourselves in a simple world where everything is on one side or another to recognize the ramifications of right/left symbolism. Granet's lucid demonstration of Chinese etiquette makes the point. For example—and this gives only a hint of its exquisite complexity—while it is proper to use the right hand for eating, the side to which honour and status belongs is the left. In greeting, boys are educated to cover the right hand with the left when they bow and then present the left hand; while girls should cover the left hand and offer the right. However, in time of mourning, men make their salutations as though they were women, concealing the left and extending the right hand. The pattern of the greeting is furthermore related to the phases of ceremonial time, and thus in China: 'A left-hander is worth as much as a right-hander. More exactly, there are cultural eras, or physiological phases of the Universe, in which it is fitting to be left-handed, and other phases in which it is appropriate to be right-handed.'[16]

The notion that underlying our social lives and cultural ideas are still pervasive patterns of classification of which we are only partially aware has remained a powerful one in modern anthropology. Two writers in particular have put forward fruitful theories about what we could call the underlying grammar of social thought-and-action. Mary Douglas's book *Purity and Danger* was a landmark in this field, and has been very widely read outside anthropology. Following a trail already indicated in Franz Steiner's *Taboo*, she explores the way in which systems of symbolic classification, even in modern circumstances, can carry with them tremendous implication for the way that people organize themselves socially, constructing boundaries and distinctions with moral and religious implications.[17] She focuses moreover, in a strikingly original manner, on the incompleteness and provisionality of actual classifications with respect to the material world. Previous discussions of classification had assumed a kind of closure, of self-sufficiency. Douglas points to the fact that any classification comes up against things which do not fit, which threaten or breach the external or internal boundaries it has set up and thus the basis of the system. Such threats are conceptually a fertile source of impurity and danger, and require, in terms of the moral logic of the classification itself, to be given special attention: to be co-opted, or purged, exorcised, purified. A famous example from her own fieldwork among the Lele of the Congo basin is the creature known as the pangolin, a scaly anteater. It defies the regular rules of Lele animal classification, since, for example, it climbs trees, lays eggs, but does not fly or have feathers. It is impure and defiling, but partly because of this lends itself to transformation into something 'sacred'. It has become the centre of a special religious cult of fertility; when one is found in the forest, it is brought home and ritually killed as part of the cult.[18] Mary Douglas was one of the first anthropologists seriously to apply her analyses to biblical evidence, to the history of Judaism, Christianity, and the modern West. One of her provocative arguments is that the common Middle Eastern prohibition on pork derives ultimately from the fact that pigs do not fit into the classes of animal creation as set up in Genesis.

They are anomalous with respect to the original scheme of creation, being cloven-footed but not chewing the cud, and along with similar anomalies they have therefore become the object of dietary prohibitions as laid down in the Book of Leviticus.[19]

Victor Turner, also an anthropologist originally working in Africa who came to extend his theories to the wider world, approached the idea of basic classifications with particular focus on ritual practice in the context of bodily growth, and also on the key place of ritual and drama on the stage of politics and public life.[20] His work on initiation ritual and on politics as theatre will be discussed again; here I would like simply to note that his concept of basic classifications underlying our ways of seeing the world was less an 'intellectualist' construct than an experiential one, rooted in our knowledge of our own bodies, the processes of organic ingestion, of decay, of sexuality and the making and shedding of blood. His primary analyses drew on his knowledge of the Ndembu people of central Africa, and the triadic schema of black/white/red, referring variously to bodily experience, to spiritual relationships, and to artistic production, which in various permutations and combinations pervaded their rites of passage and of healing. Turner provided not only an exemplary insight into the inner connections of the symbolic logic and affective response of the Ndembu as a people who actively lived their tradition, as it were, but also included in his ethnography a range of crit-icial conversations he held with his informants, some of whom commented upon that tradition in sophisticated and reflective ways, developing their own metaphors as they did so.[21]

'Classification' has also been treated with respect to specific fields, for example in analysing the zoological or botanical knowledge of a particular people,[22] or with respect to colour. There are built-in difficulties, however, in isolating a field of phenomena of this kind for systematic and comparative study. For example, in relation to colour, the interesting and important question has been asked as to how far our perception of colour is a human universal, and how far culturally arbitrary, according to the words present in a particular language and the way these divide up the spectrum. A further question arises as to whether, over long-term history, there has been a developmental trend in the way that colours are perceived or named; are certain colours somehow more basic than others, going back further in human history and common to all languages and cultural traditions today? A well-known study by Berlin and Kay reaches a positive conclusion on these issues: that there are basic colours identified in all human communities, and that there has been a one-way trend of increasing differentiation as time has gone on.[23] However, social and cultural anthropologists (many of whom have tried out standard psychological colour test cards) have pointed out two basic difficulties in this kind of study. First, the domain 'colour' itself is not universally identified as a singular 'flat' quality of things. It may appear so in the paintbox or under the spectroscope but the artist knows better. Languages do all sorts of creative things with visual impression besides cutting up the spectrum sequentially like a scientist in a laboratory. There are myriad qualities that influence the way we speak about 'colour': for example, bright or dull, shiny or smooth, dark or light, plain or textured; and many things are given colour quite arbitrarily, such as the translucence of the sky, which would not be called blue in every language. Collingwood pointed this out for the ancient Greeks and Romans, who did not classify colours according to the spectrum, but by reference to something quite different, perhaps connected with 'dazzlingness or glintingness or gleamingness or their opposites'. Thus it may be natural for a Greek to call the sea 'wine-looking', and for a Roman to call a swan 'scarlet'—or the word we translate as scarlet, rather than bright white.[24] Ethnographers have found that 'models' for the differentiation of visual impression may be the world of soils and forest, or wild animals, or even cattle— David Turton, in trying to get Mursi informants to respond to the psychologists' colour test cards, was told in response to one 'there is no such beast'.[25] Jean Buxton showed how it was in the juxtaposition of things, such as grass and animals, or animals with the necessary minimal but distinctive contrast of markings, that Mandari made 'colour difference' significant.[26] It is a common experience for us all to 'see' a colour more clearly in a context of contrast, that is, to invoke its name against a model of classification which already exists in one's mind. Moreover, 'metaphors' arising from underlying classifications are profoundly implicated in the way we speak about and represent colour, and it becomes almost impossible to penetrate through such lenses to discover how colour is 'perceived' in the abstract, or what 'differences people see' between colours when presented in an experimental test situation.

In my own first field research among Uduk-speaking communities in the Sudan–Ethiopian borderlands, I tried out some rather casual colour perception experiments. I used ordinary objects to hand as reference data as I had not brought test cards with me. I noticed immediately that objects around the village tended to be vaguely coloured, browny-green or bluey-grey and on the streaky side, rather than the flat plain colours good for testing, so I used mainly my own things—book covers, Kodak boxes, clean clothes, and plastic cups. I then discovered that you could not ask, in the Uduk language, 'What colour is this?' or 'What is the word that people use in Uduk for this colour?' There was no word that meant 'colour' as such. I could ask, 'What is the appearance of this?' and get the answer 'spotty' as much as the answer 'red' or 'black'. Even in relation to these two 'colours', I found a qualitative difference of register. They were not divisions of the same kind within a uniform spectrum, but rather extreme ends of two different poles of contrast. Red shaded into various browns, yellows and these gave way to the green range. Black, however, was opposed to white; but only rarely was anything ever seen that was 'pure' white; the terms would be better translated as dark, versus light. Most blues were included in the term for dark, and most pale colours, including light blues, in the term for light. There were no names for yellow or blue as such, but within these domains (as labelled in English) fine discriminations were made between the 'green' and 'red' ranges of the former and the 'dark' and 'light' ranges of the latter. Beyond these two basic dimensions of contrast (which correspond to a fairly widespread and possibly ancient scheme), there was a rich array of 'metaphorical' terms for 'appearance', like the English term orange perhaps, mainly drawing on trees, birds, and animals in the forest. 'Butterfly' was sometimes used in answer to my test questions, referring to patterned cloth, or 'lizard' to rough book covers. A few terms drew on trade objects, especially types of beads, including a very particular blue bead, and these terms were applied very precisely to one or two of my belongings; prompting the thought that perception is more of an active, creative capacity than comparative testing can easily reveal.[27]

Giving shape to space

Anthropologists have often concerned themselves with 'cosmological' space. In comparison to the geographers they have lifted their eyes off the surface of the earth, and sought to understand the fundamental spatial schemas and formulae which organize the whole. Archaeologists too have always been alert to aspects of 'organized' orientation in the construction of settlements and buildings, especially religious buildings, and have often speculated about the ideas of ancient peoples on the basis of this external cultural deposit. A fruitful topic for speculation by professionals and lay people alike has long been the meaning of the 'stone circles' and circular embankments of Britain and north-western Europe.[28] It is inescapable that they are spatially organized, internally and externally in relation to each other. The well-known cases of

FIG. 3. Stonehenge: an ancient and special place (copper engraving from Camden's *Britannia* (1637). Photo: Adrian Arbib.

Stonehenge and Avebury have stimulated all kinds of theories about life in the neolithic or Bronze Age. Were these and other major examples defensive sites? Were they burial sites, or religious monuments? Their apparently careful shape, design, and orientation with respect to the patterns of the sun and moon at different seasons have prompted elaborate theories that they were astronomical observatories. The sheer number of such sites is awe-inspiring; in Cumbria, for example, there are over fifty. Some are associated with cairns and burial sites, or the presence of artefacts, others not. Attention has been drawn too to the orientation of the circle pattern and the way the arrangement of stones can be seen to connect with the rising sun at particular seasons of the year, and occasionally many more astronomical features. Significance has also been read into the wider pattern of links between stone circle sites. It is tempting to ask whether the mathematical precision of modern measurements has not overdone the sophistication of these layouts and their 'meaning' for the locals? What can be said with certainty is that the building of these circles involved a lot of careful planning; that they mark out a set, even a hierarchy, of ceremonial centres on the landscape; and that they last a long time, especially when built in stone rather than wood. Their very longevity means that they have doubtless lent themselves to many 'meanings' and customary practices over time. If we take as an analogy the pattern of cathedrals and smaller churches or chapels across the landscape, we can immediately recognize the plural uses, and changing meanings, for which they have provided a focus. Medieval cathedrals are carefully oriented to the cardinal points; in their elevation they provide an image of the heavenly dimension; in the earth below lie the distinguished dead. They encompass the imaginative art of successive generations, they used to be key institutions in the local political economy and they served as convenient places for markets to develop. The cathedral is perhaps a more robust analogy than the astronomical observatory for the great stone circles, and the chapel or shrine for the multitude of minor ones.

The notion of a dominant cosmic centre, a sacred place, is not necessarily a 'universal', as we immediately remember when we think of mobile hunters or pastoralists, or fishermen or traders, whose collective life is linked to a web of spatial movements rather than to a place. Nevertheless, we can be confident in saying that the experience of physical places and the journeys between them is one of the commonest underpinnings of the human being's characteristic sense of living in a 'formatted' social space from early childhood and earliest memory. This theme will be pursued in Chapters 9 and 10.

Giving shape to time

It is notoriously difficult to define 'time'; it seems to slip out of focus as soon as we try to put it into language, or to get a mental grip on its implications. But we operate easily with practical understandings of time—it is built into the way that language itself works, and all our concrete social arrangements for living. In practice, there could be no social life without shared agreement over the timing of our activities, whether by the seasons, the clock, or the religious calendar. Nor could we operate normally without a framework of common understandings about how we relate to 'the past' or 'the future'. While 'time' in the abstract seems less tangible than space, it is often spoken of and formally enacted in comparable ways, using metaphors of physical length, boundaries, zones, and so on. Geographical space itself, in a very pragmatic way, can be used as a way of fixing points in time. For example, in many parts of the old Orthodox Christian regions of Ethiopia, there is a regular cycle of markets to which people come from a wide area of dispersed settlements. The larger villages take turns, on a weekly rota, to hold the markets. In this way, the villages themselves acquire the name 'Wednesday market' or 'Friday market', using the standard weekday names of a major language such as Amharic. Place-names like this are scattered all over the map. However, in the less accessible regions where local vernacular languages are still dominant, but do not have a corresponding set of names for the days of the Christian week, the transfer goes the other way round. The pre-existing place-name of a market village may become, in local usage, a way of marking the weekly calendar, a term for the relevant day of the week. The usage may even be so local that several different village-names will come to mean, for example, 'Wednesday'. This was found to be the situation in the Konso area in the far south of the country, when efforts were being made by education committees to standardize the Konso language for use in schools. It was very difficult to decide which village's name should go in the new dictionary as the word for Wednesday or Friday, as there were so many candidates.[29]

The managing of social time in this kind of way may be very 'visible', and an obvious part of what the ethnographer describes. Timing, as a part of practice, has other evident features—for a start, it is tangible in a direct bodily way and the fieldworker (like the jet traveller) immediately notices the change from accustomed habit, in mealtimes, bedtimes, the rhythm of occasions, and so on. In this respect it is rather like other abstract notions like 'light', which is a difficult abstraction to conceptualize, but also part of the everyday medium in which we feel ourselves to live. Those idioms of action and speech which mark out the domain of 'time', like those which mark the 'spatial' or the 'visible', are part of the essential makings of our social lives together.

Despite local differences in the experience of space, we can immediately accept that we all inhabit in an important sense one spatial world. It is less easy, but no less important, to assimilate the notion that humanity shares the same 'time-world', given the contrasts in the way that 'time' is understood from one historical period to another, from one gendered or aged perspective to another, or from one scientific or philosophical system to another. Johannes Fabian has shown how anthropology itself, along with popular historical attitudes, has tended to view the remoter peoples of former empires as belonging to another time, an encapsulated time, often failing to appreciate the coeval status of the anthropologist and the informant.[30] Anthropologists have approached the 'problem of time' by two different routes. First are those who have explored and emphasized specific, culturally embedded, and qualitative ways in which time is marked, spoken about, acted on and evaluated, including those of modern Western history. Second are those who have sought to escape 'relativism' by the application of rough common sense, on its own or combined with rationalist philosophical argument.

The Durkheimian vision of time as something emanating from the social experience of regularity in gatherings and festivals can be traced back to the early twentieth century, among other things to an essay of Henri Hubert, prepared in collaboration with Mauss, and to the better-known essay of Robert Hertz on death, in *Death and the Right Hand*.[31] These studies, emphasizing qualitative rhythm in the recurring patterns of social time, have much in common with Arnold van Gennep's classic model of the marking of stages in the life of persons and groups, as well as the celebration of seasons or changing phases in the life of kingdoms or nations (discussed in the previous chapter).

The idea of socially defined cycles in the seasonal, ecological sense also became influential in anthropology from the time of Evans-Pritchard's exemplary presentation of this phenomenon among the Nuer. He showed how the collective representation of time, through rhetorical evocation, did not follow an abstract schema of the relation between lunar months or other external markers but rather the passage of the climatic seasons themselves and the work they entailed. It was not time to plant because a named season had arrived; it was the relevant season because the time had clearly come to plant. However, 'ecological' time is a little more complicated than we might at first think. We may imagine peasants to drift along with the next agricultural task and label the season accordingly. But in practice, and with conscious individual and social effort, adjustments are always having to be made between expectation, practical conditions, and scales of marking time. In the West we add the odd day in Leap Years, to try and keep things aligned properly; and the Mursi pastoralists of south-western Ethiopia do something not so very different. According to David Turton, they speak of a year as *bergu*, and conceive of it in lunar intervals characterized by particular tasks and movements of the herds. There is also an extra 'month', *gamwe*, which is when the Omo river floods, and the cycle starts again. Each time the new moon appears they renumber the next interval as *bergu* 1, 2, etc., up to twelve, but there is no overall pronouncement. They check on the position of the rising sun on the horizon to give a rough idea of where they are in the year, but there is no fixed calendar. We can easily see how Mursi often disagree as to which *bergu* it is at any given time; some may say number 6, and others number 7, while all defer to elders with supposedly special knowledge, and in the course of time things resolve themselves. When the river floods, it is clearly *gamwe*, and then the cycle starts again. Occasionally a 'month' is missed out, while sometimes there are 13 markers in the year.[32]

Ideas about the underlying rhythms of social time have been taken up by several anthropologists. Edmund Leach in *Rethinking Anthropology* explored the formal logic of contrasts in sacred versus secular time, provocatively using the image of zigzags, rather than cycles, as the key to festival-markers in social life. The formal way in which rites of passage can signal 'time passing' was shown by Rodney Needham typically to include—perhaps universally—coded percussion sounds: bells, striking clocks, guns, drums, cymbals, and so on.[33] Sound is, inescapably, a phenomenon 'of the moment', an experiental *now*, peculiarly appropriate for marking the way that the present moment is here and then gone. It is also clearly good for marking patterns in time, for *making time* even, through its extension into the rhythms of speech or music. The basic model of social time as rhythmic passage has survived well, as shown by works such as Bloch and Parry's *Death and the Regeneration of Life*, and the forthcoming volume *The Qualities of Time*, in which these rhythms are shown to relate to the future as much as the past, and through collective expectation, to affect historical events quite directly.[34]

The sceptics, who are suspicious of a slide into cultural relativism by those who emphasize local and qualitatively rich ideas, seek a more general framework for the human understanding of time. An important example is Alfred

Gell's book *The Anthropology of Time*.[35] He insists that there is no fairyland where people experience time in strange ways, where time stands still, or chases its own tail, or swings back and forth like a pendulum. He seeks rather a minimalist approach to 'time as such' in order to assimilate diverse ethnographic accounts under general explanatory categories.[36] His approach begins with the viewpoint of the individual as an experiencing actor, rather than with the framework of shared understandings and activities in which he or she necessarily lives. Rather than starting with the formative impact of social practice upon individual experience, Gell favours the clean, clear, we could say 'culture-free' metaphysical categories of Kant, and the 'action-frame' of reference. He insists that time is an asymmetrical category and we all face it in the same way in our practical lives. The ethnographer should not, at least initially, seek out 'concepts of time', but plot what choices people make in the morning about how they will spend their day, or the next few days, in the light of the 'opportunity-costs' facing them. We could respond, however, that this very notion is a modern 'Protestant ethic' motif which might tell us a lot about the pragmatic priorities of people in a productive economy geared to manipulating prices or at least meeting survival targets. But how far in reality will it do justice to people's multiple 'notions of time' even in these circumstances, let alone helping us with, say, hunters and gatherers—where Sahlins pointed to the total lack of a puritan attitude to time in dubbing them the 'original affluent society'.[37] Moreover, there are many aspects of structured timing that are socially imposed upon us, even in modern circumstances; it is very difficult to escape Christmas, or Ramadan, or the school holidays, or the examination timetable, or the anniversaries of public events. At least in Euro-America, children are made aware of personal birthdays at a very early age, and know exactly where they are and how they are defined on this time-scale in relation to all their friends. They internalize other attitudes to time as well, especially through education. This highlights the difficulty faced by the ethnographer who tries to stand outside people's time frames in order to make abstract comparisons in a culture-free common medium. Pioneering work by psychologists in West Africa came up against this problem, when they realized that the whole idea of the 'intelligence test' failed to stimulate the Liberian child in the way it did the American child, trained to work against the clock, competitively and without consulting others.[38] In these circumstances, laden with motive, purpose, and second-guessing of one person by another, social timing becomes a *moral idea*.

The topic of 'historical time' is not discussed in Gell's book, but even considering my examples of public anniversaries and children's birthdays it is difficult to see how social timing in the immediate 'phenomenal' present can be separated from a sense of history. Gell does recognize that people everywhere are obliged to live by combining (at least?) two kinds of time-perspective. One is that of an immediate consciousness of the present, as it moves forwards to the future as it were, a perspective the philosophers call the A-series of time-reckoning. The second derives from the application of a scheme of standardized and successive intervals, such as a system of dating or of named seasons, to one's own circumstances; this kind of time-reckoning is called by philosophers the B-series. In practice, we are continually engaged in relating the one to the other, which is where we might add the social and historical matrix of cultural communication to Gell's individual actor. Just as there is no such thing as one person's time, there is no such thing in social life as an understanding of time which excludes social memory and expectation: or the placing of oneself and current events against the patterns by which we have come to understand what went before, and what should, or could, happen next.[39] It is by placing ideas about timing back into their historical context that we can appreciate something very important: that no society operates with only one, robotic schema. In all circumstances, even the most 'traditional', people juggle several different kinds of time-scale; the seasons, the phases of the moon, the succession of the generations and of the kingdom's rulers. These do not necessarily fit among themselves; demographic and environmental irregularities upset calculations and timings; and micro-politics everywhere introduce all kinds of problems arising from differential expectations. All of us are conscious of different but co-present principles of timing and their contradictions. The intellectual apperceptions of time themselves depend upon a realization that the wheels are not aligned properly, and that effort has to be made to try and synchronize them. The social experience of time as often as not is the effort involved in readjusting rhythms and reconciling expectations as events erupt out of season.

We too easily forget that the 'abstract' nature of time measurement itself is partly an artefact of technology, and that itself has often been spurred on by deeply symbolic and religious imperatives. The oldest time-technology depended on the changing light of the sun and did not work at night. In the medieval monasteries, handbells were rung at the hours of prayer, and monks had to be detailed to stay awake in order to perform this duty in the night and early morning. The invention of mechanical clocks, with a ratchet and a weight, which could ring bells automatically at these times was a break-through, and spread extremely fast throughout Europe in the seventeenth century, helping fuel the work ethic in early modern businesses, and no doubt also philosophical speculations on the nature of time and the moral signific-ance we have given to it. Clocks, calendars, metronomes, and more recently radio and travel timetables provide a series of interlocking, and not always com-patible, frames within which we check our position (how many of us do not wear watches these days?) and adjust our activities. Time is not homogeneous, but full of markers on different scales—often sounding bells, alarms, pips, and ceremonial guns, as well as changes in the weather or rising and falling levels on the stockmarket, none of these necessarily working in harmony.

The realm of time is not agreed even by the specialist physical scientists and philosophers to be one thing, one field.[40] As lay people we are conscious that even our most seemingly basic modes of reckoning time are arbitrary and do not fit the world exactly. Since Einsteinian relativity we have gradually accepted that time is not best conceived as uniform and undifferentiated. Together with space, one understands from popular scientific debate that it is *shaped* in a curve, and it is perfectly acceptable to speculate about unique beginnings and endings. My point is again, simply, that time 'exists' for dis-cussion, speculation, and comparison, only in the interplay of idioms we pro-vide or invent for it through our languages and other 'cultural' codes. These include not only visual but sound codes like music, and draw in multiple ways on the models of rhythm, duration, and ageing we find all around us in the annual seasons, the life of animals, and their communication systems. Time is not simply *marked*. We *make* it. The way we make it is itself a histor-ical phenomenon. Taking our lead from Mary Warnock's book *Imagination and Time*,[41] we can confidently ask the question as to how far Kant's category of universal time is itself historically situated; and we can recognize that recent developments of science and the understanding of the universe give us a clarifying focus on this point. The very idea of the modern, of moderniza-tion, of modernity—these have arisen alongside the supposedly universal category. 'Modern' time is certainly asymmetrical; always moving forward, in measurable stages, leaving things behind and inventing new things. However, it is not free of extraordinary expectations of the future; indeed it seems to 'bring the future closer' in an oddly millennial way. Modernity is more than the individual consciousness on which the intellectualists like Kant and Gell have focused; it has its own social rhythms—as we notice when these rhythms fail to fulfil expectations, or when they actually clash.

CHAPTER FOUR

Life in Motion:
Daughters of the Dance

THERE has recently been a flowering of the anthropological study of the forms of sensual expression: of the visual, of art, of aesthetics; of 'performance', of body language; and of the aural—the interpretation of sound, of music and song. It is becoming clear that set pieces of patterned rhythmic sound and movement, quintessentially the phenomenon of the dance, can be traced through history. Something arguably similar is even reported from the world of the other primates—Vernon Reynolds discusses 'chimp carnivals'.[1]

The technical and methodological difficulty of analysing the dance as such means that it has frequently been left aside for serious study by specialist students, just as music and language are nearly always set aside for the ethnomusicologists and the linguists or linguisticians. There have been some very thought-provoking specialist treatments of dance, which examine its internal structure, techniques, and enactment. Drid Williams writes of the 'deep structures' of the dance, for example, and Judith Hanna has designed a theory of the 'semantic grid' of dance, as a potent non-verbal mode of communication. Both have discussed the problem of creating an effective dance notation as we have written forms of language or musical scores.[2] The language analogy, however, whether for dance, or for music, or perhaps especially for visual and plastic art, cannot be wholly satisfactory, and some of the most distinguished recent commentators have moved away from it altogether (in particular, Alfred Gell, whose work is discussed below). The importance of the dance for general anthropology is not so much in its internal intricacies of design, but in its resonance with aspects of the wider social world.

I. DANCE AND SOCIAL FORM: ETHNOGRAPHIES

In this context, we can ask whether the 'idea of dance' or, deliberately to give it a special aura, Dance, has received its due from mainstream anthropologists? Does it not deserve at least equal attention with art and music, and in some ways perhaps more attention, as it encompasses them in suggestive ways? I return to review some current work in the anthropology of the visual and the aural later in this chapter, but I wish to set these domains initially against an all-encompassing, iconic image of Dance. I treat language in the next chapter as something also emergent from Dance, but as potentially a source of intellectual analysis and criticism of society beyond the capacity of art and music. My approach differs a little from that of Maurice Bloch in his study of the relations between symbol, song, and dance. Whereas he treats song as a highly stylized form imposed upon the freedoms of ordinary language, I prefer to follow a different tradition, regarding ordinary language as a specialized *distillation out of* song and formal movement. However, I agree with him over the deep affinity between song, dance, ritual, and religion, on the one hand, and the forms of authority, on the other; and the gulf between these kinds of collective assertion and ordinary language. He sums this up by observing that reason and argument belong with ordinary language, while *'you cannot argue with a song'* (his italics) any more than you can regard religious practice as a way of 'explaining' the world.[3]

Dance appears in quite a wide range of ethnography as illustrative of 'culture' or 'society' in an unproblematic way, as one might expect a war dance in a warlike society, or a minuet in an eighteenth-century Parisian ballroom. Ruth Benedict included the movements and choreography of dance in her exploration of the pervasive themes that give an overall character to the cultural ethos and even personality traits of particular communities. She drew, for example, a sharp contrast between the quiet, co-operative patterns of Zuñi dancing and the agonistic energies of the Plains Indian dance (referred to in Chapter 2). Radcliffe-Brown, on the other hand, notoriously interested in social structure rather than culture, devoted a part of his argument in *The Andaman Islanders* to the dance as a general social phenomenon, constituting in its shared rythmic performance the type case of social solidarity.[4] This interpretation was itself a rather flat-footed attempt to use some of Durkheim's insights into the prototypical significance of the collective gathering of the clans for the generation of a shared conception of the social whole.

FIG. 4. Preparing for the dance: Zande drums. Photo: E. E. Evans-Pritchard, *c.*1927. Pitt Rivers Museum, Photographic Archives (EPA 408).

Radcliffe-Brown's literalness over dancing as both creating and representing social cohesion was ridiculed by Evans-Pritchard in his earliest publication, which happened to be devoted to the Zande dance; in a much more sensitive portrayal, he pointed out how dancing produces conflict as much as solidarity.[5] For the Azande at least, dance emerges as a rich arena of social life and human expression in itself, related in complex ways to the wider context. The dance has a particular structure, prescribed form and mode of performance, leadership, and elaborate organization.[6] The Azande have a large variety of dances, old, new, regional, linked to various musical instruments or the human voice, and performed on many specific occasions, including work parties and ritual occasions such as circumcision or funerals. Some are restricted to the sons of chiefs, some to the secret societies, some are the special preserve of women. One common style, the beer dance, is analysed in detail. The music is made by large gongs fashioned out of a tree trunk in the shape of a buffalo and leather-topped tall wooden drums. They must both be played, an initial 'division of labour' in making the dance. The accompanying songs are antiphonal in structure, in the 'call and response' mode requiring at least one soloist and two overlapping choruses. The lyrics are ephemeral, often commenting on gossip of the day, but as Evans-Pritchard notes, 'the song is often a weapon of some power'.[7] The dancers, who may number some hundreds on a big occasion, move around the musicians in a series of great concentric circles, the men in the inner ring and the women in the outer, this pattern sometimes replicating itself to make two or three more circles. Individual movement is quite free in the sense that steps come in and out of fashion, and people may develop their own style to some extent. There is plenty of sexual innuendo and, while the whole occasion is a disciplined one, discreet affairs may result. There is a lot of competitive display between the young men in particular, and rivalry over the privilege of singing solo or beating the drum. Some men achieve special recognition as song-leaders, and their apprentices may take titles referring to ranks in the government police—sergeant, lance-corporal, etc. This brief sketch of the Zande beer dance does not begin to compare it with other local forms or even to relate it to what Evans-Pritchard called the larger 'ceremonial complex' of which it is a part (here, primarily the cycle of mourning and mortuary feasts). Moreover, the dance was increasingly being performed as an entertainment for visiting government officials—something which is echoed around the world in per-formance contexts, and reminds us of the wider historical processes in which dance can get caught up.[8]

A well-known study of this kind is Clyde Mitchell's book on the *kalela* dance of the Zambian Copperbelt towns in colonial times. He presented this as an innovative urban phenomenon, in which groups and individuals from different rural areas come together, to recreate their distinctiveness in town. Through costume, song, and choreography, the new social identities and behaviours of town life were articulated and brought into one arena of per-formance and satirical enjoyment.[9] Terence Ranger's study of the military-style musical marching known as Beni-Ngoma which spread as a popular dance form through colonial East Africa, ridiculing authority in subtle songs and gesture, offers an interesting comparison.[10] It derived its effect quite specifically from its ironic play upon the serious parading of the military forces. Upon these, in point of fact, the power of the colonial states actually depended. Many of their people had played a physical part as recruits into the colonial armies of Britain, Germany, and Belgium; or they had played a physical part in resistance to those armies. These historically placed studies remind us that 'dance-events' are not just tradition but may be an active part of history too. Like a theatre play, or a work of art, they may create a world within themselves, but have a distinctive orientation, often ironic, to the adjacent activities of the wider world.

Paul Spencer's collection of papers on *Society and the Dance* illustrates these points from several angles. For example, he himself writes on the subversive element in the dancing of young Samburu warriors, a constant source of political challenge to their elders. While focusing on dance, and reminding us of its irreducibility to anything else, the various studies in this collection show how intricately it is related to the other performative genres of ritual, song, music, costume, and conventional modes of personal display, not to mention the world of productive work. The book as a whole leaves us, quite rightly, with a question as to whether our conventional dichotomy between the forms of art in social practice, and those of non-art, is far too rigidly drawn. Have the social sciences concentrated too much on the apparent common sense of economic and political life, and missed the overwhelming presence of 'art' in our shared social being? Is there in fact any domain of 'ordinary' bodily activity, in field or factory or stock exchange, which has not been shaped to some extent by shared understandings of the counterpoint of style and rhythm in work, not to mention the vital etiquette of personal encounter?[11]

The study by Alfred Gell in this collection makes this point explicit. He draws our attention to the way in which dance movements among the Umeda people of Papua New Guinea are not simply different from ordinary movements. They are highly stylized versions of these same movements, of 'normal' walking as undertaken by men, women, and warriors in their occupational lives. However, even these 'normal' patterns are not simply given as natural to the human organism. They are already culturally patterned to form a recognizably local set of ways of walking, different from what might be found in the Wild West or the streets of Paris. Gell's analysis does not depend on a contrast between natural and stylistic movement, but on the contrasting juxtaposition of related styles. We could develop this insight, and say that dancing everywhere has a dialectical relation to non-dance, not so much because the one is framed and set apart as expressive, artistic, and emotional against the other which is mere utility, but because the world of non-dance is to a large extent a bodily world too: a world of muscular work, of sexuality, a world of physical effort in battle, a world of submission to the imposed disciplines of timing and spatial movement. We could suggest that (as in the case of the Beni-Ngoma) the performative and experiental aspects of the various formal genres of patterned movement, ritual, marching, and dancing are not just a spill-over from the 'ordinary' *habitus*, but derive their power partly by speaking against, resonating ironically with, this very base. The various genres of dance, and comparable dance-like patterned performances, also play upon each other, maintaining distance and contrast while often copying, mimicking, and transforming each other in a set of modes which can even become a vehicle for the 'political'.[12]

'Dance' cannot be set against some plain notion of 'society' which might be imagined to exist without it. Dance is within the set of practices that in their overlap and interplay constitute society, or to use a less 'fixed' concept, social form or the world of sociality. It is a clear example of those living, felt, and performative occasions which have moved centre stage in recent anthropological studies to emphasize subjective engagement through 'embodiment'. A fine example of the treatment of dance-events as a key arena for the living expression and negotiation of gender, generational and community relations is Jane Cowan's book *Dance and the Body Politic in Northern Greece*. As Cowan learned Greek dancing 'in the choreographic, if not the social, sense', she came to realize that the dance was 'an ordered form of sensuality'; it was an embodied form of action and experience. 'It was, as well, a first encounter with that paradoxically double sense of engrossment and reflexivity that characterize the experience of the dancer as much as that of the good ethnographer.'[13] She 'learned that in a society where most people dance, dancing is much more than knowing the steps; it involves both social knowledge and social power'.[14] The book is concerned with the social constructions of gender in the 'non-ordinary' domain of dance-events, which constitute a site where pleasure, sensuality, sociability are a part of the constitution and celebration of gender and other social inequalities and hierarchies. Dancing provides a wealth of imagery, in a series of shifts and counterpoints, and in everyday talk the dance may be used as 'an apt metaphor for the community itself'.[15] Cowan draws on Mauss's ideas concerning the 'techniques of the body' and Bourdieu's elaboration of the idea of durable dispositions and bodily practices which as part of 'habitus' are cultivated within specific social environments. Cowan mentions her aunt's wistful reference to her 'Methodist feet', which having been brought up in a small town in rural Ohio, simply would not dance.[16] It seems there are no such feet in Greece: everyone is expected to dance, though in quite specific ways on very specific occasions. The space of the small town of Sohos is highly 'gendered', and reflects an older pattern where girls and married women were more strictly confined to the house, and the public spaces of the streets and coffee-houses were for men. Today there are new Italian-style cafeterias where the more daring and advanced younger people meet, provoking all kinds of arguments about the conflict between propriety and modernity. But the coffee-houses are still used by men only; the wedding procession led by the *young men* of the groom's party makes free with the expression of emotion and individuality through dance in the streets, but the dancing and behaviour of the *girls* within the groom's party is still relatively decorous. Throughout, the groom's party displays masculinity, actively 'dancing the bride' when they bring her out from her house, and later for the admiration of the crowd in the churchyard after the service.

While the wedding dances are strictly conventional, other sets of dance-events are closely bound up with changing patterns of local social and political life. Cowan describes the evening dances of local associations, including business associations and political parties. Those aspiring to European modernity will include ballroom dances such as the tango, waltz, and foxtrot but on the whole these Sohoian evening occasions consist of Greek forms—*kalamatianos* (a circle dance) and *karsilamas* (a face-to-face dance).[17] Everyone is drawn in by the end of the evening, including the most staid petit-bourgeois head of family and his 'lady', presenting the very image of conservative patriarchy in the flesh. The elderly, especially women in their old-fashioned long dark dresses, would, however, be out of place here. So would many consider the male solo virtuoso performance *zeibekiko*, which belongs rather to the marginal, drifting world of *rebetika* music, port cities, underground political rumblings, pain and sorrow: a style which has been known in Sohos since the 1940s and is very popular. It finds a 'proper' outlet in the annual cycle of public festivals, including Carnival, and in private parties; but its capacity to inflame, arouse, and provoke emotional upset and misunderstanding is never far from the surface, as Cowan shows. It is a part of the 'hegemonic' regime of collectively held assumptions about the asymmetry of gender within which people's lives, and here the often fraught nature of young women's lives, are lived.

How 'political' can dance be, apart from the way it can be used as a kind of indirect resistance in connection with satirical and critical songs? Katrina Hazzard-Gordon offers an intriguing historical story of the origins of African-American secular dance in the social conditions of life under slavery in the New World.[18] She traces the spread of common working patterns of the 'cotton culture' across southern regions of America, especially after the ending of the trade in the early nineteenth century. Dancing often accompanied types of agricultural work, such as corn-shucking or husking. There were competitive teams, and a caller-out—'genmen to de right'—evoking the call and response pattern of African music. Corn-shucking brought together people from different plantations and 'was not without its strains of resistance . . . The dances as well as the songs often turned to satire.'[19] The dance was an even safer form of self-assertion than songs.

Secular dance became at one and the same time a medium of assimilation, and of political expression. 'For the African, dance was both a means to camouflage insurrectionary activity as well as other kinds of resistance behavior; for the masters it was a means to pacify the desire of their bondsmen to rebel.'[20] Hazzard-Gordon also examines the development of a dichotomy between sacred and secular dancing and music in the context of Protestantism. What were taken for African forms of pagan worship were banned and survived only precariously in circle dancing or 'shouts'. Line dancing became the main form of permitted secular dance. Under the slave regime, a dance culture developed which thus served many ends. African-style instruments were often made or improvised; an ex-slave recalled, 'When we made a banjo we would first of all catch what we called a ground hog, known in the north as a woodchuck. After tanning his hide, it would be stretched over a piece of timber fashioned like a cheese box, and you couldn't tell the difference in sound between that homely affair and a handsome store bought one.'[21] Slave masters provided the opportunity for slaves to dance even though it violated their religious principles; but it was 'clear from the amount of insurrectionary activity that took place during slave holidays . . . that the role of dance . . . was not limited to escapist entertainment'.[22] This is why drums were forbidden, and different instruments had to be substituted, ones that would not be seized—and could not be used to incite or signal rebellion. Inter-plantation dances were a particular source of worry to the slaveocracy; there is ample evidence of plotting on such occasions, 'giving these occasions a striking resemblance to war dances, or dances in which preparation for battle was the central theme'.[23] There were large public dances on the edge of towns, and while plantation owners tried to restrict the movement of their slaves, it was in these public spaces that the African-American dance could be celebrated. Crowd control was difficult; Hazzard-Gordon quotes some vivid eyewitness accounts from eighteenth-century South Carolina. By 1817 in New Orleans dancing was restricted to Sundays before sundown at one place, Congo Square.

This story of American dance history is not one of total prohibition, but of attempts over three centuries to restrict, reshape, and effectively to defuse the power of dancing, to co-opt it into the usefully productive rhythms of work, and to allow it into the social lives of the slave communities as part of a package which kept the peace (mostly). This story is full of ironic echoes for the history of dance in other regions marked by a history of slavery, and by modern forms of military enlistment, migrant labour, forced migration, forced settlement, and other kinds of imposed social control. Where people are without much power or influence in the conventional sense, they may find satisfaction in the elaboration of worlds that do not depend upon it; home-made music and dance is there for anyone to make and remake, and even control through definition and redefinition. Gerd Baumann has shown how the people of Jebel Miri in the Nuba Hills in the Sudan, a classic labour source area with a long history of being at the wrong end of the Nile Valley slave trade, were living in the 1970s with a profound division in their world.[24] His book is about the way people could live both as locals and as Sudanese nationals; but this complex 'identity' is more than a matter of formal political or workaday affiliations. It is constituted in part by the performance— and real enjoyment—of both local, and national, forms of music, song, and dance. However, a separation was deliberately maintained. A large proportion of the men were labour migrants in the towns, and of these many were Muslims, spoke good Arabic, and were familiar with the music and dance of the northern Sudan. Even back at home in Miri, although the mother tongue and vernacular songs of Miri were still vital, many women also knew some Arabic, and the young girls would play and dance to love songs (*daluka*) they had learned in some local market place or from the radio. When the young girls married, however, a boundary came into view: they had to forsake the Arabic romantic styles for Miri grindstone songs and other 'autochthonous' forms of music and dance. These contrasting and mutually exclusive styles of dance and music reflected a certain balance between the national and local belonging of the Miri people at the time of Baumann's research in the late 1970s, but there were tensions too and Miri has since been destroyed by civil war. Any state of 'balance' must perhaps be a fragile illusion, and a more realistic picture of the competing rise and fall, convergence and divergence of practices and genres of dance and music would often serve us better. In the peripheral regions of the south-eastern Sudan, bordering Ethiopia, this has certainly been the main pattern.

Among the displaced communities and refugee schemes of the Sudan–Ethiopian borderlands can now be found the survivors of those Uduk-speaking Sudanese communities among whom I carried out fieldwork in the 1960s. One of the most persistent choreographic forms I noted at that time, common to several genres of music and dancing style across the region, was that of an all-embracing circle, with the musicians blowing flutes in the middle and the dancers, men, women, and children, circling around in a great anti-clockwise whirl. It is a spatial form defined by the relations between the dancers themselves as it sweeps them all in. It is not addressed to an external audience. 'Outside' powers-that-be have often tried to modify this form of dancing in the region, kings and chiefs and military authorities omitting women and children and transforming it into a regimented court performance or processional line-up. Quite a few travellers regarded it as highly erotic and missionaries tried to abolish it. It is not so easy, however, as the slave plantations in the United States found, to get rid of the circle dance, which so directly seems to challenge external definition and control by articulating its own internally referential space. Some thirty years after my fieldwork originally started among the Uduk, I first heard the music and saw one of their key circular dances, the *barangu*. I had heard about this dance, mainly in the context of myths about the beginnings of the world. At that time, everybody went along to the big dance, the giraffe stepping out *tuku, tuku, tuku*, the elephant calumph, calumphing, etc. etc.; this happened, and that happened, people took sides, iron and fire appeared, human beings began to hunt the animals, permanent death overtook the older cycle of return to life, and so on. Although people told stories and sang songs in the 1960s recalling this time of the great primeval dance, the actual dance of the *barangu* was said to be obsolete. It was surprising to find that decades later, in a settlement for war refugees across the Ethiopian border, not only was there a general programme of circle-dancing but the 'primal' *barangu* had suddenly resurfaced.[25] Was 'something being said' here? If so, we need to take a broad view of what is 'political' and accept that even the way that shape and rhythm are given to the temporary circumstances of displacement can be read as part of a long-term political story.

These historical examples illustrate the way that dance is distinct from, but also profoundly connected to, other areas of social life; they also show how many-layered are the implications of the dance, and how it can be less straightforward, less innocent than it might seem.

2. DANCE AND SOCIAL FORM: PROTOTYPES

In his quest for the principles behind the 'logic of practice', Bourdieu explicitly sought an alternative formulation of 'logic' to that of the word, or of mathematics, embracing rather the language of the body. Where others referred to algebra, he invoked more than once the notion of the dance, or of a gymnastic exercise, as an image of social practice. He considered that the intellectualism of academics—including ethnologists—prevented them from seeing their own everyday practice in the same way.[26]

Nick Allen has offered a vision of primal social form very much in sympathy with this claim. He has invited us to think of a clearing in a tropical forest, where a formal dance is in progress, a dance of relatives.[27] Four pairs of figures form a circle, each a brother and sister representing their own section, who set to the other couples in various combinations. We could visualize the scene perhaps (and here I am going beyond Allen) if we think of the sections as dance teams, and allocate them distinguishing colours—perhaps the two pairs of what have been regarded as elemental opposites, dark/light and red/green (see discussion in the previous chapter). One figure, say the young man of the Dark section (though it could equally be his sister), speaks to the imaginary audience, itself composed of anthropologists; and from no particular point in geographical space or historical time (though there is a heavy ethnographic record of circumstantial evidence) explains the pattern. He describes how he and his sister circle around each other and then move together around the wider formation, to face the three other dance pairs in quite different ways. Those opposite, the Lights, are actual or potential sexual partners, his fiancée and his sister's fiancé, with whom erotic engagement is in order. The other two pairs in the square are of the parental generation, so greater formality prevails. The Reds—our informant's father with his own sister—may be on the right, say, and the Greens—his mother and her brother —on the left. When the children of our informant and his Light fiancée are born, they grow up to join the Red team, and when his sister has children with her fiancé, they will be recruited into the Green team. In turn, when the reciprocal partnerships take place again in the next generation between these newly-recruited Reds and Greens, they give birth to children who will rejoin their grandparents in the Dark or Light teams. The dance, our 'informant' tells us, is a model of his society; and for the benefit of his audience, he explains how it dramatizes what they already know as the two generation moieties that compose a four-section system. Its underlying principle is that each generation moiety, through mating between members of the two sections that compose it, gives birth to children who, according to the section membership of their mother and father, join one of the diametrically opposed sections that compose the other moiety. Another way of putting this is that the membership of sections is replenished by the exchange of spouses and children between them. Allen envisages periodic formal exchanges of children as a kind of initiation into the appropriate sections, marked by ceremonies and dancing (which he likens to Durkheim's 'effervescence' or the kind of 'totality' envisaged by Mauss for archaic systems of prestation). I return to the relevance of this imaginary scenario for comparative kinship studies in Chapter 7.

There are several anthropologists and other writers who have evoked Dance, or dance-like gatherings, as a way of thinking about social form. Durkheim had very little to say about the dance, or even music and song, as such, but included these practices as part of the occasion of the ritual gathering. In fact his treatment of the dance-element in the Australian *corroboree* is very crude, and wrongly assumes a loss of signification and self-control: 'The very act of congregating is a very powerful stimulant . . . from every side there are nothing but wild movements, shouts, downright howls, and deafening noises . . . these gestures and cries tend to fall into a rhythm and regularity, and from there into songs and dances . . . The effervescence often becomes so intense that it leads to outlandish behaviour . . . The sexes come together in violation of the rules.'[28]

Marcel Mauss mused in quite a different way on the exchange and circulation of affective gestures, seeing in them a discipline of signification. 'The cries and words, gestures and rites—for example of etiquette and morality— are signs and symbols. . . . Words, greetings, presents solemnly exchanged and received and obligatorily returned on pain of war, what are they but symbols? . . . For we have . . . cases . . . in which the image is endlessly multiplied, so to speak . . . For here is one of the fundamental points both of social life and of the life of the individual consciousness: the symbol—an invoked genie—has a life of its own; it acts and reproduces itself indefinitely.' Mauss goes on to discuss rhythm, that is the collective or social nature of rhythm. Its expression is simultaneously physiological, psychological, and sociological. The study of rhythm, particularly its contagious character and its connection with replicating images, makes it possible to go beyond what happens in a single individual. Mauss writes of the dance: 'Is it not obvious, for example, if one studies dance, even superficially, but from a sociological point of view, that on the one hand it corresponds to respiratory, cardiac and muscular movements which are identical in all the individuals and often shared even by the audience, and that simultaneously it presupposes and follows a sequence of images; this series being itself the one that the symbol of the dance arouses both in the performers and in the audience?'[29]

A number of other writers in the 1930s–1950s, when a quest for 'wholeness' of pattern in human life engaged so many in different fields, pointed to the evocative and fertile idea of the dance. For example, R. G. Collingwood in *The Principles of Art* drew attention to the rich repertoire of non-verbal modes of communication to be found in social life, noting that spoken language is only one such mode.[30] After pointing out that the sound contrasts between French and German have no basis in biological inheritance, he evokes for us a dispute between Italian peasants. 'Italians do not possess more sensitive fingers than northern Europeans. But they have a long tradition of controlled finger-gesture, going back to the ancient game of *micare digitis*. Vocal language is thus only one among many possible languages or orders of languages. Any of these might, by a particular civilization, be developed into a highly organized form of emotional expression.'[31] If one simply listens to a speaker, one thinks of speech as essentially a system of sounds; but Collingwood suggests it is not. It is essentially a system of gestures made with the lungs and larynx, and the cavities of the mouth and nose. Even a writer or reader must 'speak' them soundlessly. 'The written or printed book is only a series of hints, as elliptical as the neumes of Byzantine music, from which the reader thus works out for himself the speech-gestures which alone have the gift of expression.' Collingwood goes on to generalize this picture of the relation between the different kinds of language and bodily gesture. The art of painting is intimately bound up with the expressiveness of the gestures made by the hand in drawing, and the same movements are echoed in the act of appreciating art, with its 'tactile values'. 'Instrumental music has a similar relation to silent movements of the larynx, gestures of the player's hand, and real or imaginary movements, as of dancing, in the audience.' Collingwood concludes: 'Every kind of language is in this way a specialized form of bodily gesture, and in this sense it may be said that the dance is the mother of all languages.'[32] All orders of language are offshoots of 'an original language of total bodily gesture', in which every movement had the same kind of significance as movements of the vocal organs have in speech, and a person using it would be speaking with every part of themselves. 'Now, in calling this an "original" language, I am not indulging (God forbid) in that kind of *a priori* archaeology which attempts to reconstruct man's distant past without any archaeological data. I do not place it in the remote past. I place it in the present.'[33] We speak all the time with our whole bodies. 'This "original" language of total bodily gesture is thus the one and only real language, which everybody who is in any way expressing himself is using all the time. What we call speech and the other kinds of language are only parts of it which have undergone specialized development.' It is the motor side of 'our total imaginative experience', and a part of what enables us to recognize our individual selves as part of a 'world of persons'.[34]

Johan Huizinga, professor of history in Leiden from 1915 to 1941 and specialist in Indo-European linguistics and the Middle Ages, published a magisterial and innovative book towards the end of his career on the idea of 'culture as play', entitling it *Homo Ludens*, and deliberately setting the idea of 'Man the Player' against Homo Sapiens and Homo Faber, the 'Wise' and the 'Maker'.[35] Within his broad canvas, dance has a privileged place. It is 'the purest and most perfect form of play that exists', even more than its 'twin-sister' music. He regrets the seeming cultural decline towards dancing *a deux* in the gyrations of the waltz or the polka (let alone the 'slitherings and slidings' of his contemporaries) since the days of the Greeks, the dancing of King David before the Ark of the Covenant, or festival and figure dances generally; but emphasizes that even the solo dance of today is just as much a performance, an exhibition, a display of rhythmical movement. He also makes the point that play is found in the animal world and clearly pre-dates language. In introducing the book for a later English-reading audience, George Steiner has some criticisms, but considers the work still worth reading. Huizinga's 'trust in the ultimate validity of art' is something of which 'our acid present has obvious need', and the relevance of a theory of 'cultural play' is not yet spent—as remarkable studies of children's games have also suggested. 'Man is at his most inventive, he is most enfranchised from the determinism of mutual enmity or gross need, when he is "playing the game". It is only death that knows no rules, that insists, always, on winning.'[36] Steiner also notes the difficulty of defining what is *not* play in Huizinga's scheme, except for technological progress and utilitarianism. Of course in the present book I am suggesting that even these plain, puritan fields of life have their game-playing aspect too, their 'ceremonial' dynamic.

Suzanne Langer's writings on symbolism, art, and the dance are also very illuminating for anthropology. In her first major book, *Philosophy in a New*

Key,[37] she argued (independently of Collingwood, whose work she did not know at that time) that dance, song, and ritual gesture antedated language. The nature of language should be sought in its affinities with that performative and symbolic domain, rather than in the beginnings of individual rational intention and utility. Drawing on available scientific literature she offers some admittedly speculative ideas on the transition from animal (specifically chimpanzee) communication in dance-like forms of organized gesture and song to human language. Some of her sources, even from the 1890s, prefigure to a surprising degree recent research in the field. In a later book Langer writes on the various forms of art, and how they are shaped in analogous ways in different imaginative media; painting creates 'virtual' space, music 'virtual' time, dance 'virtual' gesture.[38] Dance is not merely emotional expression, or primarily expressive of the accompanying music. Nor is it just a shifting picture, or pantomime/drama. '*Gesture* is the basic abstraction whereby the dance illusion is made and organized. . . . it is seen and understood as vital movement. In actual life gestures function as signals or symptoms of our desires, intentions, expectations, demands, and feelings. Because they can be consciously controlled, they may also be elaborated, just like vocal sounds, into a system of assigned and combinable symbols, a genuine discursive language.'[39] The dance has an overall, collective shape, particularly evocative of a field of power: 'One sees the dance driving this way, drawn that way . . . and all the motion seems to spring from powers beyond the performers. In a *pas de deux* the two dancers appear to magnetize each other; the relation between them is more than a spatial one, it is a relation of forces; but the forces they exercise . . . are dance forces, virtual powers.'[40] 'The prototype of these purely apparent energies is not the "field of forces" known to physics, but the subjective experience of volition and free agency, and of reluctance to alien, compelling wills. . . . It is *imagined feeling* that governs the dance, not real emotional conditions. . . . Dance gesture is not real gesture, but virtual.'[41] Elements may be taken from animal movements, and from other fields such as sports, as motifs or models for the dancer's art.

The enactment through gesture of a 'play of power made visible' for Langer lifts the concept of Dance out of all its theoretical entanglements with music, painting, comedy, carnival, or serious drama, and provides its unmistakable and essential character.[42] The individual dancer shares with the spectators, if there are such, the illusion. While the individual dancer never has the actual impression of the performance as a whole,[43] even a solitary dancer '*sees* the

FIG. 5. *Pas de deux*: Margot Fonteyn and Rudolf Nureyev in rehearsal for the Athens Festival, 1963. Keystone collection, Hulton Archive HT1438/Getty Images.

dance sufficiently to let his imagination grasp it as a whole; and with his own body-feeling he understands the gestic forms that are its interwoven, basic elements. . . . He sees *the world in which his body dances*, and that is the primary illusion of his work; in this closed realm he develops his ideas.'[44]

Langer writes that the primary illusion of dance is a peculiarly rich experience, just as immediate as that of music or the plastic arts, but more complex. 'Both space and time are implicitly created with it. Story runs through it like a thread, without linking it at all to literature; impersonation and miming are often systematically involved in its basic abstraction, virtual gesture, but dance pantomime is not drama; the mummery of masks and costumes, to which its thematic gestures belong, is depersonalizing rather than humanly interesting. Dance, the art of the Stone Age, the art of primitive life par excellence, holds a hegemony over all art materials.'[45]

FIG. 6. The dancer 'sees the world' in which her body moves: Fonteyn, multiple exposure, c.1949. Hulton Archive HE6719/Getty Images.

The speculations of Mauss, Collingwood, Huizinga, and Langer on the radical social nature of dance, both as practice in the literal sense and as an iconic image of the process of social life, are thus complex, and suggestive for anthropology. One aim common to these writers was to play down language as the dominant or defining mode of human communication, and to articulate rather a conception of social life which focused on an aesthetics of embodied action, visual signs, music, and art. In specifying dance, or play, as an encompassing image of their conception of human life, they were proposing to encompass language 'as such' within it. These perhaps rather 'amateur'-looking ideas of the 1930s–1950s about art and feeling and embodiment were not taken up by the systematic modernizers building 'social science', but then anthropology has never been comfortable for very long about modernizing itself, and the older and 'softer' visions of humanity are now looking very appealing.

What makes it difficult to slot dance into serious social science is that being non-productive and non-verbal, in an odd modernist way it 'does not have meaning'. It may of course contain words, and even be integrally partnered with song, but it is true that it cannot be read as a text in a uni-dimensional way; it does not 'explain' itself. A logocentric anthropology is not easily able to specify its full significance. There are things going on in the dance which evoke from us wordy interpretations and explanations: and not only from us as observers, but from us as participants. The dance may reveal, but also conceal. An occasion may demand a festive dance, though individuals are sad; a glad victory celebration, while applauding no doubt Langer's 'play of power made visible', may cover up the true extent of the cruelties of kings and the sufferings of war. For ceremonies understood as analogues of the dance, there may be concealment too: the fulsome greetings of high society may hide hostility; the coronation of a new monarch may veil or even silence the parliamentary opposition; even the advanced democratic rituals of a presidential election can conceal a wasps' nest of contradictions which some might see as injustice. The much celebrated fairness and accountability of capitalism can conceal 'rotten apples' and crumbling institutions, while money itself is at bottom merely a set of counters in a game.

The analogy of the dance, and of the layered 'choreography' underlying lived activity, can be creatively extended to a whole range of social phenomena. Examples go well beyond obvious religious occasions or public ceremony to include the patterning of daily work, of family meals, of national politics, or the routines of the prison and the refugee camp. The patterning itself may be imposed in stone or concrete upon the land, and future generations may have to weave their networks within a historically fixed frame. We do this with the traffic circulation, flowing into the city in the morning and out at night, more or less keeping left (or right, according to nation), dodging in and out of lights and junctions, guessing (*nearly* always accurately) at the intentions of the other drivers to achieve an overall smooth progress—a gestural 'Will you, won't you, yes please do'; city traffic sometimes seems a weird motorized version of Alice in Wonderland's caucus race, with nobody really in charge, though the planners try. A lot of social life is rather like this, accompanied too by non-verbal politesses or splutterings, occasionally enlivened by swearing but only rarely put into articulate letters to the council.

Inevitably perhaps we have to return to language, and the difficulty of making it *effective*, unless it is enshrined in formality to the point of constituting a part of ceremonial action in itself. We have sophisticated recursive ways of talking and writing about language, and the historicity of its underlying grammar or what Wittgenstein described as 'forms of agreement' in language. But language is not the whole of human life. What can be said in language does not fully match all that is going on in life. A theme of this book is to explore aspects of what we could call 'ceremonial grammar', that is forms of agreement not in the 'grammar' of how we speak to each other using words as such: but forms of agreement in the way we 'dance' together, forms of agreement in ceremonial participation. 'Natives' are notoriously unable to explain their ceremonies and rituals; could any lay person do better with an ordinary church service or a disco, let alone the outpouring of the public onto the streets of London at the time of Diana's funeral? It is the highly specialized task of the academic to try and explain ceremony in language, but this does not mean we should reduce ceremony itself to a pale reflection of language.

I believe that some of the ethnography quoted in this chapter resonates effectively with some of the older general writings about art and dance, themselves foreshadowing Alfred Gell's arguments that visual art, music, and dance are not best understood as languages or as like languages, but are quite different. Collingwood's image of Dance as 'the mother of all languages' tempts us thus to see its derivatives, music, art, and so on as 'daughters of the dance'. Is language simply one of the offspring of the Dance too? Its special status will be discussed in the next chapter, but the present chapter concludes with a review of some recent work, first on music (so close to dance) and then on visual communication and art, by anthropologists who are seeking to present these on their own terms, from first principles as primary phenomena of human life, rather than as sub-varieties of language.

3. MELODIES OF THE AIR

Music is everywhere around us, though we are not always aware of it as such. We do not have to play to be a part of the musical world. Kariamu Welsh Asante's volume of essays reminds us of the way that African dance music is played in counterpoint with the movements of dancers; their feet and bodies accentuate beats, even main beats, which are not necessarily played by the drummers.[46] 'Silent' participation, even calm listening, can also be rhythmically responsive—in the imagination. Not only can we can play the official role of audience to a musical performance, but even more often, we are attracted as eavesdroppers, especially with today's radio, cassettes, and television. There is more music in the everyday lives of us all than the social sciences commonly recognize. Anthropologists traditionally tended to leave the study of music to musicology (in the West) or ethnomusicology (rest of the world). Arguments for the integration of music (and dance) studies into general anthropology, however, were pressed by John Blacking in the mid-twentieth century and this approach is now bearing fruit.[47] In a pioneering study for its time, Peter Lienhardt showed how Swahili society on the East African coast was riddled by 'moiety-style' competition between rival football teams, and everything that went with the supporters' clubs—including bands and music-making of all kinds.[48] All fieldworkers need to decide, whatever their particular speciality is, how far they should be aware of music and song, and how far to be systematic about it, to prepare themselves in advance with training and equipment. The music and the song will be there around them, almost certainly integral to the 'society' they are trying to understand. They will have to judge how far to take it into account in their analysis. A. Seeger has offered a 'musical anthropology' from the Amazon, arguing that music does not happen 'in society' as much as society is given shape, at least in the Suya case, through musical and dance performance. In this way major organizational features such as moieties are made recognizable, social time is ritually articulated, and cosmology grasped.[49]

Three recent edited volumes illustrate how fruitful the inclusion of a musical component in anthropological study can be, after a long period of domination by language and textually oriented methods. Anthropologists are increasingly noticing how musical experience and memory is associated not only with personal identity but social groupings and places. A pioneering collection of studies on these lines has been edited by Martin Stokes, and his introduction to the book is a very helpful guide to this theme.[50] The studies themselves are quite provocative for mainstream social science, offering new thoughts, for example, about nationalism and classical music (as with the case of Chopin and Polish nationalism), the evidence for associations between music, status, and class in Hélène La Rue's literary study, the musical styles which help define local ethnicity (explored in different ways by Malcolm Chapman for the Celts and Peter Parkes for the Kalasha of the Hindu Kush), the precise location in time, place, and style of the 'Liverpool sound' as traced by Sara Cohen. Stokes himself contributes an essay on the kinds of social-and-musical exchange stimulated by a visit of Black Sea musicians from Turkey to the West of Ireland. His work in other ways has always been sensitive to hybrid forms, displaced forms, different levels of reference between kinds of music, and the way that music spreads around the world.[51] In Chapter 11 I return to his account of musical tensions on the Turkish–Syrian border, as a part of the sociology of nationalism and ethnicity. Musical performance can of course heighten political anger or even be in itself a cause of political anger, as Stokes shows for Northern Ireland.[52]

Gregory Barz and Timothy Cooley have brought together a collection of essays emphasizing for regions literally from the Arctic to the Equator the way that 'participant-observation' as a research method can be brought to life through the appreciation, playing, and teaching of music on both sides of the research encounter.[53] A visitor can come to 'know' people through joining in their music, in ways that bureaucratic investigators with their clipboards rarely do. Music has emotional appeal and can tap the sources of our well-being, and the third collection I would like to mention here concerns its potential in the practices of healing. Penelope Gouk brings together essays by anthropologists, medical people, and music specialists to reflect on this theme. A particularly interesting chapter is by Lyn Schumaker, who takes up the *kalela* dance of central Africa (made famous, as mentioned above, by Clyde Mitchell) and shows how its performance is linked with the promotion of cleanliness and hygiene, almost becoming a protective health measure. More familiarly, there are many kinds of music for the mind and spirit; Cheryce Kramer's essay, for example, traces the place of soul music in German psychiatry.[54]

A rather different kind of study also reveals music as an unexpectedly central preoccupation in a very 'modern' place. Ruth Finnegan has written a fascinating book on the 'new town' of Milton Keynes set down in the 1950s in a fairly unremarkable stretch of midlands on the fringe of the London commuter belt, not a place people associate with any high form of culture, nor one where we might expect much in the way of authentic country singing and dancing.[55] In fact even the rather anonymous population of Milton Keynes turns out to be riddled with music-making. An extraordinarily large number of people take part in choral groups, church choirs, rock bands, string quartets, school concerts, and so on (quite apart from those who form the audiences), and Finnegan wryly points out how much 'work' is involved—in practice sessions, in driving people around from one place to another, in acquiring and caring for instruments. All this work is out-of-hours and unpaid, even personally funded, and any money earned goes mostly into local charities and does not appear in the statistics of the national economy.

Studies of this kind demonstrate beyond any question how music is associated with moiety, or class, or place, or ethnic or national or personal identity. But they go beyond showing simple association. Running through them all is a picture of the human condition with a capacity for making and responding to music at its core, not as an add-on extra. Music touches a more 'instinctive' level in us than language, and of course styles move easily across language barriers. Lévi-Strauss seized on music as a model for our reponsive-ness to the structural principles underlying myth, and by implication culture in a range of other forms.[56] The image of the jazz band nicely combines form and the creativity of improvisation. A jazz performance is always unique, and yet part of a tradition as much as the classical tradition based on written scores. Stokes discusses the ways in which music can open up boundaries and, 'depending on how we are placed by other social facts', either entrap us in a narrowly chauvinist or sexist sense or, alternatively, 'leap across boundaries and put into play unexpected and expanding possibilities'. In his view, the widespread disillusion with 'grand explanatory schemata' and renewed attention by anthropologists to 'the resourceful and prolix creativities of everyday life' provides them with an opportunity to engage with music as a vital form of social creativity.

4. FROM 'WAYS OF SEEING' TO THE PRODUCTION OF ART

The gift of sight is important to us. Metaphors of sight reflect this; in English, but in many other tongues as well, 'seeing' indicates understanding, knowing. As scientists or ethnographers, we 'observe', though that word is very flexible; 'light dawns' as we get the point of an argument, we 'perceive' grammatical rules in a foreign language, we remember things 'in the mind's eye', and so on. Although a strong line of current criticism suggests that anthropology has been too 'logocentric' in its methods and analysis, others have pointed to the hidden ways in which our work has depended upon visual metaphors which run, sometimes quite unconsciously, through our language. Do we slide too easily from one to the other? Can the visual always be translated into the lin-guistic (as for example Jim Faris attempted to do for the 'grammar' underlying the designs of Nuba body art), and vice versa, or are these profoundly differ-ent dimensions of our experience, knowledge, and creativity?[57]

At an earlier period in anthropology, the art of tribal peoples tended to be taken 'at face value' as a matter of cultural style, technique, possible religious significance, and even beauty in an abstract sense.[58] Art objects from Africa and Oceania, exhibited in London at the start of the twentieth century, stimulated developments in Western modern art, something especially evident in the work of Picasso. Until recently anthropologists have been a little suspicious of the way that the indiscrimate importation of form and style through objects from exotic places leaves behind their 'real' meaning, their local cultural significance and associations, and local aesthetic principles of appreciation. Surely a Congolese mask, they ask themselves, does not 'look' the same to a Western artist or gallery-goer as it does to the people who made it. The role of the anthropologist must surely be to explore local cultural evaluations, including socio-religious aspects and aesthetic criteria, and set them against those of the global aesthetic or commercial interest. Out of these concerns has developed a rich debate about how far there are, or are not, universal aesthetic standards, and as we might expect, the answer has tended to rest upon 'what you take to be aesthetics'. Jeremy Coote has argued strongly that mobile pastoral peoples like the Dinka and the Nuer, who make few art objects, nevertheless have a deeply visual aesthetic we can connect with in their appreciation of colour and shape in animals and in body movement, including representational dancing.[59]

The growing use of visual methods in recording the ways of life of peoples across the world has thrown this issue into sharp relief through helping foster 'visual anthropology' as an important sub-discipline in itself. Photography, and film, have helped sensitize all of us to the specifically visual side of representation and thus of knowledge. The sophistication of film-makers in creating visual experience (not always reducible to language—a film whether good or bad is definitely different from a book) has sensitized professional anthropologists to the possibility that 'ways of seeing' are founded in culturally and historically specific contexts. Jim Faris has argued that one can read the exploitative and subordinating role of internal American colonialism as well as its changing aesthetic styles in the photographic record of the Navajo peoples of New Mexico and Arizona.[60] The Navajo were represented at any given time *in a certain way* through the camera, even with a Navajo person behind the lens. In circumstances of less obvious ideological domination, perhaps the eye of the photographer does engage with that of the photographed. Anna Grimshaw has shown how the pioneering West African films of Jean Rouch capture visually the confused but celebratory moment when African nations were throwing off the colonial yoke, and how Melissa Llewellyn's films of the Masai over some twenty years of the developing feminist movement adopt an increasingly sensitive and engaged perspective upon the lives of women there. Her arguments certainly concern the perception of the film-makers, the 'ethnographic eye' (along with changing camera technology), but even so also open up the question of the 'native eye', as it were.[61] That question itself has taken centre stage in some quite dramatic ways, as 'indigenous art' has been fostered in many parts of the world and has stimulated Western tastes for the 'ethnic'. Clare Harris has explored the extraordinary range of different styles in which things 'Tibetan' have been portrayed by Tibetan artists, in the shifting historical and geographical contexts of their lives, especially those living in exile since 1959. Can we still conceive of such a thing as a Tibetan eye, or has the image of Tibet been refracted through so many lenses that we cannot follow an essential trace?[62] Is the production of pictures by artists in the diaspora of any of the world's displaced people the same activity as painting in the homeland once was? Has the activity itself become more significant than the representation? Are 'ways of seeing' perhaps broader than a matter of the composition of pictures but built into our lives, in a manner not necessarily obvious to the person who has the privilege of wielding the paintbrush or the camera?

This is indeed the argument of Marcus Banks and Howard Morphy in a recent edited volume which seeks to extend 'visual anthropology' beyond photography and film, indeed to reintegrate the visual dimension into mainstream anthropology, as David MacDougall argues powerfully in his contribution. The studies brought together do this first by deepening our awareness of the wide range of visual codes and techniques we employ in the 'modern' sector through using computers; making and watching television— for instance, in Bali and Japan; and in the deliberate efforts now made by some ethnographic film-makers themselves to escape 'observational realism'. Secondly, the collection boldly recaptures something of the older territory of the anthropology of art while problematizing, in a range of cases from India, Melanesia, and Oceania, what might be constituted as criteria for visual significance in local crafts, theories of perception, proper visibility and invisibility in a ritual sense, and the contextual transformations of actual 'art objects' as they pass from one setting to another.[63]

An even more radical work is Alfred Gell's *Art and Agency*.[64] Gell insists that the anthropology of art is not a question of 'ways of seeing', of a diagnosing a variety of language-like codes which help us discern significance in cultural styles. For him, this is itself an approach which belongs to Western academic art history. This tradition, a very visual one indeed, overvalues the 'art object' as such and overemphasizes its representational aspects at the expense of its actuality in a social process of production and circulation. He seeks, and puts forward, an anthropological theory of art which like other anthropological theories goes to the heart of relations between people, and the material things which they make and exchange among themselves. Anthropology for him is not about things said or represented, but about *things done*, and characteristically focuses its analysis within a biographical time-span, that is, the real time of people's lives and their interactions with each other. Placing the making, reception, and wider ripple effects of art in this frame, he adopts Peirce's use of the term *index* for the 'work of art', rather than 'representation'. A variety of relations can be traced between the patron of the work, the artist, the thing (landscape, god, even person) 'indexed', the recipient or audience, and so on, in ramifying ways which can form a complex network. From the index, we proceed to guess at, hypothesize, or 'abduct' this context of relations beyond it. There are many further ramifications; the index itself may have a sort of rebounding effect on the artist, or the commissioner, or the person portrayed; the index ('work of art') can be said not only to carry something of the agency of any of these with it, but to acquire a kind of agency in itself. Indexes develop networks of linkage of their own, artists copying other artists, preparing for and recapitulating their own work, and constituting thus a set of 'distributed' elements of the original artist's own agency, and indeed the mutually interacting agency of many other artists.

Gell draws attention to the interest of John Layard in the affinity of graphic art styles on Malekula in the New Hebrides with local dance choreography; an interest 'utterly foreign to the mind-set of his anthropological contemporaries' in the 1930s (though interestingly matched by Collingwood's attention to the inscribed patterns of dance in Celtic art[65]). A complex maze-like pattern in the sand was drawn as a kind of performance, to show a journey through obstacles faced by a ghost outwitting a demon on the way to the land of the dead. The pattern was echoed in the ceremonies of induction into the men's cult, in which a single dancer 'has to thread his way through the ranks of the main body of dancers very much indeed as if he were negotiating a maze'. Gell thinks it is useful to consider the act of drawing as 'akin to dancing', and the design itself as a residue of this ballet of the hand. He reminds us that this analogy evidently suggested itself to Merleau-Ponty, after watching Matisse's hand and brush in slow motion (and I have noted above a very similar observation by Collingwood on the manual action of the painter). Insights such as these confound the conventional aesthetics which deals separately with the art forms and modalities of expression 'because they give pleasure to separate senses, the eye (visual art), the ear (music), or the kinetic sense (dance)'.[66] Patterns and designs moreover have a way of exerting an independent agency; Gell shows how the eye can be captivated by intricate, puzzling, and ambiguous lines, whorls, and pathways. This mode of decoration is not peculiar to any particular culture, but very general, and used to confuse enemies and evil spirits very widely. It seems almost to have magical power. We are 'hooked', enchanted. The exquisite geometrical designs made by Marquesan people on their bodies and artefacts, recorded in the nineteenth century, exert a fascination on us even through the filter of museum collections and books, the only places today where they have left a residue. We can trace how they 'speak' to each other too. Subtle transformations were being made all the time between the design elements, achieving fine but essential distinctions. The designs were not produced simply for art's sake, however, but in the processes of the life-course, a struggle to maintain and protect personal and social identity against dispersal in a context where pedigrees were known to be political fictions.

Further striking examples among those offered by Gell include that of the way Melanesian operators in the famous inter-island ceremonial exchanges known as *kula* seek to build up their fame through associating their name and thus agency with the shell treasures in circulation; and the competitive proliferation of beautifully decorated Maori meeting houses in the late nineteenth–early twentieth century which 'indicated' (were a *collective index of*) the assertion of Maori communal agency at this time (which we might point out has obviously had powerful consequences across the world and especially on the politics of indigenous peoples globally). Perfection was not achieved; each meeting house was 'a project for future houses, a "sketch" towards a series of as yet unbuilt houses'. Building on memory, looking to the future; the whole phenomenon, like other areas of artwork, was set in networks over time, rather like the oeuvre of a great Western artist. Houses, however, are not just to look at, they are to live in. The Maori meeting house (in its collectivity) is an object we can trace 'as a movement of thought, a movement of memory reaching down into the past and a movement of aspiration' and through the study of such artefacts we are able to grasp 'mind' as an external disposition of public acts, 'transcending the individual *cogito* and the co-ordinates of any particular here and now'.[67]

CHAPTER FIVE

Ritual, Memory, and Religion

ANTHROPOLOGISTS have struggled very hard to appreciate things from the participant's point of view, and in the native language, as far as possible. A sensitivity to indigenous expressions and their translation has greatly improved the ethnographic reporting of religious phenomena in particular, but 'beliefs and rituals' are more than a matter of words. Language and the collective morphology of signifying action are best teased apart, before we can explore more lucidly their interconnection. Many of the shaped ceremonial actions of mundane life have a quasi-religious aspect; and religious phenomena, however defined, if we are to use the word as a general category, must share much with the ceremonial qualities of the mundane. From considering first some topics often regarded as secular and distinguished sharply from the study of religion, I move on to consider how anthropologists have tackled the key challenge of religion and try to persuade any sceptics who may read this that we should seek continuities rather than distinction here. In my view, the Durkheimian dichotomy of sacred versus profane in human affairs obscures the shadings of ceremoniality that pervade all the arenas of social action.

I. SOCIAL FORM AS DRAMA: MEMORY, EXPECTATION, AND THE TENDENCY OF WORDS TO FAIL

Memory is more than intellectual knowledge of the past, but is a lived framework for the partial revisions of the present which go on around us all the time, and for changing expectations of the future too. Moreover, individual memories are inextricably part of a shared network.[1] We spend a lot of time in daily life or in academia trying to capture memory by telling stories or 'history' in personal, linear narrative; but language rarely seems enough in itself to access the three-dimensional riches of shared memory or anticipation.

An illuminating illustration of the way in which the circulation of words can fuel expectation, and yet be very misleading if literally understood, is Peter Lienhardt's study of rumour.[2] All sorts of bits and pieces of language, including quite contradictory statements, feed into rumour. For example in the 1950s there was a rumour in Bahrain that the British government had forced the Sheikh of Bahrain to legalize the selling of alcohol to Muslims. This rumour had something in it for two constituencies: the conservatives who objected to alcohol and the modernists who liked to drink it at that time but opposed colonialism. For both groups it was a British outrage, and provided an opportunity for them to unite for motives that were ambiguous and incompatible, even opposite. Rumours may represent 'complexities of public feeling that cannot readily be made articulate at a more thoughtful level . . . they join people's sympathies in a consensus of an unthinking, or at least uncritical, kind'. Rumour may not be rational language, but it can lead to spontaneous demonstrations on the streets: Lienhardt dubs rumour 'the voice of the mob, before the mob has gathered'.[3] Although explicit in themselves, the actual words of rumour can be tangential to the social movements of feeling and shared purpose on which they are borne.

A study by Robert Borofsky of the interplay of action and narrative in articulating social memory on the tiny islands of Puka Puka in Polynesia illustrates the 'marginality' of words beautifully.[4] His study shows how even the verbal work of conversation between anthropologist and informants, and the written investigations provided by a series of ethnographies, are incomplete. These methods can leave untouched large areas of social memory, and *possible choreographies* of future practice, which can be transmitted over time without surfacing in so many words. His analysis illustrates how deep the unspoken archive of social memory can run.

At the start of his field investigations between 1977 and 1981, Borofsky encountered a form of moiety organization known as Akatawa. This was a little surprising because Puka Puka consisted of three physically separate coral reef villages, rather than two geographical communities. 'Akatawa' literally means 'becoming sides', and while it was in force, land resources and social alignments fell into opposed halves, each including the whole population of one village and a portion of the third. People claimed that the system was an ancient tradition validated in myth. Borofsky found them organizing sports events such as cricket and public celebrations on this model, as well as debates in the island council. He was surprised to find out that the Akatawa moiety-system had not always been in vogue, but in fact had just been 'revived' in 1976. Why had this apparently traditional ceremonial set-up not been mentioned anywhere in the previous five ethnographies of Puka Puka, published from the 1930s on? Islanders replied that the earlier anthropologists had not asked about it. There was nothing in the government archives about it either; in fact these records seemed to suggest that the three-village structure had formerly been the only basis of administrative and economic organization. Borofsky even consulted a fictional account of the islands, which again mentioned the three villages but no Akatawa rival 'sides'.[5] To add to the puzzle, Akatawa was abolished in 1980, to be replaced for all practical purposes by the three-village system again.

In pursuing his inquiry as an exploration into 'anthropological ways of knowing', Borofsky outlines the ways in which social life is organized on Puka Puka. There are some relatively low-key ideas which do not relate to the three-village pattern. These include an egocentric conception of matrilineally connected 'kinsmen' which can be used in many adaptable ways, cross-cutting the patrilines relating to public discourse and officialdom.[6] 'Double-descent' on Puka Puka was not a fixed social structure, but the option of organizing things in a matrilineal way was part of the Pukapukan archive of cultural possibilities (in my words rather than Borofsky's), one of a number of often rather fluid ideas in an evolving situation.

To locals, the temporary adoption of Akatawa was not as much of a revolution as it might have appeared to outsiders. One of the themes of Borofsky's book is that verbal accounts provide only partial perspectives on the past, and much can be sought in their discrepancies and ambiguities as they relate to learned and remembered forms of practice, whether in productive work or in collective ceremonial. Throughout his account Borofsky emphasizes the pragmatic attitude the people had to learning and to knowledge, as reflected in the way they learned crafts by visual attention and bodily practice. In this context the revival of Akatawa, the matri-moiety structure, can be looked at again as one among many other experimental ways of doing things. At first in 1974 it had been a temporary measure just for sports, but in 1976 it was 'called into being' by the Council of Important People 'to teach the younger people about tradition'. It was a great success, and gained a 'kind of authenticity' as people talked about it. The anthropologist happened to be present at the 1980 meeting of the Council when it was abolished; he recognizes how his own questionings had helped to produce an agreed view about the Akatawa, to create 'traditions' that did not appear previously (from the evidence of previous ethnographers) to have become set into explicit verbal form.[7]

Social memory and structured plots

Novels certainly can invoke large scenarios set in space, time, and social history. But their space remains that of the individual imagination, as the pages written by one person are turned over and read in silence by another. It is the stage-play rather than the novel which *enacts* such scenarios, in 'real' space and human encounter (with implications explored by Kirsten Hastrup in her study of stage-acting as a species of self-reflective social action in general).[8] A play is a collective product, and offered to a collective audience by contrast with the one-to-one relationship of a novel to its readers. As with the opera, staged encounters are not necessarily just between individuals, but moral forces, representatives of destiny, love, or the gods. Moreover, plays like Shakespeare's go beyond speech—they are wonderfully enlivened with music, dance, and violent action, not to mention plays-within-the-play. All the arts since Shakespeare have drawn on his plots as well as his language, as he himself used earlier sources (there are apparently *twenty thousand* pieces of music linked to Shakespeare in one way or another). Some of the plays have been turned into independent ballets and musicals. What makes great drama so 'translatable', in a way that novels perhaps resist? The details of personal life and inward character (often so crucial in novels) can be dissolved away, but the primary plot-shape endures: the driven encounters between kings and fools, soldiers and priests, fathers, mothers and children, lovers and spouses, rival great families pursuing their intrigues at the heart of political affairs, as in *Julius Caesar* (which has been rendered more than once into African contexts—see Fig. 7). *Romeo and Juliet* is another outstanding example: the structural clarity of this story, itself borrowed by Shakespeare from earlier sources, has famously been translated into *West Side Story*, one of the most successful musicals of all time, set among Puerto Ricans and the white working class in New York. The story of romantic love across the barriers of family and caste, leading to tragedy, scarcely needs the embroidery of language or the introspection of the modern novelist to be understood; its lastingly 'mythical' quality translates well from production to production—as Figs. 8–10 illustrate—even into the haunting music of Prokofiev and 'virtual' emotion as captured in the movements of pure ballet.

FIG. 7. *SeZaR*: once translated into Swahili by Julius Nyerere, *Julius Caesar* is here transposed to South Africa, where the play has inspired other leading figures like Nelson Mandela. This adaptation, which was first performed in South Africa, has also toured Britain. Directed by Yael Farber, it is based on Sol Plaaitjie's translation of the play into SeTswana, rendered back into English but retaining some conversation and song in the Tswana tongue. In this scene Brutas talks to Sinna, with Kassius looking on from behind. Brutas is played by Menzi 'Ngubs' Ngubane, Sinna by Siyabonga Twala, and Kassius by Tumisho Masha. Photo: Ruphin Coudyzer, courtesy Leigh Colombick.

FIG. 8. A minimal version of dramatic form: the Tybalt–Benvolio duel in *Shakespeare's R & J* by Joe Calarco, a production with four actors, directed by Danial Yurgaitis, 2002. Photo: Larry Wild, Northern State University, Aberdeen, South Dakota.

FIG. 9. *Romeo and Juliet*: classic Elizabethan style with Reginald Denny and Basil Rathbone, 1936. General Photographic Agency, Hulton Archive HE5945/Getty Images.

FIG. 10. *West Side Story*: with Rita Moreno and George Chakiris, directed by Robert Wise and Jerome Robbins, 1961. Photo: Ernst Haas/Hulton Archive JC8132/Getty Images.

The structured plots of myth

Anthropologists have long concerned themselves with 'myth', agreeing this to be a kind of storytelling which transcends ordinary narrative. What makes myth so special? Why are there extraordinary similarities between myths drawn from all over the world? Efforts have mainly tended to define myth in terms of its content: either its concern with sacred topics, with the gods and spirits, or with its focus on explaining 'origins', how things came to be. Malinowski adopted both these elements in his characterization of myth as a genre of sacred tales relating to the origins of the world, but added, from the sociological point of view, that these tales also served as explanation and justification for the social order as we find it today. He suggested that we could regard myth as a sacred constitution or validating charter for the way things are, for the legitimacy of the chiefs and the division of land among the clans. Malinowski's analysis (illustrating his 'functionalism') addressed itself to the literal level of the events and explicit moral of the story, but most other anthropologists have sought something deeper, psychologically or culturally. Lévi-Strauss set aside the surface level of stories as told by individual speakers, and demonstrated, famously for the Oedipus tale and for myths of the Americas, that beneath the narrative surface we can identify key elements of the story that combine and transform themselves in comparable ways across vast regions. To reveal these structural patterns we need to survey together, as one might today using a computer, whole sets of stories. Now the elements and patterns that Lévi-Strauss identifies are characteristically those of *plot*: of key encounters between representative moral figures, often establishing contact or separation between regions of space—sky and earth, north and south, water and land, etc., or between other opposed elemental principles such as male and female, nature and culture, animal and human. Lévi-Strauss maintains that it is the philosophical paradoxes of identity, difference, and transformation underlying good myths that make them 'translatable' and explain their widespread affinity over many centuries and continents.[9]

My hunch as to why myths are so appealing and capable of extraordinary transmission over time and space, on a metalevel quite unlike ordinary language or poetry or novels, is not so much their intellectual but their 'dramatic' character. They dwell on *enactable* paradoxes—seemingly impossible transformations and encounters we could nevertheless stage in three dimensions and in technicolour. Poetry does not always travel well, it is very difficult to translate as it has to be almost re-composed when put into another language, but the plot of a myth, like a strong Shakespearean story, is so robust it can be transposed. If we ponder specific myths, whether from the Greeks, the Bible, the Australian Dreamtime, or the tales so common in the Nile Basin about the moral faults in humans which cause the primal separation of earth and sky, we can see how they might lend themselves to *enactment* and preferably so with extra music and sweeping choreography. The myths of Asdiwal portray a hero of the Pacific Coast of North America, who moves between sky and earth, winter and summer, plenty and famine, sea and land, a succession of encounters with female kin, to present finally an irresolvable paradox, an imaginary counterpoint to reality, of the tension between such principles as matrilineal filiation and patrilocal residence. What gives this story-cycle its momentum is the cosmic scale of the imagined action. It could be made into a marvellous opera, or a film—because of the special ability of the big screen to create large-scale virtual reality. In its capacity to invoke virtual spaces and transformations, we can associate myth again with 'ritual', as several early anthropologists did, though on a rather different basis—of 'form' rather than of literal meaning.

The structured plots of everyday memory: enactment in space, time

Whatever we mean by 'ritual', we include the idea that it is deliberate ceremonial performance, physically enacted or enactable, and transformative in intention or in effect. Thus rituals (again however defined) entail use or treatment of the body, controlled use of space and specific timing of actions. The bodily aspect has been emphasized in recent anthropological writings on performance, and on medical treatments. The spatial aspect of rituals has been given particular attention by David Parkin, who draws attention to their common feature of patterns of prescribed movement, as well as their typically invasive effects upon the body.[10] We recall van Gennep's spatial metaphors and ritual enactments of passage 'across thresholds' through time (Chapter 2 above), the spatial form of circulation in ceremonial exchange systems such as the Melanesian *kula*, and the typical orientations and central points of religious observance and religious journeys. Some anthropologists, for example Leach, have suggested that ritual is like language, but then have to emphasize what a very special language it is, to the point where the similarity disappears. It is perhaps less like language than like music or dance. More recently Caroline Humphrey and James Laidlaw have insisted on the autonomy of ritual in its distinctive frames of action, emphasizing the timing and sequencing of its 'archetypal' elements.[11] In these respects, as in the manner of framing, or setting off from other domains of life, and in the self-referential criteria which are thus defined, ritual stands up well to the analogy with drama.

A good example of how ritual is both set apart from, and yet intimately connected with other domains, including social memory, can be found in Bloch's work on the Merina kingdom of Madagascar. His general approach to cognition, ideology, and ritual rests on four assumptions. In summary these are as follows: there are universal psychological characteristics of human beings; knowledge results in part from their direct interaction with the environment; but it also derives from cosmological and ritual schemes which present ideological *alternatives* to everyday knowledge, to be understood as transformations of the latter; these schemas and their relation to everyday cognition are crucial in the operations of power and political domination.[12] His argument is vividly set out with reference to the Merina ceremonial of the royal bath.[13] Royal symbolism is created out of non-royal symbolism, logically and probably also historically. It often represents an unchanging order, over and above the continual movement, exchange, and decay of ordinary life, but the royals themselves have to move between the two. There were many reports from the nineteenth century of the ritual of the royal bath as practised in extremely elaborate form by the rulers, at a time when the kingdom was expanding.

The ritual should occur at the beginning of the agricultural year, and at the beginning of the calendrical year (on the Malagasy version of the Arabic lunar calendar). While these obviously did not often coincide, the idea of 'the new year' and a period of growing strength and sanctity was important. One part of the ritual was concerned with the growth of the new moon, represented as a young chick emerging from the shell. A period of restrictions began two weeks before the actual bath: no animal could be killed, there could be no funerals—if a person died, the matter had to be hushed up; and the weekly market and other cyclical activities were stopped. Various taxes had to be paid to the sovereign, called, for example, 'the price of life', 'the new year present', heightening the normal pattern of tribute to superiors. The night before the actual bath, there was a state-wide orchestration of weeping by women, each house mourning those of its own who had died. In the morning everything was washed and people, including the king, went to their family tombs, asked for blessing from their ancestors, and collected a little soil to add to the water of the bath. The night of the royal bath, some sources indicate, began with 'disorder' and a discreet orgy of sexual activity, but later in the evening everyone had to be in their proper place. Youths fetched water from special sources, across the kingdom, associated with spirits from the past. In the middle of the night, the king stepped in and out of his bath, put on new clothes and sprayed his subjects with the water; this blessing conferred symbolic filiation, and if a slave was splashed, freedom would follow. After the king's blessing, the head of every household in the kingdom would also take a bath, though not a complete one, and bless his family and dependants. A special meal followed. The next day, there was a distribution of cattle, and many were killed for the feast.

Bloch emphasizes, as I cannot in this short summary, how the ritual aligns society, royalty, and astronomy, especially through the chains of 'blessing' which transfer fertility and life. He analyses a set of internal contrasts and paradoxes he finds in the details of the ritual, and points to the way that like theatre, rituals create images by means of contrast—here, for example, as we move from the house of weeping to the tomb of rejoicing; in the sexual orgy later transcended by the re-establishment of order; and the beginning of new life in the middle of the night, following from the powers of the king's blessing. The exegesis could go on for ever, as does commentary on a good opera, but the profusion of resonating detail only confirms the clear underlying theme—essentially about the struggle of the kingship to retain control over and preserve for all time the vitality of the kingdom. The royal ritual has the emotional and ideological power to move and organize the people because its elements on a grand scale recognizably echo and co-opt the elements of ordinary family rituals and symbolism. In a later study, Bloch shows how the related rite of circumcision can be traced over a two-hundred-year trajectory among the Merina, powerful royal forms probably being transformed in scale and emphasis from domestic forms and subsequently lapsing back into them.[14] Such rituals are not just 'spectacle' but potent and memorable because of their place in hierarchies of other social performance. Rulers play on the elements of ritual practice already known to the people, and can sometimes make them weep.

New work on Madagascar is taking further the question of relations between the past, the memory of the past, and the life of the present. Michael Lambek's study of the formerly powerful kingdom of Sakalava in the northwest of the island offers fruitful insights into the way everyday practice and ritual alike, especially possession by spirits of former royals, make the past 'present' to the people in deeply affective ways. They talked of 'bearing the weight' of their own history. Lambek suggests that this shared 'burden' makes Sakalava people who they are. The annual Great Service at the royal capital of Mahajanga is the heart of a living consciousness of history which defies any simple contrast between past and present. Sakalava people are portrayed as 'making' their world, a phenomenon for which Lambek draws on Aristotle's conception of 'poesis', out of the living memory and fresh manifestations of the past of the kingdom and its emblematic characters or personalities. The cult of Sakalava royalty is not being displaced by modern economic or political developments, or the mobility of its adherents— including foreign travel; it may contradict the conditions of modern life in theory, but coexists with them in practice. It has, in Lambek's analysis, something of the Maussian notion of the 'total' social phenomenon about it, even though the way that people 'take their bearings' from it is often not evident to the stranger passing by, or explained in ordinary conversation.[15]

A link with social memory can be made from here back to Bourdieu's use of the idea of *habitus*, in which practice is the key to understanding the way that symbolic resonance is generated in us as we grow up within a particular context. Even patterns of movement and social manners can be internalized as a part of 'social memory', reflecting the hierarchies and deference of earlier times. A similar observation of the way in which we can unconsciously echo the past in our bodies is given in Paul Connerton's book *How Societies Remember*.[16] He contrasts this with the politically deliberate mounting of ceremonial markers of the birth of nations, and notes the difference between the two kinds of social 'remembering'. In Lambek's account these two kinds of remembering are not really separable. There are visitors to the Sakalava rites even from the central parts of Madagascar; there is a growing sense of the performance of nationhood here, in this otherwise provincial area.

A note on Wittgenstein's distinction between language and ceremonial action

Wittgenstein spoke of a tendency in himself and others who tried to write or talk Ethics or Religion to 'run against the boundaries' of language. He is quoted as saying to a friend, 'I can well imagine a religion in which there are no doctrinal propositions, in which there is thus no talking.'[17] A number of commentators, of the kind who like to see some philosophical significance in anthropology, have sensed the power of these ideas.[18] Herbert Fingarette declared on the basis of his study of Confucius, 'What we have come to see

. . . is how vast is the area of human existence in which the substance of that existence *is* the ceremony. Promises, commitments, excuses, pleas, compliments, pacts, these and so much more are ceremonies or they are nothing. It is thus in the medium of ceremony that the peculiarly human part of our life is lived.'[19] Fingarette's treatment, however, accords ritual a rather benign and non-violent place in the range of human action, while Wittgenstein acknowledges its potential fearfulness and echoes of cruelty.

Wittgenstein's most sustained commentaries on ritual arose from his reading of Frazer's *Golden Bough*.[20] He starts with the point that we should not approach ancient practices like killing the priest-king with a view to *explaining* them away in terms of one or other theory, whether indigenous or Frazer's own. Native ideas about magic, treated in this way, inevitably appear just as 'mistakes', while Frazer's explanations merely make such practices 'plausible' to people who think as he does (a rather narrow circle—Wittgenstein scorns Frazer as someone unable to imagine any priest who is not basically an English parson). When it is claimed that the king must be killed in his prime, because otherwise his soul would not be kept fresh, 'the practice does not spring from this view, but they are both just there'. We are not faced here with an error. What is happening is described as strange and dreadful, and the question as to why it happens 'is properly answered by saying: Because it is dreadful'. 'Here one can only *describe* and say: this is what human life is like.' 'Compared with the impression which the thing described makes on us, the explanation is too uncertain.' To place the life of the priest-king and the phrase 'the majesty of death' side by side, is to show they are the same. This is no explanation, but 'merely substitutes one symbol for another. Or: one ceremony for another. No *opinion* serves as the foundation for a religious symbol.' We act in a particular way, for example burning something in effigy, or kissing the name of a loved one, and feel satisfied. Here, as in the case of baptism as 'washing', it does not make sense to speak of 'error'. The principle according to which such practices are arranged is a very general one, present in our own minds; we could invent possibilities ourselves and 'it would be pure luck if they were not actually found somewhere'.

For example, we could easily imagine a tribe where the king is always hidden but must be *shown* to the people on special occasions; perhaps no one should touch him, or everyone *must* touch him. After Schubert's death his brother cut some of his scores into small pieces and gave them out to his favourite pupils. 'This act, as a sign of piety, is *just as* understandable to us as the different one of keeping the scores untouched, accessible to no one.' We could also understand it if Schubert's brother had *burned* them as a sign of piety. Considering further the idea of fire, Wittgenstein asks how it could have failed to make an impression on the 'awakening' human mind? Does an 'explanation' make it less impressive? There follow the observations quoted in the opening pages of this book, on the prevalence of 'ritualistic' actions in human life, how they do not arise from faulty scientific theory, and how we could almost regard our own species as the 'ceremonial animal'.

Wittgenstein suggests that Frazer's collection of facts almost points to a 'secret law', which we could consider by means of 'the arrangement of its factual content alone, in a "perspicuous" representation'. He glosses this as 'a kind of "World-view"', in which understanding consists of the fact that we 'see the connections'. Veneration of the oak tree in the past had no particular *reason*, except that human beings and the oak were united in a 'community of life'; if fleas developed ritual, it would be based on the dog. It was not so much the union of humankind and the oak but their separation that gave rise to rites; 'for the awakening of the intellect occurs with a separation from the original *soil*, the original basis of life'.

Later elaborating Frazer's themes of fire and sacrifice, Wittgenstein is struck not only by the similarities but also shades of difference between the fire festivals of Europe, like a variety of faces with common features showing up in one place or another. He asks what connects this picture of 'an association of practices' with our feelings and thoughts. At the Scottish May Day festival of Beltane, one unlucky person finds they have chosen the wrong piece of cake. Seized by part of the company who made a show of putting this person in the fire, the quickly rescued victim might be spoken of as dead. Wittgenstein asks whether this practice is intrinsically sinister, even though just a game? What makes human sacrifice something deep and sinister anyway? It is not just a question of the suffering involved, for there are many other kinds of suffering, nor a matter of possible historical evidence for the gory prehistory of this or that game. *We* ourselves ascribe the deep and sinister impression made on us by the festival from an inner experience, which he implies is general in people, and notes the importance of 'the surroundings of a way of acting'. Even though it is like a game of robbers or children's play, or like a theatrical production, or a practical joke, the festival provokes an uneasiness of action and mood which distinguishes it from these. 'Just as the fact that on certain days children burn a straw-man could make us uneasy, even if no explanation for it were given. Strange that they should burn *a man* as part of the festivities! I want to say: the solution is no more disturbing than the riddle.' I am

FIG. 11. Baal dancers:
May Day, Northumberland,
c.1910. Hulton Archive
HE0149/Getty Images.

G. 12. The shape of expectation: the Baal fire ready for lighting, Northumberland, *c*.1910.
fterwards there is a scramble for sweets. Hulton Archive HE0148/Getty Images.

sure I am not the only one who recalls as a child the sudden roar of flames against the dark as they fastened onto the Guy Fawkes effigy. The 'popularity' of rites of this kind is spreading, if anything, partly for fun and festivity as in the case of modern Santa Fe's invention of the burning of Zozobra (described later in Chapter 10). It is also spreading as a mode of expressing political anger as in the burning of effigies of world figures at political demonstrations, an act which scarcely needs a reporter's commentary on top of the filmed image. The occasional real burning of a human being is usually deemed too awful to screen on the television news.

Ceremonial action, form, and human context: the Sudanese zar

Rituals that last, that have an enduring character in a historical sense, almost by definition have complex resonance or 'connections' in Wittgenstein's sense above, and in addition, we might add a certain quality of political potency, often not unconnected with images or bodily practices of a violent kind. Such rituals, most obviously those of monarchy and established religion, but also many which inhere in personal and family life, are not easy to 'reform' through the arguments of reason.

FIG. 13. The *zar* spirit responds to its call: 'Hofriyat' village, northern Sudan, 1976. Photo: Janice Boddy.

In the central Nile valley, and some adjoining regions, a dramatic ritual can be seen which illustrates all these points: the *zar* ceremony of spirit possession and exorcism. Its major 'staged' performances attract large numbers of guests and hangers-on. Under the guidance of a woman expert, a range of exotic spirits or *zar* are called down by the playing of drums and songs. A number of persons, mainly women, are already diagnosed as being the human vehicles of ('possessed by') these various beings, who take on a range of characters from Sudanese history and legend. These include Ethiopian princesses, Arab sheikhs, Zande cannibals, and British district commissioners. As their spirit comes to the call of the songs, the host goes into trance, dons the clothes and paraphernalia of the *zar*, and dances or staggers around making demands, including demands for gold bangles or cigarettes and whisky, until the spirit, satisfied, leaves her again. A full *zar* event can last a week, and attract a lot of attention especially in towns—on one occasion many years ago when I was present, a large marquee for some hundreds of guests had been erected on the outskirts of Port Sudan. Many commentators have witnessed these ceremonies, and been struck by their theatricality, on the one hand, and, on the other, by the way that women appear to manipulate their husbands through voicing 'the spirit's' demands for jewellery, watches, and perfume. The *zar* was originally regarded by scholars as an age-old tradition, partly a survival of the ancient pre-Christian religion of the Agaw people of northern Ethiopia. By the 1960s, however, the standard explanatory approach by anthropologists and sociologists both for the *zar* case and for similar cults in West Africa was to 'explain' these rituals in terms of their social function. For example, they were often seen as an indirect response to a problem, either as a psychological outlet for the tensions of modernization, social change, and urbanization, or as a means for women to seek compensation for their relative powerlessness—along with down-and-out men—in the social structure.[21]

A new generation of studies in the 1980s and 1990s began to reveal much greater psychological complexity in spirit possession cults, and to hint at the stubbornly deep roots which connect them with other levels of social and symbolic practice. An outstanding example of the new approach is Janice Boddy's work on the Sudanese *zar* cult.[22] Through extended fieldwork in two periods between 1976 and 1984 in a village on the Nile, north of Khartoum, she was able to explore the deeper connections behind the public exorcism performances. Earlier studies had tended to try and explain these as self-contained rituals, something quite apart from ordinary life. Boddy showed that they were only the tip of an iceberg, if such a metaphor can be allowed in the desert heat of 'Hofriyat', the fictional name she gave to the village portrayed in her work. She opted to give a pseudonym to the village and the people who live there because her book unveils a world of women's secrets. The openly staged dramas of the *zar* cult enact, not so much an escapist fictional alternative to the mundane everyday life, as a heightened elaboration and ironic theatrical insight into that very reality.

Using the 'ethnographic present' of Boddy's study, we can say that the women of Hofriyat are Muslims and Arabic-speaking, largely occupied with domestic duties, while their menfolk work outside the home and even in the towns and cities. As in other parts of the Arabic-speaking world, favoured marriages are those which tie people in to the productive local community, binding in both existing kin and strangers. The explicit ideal is for a young man to take, as his first wife, his father's brother's daughter. Many marriages in Hofriyat are indeed endogamous within the village. Thus, the village, and even a particular family compound in it, will be a girl's home throughout her life. Women are not able to travel much; they see their own existence as 'enclosed' and sometimes speak of themselves as like cattle tied up in a pen. Facing inescapably 'traditional' expectations they know that their ideal accomplishment in life is to give birth to a line of healthy sons. To this end they accept that they must achieve and maintain standards of great personal purity, discipline, and self-containment, and avoid if they can the contamination that is caused by the threat of *zar* spirits entering their bodies. Part of the nexus of ritual which literally shapes their life course is 'circumcision' during girlhood, an operation carried out usually by an older close female relative. This entails the cutting away of all the soft flesh in the genital area, and sewing up the wound, leaving only a small opening for urination. This operation, understood as purification, is very dangerous in biomedical terms, giving rise to easy infections, difficult births, and (in the judgement of many in the West) depriving women of the possibility of a relaxed and fulfilling sexual life. A succession of Sudanese governments, from the colonial period onwards, have attempted to ban it, and a movement has existed for many years among educated Sudanese women themselves to achieve some kind of reform, even a reduction of the severity of the operation. Liberal argument has had a tough problem in making much headway, however, and even the Islamic fundamentalist regime which took power in 1989 has tried to stamp out both the *zar* cult and female circumcision without much success.

What is the connection between these things? Boddy shows us how girls in Hofriyat fear the way in which contamination might enter their bodies through any orifice, particularly where there is any trace of blood; how they take all kinds of care to keep clean and whole and smooth; how a substantial proportion of young women, both before and after marriage, do indeed remain vulnerable and fall to possession by a *zar* spirit. The signs include problems with pregnancy, childbirth, the poor health and even death of infants, and the lack of sons even where daughters are born. General illness can take charge of a woman's life, and sooner or later the experts will arrange for the spirit to be explicitly recognized and thus to become manageable. It is rare for the *zar* to be totally exorcised—more often, a mutual accommodation has to be reached through the calling down and acceptance of the troublesome spirit. Although this is a Muslim community, the Islamic authorities (at least locally, and until recently) have managed to maintain a working coexistence with these practices, and to an extent some scriptural validation for the existence of 'red' and 'black', acceptable and dangerous, *jinn* spirits can be found. The elaborate staged ceremonies of dancing out the foreign spirits provide an opportunity for the women to enact an ironic play upon their situation, which on one level they see from the outside: they know they are relatively contained and defined by marriage, by Islam, by the male world of power and public experience generally, and the *zar* performance articulates this self-knowledge. Their self-consciousness has a historical dimension and operates on more than one level; they are acting not merely 'as women' in this deeply gendered social world, but acting out the premises of a world they share with men, and with the tenets of Islam. There is more than a hint of collusion in the ritual enactment. Part of this collusion lies in the fact that the *zar* performance itself is a counterpoint to the regular performances of social life: in particular, to the template of the marriage ceremony. In detailed ways, the characters, colours, costumes, and husband's gifts in the *zar* offer a bizarre 'alternative' wedding ritual, the bride transformed into a sacrifical ram. The wedding and the *zar* are different but part of the same symbolic universe.

The capacity of such ritual to 'speak' to other performances and to different settings is illustrated by Boddy's later encounter with the *zar* in Toronto. It is 1993. Educated women, now refugees from the severe regime in the Sudan, are looking for a way to celebrate International Women's Day. They hear of a book about the *zar* by a Canadian, and contact the writer for advice about its performance. A fine 'musical drama' is staged with Janice's help and her *zar* costume for Luliya Habishiya, the Ethiopian prostitute spirit who tries to pass herself off as a Sudanese bride. Speeches of a distinctly political cast are made not only about women's rights but also about Sudanese and Nile Valley heritage and its 'Nubian' roots (that is, pre-Arab, in this context). Canadians appreciated all this partly because there was a Nubian archaeology exhibition on at the Royal Ontario Museum.[23] The 'ritual enactment' retains its essential form, while the multiplicity of individual, social, and political readings have shifted. You cannot give a one-dimensional 'explanation' of the *zar* cult; you have to 'see the connections'. As with the old European fire-festivals, perhaps an ill-defined sense of threat and violence hangs over the *zar* practices—felt as dangerous, however, in a range of rather different ways by the 'traditional' Sudanese woman and by the liberal reformer. But the arguments of language do not easily dislodge the ceremonial performance itself, which can be given a harmless gloss, as in Toronto. Memories and expectations of collective symbolic action lie deeper than language and the arguments of reason. They have a momentum of their own regardless of verbal commentary, as we saw at the beginning of this chapter in Peter Lienhardt's sketch of the deep and contradictory social currents that may propel the meaningless verbal fragments we call rumour.

2. MAJOR THEMES IN THE ANTHROPOLOGY OF RELIGION

There is evidence that the role of priests, and the domain of priestly activity, is ancient—going back some six thousand years in the Indo-European region, for example. However, even this evidence does not constitute proof of universally comparable phenomena of a religious order, and leaves important questions quite open with respect to the specifically modern ways in which the domain of religion has been defined as set apart. Modern understandings have developed no doubt in parallel with the rise of the (more or less) secular state. The rationalisms of the late nineteenth century allowed plenty of space for the development of specialized studies of religion, in subjects such as theology or church history or oriental studies which took it for granted as a valid institution of any civilization. But the rationalist stance also led to questions about the point of the institution as a whole: why was a degree of unquestioning faith in (mostly false) gods such a prominent part of history, and given the powerfulness of its appeal (now thankfully weakening), what was its origin and evolution? The ancient Greeks might have been pagans, but they had at least left us a rich literature explaining everything. The Old Testament also provided vivid accounts of ancient belief. Beyond this, religion in general, however, or 'primitive religion' specifically, raised problems for rational explanation. The history of anthropology reflects very well the internal dialectic of religion and science in Western history, and the root question as to whether we are, and therefore are studying, God's creatures or nature's creatures.

Anthropology, like 'Orientalism', is a scholarly tradition that has been formed over the years in a kind of tension with the self-understanding and internal debates of modern Western society. Questions of the sources of religious experience and authentic spiritual knowledge were becoming prominent in the early decades of anthropology's formation, when the authority of the Church was being challenged and privileged access to truth and knowledge was being claimed by science and rationalism. A degree of what we would call today 'reflexivity' and personal opinion inevitably entered the scholarly debates about religion, and a degree of objectivity could best be obtained, it seemed, by focusing on the remoter tribal peoples and constructing a scientific-looking terminology for 'primitive' religion. This became anthropology's speciality. It was not always recognized that the prejudices of those belonging to the civilizations associated with the Judaeo-Christian tradition, regardless of their personal views, tainted the supposed 'objectivity' of their perspectives upon their own periphery. Here were the peoples and 'beliefs' perceived as historically prior, closer to nature, culturally simple, peoples and beliefs for whom and for which Western civilizations already had a range of terms to hand, even in their sacred texts. The anthropology of religion thus originally developed as a specialized study of the pre-defined category of 'the pagan', rather than as a broad-based study of the religious aspect of human life (however defined) in general. I shall give a thumbnail sketch only of the main approaches and developments; there are good surveys and collections of readings from Evans-Pritchard to Fiona Bowie and Michael Lambek which give more depth and detail.[24]

Introspection: Tylor

Edward B. Tylor began teaching courses in anthropology at Oxford in the 1870s, from his position as curator of the Pitt Rivers Museum. He did travel, specifically to Mexico, but most of his work was in the 'armchair' and drew on museum collections as well as published ethnography. Tylor adapted an old Latin root to fashion his theory that 'animism' was the earliest form of religious belief. As a way of making some coherent interpretation of his survey of ethnographic evidence about religious beliefs, he speculated upon the experiences of early human beings, as they themselves wondered about the meaning of their dreams, and what could be the nature of their own consciousness which seemed to be detachable from the body. In the morning a person might well wonder where they have been while their body was inert; they might ask themselves whether perhaps there was a special consciousness within, a vital or 'animating' element, quite different from the body. Perhaps other people had this counterpart 'soul' too, and perhaps animals and trees and even the wider universe had such a counterpart which animated the whole. From these speculations originated the notion of the soul, and the notion of spirits of the wild, and the notion of an overall divinity.[25] Tylor's vision of a kind of spiritual agency permeating the world of things has not only Romantic—distinctly Wordsworthian—echoes, but even modern 'phenomenological' overtones that have lent it a fresh lease of life in some current specialized anthropological debates. In general use, however, the term has a stultifying effect in missionary discourse, or in journalistic accounts of situations like the civil war in the Sudan, where northern Muslims are often said to be pitted against Christians and 'animists' in the south.

Myth and ritual: collection and comparison: Frazer

Western scholastic ideas about the special interest of 'pagan' civilization derives from the important place of the study of the ancient Mediterranean civilizations, especially the Greeks, in scholarship from the Renaissance onwards. The Greeks offer a model of sophistication in ancient times, and a world we can enter through the study, especially, of their own language, literature, and art. Greek myths were not only prominent within their own context, but they resonate down to the present day. It is partly because of this that the study of 'myth' acquired a special status in the comparative anthropological study of religion. Not all peoples have myths of the kind that the ancient Greeks did, but James Frazer (originally a classicist) sought to collect and synthesize a great body of stories from all over the world as a foundation for the study of the origins and development of religion in his monumental series of volumes *The Golden Bough*.[26] There were other outstanding scholars who devoted themselves to the widespread affinities of myths over large regions, for example Georges Dumézil, who developed provocative theories about the inner connections between civilizations across the Indo-European language region, using formal written scriptures and literature but also oral tradition and myth as his sources.[27] This 'text-based' approach to the spoken literature of the tribal cultures of the world paralleled the growth in 'folklore' studies which were devoted mainly to exploring the riches of local tradition in the rural hinterlands of Britain and Europe.[28] The collection of narratives of all kinds has continued to be an important strand in anthropological research, a task made much easier with the advent of tape-recorders.

The community of believers: totemism: Durkheim

The first question in the minds of early anthropologists was a self-reflexive one: what are the historical and spiritual roots of religion, as we know it today in the Judaeo-Christian world? Durkheim's *The Elementary Forms of Religious Life* (introduced in Chapter 1), drew on the fresh ethnographic accounts coming out of Australia at the turn of the twentieth century, to investigate the roots of religion in the light of this concern. He gave prime place to people's *social* experience of the world through their shared, and patterned, life together, seeing this commonality of life itself as the grounds of reality as understood by any human being. For him, the way that the sacred was constructed in practice through the ceremonial gatherings of local groupings among the Australians was the epitome of religion. The distinctiveness of each grouping in its relations with others was expressed through the idiom of differentiation among the natural species. The special ritual attention to the emblem of one's own group and its symbolic elaborations was the core of the religious system that had already come to be known as 'totemism' in anthropology (the word totem itself having first been noted in 1791 as used by an Ojibwa speaker).[29] In the gatherings of such totemic groups, Durkheim saw the elements of a 'church'.[30] This sociological dimension of Durkheim's inquiry sets it apart from the introspective approach of many other scholars writing on the anthropology of religion, or the question of 'primitive religion', in the period from the 1870s to the 1930s.

However, Durkheim's bid for objectivity is open to several criticisms, not least the point that in applying the image of a church to the *corroboree* he is grafting a ready-made modern idea of the sacred into a rather different context. It is a continuing dilemma for anthropology that it has to keep

returning to images from the Judaeo-Christian tradition to try and understand practices which do not necessarily depend upon claims to exclusive
truth, revelation, or salvation, nor upon a clear separation of sacred and
mundane. Anthropology has inevitably worked, to a large extent, within the
self-referential space of the main scriptural religions of the West.

The Bible as a source and an inspiration

The Bible itself, essentially the Old Testament, was a key source for anthropologists first starting to search for the early forms of religious life (and it continues to strike chords). For some, its record of the life and cultural traditions
of the ancient Jewish people has a special status as a part of 'our own' heritage.
And even for agnostics and sceptics, the Old Testament is a goldmine of
possible models for the way that modern tribal, as well as ancient society,
could be understood to operate and to represent the world. For Durkheim and
the *Année Sociologique*, the Old Testament was both ethnographic evidence,
and a source of many interpretative models. Edmund Leach, an avowed
agnostic, tried to escape religious bias by using the materials of the Old and
New Testaments as ethnographic evidence like any other source for structural
analysis, debunking the special status of the Bible and infuriating many
believers.[31] Mary Douglas, on the other hand, a lifelong Catholic, has drawn
inspiration from the formal religious prescriptions and prohibitions of the
Old Testament, and most recently has worked in detail on interpreting its
stories and imagery. Her writings, more than those of any other modern
anthropologist, have attracted the attention of theologians and biblical
scholars.[32]

Even those anthropologists who do not explicitly claim to be using the
Bible as a source, an object of study, or as general inspiration, find themselves
working with supposedly general terms and ideas which ultimately carry a
'biblical' aura. Plenty of examples come to mind: first is the very notion of
an anthropomorphic and all-powerful male God, which even the agnostic
ethnographer as well as the missionary is predisposed to recognize on the
slightest evidence—see, for example, the essays in a 1954 collection, *African
Worlds*, dealing with values and cosmology.[33] In more subtle ways, biblical
images of sin, soul, and sacrifice work their way into ethnography and comparative anthropology. 'Sacrifice', for example, might seem at first to be
an unproblematic, descriptive word under which comparative cases can be
brought together. Mauss and Hubert crafted a fine comparative analysis of

sacrifice with specific reference to ancient Indian and biblical cases, revealing the 'grammar' of the rite as the sacred and profane are brought together in a revitalizing exchange, drawing on the analogy of the gift. Evans-Pritchard used this model in his analysis of Nuer sacrifice.[34] But do all 'ritual' killings of animals constitute 'sacrifice' in the full biblical sense? What about the 'ritual' killings of wild animals, which may be thoroughly imbued with ceremony and meaning, but are not really 'gifts to the gods' (such as the case of the Lele pangolin, introduced in Chapter 3)?[35] To clarify what it is that we easily take for granted in the idea of 'sacrifice' is an effort, but if we make the effort, we can recognize how much our concept depends on the model of the ancient Israelites. They did have domestic animals, whom they had reared and thus who belonged to their various lineage groups, and they lived in a dualistic world of God and humankind; it therefore made sense for animals to be 'given' to God in some way. Wild animals, by definition, do not *belong* to you, and so cannot be 'given away' even if you wished to give them. These and other points have been made by anthropologists as the subject has become more aware of its own biases, including the history of its own language. Even domestic animals can be killed by pious pastoralists without the theological implications of sacrifice; Paul Dresch has very usefully picked up the old Anglo-Saxon word 'hock' for the killing of 'slaughter-beasts' by Muslims in Yemen.[36]

There has been an increasing realization within anthropology that the very terms of comparative study necessarily have a particular history, located in a particular ideological and political context. This realization is nowhere more crucial than in the study of religion, where so many of the discipline's comparative categories, following lay usage, lie in the Judaeo-Christian tradition itself. Rodney Needham criticized the very description of 'belief' as a neutral term for all that people claim to know and affirm or appear to take for granted. 'Belief' as a species of internal creed is not a 'natural' human capacity, but a component of the way that images of human psychology and of the nature of knowledge, especially of the divine, have been constructed in the course of Western history.[37] Malcolm Ruel has pursued a parallel argument, locating the notion of 'belief', as something to be opted for by the individual person, in specific periods of Christian history. He comments on the 'monumental peculiarity of Christian "belief"', as it emerged from the older Hebrew sense of 'trust' to become an 'acceptance of teachings' after Christ's death and resurrection.[38] Belief in the sense of required personal commitment is a relatively modern, post-Reformation idea; it has a close connection with the modern spread of Christianity and missions in the context of imperial rule.

Another powerful key term in the anthropology of religion today is 'ritual', whose meaning we frequently debate and modify but whose use has become almost unavoidable in academic anthropology as it has in lay usage, to the point where we now speak comfortably of 'secular rituals'.[39] There is a special 'aura of incense' to the word ritual. Its origins too lie in the history of Western Christianity. We may well wonder what is the nature of that specialness, and what is therefore the essence of ritual. A strong theory here is that the sense of a magical, intensifying quality actually comes from the history of 'the church', in which there are specific prescribed actions—such as the sacraments—affecting the relation of human beings to God; and that this concept has leaked out of its original setting. Talal Asad, who originally worked on the modern Arab societies of the Middle East, later took up the topic of medieval Christianity, partly in order to demonstrate that the unselfconscious naturalism of his contemporaries about religion needed itself to be placed in history. 'Ritual', he points out, originally meant a book, a manual giving the rules for performing the liturgy, and hence helping to educate the proper dispositions of the monks and to establish the monasteries' 'regime of truth'. Though it retains a residue of the medieval sense, the term has spread far and wide, introducing a generalized religiosity into what were previously 'secular' settings.[40]

We talk today of the rituals of parliament, politics, football etc.; but to call something 'secular ritual' remains a contradiction—itself invoking the sacred/profane opposition, it seems to call for endless redefinitions of what we mean by 'ritual'. However, whatever effort we make to redefine and relocate 'ritual', it seems to me, we have not managed to escape the theistic framework of the world religions which gave rise to the category in the first place. A recent book by Roy Rappaport tackles this problem head on, arguing that we should recognize how widely aspects of the sacred have spread to colour much outside the domain of the official world religions. The substance of much of his work overlaps with my project in this book, though he approaches the question from a different angle.[41] In their subtle and important book, Caroline Humphrey and James Laidlaw argue that there is something 'primal' about ritual, especially in their key case study, the *puja* rite of the Jains. But while defending the separate character of 'ritual' as a distinctive ontological *genre*, they do not deal with the basic problem of having to construct a *generally applicable* category of social being from a specific world-religious tradition. Their focus is a very actor-oriented one, concentrating on 'the ritual commitment' and 'ritual stance' on the part of the agent towards a given action.[42] But how far does this agent's point of view give an adequate perspective on the collective and historical character of rituals, and the way that the 'ritual' domain, however distinguished, relates to other formal or informal areas of life?

Other recent anthropologists have blithely abandoned all discrimination between the sacred and the secular, even very carefully and deliberately doing so in the case of Danny Miller's treatment of shopping as religion, specifically as sacrifice. Interestingly, he also places the intending and experiencing agent, here the everyday shopper and his or her (mainly her) moral feelings and symbolic motivations, at the heart of the analysis, as a justification for calling this activity 'religion'.[43] This seems to take the modernist idea of individual moral opinion as the basis of religion to an absurd extreme. The domain of 'religion' in the modern context, or rather the stretch of distinct territory today occupied by specific and competing religions, still has to be specified on a collective and institutional basis. Liberal discourse typically differentiates the domains of religion, economics, politics, and even morality; though the new fundamentalisms are making efforts to collapse these distinctions. Anthropology, like the other social sciences, should try to see clearly the way in which the domain of religion is defined today *as a part of the field of coeval social phenomena to be studied*, not as a given condition of human life to serve as a starting point for comparison with the various forms taken by 'the sacred' in other ages and places.

Ethnography, translation, and personal commitment: Evans-Pritchard, Godfrey Lienhardt

One of the ironies of the anthropological study of religion is that the best ethnographic studies often reflect the very dilemmas we are discussing: dilemmas of perspective, of definitions, of religious conviction itself on the part of the ethnographer as well as the people studied. Bold decisions about how to present empirical findings, informed by passion and an ambition to convince, perhaps produce the monographs with the most vitality. For example, Evans-Pritchard wrote very little on the mainstream world religions though he did some ethnographic work among Muslim Bedouin in Egypt and Libya, focusing mainly on politics and history rather than Islam. When he undertook his main field studies of the Azande and the Nuer in the 1930s, he was not a practising churchgoer although son of an Anglican clergyman. During the War, however, he was received into the Roman Catholic Church, and his later writings displayed a new religious dynamic. In his Aquinas lecture of 1959, on 'Religion and the anthropologists', he offered a much more personal commentary than was common in anthropology at that time. He pointed out (somewhat disparagingly) that most anthropologists were either atheists or agnostics; and therefore did not have 'an ear' for the religious experience of others—using the analogy of a 'musical ear'.[44]

In his magisterial and quite unprecedented study of Nuer religion, he strove to avoid the special anthropological language prescribed by standard academic scholarship for the beliefs of the pagan periphery.[45] It was not eliminated entirely—'totem' and 'fetish' survive, for example, but only as a literary technique for subordinating their place in the hierarchies of Nuer spirit, as we might deprecate a bit of magic. Otherwise, Evans-Pritchard appropriated the language of the Bible as a part of his serious project of presenting Nuer religion as one way of understanding the nature of God; and thus claiming the attention and respect of Christian believers, academic theologians, and even the ordinary Western reader. Here is 'a religion' with all the elements 'we' can recognize: the translation of Nuer *kwoth* as one name for God; the human soul, sin, belief and trust, expiation, sacrifice, and prophets. Is there an exaggeration of the religiosity of the world of the Nuer, along biblical lines? Was there an element of wishful thinking in Evans-Pritchard's portrayal of the Nuer trust in their divinity, the coherence of their theocentric cosmology, the piety behind their practices? Some have thought so, but is their attitude any less ethnocentric or prejudiced than Evans-Pritchard's own? By using the language of the Bible, especially perhaps the Old Testament, he was at least encompassing the Nuer in the same moral world as his own, allowing to them and peoples like them the same option of salvation as he believed was open to him. Just as, perhaps, he had used his ethnographic work among the Azande to mount an argument for the recognition of reason as a common human capacity.

Godfrey Lienhardt's *Divinity and Experience: The Religion of the Dinka*, published in 1961, marked a further turning point in the anthropological study of religion, for he engaged more directly with the specifics of events and their experiential impact, narratives, interpretations, and poetic imagery, leaving the 'system' of Dinka cosmology and knowledge of divinity to emerge gradually in the mind of the reader. In this study, 'the field' seems to take over from a priori concerns of the author, despite the biblical echoes which are carried over from Evans-Pritchard's work, even the New Testament resonance of the voluntary sacrificial death of the Dinka spearmasters. We absorb the stories of great prophetic leaders of the past as Dinka refer to the inspiration they still seek and find in their current spearmasters, men embodying special insight and wisdom. We see how cases of strange behaviour, even fainting and trance, are at first puzzling, and how a diagnosis of possession emerges through debate. We are gently inducted into the richly reverberating imagery of the river and the sky and the life of cattle, and into the connections between 'religious' dispositions and 'social relations' (to put this point more crudely than Lienhardt would ever have done). For example, Dinka say that one should not harm one's clan divinity, or 'emblem' (Lienhardt finally abandoned 'totem'), by killing or eating that particular animal. One should respect it, *thek*. This attitude is not a superstitious fear, as we come to understand: *thek* is also the respect one should pay to one's mother's brother, and his whole set of clan relatives, because they are the source of one's own life; without their sister having married one's father, one would not exist. There is a debt of life, and a special kind of respect is in order; in conflicts, therefore, one would never attack the people of one's mother's clan. Insights of this kind make Dinka 'religious' notions accessible while at the same time showing how deeply rooted they are in the social life of the people as a whole.[46]

Later historical research has shown how intimate the connections between Nuer and Dinka, and indeed other peoples of the Upper Nile basin, have been and still are. Douglas Johnson's study of the Nuer prophets, and the general history of prophecy in the region, reveals how many themes in the myth, symbolism, and ritual of the Nuer echo the Dinka world; and how over time, the prophetic tradition of both peoples can be seen to draw on the same sources of inspiration. The historical perspective shows continuity, rather than difference, between these peoples, and with the passage of years we can see that the real contrasts between the published ethnographies are a product of their own time, the different circumstances of fieldwork, and the academic concerns and literary intentions of their authors, as much as any difference between the two peoples studied. Johnson has found it useful to collapse the difference in terminology for their various spiritual representations, for example, using Lienhardt's 'Divinity' for the Nuer *kwoth*. The historical perspective of his work also lends a convincing modern presence to the Nuer and Dinka: they do not simply inhabit the anthropology books, they have grappled with the British, the Ethiopians, and the Arabs, and as co-citizens of the same world we all inhabit today, their representatives, some drawing on the still-living prophetic traditions, have appealed to the international community to help bring peace to their lands.[47]

Post-colonial changes: liberal anthropology in 'the third world'

It was really the end of the colonial era, and the transformations of anthropology that followed, that eroded the old us/them distinction in the anthropology of religion as in other domains. The changes included the spread of anthropology into the education and academic life of universities across the world, including regions outside 'the West', and specifically outside the zone where 'the church' was taken for granted as the type case of religion. Inner biases of which we were once unconscious have suddenly become visible, and audibly criticized, as problems of translating the very language of anthropological description and a need to face unspoken attitudes and judgements have imposed themselves. My own experience of growing self-consciousness as an anthropologist not only researching but teaching in an African country with a large Muslim population, reflects these dilemmas.

I should explain something of my own personal background, from a family combining actively agnostic rationalism on one side and gently lapsing Quakerism on the other; and my professional background, a training in geography and social anthropology at Oxford, followed by research in the Sudan, mainly among the minority Uduk-speaking people of the Ethiopian borderlands, during a five-year position as a lecturer in the University of Khartoum. Both research and teaching in the Sudan of the 1960s were engagements of great complexity, uneasiness, and volatility during the country's first post-independence civil war (foreshadowing the descent from 1983 onwards into the mega-deaths and tragedy of the second war). I remember taking a class about Somali society, using I. M. Lewis's work, focusing on the ways that Islamic observance took different organizational forms in the northern, pastoralist regions from the southern, settled regions.[48] The students, mainly young northern Sudanese men, became a little restive, and then suddenly went very quiet. Questions were asked: they did not understand what I had said, and would I please explain again. I did so at some length, before sensing the slightly hostile atmosphere and realizing that a more basic point was being made—about my right, as a young Western woman, to be lecturing them on the forms of Islamic society. A good number of hands were raised when I asked who still did not understand what I had been saying, and so I packed up my papers quietly and drew the session to a close. Today, in that country and that university, a militant Islamic regime officially questions the presuppositions of the Western social sciences. At that time, my own research looked calmly at the spreading influence of both Christianity and Islam upon the Uduk people, who did not previously live under a regime of hegemonic truths. In the transitional zone where they lived, it did seem as though they would either follow the model of the southern Sudan in embracing Christianity, and the assumed individual freedoms of Western modernism; or the northern, in accepting the tenets of Islam, along with socially conservative practices which seemed to subordinate women, such as endogamous marriage, veiling, and circumcision. Twenty years after my original research, all the villages in which I worked were destroyed by the armies and popular militias of the Sudan, pursuing in part a holy *jihad* against the infidel, and the surviving Uduk have passed through a series of refugee camps swearing allegiance to Christianity as they went. A further decade on, some were being permanently resettled (with the indirect support of Christian evangelical groups) as far away as North Dakota and Salt Lake City.[49]

Against this background, as well as in the continuing context of my other teaching and research, I have slowly come to understand the rootedness of the anthropological profession in contemporary (in the sense of coeval) Western concerns. We were trying in Khartoum back in the 1960s to provide a helpful glossary for students, of anthropological terms translated into Arabic. For pragmatic conceptions such as matriliny, it was difficult enough. For religious ideas, it was almost impossible, for the efforts to produce a neutral working vocabulary for the comparative study of religious phenomena in English have simply not been undertaken in Arabic. We do not always realize how closely the language and assumptions of anthropology are associated with the historically Christian discourse of the West and its engagement with liberal modernity. What is ritual, what is the soul, what is totemism, how can you define an anthropological notion of 'belief' that can apply both to Muslims and to non-Muslims, within an Arabic-language anthropology? How do you put even the phrase 'the anthropology of religion' into Arabic? 'Customary practices of the various races of people' possibly. But religion? *Al-din* can be translated 'faith' but not any old faith—it means exclusively the Islamic faith. What is evidently not Islamic, to a scholar, and sometimes also to a local population, is *al 'ada*, meaning relatively unproblematic local customs and traditions. The observances of non-Islamic tribes, at least in Sudanese Arabic discourse, are the equivalent of pagan mumbo-jumbo, and can be dangerous, bordering on the satanic. We can consider also the case of language: *lugha* is a dignified term embracing written tongues such as Arabic or English, but this does not apply to the Nuer, or Zande tongues—these are *rutana*, often translated 'dialect', rather than 'language'. The name of God,

Allah, and the holy Koran cannot properly be translated into other respected languages, let alone bush dialects of the uncouth. How could we write of the general conception of the sacred, as it has developed in Western scholarship, in an Arabic setting? The term 'spirit' may sound fairly neutral in modern English language anthropology; but in Arabic, it could only be translated prejudicially as *ru'h*, or *jinn*, or *zar*, etc., fading off into devilish conceptions like *iblis*, all with a potentially negative moral meaning. None could be assimilated to God, as Evans-Pritchard transcribed the Nuer *kwoth* as Spirit and (even in its pluralities) equated it with God. Nor could we find any suitable Arabic parallel for Godfrey Lienhardt's judicious use of 'divinity' and 'powers' as lower-key terms for Dinka religious conceptions.

A very glaring illustration of the problem is the anthropological use of the term 'prophet'. Evans-Pritchard drew on the biblical scholar Robertson Smith's study of the pre-Islamic religious traditions of Arabia, in identifying Nuer religious figures as 'prophets'.[50] Indeed he made the Nuer prophets famous, and drew them into the discourse of ancient Arabian and Old Testament scholarship. To Arabic-speaking Sudanese students of Evans-Pritchard's work, however, there is the problem of how to study modern 'pagan prophets': you cannot call them *nabi*, for Mohammed was the last of the prophets in Islam. Douglas Johnson tells me how a confident Nuer friend once deliberately teased an Arab trader with a remark about the fame of the Nuer prophet Ngundeng, using the phrase *al nabi* Ngundeng—which is blasphemous in Arabic. To ordinary Sudanese Muslims, the Nuer prophets were *kujur*: a term from one of the languages of the Nuba Hills which has been absorbed into colloquial Arabic and widely used of local men and women of occult power. *Kujur* has the aura, in Sudanese Arabic, of magician, medicine man, or witchdoctor in English. Could a fair translation of Evans-Pritchard's or Lienhardt's books ever be rendered into the dominant language of the country in which most of the Nuer and the Dinka live?

Towards the anthropology of the world religions

On top of the collapse of European colonial empires, and the rise of the Civil Rights movement in the United States, there were two main reasons for the transposition of the anthropological study of religion from the pagan fringes to the world's great traditions. One was the broadening out of the 'social science' base of anthropology itself. While Durkheim has long been the mainstay of social theory in the anthropological tradition, integrated as well as can be managed with the evidence of ethnographic research and museum studies, in the 1960s anthropologists began to pay serious attention to some of the other key figures in the theoretical analysis of society; in particular, Marx and Weber. Here were large comparative horizons and analytical challenges for the local case studies of most anthropology; here were political processes behind social institutions, here were frameworks for the analysis of change and history. With respect to religion in particular, Weber's writings on the puritan ethic and on religious authority, both traditional and charismatic, provided some fresh air for anthropologists brought up on functionalist ideas of religious 'sanctions' on the social order; and Marx's wide horizons on ideology and power were seen by some as a way of refashioning anthropological questions about religion altogether.[51]

The second reason for the widening out of anthropological horizons was, ironically, a shift away from institutional forms towards the perspective of individual experience; towards feeling as distinct from intellect, psychological insights, and modes of consciousness in the field of religious phenomena. This move was taking place across the social sciences generally in the late twentieth century, and went together with a growing recognition of the 'reflexive' aspects of research, that is, the way in which the perceptions of the observer affect what is observed and recorded. Anthropologists did not write directly about the world religions much at all, until very recently. There was a move of anthropology closer to home in the 1960s: to the literate and historically known parts of the world, starting with India, the Mediterranean, the Middle East, and northern Europe. The first generation of such studies looked mainly at pragmatic aspects of social life and structure: the mores of family, marriage, household, agricultural patterns, village studies, and local history.[52] India was perhaps a special case, in that there was the orientalist tradition of studying the Indian-based religions to give anthropologists a start, and here we should note the classic work of Louis Dumont which gave pride of place to religious hierarchy in any social analysis of Hindu life. But in the first anthropological studies of European and Middle Eastern communities, Christianity and Islam, and even Judaism in the first studies of Israel, were left in the background. Questions of religion were more or less left to the other scholarly disciplines, and anthropologists focused on pragmatic aspects of community life.

In fact, it was the pragmatic aspect of mission conversions, and the social turbulence they caused, that first caught the attention of anthropologists in the colonial territories of Africa and elsewhere. They initially wrote about the disruptive effects of missions on local social structure, and about breakaway churches, cargo cults, and so on as destabilizing movements. Changes were seen as ripples caused by the spread of world religions and their agents, but these religions and their own social formation and modes of experience were not initially the focus of anthropological analysis. Attention was mostly upon the specific local reasons why conversion did or did not take place. For example, Mary Douglas in her early work offered an elegant social-structural rationale for the way that missionaries finally got through to the Lele people of the southern Congo. By attracting girls as well as boys to their school, they were in the end able to break the firm control that older men had exercised over the marriages of young men through bridewealth and brideservice; mission students could marry each other without having to seek the economic and symbolic patronage of their elders, and could found independent (and Christian) families who were free to enter the modern economy.[53]

A collection of anthropological studies on religion edited by John Davis in 1982 helped to set a new agenda.[54] This collection focuses on experience, rather than on institutions, systems, or creeds; and not on the experience of individuals in a vacuum, but on historically placed experience—such as religious weeping in sixteenth-century Spain. Lienhardt's chapter on the Catholic fathers among the Dinka is very different from earlier studies of missionaries among African peoples; the missionaries themselves begin to be a part of the picture, and the moral and intellectual judgements of the Dinka are shown to be partial, subtle, responsive not only to the mission enterprise as a whole but to individual missionaries.

Since the early 1980s, there have been more field-based studies viewing the world religions from below, as it were, and in many ways humanizing the prescribed framework of sacred places, times, texts, and rituals. The intermingling of different perspectives in a given community has tended to become more visible. Internal ironies and ambivalences have been emphasized. Lines of distinction within a religious world have become the axes of analysis, not only between say Christians and Muslims, but between the literate and non-literate within one of these religions; between the folk and the clergy; the traders and the farmers; between sects; between rich and poor; pilgrimage centres and periphery; older and younger; between men and women. In the Muslim world, anthropologists have been able to complicate and at the same time make more sympathetic the rather stolid image of 'Islamic society'. It was in the periphery that anthropological studies of Muslim communities *in context* got under way, for example with Clifford Geertz on Indonesia and on Morocco, and Abner Cohen on the entrenchment of Muslim trading communities in West Africa. In the periphery, we can see that the rigid pre-scriptions of Islamic allegiance: prayer, fasting, and pilgrimage, can coexist with all sorts of other things. There are saints, tombs, pilgrimages, competing religious orders, all very community-rooted, specific to place and to the rhythms of the annual calendar (and see my discussion above of Janice Boddy's work on spirit possession in the Muslim Sudan). As a tribute to the work of Peter Lienhardt in the Persian Gulf, in Isfahan, and on the East African coast, Ahmed al-Shahi brought together a collection of studies under the title *The Diversity of the Muslim Community*.[55] Michael Lambek has offered a micro-study of a long-standing though peripheral Muslim society, on the island of Mayotte in the Comoros. He sets Islam within the practices of a small island, drawing attention to interactions between kinds of knowledge, based on official Islamic learning, on Middle Eastern divination systems, and on locally derived possession cults. One route to knowledge is through Koranic study; one is through the kinds of specialist divination which circu-late throughout the Islamic world; and one is through the direct experience of spirit possession. These three paths to wisdom are not congruent with each other: they are contradictory in several respects; the individual is con-scious in various ways of resulting dilemmas, and while everyone is more or less a good practising Muslim, people are able to preserve some intellectual and moral distance from any particular kind of knowledge and its relation to them personally.[56]

Studies of Muslim societies in the heartland have adopted a much more experiential focus than previously. The work of Michael Gilsenan is out-standing here; on saint and sufi, on 'recognizing Islam'. He writes of the qualities of religious experience in the mosque, stimulated by memory, expectation, the chanting of sacred language, bodily deference in prayer, and what he has pinpointed as the total experience of the colour green as deployed in the mosque.[57] Studies located within the 'Christian world', too, now seek a more personally grounded perspective on the complicated ways that institutionalized religion relates to other areas of life. Roger Just's study of the ironic nuances of Christian identity and faith in rural Greece, where people may not be very pious or respect their local priest, but nevertheless are very possessive, as Greeks, of the Church itself, is a wonderful counterfoil to anthropological studies which have concentrated largely on mission Christianity and local responses to it in the context of Western imperialism.[58] Larry Taylor has shown how socially and symbolically contradictory the old

FIG. 14. Shia Muslims on the road to the holy city of Karbala, Iraq, April 2003: a pilgrimage banner during Saddam Hussein's rule. Photo: Yannis Behrakis/Reuters.

Christian landscape of Ireland is; and John Eade and Michael Sallnow have offered a pioneering set of studies in the anthropology of Christian pilgrimage, echoing in their recognition of ancient complexities Richard Werbner's earlier insights into sacred geography and movement in religious activity in *Ritual Passage, Sacred Journey*. Public manifestations of religious activity, including pilgrimage, have become increasingly visible and ambivalent in their political meaning in today's world of easy visual communication (see Fig. 14).[59] Anthropologists once left missionaries and imams out of their accounts; now, missionaries and religious orders themselves have been integrated into anthropological study.[60]

Recuperating the 'human science' questions

The movement towards studying world religions has certainly brought many anthropologists closer to that reflexive awareness of the observer's perspective and the singularity of experience which characterizes the humanities. However, the search for 'human science' insights into religion as a general phenomenon, with particular reference to the ethnography of remote peoples, still goes on in tandem. Pascal Boyer, for example, has pressed questions about the natural basis of religious belief, arguing from the supposition of a universal psychological set of dispositions. Using evidence from his own work in West Africa, he has focused attention on the way that the repetition of practice (rather than verbalized learning) is an essential in the transmission of ritual, and culture in general, and has developed a theoretical approach to this question.[61] This insight helps us connect some of the work of the developmental psychologists with that of sociology and anthropology. Dan Sperber, drawing on his ethnographic research in southern Ethiopia, has investigated the way in which religious representations spread; again finding a way of combining the psychological with anthropological angles, he suggests we trace this spread as a kind of epidemiology with social rationale. Harvey Whitehouse has drawn the attention of ethnographers and psychologists to each other's work, and his own research in New Guinea is stimulating some important new debates in the area of the anthropology of religion and cognition.[62] Maurice Bloch's work stands out as combining a concern for socio-centric practice with cognitive phenomena, and he has offered a powerful argument that there are common features to the core images of religion, constituting as they often do transformations of natural kinds from one domain to another, partly through ritual acts including sacrifice (see my earlier discussion in Chapter 3).

Whether we are thinking of the anthropology of religion in the 'humanities' mould or in its neo-scientific forms, the relevance of personal convictions often arises. Do Christians, for example, make good anthropologists, or are they handicapped by their particular bias? Is it better for anthropologists to be atheists? Can Islam or Buddhism be best understood by Muslim, or Buddhist, anthropologists? Do African scholars have special access to the realities of traditional African religion? The question is no doubt important, but becomes absurd if taken too literally. Can *only* a Muslim understand Islam—and then what about 'other' faiths he or she might contemplate, even those of neighbours and fellow-nationals? Even a Sudanese Arabic-speaker can surely see the possibility of a more sympathetic investigation of the world of Nuer spirituality than is possible in the standard discourse of the country, and at the same time see that it is more than a matter of learning the technicalities of Western anthropology as a social science. The anthropologist, whether believer or not, needs to find a little scholarly distance, to see in some way the complex place of 'religion' in the history of his or her own part of the world as well as 'other' parts. I think the question should be depersonalized as far as possible; your findings are framed more by the moral and intellectual frame in which you cast your investigation, than what personal allegiance you have.

One of the basic problems, introduced at the start of this chapter, is the fact that 'religion' is a domain of life which has only in modern times been identified as fundamentally different from others. Fredrik Barth once remarked on the fact that he had not paid much attention to Islam or to ritual and symbolism in his study of the Basseri pastoral nomads of southern Iran.[63] However, he pointed out, the Basseri themselves did not seem preoccupied with Islam; while the drama and excitement of the seasonal migration across the high mountains in spring was arguably a kind of 'ritual' in itself, emotionally very satisfying (the irony of Barth's own perspective as a good Norwegian, romantically oriented to the mountains, would not have escaped him). In the context of my present argument, this pragmatic perspective on the ceremoniality of ordinary life is very helpful.

PART III

Language and the Making of Persons

CHAPTER SIX

Speech and Social Engagement

T HERE are many respects in which spoken language can be treated as an aspect of social ceremonial, and thus (to stay with Collingwood's metaphor) as one of the 'daughters of the dance'. There are some striking cases. For example in the Yolngu area of North-East Arnhem Land, there are two sets of dialects. The first is the usual geographical spread of variants. The second set, the styles of speech known as Thuwala and Thuwal, better termed 'sociolects', are not related to geography but to the conceptual division of the Yolngu people into two complementary and exogamous moieties. These moieties cut across all local dialects, and are always found paired within marriages and across the generations. Children grow up speaking according to their mother's moiety style, but later switch to their father's. The actual difference between the 'sociolects' consists of a rule about vowel deletion in certain grammatical morphemes, resulting in a distinctly different rhythm of speech. The difference, obviously, is a consciously maintained matter of style, and everyone is engaged in the same everyday game-playing which thus keeps alive the most basic of social structural principles.[1] A moment's reflection reminds us that there are conventional structural qualities to a whole range of our ordinary encounters where we adopt lavish greetings, slip into suitable accents, gender, or class styles, or into the (deceptively) casual styles of intimacy.

However, the main point we shall explore in this chapter is that language is more than a conventional game of social positioning. It is a potentially sharper tool of individual and shared consciousness than that. This applies even to the most gestural of languages: the sign languages developed for and

FIG. 15. Sign Language: Actors Ricardo Montalben, Clark Gable, and John Hodiak rehearse India sign language with technical adviser Chief Nipo Strongheart on the set of the MGM produ tion *Across the Wide Missouri*, 1951. Photo: Kurt Hutton/Picture Post collection, Hulton Archi HS7028/Getty Images.

by deaf people. These can become more complex and subtle than is realized— and there are many of them. For example, a form of hereditary deafness existed on the island of Martha's Vineyard, Massachusetts, from the time of the first settlers in the 1690s. Not only did sign language develop among the deaf islanders, but because they were so many, by the mid-nineteenth century the rest of the population had picked it up too and used it freely, so that the deaf did not stand out as a separate 'handicapped' community. Even after the last deaf person died in 1952, the hearing went on signing among themselves in an easy and intimate way, telling off-colour jokes and talking in church. Oliver Sacks was so moved on hearing this news that he immediately went to visit the island. He found elderly people still mixing sign language in with their gossiping on the porch, and was inspired to write passionately of its 'intrinsic beauty and excellence sometimes superior to speech'. As television viewers, all of us are beginning to sense something of its fluidity and effectiveness as we notice interpreters performing for the deaf in the corner of our screens (something more common in the USA than in Britain).[2] Sign languages have a long history, and not only for the deaf, but for other kinds of communicative need and play, as the older ethnography of Native American peoples testifies.[3] Today there are many recognized varieties, including, for example, Irish and Icelandic Sign Languages, and also a developing International form. American Sign Language (ASL), or just 'sign', has gained particular recognition as a fully autonomous and intricately expressive mode of communication, able to free deaf people from the isolation they can experience if left to struggle alone in a hearing world. No one on their own develops a sign language spontaneously; this requires communication with others, whether in an informal community or through specific education. The acknowledgement that a signing system like ASL is indeed 'real language' reminds us of how very *specific* all 'natural' languages are in a cultural or historical sense. We talk a great deal about language in general, but in practice we have to grapple always with concrete languages in the plural, and the way they change and interact over time. A very substantial proportion of us, taking the world's population as a whole, happen to grow up in multilingual or transregional contexts and are therefore very conscious of languages as discrete social phenomena. Those of us who tackle foreign languages in school also gain a sense of this, and in the course of everyday life, quite apart from work contexts, an enormous amount of human time is spent moving between languages or consciously translating them.

David Dalby, who has attempted to track and map languages across the world, has no sympathy with the image of the Tower of Babel as a mountain of confusion and disaster. He considers diversity of languages a good thing and multilingualism a normal and healthy part of the way human society is organized. He has pointed to bilingual schools in Wales to illustrate how learning in two languages sharpens the wits, and noted that some 275 languages are used at home by London schoolchildren. He even considers monolingualism a disadvantage in life, like illiteracy, and warns this is a serious danger for anglophones.[4] Young children are known to 'pick up' languages around them with ease, but as we all know, we lose this flexibility as we get older. The historical stability of languages over time owes something to the way we settle down linguistically as we grow up, losing our infant gifts.

I. APPROACHES TO LANGUAGE[5]

The 'ethnographic history' model

Language is a primary feature of the human condition, and still the most distinctive single criterion for defining what sets us apart from our closest relatives in the animal world. At the same time, languages are plural and concrete. All of us, even in very 'traditional' contexts, are conscious of differences between languages or at least dialects, of a flow and flux in use over the span of our lifetimes, of shifts in vocabulary and fashions in ways of speaking. While these changes are often minute, they can add up to substantial change over longer time periods. Direct investigation of the way people spoke in earlier times is impossible, but careful comparative work on today's languages and those for which we have good historical written sources can suggest the lines of long-term development. Historical linguistics is the discipline which attempts to model the long-term drifts and borrowings in language change which, together with population movements, can eventually produce separate and mutually unintelligible tongues. It is difficult to give an objective estimate of the number of such languages in the world, because of the way that dialects vary and the fact that not all languages have standardized written forms which give a fixed point of reference. Andrew Dalby gives 5,000 distinct living languages as a conservative figure, while technical analysis yields around 7,000, and if local 'inner-language' dialectal variants (such as Scots or south-eastern United States English) are taken into account, the number rises to over 13,000.[6] Many others have been lost, especially in the course of the last century or so, and many are spoken only by small 'remnant' populations and are very vulnerable. The spread of the world's dominant languages through nationalism, education, and the media does not necessarily mean the complete displacement of minority tongues, as human beings have the remarkable capacity to use more than one language comfortably; but clearly the technical or philosophical standing and social value of a vernacular language are affected when all its speakers adopt a lingua franca and use it in parallel.

Thought-frameworks

The most obviously 'anthropological' approach to language is perhaps that which relates to the specificity of languages and their integral connection with thought and action. If we regard language as deeply implicated in our ways of thinking and feeling and 'being in the world', as anthropologists quite rightly do, the fact that there are thousands of different languages in use might suggest an extraordinary and even arbitrary diversity in the ways we think and feel. The pioneering scholars here were the American linguists Edward Sapir and Benjamin Whorf.[7] The basic theme that language is a key currency of human expression, and of the representation of the world, even to ourselves and about our personal experiences, is still a starting point in anthropology. However, most would avoid the degree of cultural relativism implied in strong forms of the 'Sapir–Whorf' hypothesis, which hold that one's language imposes 'a hidden metaphysics'. There is little room, in their terms, for the universal self-consciousness or irony of human beings towards their own language as an artefact, and yet the appreciation of poetry and song, of wit and humour, and the power of logic or rhetoric depends upon this 'distancing' capacity of every language user.

Given the variety of natural languages, we therefore have to ask the question: Do we live in five (or seven, or thirteen) thousand exclusive culture boxes? The answer has to be 'No'. This alarming picture has to be modified in three main ways. First, a surprisingly high proportion of the world's people are bi- or even multilingual and processes of translation are effectively going on all the time between languages. Second, language does not dictate or imprison our cultural being; many non-linguistic cultural practices, including work techniques, art, and music, all imbued with pattern and meaning, cut across language difference and complicate the situation. No language as such is innate, it is the capacity for language-learning which is innate. We are individually capable of learning any of the world's languages, especially when we are infants. Third, languages do not exist in isolation, but are linked with each other over time. Despite a continual give-and-take even between quite different tongues, we can recognize 'families' of languages which have remained fairly stable over long periods. The question of a relation between language and 'thought' or cultural ideology therefore has to be posed in a more general way than the exclusively local. Scholars have pondered, and still ponder, the possibility of a shared, historically basic, original ideology in the world of the Indo-European languages, for example, or the world of the Bantu sub-family of languages of central, eastern, and southern Africa, or that of the Austronesian language family, distributed around the Pacific basin. If we are to accept the connection of language with human modes of consciousness and knowledge, including self-knowledge, as well as with social forms and practices, and if we acknowledge the persistence of these forms through time, there is a good argument for taking as a starting point the stability of language families and the deep-level links between members of these families.

The quest for universals

A very important approach to comparative language study, however, looks at similarities, rather than at differences, probes the common underlying principles which structure language in general, and asks (by implication if not explicitly) how far these common principles are innate in the way our brains are built to learn culture.

There are key writers who have investigated the 'universals' of language structure, using the evidence around us of the complexity of natural languages themselves. The Swiss linguist Ferdinand de Saussure developed a very fruitful line of analysis which made an important distinction between the enduring interiorized patterns of grammar and syntax (*la langue*) and the 'free' flow of actual speech and writing produced by users of the language (*la parole*).[8] The Prague school of structural linguistics in the 1930s pursued the question of common properties in the basic grammatical structuring of language, including the minimal level at which we pattern the elements of significant sound in a given tongue and across tongues. American linguistics had already offered the concept of the phoneme as the minimal significant sound component in the set of such components that speech in a given tongue employs. It was suggested by the structuralists that the set of phonemes in a given language, whatever its number, could be described even more simply. It was an artefact of the way that quite a small number of oppositional contrasts were systematically made at a series of points in the vocal tract. The 'significance' of the phoneme did not lie in the physical sound made, the recording that might be picked up on a machine—which would not easily recognize words as the same when variously whispered or shouted, or spoken in different regional accents. It lay rather in the way that a native speaker would recognize without thinking the contrasts being set up by one sound against others in the pattern of language-as-a-whole. At the same time, it was shown that contrasts made in the quality of sound as the breath passes along the vocal tract, by the shape of the tongue relative to the palate, by constriction of various degrees in the throat or at the lips, by allowing or preventing the passage of breath through the nose, etc., were not peculiar to particular languages but very widespread. Many were common to large numbers of languages, and only a very few were specific to particular languages or language families.[9] The idea of overlapping sets of 'distinguishing features' based on simple binary contrasts was a fruitful one for comparative anthropology and was applied with dazzling results to different levels of cultural as well as linguistic communication in the structural analyses of Lévi-Strauss.[10]

The vision of a foundational set of structural principles common to all natural languages was developed by Noam Chomsky. He formulated the notion of universal grammar based upon the way that phrase structure everywhere replicates and transforms itself in a similarly hierarchical way to create the finished 'meaningful' exchanges of speech. While giving full recognition to the way that specific languages were created and transmitted culturally, he argued that their basic similarity or deep structure must emanate from a dedicated capacity in the physical brain.[11]

Academic models and logocentric analogies

Language has exerted a thoroughly bewitching spell over anthropologists, and as one of those affected, I understand how it has come to be seen as a key to so many other aspects of life, even being adopted as a model for society and culture as such. Durkheim used the image of language as almost a test case of what a 'social fact', or in the more user-friendly translation, 'social phenomenon', could be.[12] Lévi-Strauss used the analogy of language for the communication of women between groups in marriage; and for the more complex patterning of myths. The application of the idea of 'grammar' to non-linguistic spheres has always exerted a strong appeal. Leach claimed that language-like structural codes lay behind all communication, applying this in his early work to ritual and in some of his later work to things like traffic lights, arguing that they could all be reproduced on the binary computer. Jim Faris experimented by applying Chomsky's principles of transformational grammar 'literally' to body-painting among the south-eastern Nuba. Such efforts have since been criticized by Alfred Gell, as I noted in Chapter 4—for Gell, art, like music and dance, is not congruent with the workings of language at all.

Language has been used in some very general ways as a model for social life. Clifford Geertz has developed the analogy of culture 'as text', something to be read and interpreted as one would language (an approach touched on already in Chapter 2). The idea of 'discourse', that is basically the exchange and circulation of spoken language, or in a distinctive older usage, a piece of reflective oratory or writing, became a powerful metaphor for hegemonic forms of cultural practice in the work of Michel Foucault. His work shadowed earlier Marxist conceptions of ideology but shifted the emphasis away from generalized forms of belief and ideals to details of varied local and individual action which were nevertheless complicit in a wider political and cultural whole.[13]

There is a marked bias towards textuality in scholarship generally, a 'logocentric' approach to culture and experience, stemming in part from intensive academic education itself. Bourdieu has drawn attention to the key place of formal language in the creature he dubs 'academic man'.[14] The place of language as an *object* as well as a *medium* of study has certainly been a dominant one in academia, in respect of grammar, translation, and the study of literary or historical texts, as well as in the production of yet more books.

While anthropology is a discipline that has attempted, more than most, to get out into the fresh air and away from the library, and to focus on language in use rather than preserved as a specimen, it has followed the model of the other disciplines to some extent in relying on textual passages from informants in order to illuminate concepts and explain action. Have such methods over-formalized our understandings of systems of 'thought' in non-literate communities, and in the more spontaneous areas of social life in literate communities? Have we gone too far in endorsing a 'logocentric' approach to society and culture? Have we exaggerated the difference between pre-literate and literate communities? A conventional assumption on the part of historians and anthropologists has been that the invention or acquisition of writing makes a tremendous difference to culture and civilization. Jack Goody has powerfully defended this view, and writers such as Ernest Gellner and Benedict Anderson are quite right in pointing out that the history of nations and influential international communities is linked with mass literacy and the spread of ideas through technological means like printing. Talal Asad has characterized the world's languages as 'strong' or 'weak' on this kind of basis.[15] Even so, literacy, however 'strongly' promoted, does not displace oral communication, and indeed can only be taught through it. Spoken language has a special vitality, which anthropologists are well placed to spot, and Goody himself has provided us with rich materials of oral myth from West Africa.[16]

Oral narratives

Beyond the conversational context of anthropological field research, more or less formal spoken narratives have been solicited, and systematically collected or recorded in various ways since the days of Frazer. These narratives have fallen into such categories as myth, legend, history, autobiography, exegesis of customary practices, and so on. Increasingly, 'native voices' have appeared in ethnography. With the shift away from 'function' to meaning, and to history, in the later twentieth century, oral narratives have gained pride of place in much anthropological research and analysis, some even arguing the extreme position that ethnographers should not indulge in fanciful analysis of their own but limit themselves to a commentary on the texts they have collected and translated.[17] The study of oral literature, of poetry and storytelling and song, flowered with the increasingly 'literary' sensitivities of anthropology from the 1960s on, rejoining an older tradition of folktale studies.[18] Historians too, such as Jan Vansina in Africa, were pursuing spoken tradition, and seeing in the comparison of narratives the possibility of reconstructing the past in regions where there were few conventional sources.[19]

The anthropological question of context stimulated some creative work on the entanglement of 'past' and 'present' in spoken historical narratives, for example in John Davis's work on the social relations of the production of history, and on the articulation of identity, memory, and history. Memory is always nourished by conversation, and this itself is set in social relations, within or between cohorts, rival generations, or age sets, or communities of shared experience. Language, including accounts of the past, can entrap and entrance you; even in memory, in privacy—Wordsworth's 'recollection in tranquillity'—verbal formulations can distil something rather different from the immediate confrontation with experience. In my own work on the social circulation of accounts of shared danger I have found it helpful to draw on George Steiner's portrayal of the 'family of remembrance'.[20] Narratives are not the whole of memory, as I have demonstrated in the previous chapter. 'Social memory' specifically, as a 'shared' concept, is not easily visible or audible to the anthropologist, nor can it be captured in a straightforward way on her audio- or video-tape. But the possibility of recording, of 'capturing' what is actually said by different people, and of re-recording at different times, has certainly opened up the treasures of memory to new kinds of study.

I, Thou, and Language: a model of sociality

Can there be a non-logocentric approach to language?—one which treats of language in life, in use? The writing down of spoken texts seems to offer only a spurious objectivity, for all spoken language is part of an ongoing stream of wider reciprocities. A lot of ordinary conversation serves less for conveying important information than for 'grooming' and twittering. Even calling people by their particular names is a way of keying them into a relational link. All names are self-refential to the namer in the first place, as Lévi-Strauss pointed out.[21] Even the naming of places has a reflexive aspect: for example, in examining the names of places on African maps, you learn more about explorers, conquerors, and later national leaders than about the places named. David Zeitlyn has emphasized, too, that the terms we juggle and select in use as pronouns and kin terms are not so much fixed 'nominals' as always relative to situations of usage and reference. A term borrowed from linguistics and now gaining currency in anthropological analysis for this relational and reflexive quality of words, a context of 'speaking' rather than a dictionary approach to language, is *deixis*. Put simply, the word indicates the relevance of the identity and situation of the speaker to what is being said: 'here' and 'now' are obviously deictic.[22]

Some philosophers have even imagined language as essentially stemming from one speaker, and expressing the inner thoughts of one mind—a view associated strongly with the French philosopher Descartes's claim 'I think, therefore I am'. However, current research has pointed to its primary nature as *linking* two or more speakers: a neat expression of its social quality is to imagine as a minimum two persons engaged in a conversation with reference to, or in the hearing of, a third. A productive scenario in infant learning is in fact a trio: mother and baby perform to each other in front of an admiring visitor. 'Semantic' anthropology places emphasis on the 'shared' nature of meaning, which of course includes not only those who speak, but those who hear. C. G. Fiumara in an interesting book *The Other Side of Language* has revealed something of the complex depths of exchange in a conversation; just as much is going on in the mind of the silent partner at any one time as in that of the person whose turn it is to speak. Our *understanding* of language lies in listening, perhaps even more than in uttering.[23] Our participation has much of game-playing about it, and in any game we reveal only a part of ourselves. Michael Herzfeld has plumbed successive levels of living, shifting language use among Greek speakers, and developed sharp and interesting ideas about socio-linguistics from this insight into multiplicity.[24] A recent anthropological volume has explored the social relations of 'indirect' communication, a field of subtle signals picked up in all sorts of different intimate circles, rarely 'read' by outsiders. In fact, a lot of language is like this, rather than being openly and maximally communicative of useful information.[25]

2. LANGUAGE WITHIN THE 'DANCE' OF SOCIAL LIFE: BARBER ON *ORIKI*

Recalling my discussion in Chapter 4 about music, we should not forget how often language is partnered with music and rhythm; even the plainest speech in foreign languages has a different 'music' to one's own, and in song the voice itself is explicitly encompassed within musical form. Without the living expression of the musical voice, song is a poor thing when reduced to paper. We sing as we remember the previous living performances we have heard. Ruth Finnegan has revealed the extensive and elaborate worlds of song and oral literature in Africa; Lila Abu-Lughod has shown how a perspective from women's songs among the Bedouin can unveil many often-hidden sides of Arab society. A particularly lucid portrayal of the life of words within musical forms of social life is Karin Barber's work on the Yoruba of Nigeria.

Based on her fieldwork in the small town of Okuku in northern Yorubaland, Barber celebrates the ubiquitous oral text *oriki* as a 'master discourse'.[26] *Oriki*, a spoken form of pithy epithet about persons or topics, are performed mainly by women. Short, or long, they are sometimes collections of riddle-like, partially complete allusions, which the addressee will pick up better than any outsider. They are composed for all kinds of subjects, human, animal, and spiritual, and occasionally encapsulate fragments of quite ancient historic text and juxtapose them with new elements. *Oriki* act as an evocation and identification of people and things, and can be used to create new relationships. They may be performed in numerous modes or genres, being chanted 'as a central component of almost every significant ceremonial in the life of the compound and town' such as weddings, funerals, and masquerades; used in jokes and banter or just casually exchanged as greetings on the street. Some may be transmitted with the generations, partly in 'lineage' fashion and particularly as shared among those who consider themselves to have come long ago from one of a set of primordial towns of

FIG. 16. The Bride's lament: Okuku, Nigeria. Photo: P. F. de
Moraes Farias, courtesy of Karin Barber.

origin. Some performers acquire fame, at public festivals and even on the
television, while ordinary domestic life is permeated with the use of *oriki* as
fragments of the past continually weave into the fashioning of ordinary life.

Oriki are set within a clearly articulated structure of social hierarchy, differential occupation, lineage and family identities, marriage connections, and a
cycle of public ceremonial. However, they also exercise a free play of language
and deploy critical, ironic, and contradictory sentiments. Taking advantage
of the relative immunity built into their ambivalence and indirection, they can
play a role in political intrigue.[27] They also provide scope for contradictory

reflections upon social relations and ceremonial forms themselves: the out-standing example is that of the bride's 'laments' on the day of her 'enjoy-ment' in the course of the wedding ceremonies. This special day is a unique opportunity for the bride to express her ambivalence about leaving her child-hood home, her friends, her mother, to join the household of a husband (who, until recent decades, might have been virtually unknown to her). She may have a chorus of girls supporting her, and there are plenty of other opportunities for young girls to learn and practise the appropriate style of *oriki*, so she has had time to prepare for this day. She has to make the most of it, as married women no longer have the opportunity to comment on their position in this way. Most other forms of *oriki* are addressed to other persons, or to the gods (*orisha*), and a married woman may become an expert in chant-ing these forms, almost always in the vocative form. The bride's lament is, however, recursively focused upon herself, and her position. Here are two examples:

> I would have liked to be a hunter, but I have no quiver
> I would have liked to be a blacksmith, but I have no bellows
> When I would have liked to go on living in my father's house
> I, Abike Omotanbaje
> Child of the Okin people, I did not turn into a man
> May good luck attend me today.

In the next example, the bride feels like a sheep being put up for sale:

> They're making arrangements about the ram
> The ram is grazing in the yard
> When I was not in the house
> 'Laughing teeth', they made arrangements about me
> They plotted and planned
> Plotted and planned till they got the date-fixing fee
> got the date-fixing fee, but the rest is left to me alone
> May good luck attend me today.[28]

The skill of the expert is found both in the social and political allusion of *oriki*, but also in the literary manipulation of the shape and sounds of words. The senior woman Sangowemi was able to 'improvise' *oriki* at great length and with great subtlety. In the course of one performance in honour of Jayeola, father of a famed priest of Ifa divination and her own great-great-grandfather, she created two versions of one set of lines which illustrates something of the artistry *oriki* can involve. One of Jayeola's short *oriki* appellations is the

FIG. 17. Sangowemi performing *oriki*: Okuku, Nigeria. Photo: P. F. de Moraes Farias, courtesy of Karin Barber.

proverb-like observation 'It is the courageous person who gets the anthill', meaning that only a daring person can seize the opportunity to get what he or she wants. This image is played upon and linked with others on the basis of either 'meaning' or pure sound in the course of the performance. Barber invites us to compare two passages which echo and counterpoint each other. The first goes:

> The storm rages, it cannot carry away the grinding stone
> The gentle breeze cannot carry away the hill
> The monkey robbed the farm, it swaggered
> Jayeola, Oyedokun, my father the ferocious leopard.

The second variant is as follows:

> Child of 'The storm rages, it cannot carry away the grinding stone'
> 'The gentle breeze cannot carry away the hill'
> Wherever the gentle breeze wishes, Ayinde, it can turn the treetops
> Wherever a master wishes, he can send his slave . . .

Both passages begin a standard formulation, indicating that the subject cannot be assailed by his enemies. The first passage then follows up *ìjì jà* (the storm rages) with *ìjí já* [oko] (the monkey plucks [fruits from the farm]). The monkey, Barber explains, is another image of the big man's power, robbing a farm and swaggering away with impunity; and the final line evokes a parallel animal image of even more terrifying power. By contrast, in the second variant passage, Sangowemi picks up not the sound of *ìjì jà* but the sense of *éfúùfù lélé*, the gentle breeze. She goes on to turn this into a metaphor for a great master, whose servants bow to him as the trees to the wind. The import of the idea of the wind is, however, reversed—in the opening lines, the subject stands firm against the wind, and in the later line, becomes a wind himself, bending the treetops around him. 'It is as if Sangowemi were reminded . . . of another chunk of *oriki* . . . letting the word association stand as the only link.'[29]

Karin Barber points out in her discussion of oral literary texts, of which *oriki* are a fine example, that they are part and parcel of social life. Unlike written forms they cannot be conceived of as separate commentaries upon society; nor are they self-contained, attributable to particular authors or historical origins, or possible to understand except in the context of performance to an audience familiar with much of the genre and local circumstance. They evoke the past, but not in a narrative or explanatory historical way; they encapsulate fragments of the past into a living present, as reputations of persons and groups are competitively recreated. They speak to someone, from someone, and in this sense are almost type cases of what Bakhtin called the 'dialogic' character of language in general. Barber concludes by suggesting that Volosinov/Bakhtin foreshadows—and goes beyond—performance theory and speech act theory in seeing literary text as utterance, and utterance as attaining meaning only in and through the concrete contexts of real social existence. He writes 'as if he had *oriki* in mind'.[30] They are a form of language which does not simply reflect or parallel other kinds of signification; they 'must be apprehended as art forms' in themselves,[31] and as such are an integral part of the ceremonial life of Okuku and Yoruba society more generally.

The power of language: within and against authority

Let me return here to some of the observations which Karin Barber has made on the place of language, and literary texts in particular, in anthropological theory and practice. She writes that despite the modern dominance of interpretative approaches in anthropology, it is rather unusual for anthropological inquiry to treat literature as a key diagnostic device, a thread leading into the inner aspects of a society's imaginative life. 'Semiotics and structuralism have attempted, with partial success, to show that the symbolic and classificatory systems of signification that anthropology has traditionally concentrated on are *homologous* to language. What is much more evidently true, however, is that they are *implicated* in language and are dependent on it. Sooner or later, they are interpreted, amplified, or evaluated by a verbal commentary, and without this speech context they could not continue to operate.' Barber proposes that it is often through literary texts that exegetical commentary is directed towards these other systems of signification, pointing out that literary utterance is at once action in society and reflection upon society. 'The text, furthermore, does not just represent an already-constituted ideological viewpoint; it is in the text that a viewpoint is constructed. . . . The text itself says more than it knows; it generates 'surplus': meanings that go beyond, and may subvert, the purported intentions of the word.' Above all, literary texts are revealing because they easily lead on to further comment, to verbal exegesis, such as a historical narrative or a discussion of family taboos. Barber concludes,'The *oriki* are not just the trigger which sets off a separate discourse; they are the kernel of the discourse itself, which will not take place except with reference to the *oriki*.'[32] We may not all have *oriki* as such: but they are probably a better key to what language is all about than the propositions of the positivist philosophers ('this table is blue') or the negotiations of the rational exchange theorists ('How many bananas for this fish?'). They also hint clearly at the creative and subversive potential of language, which can speak against the context that spawned it.

In a sustained attack on postmodernism, Terry Eagleton insists that we recognize that we are not 'cultural' rather than 'natural' creatures, but cultural beings by virtue of our nature. Language, he claims, is what emancipates us to a degree from the full constraints of our biology. 'Only a linguistic animal could have history, as opposed to what one imagines for a slug is just the same damn thing over again.' Because of the capacity of language to transgress its own systemic principles, as it does in poetry for example, human existence is 'exciting but precarious'.[33] In concluding this chapter, we have to go back to retrieve its original point: that while the role of language as a tool for living in the world and representing it has been given too much weight as an analogy for all social interaction, it is both subtler and more powerful than that: it permeates all sociality, often inextricably linked with art or music as one order of ceremony among others. It can, however, become a vehicle for especially sharp communication—because it is qualitatively different, in its self-referential complexity, from the other aspects of sociality. Let us be bold and return in a way to the older academic understandings: since the beginnings of language, a hundred thousand years ago or possibly much more, it has come to claim the leading position in a hierarchy of the modes of human communication. It is Queen of the human arts, but scarcely functions in isolation from them—its richness lies in its connections with the others and arguably its greater capacity for presenting things with 'the mind's eye', as they might be rather than as they are; generating the unexpected. This is why it is worth pondering the Yoruba *oriki*—because they exemplify not only artistic performance, but can carry reflexive irony, political critique, and historical judgement. Aesthetics, politics, and the historical imagination all involve a sense of 'ought'—but they are not restricted to modern education and writing, they are found wherever there is spoken language too.

CHAPTER SEVEN

The Dialectics of Gender and Generation

O UR lives are lived, in many ways like those of other species, along the trajectories of sex/gender and of age. Both are obviously rooted in biological or organic life. But unlike the other species, human beings make abstractions out of these ideas, play around with their significance, turning them into ordering principles and arguing about their proper role in social life. The personal, experiential aspects of living our lives as social creatures are among the themes explored in the next chapter. Here, I present some of the analytical tools which anthropologists have fashioned in order to pinpoint and compare the moving choreography by which we relate to each other through conventionalized principles of gender and age, a domain of study conventionally dubbed 'kinship and marriage'.[1] It is important to remember that the links of human kinship are not simply biological facts but are life-data made salient through shared moral and theoretical perceptions. At the same time ideas about kinship are more than simply a cultural imaginary, they are the very framework in which the human community sustains and reproduces itself. The social forms of kinship are more than abstract rules and obligations and linguistic classification; they are the arena in which those abstractions become, in a direct sense, flesh: this is at base a field of bodily encounter, of life and death and the creation of patterns of give and take in life-sustaining activities.

The growing campaign over 'gender' issues and perspectives in the social sciences since the 1970s has given new life to the academic analysis of kinship, which had come to seem a little antiquated and narrowly specialist. Indeed the arguments from feminism have enlivened and rejuvenated anthropology itself, starting from its heart in the study of the family and relations between women and men, children and adults. The writings of Louise Lamphere, Sherry Ortner, Edwin and Shirley Ardener, Henrietta Moore, and Marilyn Strathern, for example, which initially helped to create a subfield of study—the comparison of women's lot across the world—were crucial in finally breaking the 'structural-functional' mould and have led directly to a more 'plural', embodied, and experiential conception of social formations in general.[2] A structural element remains, and in my view it remains of the essence. Dialectically positioned voices and perspectives, especially the interactions of gender and the passage of the generations, are the very forms within which human life reproduces itself. To accept the revolution in gender awareness is not to reduce everything to the personal, or the bodily level of experience. On the contrary, it is to sharpen our sense of how profoundly structured are the ways in which we participate in the gendered processes of social reproduction over time.

The approach of this chapter retains a typically 'anthropological' and holistic vision of underlying structure as a nesting series of *key relationships*, as against the efforts of sociology and psychology to generalize about empirical families or individuals, or the new evolutionary psychology which attempts, for example, to account for current social problems of male violence or female jealousy in terms of inbuilt drives which once had an advantage for the 'reproductive success' of a given individual in replicating his or her genes (see discussion in Chapter 2). In the face of challenges from social survey statistics, introspective psychology, and quasi-zoological models of human behaviour alike, social-cultural anthropologists have rejuvenated their core disciplinary concern with 'kinship and marriage' in two complementary ways. First, they have revived their classic interest in the worldwide comparison of the 'logic' of kinship systems, with a new emphasis on their historical context and possible relevance to understanding humanity's early history. That logic, which finds its clearest expression in the world of egalitarian, mobile, and often hunter-gatherer societies, inevitably pivots around the principle of exogamy: *marrying out*. Second, field-working anthropologists have focused in much greater depth than ever before upon the ways in which people rooted in the productive systems of agriculture or industry typically concern themselves with patterns of 'closeness' or 'belonging' to which they appeal in the making of marriages and other bonds in the deliberate conservation of community. Here, while the logic of exogamy remains, it takes a minimal form of prohibited degrees around primary kin. Taking a wider analytical view, it is overlaid in practice by the pursuit of marriage and other social bonds *within* a locality or a social class or category—that is, a definite strategy of endogamy: *marrying in*. This strategy reveals a strong concern with the aim of reproducing 'ourselves', our own kind or group. The shift from asking questions in anthropological analysis about exogamy, to questions about endogamy, corresponds in part to a shift from contemplating the classic ethnography of mobile tribal peoples to tackling intensive agricultural and industrializing communities. Both approaches are nevertheless concerned with the patterns of 'gender and generation' as transmitted social phenomena.

Before proceeding, we have to remember that the English language may be very rich in many respects, but it is poor in the lexicon and logic of kinship. Relatives are traced out in all directions, from individual to individual in a spreading genealogical framework, regardless of whether one is tracing through the father or the mother, and without respect to whether the links in the chain are between persons of the same or opposite sex. The old Anglo-Saxon system mapped these links onto the proliferating segments of the body— father and mother at the head of the 'sib', brothers and sisters at the neck, followed by cousins at the shoulder, elbow, wrists, finger joints, and nails as one reckoned further and further out. English 'uncles' and 'aunts' are treated as all related to oneself in the same sort of way, while 'cousins' spread out vaguely in all directions, qualified only by pedants as first or second or third cousins on either side.[3] Beyond the rhetorical camaraderie, one nearly always has to fall back on a step-by-step genealogical calculation to justify the cousinly warmth. However, the great majority of the world's languages have a sharper tool kit for sorting out relatives, often using principles which class people according to gender and generation sameness/difference in the links. One of the clearest diagnostic features of a terminology is the way that it classifies cousins. For example, when siblings of the same sex (two sisters, or two brothers) grow up and marry out, their children will often be regarded as very close to each other, on the model of siblingship itself. In the case of a brother-sister pair of siblings, however, relations in the next generation are quite different: when these two grow up and marry out, their children may call each other by a contrasting term often quite opposed to the idea of siblingship. The former are commonly prohibited marriage partners, while the latter are often marriageable. In anthropological language, the former are 'parallel cousins' and the latter 'cross cousins', signalling whether there was similarity or 'cross-over' of gender between the sibling pair in the parental generation. In a system like this, it follows that a mother's brother is a very different kind of relative from a father's brother, and a father's sister from a mother's sister. The principle of classifying by 'crossness' at varying degrees of distance, lineally or in ascending or descending generations, provides a way of comparing terminologies and the way they distinguish, not simply between individuals as such, but between significant categories of relatedness.[4]

I. 'MARRYING OUT': LANGUAGE AND LOGIC OF THE REPRODUCTIVE GAME

Gender and sexuality, marriage, and family-making are like games of chess in every society. While complicated, the dialectics of kinship are well understood by 'the folk' if not always by the anthropologists; people are fully aware of their internal tensions and puzzles, and explore these themes in myth, art, and homespun philosophy. Even in our impoverished kinship system in modern England, we have 'mother-in-law' jokes; most other places are much better endowed. Kinship conundrums may turn up in proverbs and riddles, or in the formal practices of 'Joking Relationships'.[5] As a total outsider in the Uduk villages of my fieldwork, I found that once having been dubbed— in play—'cross-cousin' to a particular young man with a sense of fun, my own social horizons opened up and I always had conversational gambits— 'Crocodile gap-tooth!' 'Flat-head!'—to try out with a range of other people who could be regarded as further or 'classificatory' relatives of a cross-cousin type to me.

In thinking about the intriguing games people play with ideas about kinship, we have to drop the notion of the two-up, two-down modern nuclear family in its square suburban house as a basic human norm and the minimal unit of each and every system. Nor should we cling on to today's apparently self-evident assumptions about gender dominance, or family continuity down the male line (or any other lineal principle), or permanent structures of identifiable groups on the ground and enduring links of affinity or alliance between them. A way of liberating ourselves from these starting points is to return to Nick Allen's radical imagining of a primal order of relationships based upon a quartet, the 'dance of relatives' I have already introduced in Chapter 4. Allen's 'tetradic' model merges egocentric and sociocentric perspectives, which means that everyone in this game of relationships sees their field of connections in the same way; to young or old, male or female, 'the system' looks the same. You are not *born* as a Red or a Green, a Dark or a Light (adopting my own terminology here), but you are initiated into one of these four teams as a youngster. Individuals then play the mating game according to the rules linking the two sets of 'partner' teams: for example, Dark with Light. Recruitment of their children then follows, into one side or the other of the alternative pair of teams, in this case Red or Green, according to whether their mother was Dark and father Light, or vice versa. The process is then repeated in the next generation, among new children who have to learn the rules of the game. The crucial categories are not lineal descent groupings or conjugal families, but socially created teams of individual recruits—'sections'. These are set in motion by a double pattern of reciprocity that links one section with its opposite in marriageability, and allocates the children that result between the two other opposing sections. As they mature, everyone is thus lined up with the section of their direct grandparents (containing mother's mother and father's father; while these grandparents' spouses are in their own opposite section). Using the metaphor of 'dance teams' rather than the technical term of 'generation moiety' helps us understand how all four categories of people are present at the same time, each including individuals of all ages. Was human life once more comprehensively, coherently, and cogently organized, on clear game-playing principles of this kind? Has it fragmented, or unravelled itself, from this 'germ' of a beginning (Allen's phrase)? Has it become specialized into distinctive local forms by giving heavier weight to one particular relationship over others within this model, over the long-term span of history? This is Allen's view, which draws on Durkheim and Mauss's *Primitive Classification* but also on Mauss's fertile ideas about the 'totality' of pre-modern exchange relations.

There are certainly in the real world partial patterns of marriage exchange between moieties, and sets of sections (especially in Australia and South America); and there are patterns of association between alternating generations (for example, those regions and eastern Africa); the simplest combination of all in Allen's model is a supposition only, though there is persuasive evidence from kinship terminologies that it might echo ancient human history.[6] To bring this admittedly imaginary model closer to home, or at least to bring it into line with more familiar ethnography, a helpful touchstone is Lévi-Strauss's 'atom of kinship'.[7] Criticizing the common-sense 'Western' view, though retaining assumptions about lineality and gender dominance, Lévi-Strauss insisted that the seemingly obvious nuclear family is not the

logically or biologically 'given' unit from which society is built up. The immediate family is merely a transient stage in a wider process. A way of capturing
this process is to include in a model of the 'atom of kinship' the way in which
the marriage relation of the parents was established in the first place, including therefore a representative of the group from which the woman came.
'Affinity' or 'in-lawship' is as important as the relation between siblings, or
'filiation'—the relation between parent and child. The mother's brother must
be present in this model, not because of a genealogical or consanguineous
connection, but because he is a kind of 'wife-giver', representing the dynamic
principle of give-and-take between categories or groups which generated
the kind of marriage that had been formed. Affinity, moreover, is not simply
over and done with when a marriage is made; it is transmitted to the next
generation, in that, for example, the relation between a child and his or her
mother's brother may be as crucial as that with the father. The minimal set of
relationships in this model of kinship is that between a man and his son, on
the one hand, through his wife to her brother, on the other, and finally on the
part of this latter figure to his sister and her son. While particular objections
have been made to this 'structural' model of the minimal elements of kinship
(including its male bias), social and cultural anthropologists would concur in
Lévi-Strauss's view that the field of kinship is one permeated by wide-ranging
and systematic principles of a logical and conceptual kind governing the
making of marriages.[8]

Lévi-Strauss characterized as 'elementary' structures those kinship systems
which include a pre-designated kin category as the ideal or even required one
into which a person should marry. The simplest was the dualistic model of
symmetrical exchange between two parties regarding themselves as mutually
distinct groups, and marrying only outside, that is, seeking spouses only
from the opposing group. Thus, imagine that anyone who was anyone supported the Oxford side or the Cambridge side at the Boat Race, the men of
one side always seeking a spouse from among the women on the other side.
This system would produce marriages which repeatedly linked the sides in
the same way in each generation; a man would marry where his father did,
and his son will expect to; and a woman would marry where her mother did
and her daughter will. Each marriage would thus bring together classificatory
cousins, traced bilaterally through either parent. Lévi-Strauss also wrote of
'generalized exchange' as a further variant on elementary structures. In such
a system, which Rodney Needham has described as 'asymmetrical exchange',
there would be more than two participant parties: and instead of reciprocation

in marriage being made by one party to the other, marriage would take a one-directional route between several parties. We might imagine Oxford men marrying Cambridge women, but Cambridge men going on to seek wives in London, whose brothers would go courting in Bristol, men from Bristol proceeding to Birmingham to find brides, their brothers eventually marrying the sisters of the Oxford men. Each party would stand as wife-givers to one group, and wife-takers to another. Sometimes people might speak of the system as 'marrying in a circle', as theoretically the cycle would be closed in a balanced way, even though wife-givers were often perceived as superior to wife-takers, presenting them with a gift that could never be reciprocated. In practice, it was often the case that some in such a system would occupy, or achieve, a superior position, by virtue of their ability to give wives to those below them, and so on down the ladder, marriage itself being reciprocated with valuable bridewealth serving as a kind of tribute so the hierarchy was kept in being. If one draws the diagrams it becomes clear that here, while a man is expected to marry a cross-cousin, this girl will be among the wife-giving group, the 'mother's brothers' and their children, while the wife-takers are 'father's sisters' and their children, a contrasting type of cross-cousin who is likely to be labelled as distinct. This kind of one-way system which can integrate a pattern of links over many groups has been most extensively studied in south and south-east Asia, where rules of marriage do indeed indicate at least a preference for a man's classificatory maternal cross-cousin. Good examples would include Edmund Leach's analytical ethnography of the peoples of highland Burma, and R. H. Barnes's study of the Indonesian island of Kédang.[9] It has been asked why the rule of marriage could not be reversed to indicate general preference for the other cross-cousin; but there is a lack of any convincing example; and given the gender asymmetry in which overall systems of kinship and marriage are commonly represented, and also the way in which anthropologists fit them into diagrams, we can work out how such a rule could not yield an 'integrated' pattern.[10] However, immediate one-to-one exchange, reciprocated on the spot, is certainly found in the world and has some historically robust aspects (see my discussion of the Gumuz case below).

It is not only the modern structuralists, in the wake of Lévi-Strauss, who have emphasized the need to see the family—any family, not only in 'elementary structures'—in a wider context of give-and-take, as signalled by the presence of the mother's brother in his minimal unit of the 'atom of kinship'. Anthropology has always emphasized the way in which people everywhere juxtapose the idea of a circle of primary close kin, however defined, with an external 'other' category to which sexuality and marriage potential is directed. Very few master theorists have avoided the temptation to speculate on the role of incest prohibition as the trigger for the generation of kinship systems. Tylor imagined the pragmatic need for original human groups to seek outside partners for their own replenishment—they were to 'marry out or die out'.[11] McLennan imagined the early role of 'marriage by capture', a formulation which has lasted in various ways and strikingly encapsulates the violent side of kinship and marriage. Freud imagined an early family-like horde in which the sons killed the father, and then, fearful that the same would happen to them if they took over their mothers and sisters, decided to prohibit them and seek sexual partners outside.[12] Maurice Godelier has recently put forward an imagined scenario of his own, in which he postulates that the beginnings of rules and regulations about sexuality (and thus kinship) must have come about as the result of the evolutionary loss of the periodic oestrus in females that marked the beginning of humanity.[13] Replacing a pattern of seasonal receptiveness, sexuality in women became generalized, while the whole phenomenon of sexuality became 'cerebralized' with the growing human brain and related rise in co-ordinated activities. This meant the potential for conflict was heightened within the community. Godelier imagines that in proto-human communities there would have already developed a gender- and generation-based division of labour, and that a number of such co-operating 'families' might already live together in a band society. Human sexuality arrived at a point where it was somehow a threat to the reproduction of society as such, as a whole, and this made it necessary for sexuality to be brought under management. 'Exchange' as a principle might then follow, along with the development of language and the kinds of memory upon which 'relations between relations' and human kinship systems depend. This provides an interesting counterpoint to Chris Knight's theories of the 'sex strike' origin of culture, introduced in Chapter 2; and to Allen's image of a primal four-section system with generational exchange discussed above.

We might wonder what conceivable connection these speculations about the choreography of early human kinship, or of rare tribal cases, have to do with our world today. There is a clear answer here, because the 'kinship terminologies' or vocabularies of kinship connection used in the world's natural languages are remarkably stable over time. Since L. H. Morgan's pioneering work of the nineteenth century, anthropologists have sensed how crucial are the puzzles raised by the language of kinship and how it relates to other aspects of life, especially marriage patterns.[14] Godelier and others have recently justified this kind of inquiry on the grounds that the very language in which we class kin relationships is a 'logical map' of the social world. There is no doubt that grasping the language of kinship helps us find our way, with informants, through the maze of rules and practices concerning marriage, religious beliefs, recruitment to groups, the inheritance of property, and so on.[15] But most interestingly, in spite of the seemingly endless variation of such rules and practices, kinship terminologies do not vary wildly with the thousands of languages and local cultures of the world. They are relatively stable as lexical sets, and not as fluid as actual behavioural patterns might indicate. Moreover, known kinship terminologies are built up from relatively few principles of distinction and classification, and constitute variants on a limited number of types. These can often be shown to constitute transformations of one another. Current thinking has been focused on the question of how these transformations take place, and whether there is an overall direction of change in the short or even longer term.[16] The method of comparison within specific regions is relatively straighforward. More problematic, and yet more intriguing, is the occurrence of similar kin terminologies in totally different parts of the world, which cannot be put into any known historical framework of contact or explained by obvious socio-economic factors. Some commentators have accused the enthusiasts in this field of study of making up their problems, but the kin terminologies in question are historical facts, sociological schemas created and applied by the human mind in specific contexts, and not the invention of scholars.

The distinction parallel/cross cousin in a terminology, sometimes known as 'bifurcation', is of special interest because of the way it is frequently aligned with marriage rules. In a mild form, marriage may simply be allowed with a cross but not a parallel cousin, the latter being treated 'as if' a sibling. In a strong form, marriage may be prescribed with a classificatory cross-cousin (as in Allen's model and Lévi-Strauss's elementary structures). In a system like this, a single 'kinship term' might be expected to cover a man's mother's brother, his father's sister's husband, and also his father-in-law, actual or potential. This 'equation' in the terminology would be congruent with a formal, sociocentric pattern where two 'halves' or moieties, or perhaps four sections, of a social whole exchanged marriage partners with each other on a symmetrical basis. But the same principle could operate in a multitude of ego-centred small arrangements. One of the best-known examples of this pattern in practice is commonly labelled the 'Dravidian', from its original identification in southern India. Here the pervasive distinction is basically one of kin (parallel) versus affines, present and potential (cross). Dravidian-type systems have now been recorded in various places across the world, for example in South America, which brings us back to the fascinating question of why there should be such correspondences; the 'tetradic' theory of Allen of course would see these cases as surviving traces of a former pattern common in world history.

Elements of classic reciprocity need not always be tied in to evolutionary schemas. They can be found today in all sorts of combinations with pragmatic interests and purposeful individual projects. Ken Burridge's ethnographic analysis of friendship and kinship in Tangu, on the northern coast of New Guinea, is not a formal 'elementary structure' but has many echoes of the kinds of system we have been discussing.[17] At the same time it offers a fascinating example of the way that ideal rules about kinship and marriage can be made to 'work' as blueprints for solidary social reproduction while drawing in quite unrelated persons. There was a time in anthropology when 'kinship', assumed to define the whole of a 'primitive' social world, used to be opposed to 'friendship', presumed to characterize only 'modern' society. But Burridge recognized that the two domains overlapped and redefined each other in social practice. In Tangu, the major local communities are all divided into two approximately equal halves, each led by a team of brothers in competitive feasting. Ideally, marriages take place between these halves, each man marrying a sister of a man in the other half, who will himself marry the first man's sister. Each exchange marriage is ideally repeated in the next generation, maintaining the complementary relation between the two halves (as in the elementary model of reciprocal moieties discussed above). However, there is also a wide range of intermarriage between different Tangu settlements, and also with non-Tangu. Where individual genealogical patterns do not fit the ideal scheme, people speak 'as if' they did, and in effect they are merged into it.

Moreover, there are patterns of *formal friendship* in Tangu which initially are nothing to do with kinship (at least as understood in the older anthropological literature). The word for friend is *kwav*, which can also be translated as 'self', in an objective reference to myself, as in answer to the question 'Who is there?'—answer, *kwav*, 'I'. Tangu also use the term in speaking of 'my friend', or say of two people 'They are friends'. These formalized friendships are between two men, or two women, but not between a man and a woman. Friendship is instituted by the two partners exchanging clothes, each dressing the other as they would themselves, in a ceremony which used to be performed publicly.

The relationship is carried on to the next generation, to the sons of two men friends or the daughters of two women friends. Individuals may have several overlapping friendships, and while some of these could be with people far afield, others may even be with kin. In each case, friends will help each other, even in a quarrel involving kin. Friendship involves mutual aid and gift-giving, but never economic obligation of the kind you owe to kin. Of particular interest to my present argument is the point that marriage between the son and daughter of two male friends is considered an ideal. Further, a marriage may be arranged between the son and daughter of their respective full sisters, or between the son and daughter of the full brothers of two women friends. Not only today, but even in mythical times, there are examples of *friendship* giving rise to marriage and thus connecting previously 'unrelated' groups. The 'social' reproduction of the community as a whole is thus cast in the idiom of kinship and affinity, but made plausible through a range of individual and pragmatic actions.

The theme of exchange and reciprocity, prominent in anthropological writing on Melanesia since the key works of Malinowski and of Mauss (introduced in Chapter 2), has been further elaborated by today's specialists on the region. Marilyn Strathern's comprehensive survey of the underlying ideas of Melanesian peoples about the flow, and regeneration, of social relations offers a fresh perspective which is modifying the way that anthropologists approach 'kinship' as a topic. In *The Gender of the Gift* she departs from the dominant modern Western idea that 'society' is constructed through the making of links between pre-defined individuals. Sociality is rather the outcome of the transfer of goods, of substances, of life-giving powers along gendered lines. She speaks of people as themselves acquiring identity in the milieu of these transfers. In Melanesia individuals do not exist socially except as partners in this kind of flow and transfer; she writes of 'dividuals', people whose identity is a combination of their roles in a range of different mutual links. The elemental 'dyads' out of which social relations emerge are always gendered; they are between same-sex, or opposite sex, partners, of same or different generation. Strathern's work may be seen to have inherited much from structuralism; one way in which it differs, however, is the abandonment of any assumption of gender hierarchy, or even the fixed notion of personal gender identity. In no sense are men representing groups who exchange women. There is much crossing over and participation in differently gendered processes; and because this is a social world permeated by the ideology of the gift, there are no hard and fast lines between persons and the 'things' they produce and hand on. The person is not an owner, and the goods produced are not commodities. The transfer itself is constitutive of a different kind of relation between persons. Moreover, these persons are not ciphers or holders of roles and statuses: they are living breathing organic beings, who spend their time eating, having sex, giving birth, and so on, all the time engaging, as they explicitly understand it, in a very direct flow and exchange of bodily substances. Their sociality embraces the reproduction of biological life.[18]

This renewed formulation of a classic approach in Melanesian anthropology, and the restatement of the deep difference between that world and 'the West', has found response among those who are now developing a fresh generation of fieldwork and writing in some other parts of the world: mainly indigenous communities of Indonesia, Australasia, and South America, and (as I consider separately below) Africa. These new analyses are marked by the search for the quality of relations between persons through the idioms and images of material circulation between them over time, rather than their occupation of 'statuses within society'.[19] The vision of archaic society as first articulated by the *Année Sociologique* and given depth by Lévi-Strauss is thus being given a new lease of life. This trend in today's anthropology is exciting and important. It is also, I believe, complementary to another trend which at first seems to be quite different: this is, the growing literature on *marrying in*, rather than marrying out, as a key to understanding what drives patterns of kinship and social reproduction.

2. 'MARRYING IN': MODERN KINDS OF BELONGING

The standard models for analysing kinship and marriage have been based on the principle of exogamy, of give-and-take as a key to the social reproduction of a family or a group. This approach has been very fruitful with reference to the relatively egalitarian circumstances of hunting and gathering, some pastoral, and some partially mobile cultivating communities. However, perhaps especially in circumstances of intensive permanent settlement and agricultural or industrial production, the rhetorics and practice of 'kinship and marriage' become entangled with forms of land- and property-holding and investment in industrial production. We see the build-up of networks specializing in trade or in skilled crafts, the accumulation of treasure and the creation and maintenance of elites, and eventually the formation of the controlling classes of modern capitalism and their divergence from those who (now on a global scale) supply the labour and raw materials. In the course of these historical developments, we find elites and specialist groups elaborating notions of *holding back* on exchange, of controlling the flow, conserving substance, and through variously implicit or explicit practices of *endogamy*, or marrying in, maintaining closeness within an exclusive group and a distinction of status or wealth between social categories over the generations.

While the widespread pragmatic relevance of this theme is now being emphasized, the place of formal endogamy has long been recognized. The practice received some attention from the structuralist school, but was presented almost as an exception to the rule. For example, in a famous piece 'The Bear and the Barber', Lévi-Strauss argued that 'exchange' is always a fundamental principle, even when it appears to be denied, as in the Indian caste system.[20] The classic interdependence of groups through mutual exogamy is represented by the hunting and gathering societies of Australia or native America. A group there defining itself by the totemic figure of the Bear, for example, might be economically self-sufficient, but was totally dependent on marriage exchange with others for its own physical reproduction. In the Indian system, on the other hand, marriages (with a very few exceptions) take place only within particular castes or subcastes, who reproduce themselves autonomously in this respect. Lévi-Strauss suggested that the Indian case was nevertheless an 'exchange'-based system when considered from the economic point of view: the various specialist occupations, like that of the Barber, had a complementary interdependence with other occupations, and despite its self-sufficiency in marriage, each caste was thus enmeshed in an exchange structure. This pattern he represented as a transformation of the Australian or American case; and equally imbued with religious and ceremonial symbolism. Some have suspected a bit of Lévi-Straussian sleight of hand with the double mirrors here; but what his essay does underline is that despite the engagement of different modes of reciprocity within and between the domains of 'kinship' and 'economy' in the two cases, our clearest way of gaining insight into these processes is by tracing, in the first instance, the way in which marriages are made.

Patterns of effective endogamy need not be ideologically explicit. There is always the tendency to marry the boy next door because he is around, and because you (or even your parents) never meet more than the tiniest fraction of the theoretically available population. Such endogamy by default can reinforce boundaries of class and subculture of which we may be barely conscious.

However, there are strong drives also in the modern world to intended endogamy, of marrying in to one's own community, however that may be defined. 'Marrying in' may be at a very local level of household and neighbourhood, without any intention of constructing boundaries against others, but rather to carry on the working patterns and kinds of relatedness that already exist. This style of repeated folding in of the links of relationship, and the informal repetition of intermarriage, has been the theme of important recent anthropological study in several parts of the world. Janet Carsten has pioneered this mode of approach, and formulated the useful concept of 'cultures of relatedness' to indicate the value-laden, and personal participation in, domains of local and domestic intimacy which constitute the arena of 'kinship' in many parts of the world.[21]

The political aspects of endogamy are also coming into sharp focus in recent anthropology. Pierre Clastres has criticized the whole 'exchangeist' approach, giving more emphasis to the principle of local self-sufficiency and autonomy.[22] He underlines the way in which communities, in general but specifically for his analysis in South America, do not simply await their turn in systems of exchange but are driven to assert and implement their independence of the supposed obligations of exchange. The political aspects of endogamy in particular, we could add, have always been recognized for elites, but the reach of 'politics' is now understood far more widely than it once was. The Middle East is here the classic region which seems to defy the older models of exchange and exogamy as prime keys to social relations, and along with Africa it is a region scarcely touched on by Marcel Mauss or Lévi-Strauss. It is in the Middle East that the most powerful new analyses of 'marrying in' as a key theme and formal principle of political ideology, linked undoubtedly to very deeply rooted notions of the asymmetry of male and female, are emerging (see, for example, my discussion of Janice Boddy's work in Chapter 5). The ideal type of union within what is represented as a patrilineal, or agnatic, lineage, is referred to as marriage of a young man with his father's brother's daughter, his *parallel* cousin, explicitly repudiating the need for exchange with outsiders. In practice, this actual preferred marriage with a first patrilateral cousin often figures as a considerable proportion of first marriages in Middle Eastern communities, while a much higher proportion especially of second or later marriages are contracted with persons more distant than first cousins but still found within what is regarded as the same agnatic lineage. French writers on the Middle East and North Africa, most conspicuously Pierre Bourdieu, began to transform the insights of structuralism through relocating them within the contexts of power, practice, and history.[23] This region of the world, even more than sub-Saharan Africa, was most glaringly omitted from the analytical models of kinship based on equal give-and-take. Paul Dresch has probed the Middle Eastern sheikhly ideal of lineage self-sufficiency through in-marriage and the careful control of external economic relations. He quotes from an old report about the people of Afghanistan, who praised as a well-governed country one in which each household would pro-duce all its own food *and the mothers of its next generation,* or failing that, would absorb them unilaterally from elsewhere. He also mentions tales of the odd Yemeni tribe in the old days, when values really counted, whose pride of lineage was such that they married no one—and died out; or when faced with economic dependence, sat around in a circle and starved to death.[24]

3. AN AFRICAN PERSPECTIVE: FROM COLONIAL TO POST-COLONIAL THEMES

One of the background reasons why there has been a return to classic regions of 'kinship' study, such as Melanesia and South America, and a fresh round of what we could call 'neo-structural' analysis, is that anthropologists are still trying to get away from the effects of late colonial pragmatism upon their work. Anthropological attention to kinship and marriage was dominated, in Britain at least, from the 1930s up to the early 1960s, by studies carried out in the colonies, especially in Africa where a distinctive style of research and writ-ing developed.[25] The period of conquest and pacification being firmly imag-ined in the past, these studies operated almost by necessity in a framework of concern for good administration: for the principles of local customary law about land tenure, succession to chiefship, feuding and the maintenance of order, social hierarchies, and standard marriage practice. Though there were exceptional episodes of harsh rule and even brutality, for example in the 1950s Mau Mau emergency in Kenya, there was a basically liberal concern to grant civil rights to native peoples, collectively and individually, and to treat them as deserving citizens of emerging modern nations. Nevertheless, the power of the colonial authorities was still pretty well absolute; anthropolo-gists of a radical leaning often wrote sympathetically about the colonized peoples, and even began to associate themselves with political reform and anti-colonial struggles.[26] Anthropologists who neglected these current issues were dismissed as antiquarians. Those who wished to count as relevant wrote in terms of native rights and duties, the authority of kings and leaders, economic and social development, and the need for modern courts to sort out the claims of individual parties in disputes. Many of the cases that came to court in colonial Africa were concerned, in addition to homicide and raiding, with issues of land claims, marriage, inheritance or succession, and it was completely understandable that anthropologists should study the forms of customary law, develop a legalistic or 'jural' approach to traditional social structure, and even help identify points where greater attention to individual rights could be promoted.[27] Gluckman, for example, argued in the context of the Barotse courts in southern Africa for the importance of the local concept of the 'reasonable man', whose ability to see what was essentially fair to individuals behind the conventions of custom should be recognized in the operation of the courts. His position could almost be read as advocating that a capacity to judge what might be regarded as fair and reasonable, whatever the cultural or political circumstances, is a human universal.[28]

For these kinds of reasons, the anthropological literature on kinship and marriage in colonial Africa tended to focus on customary law, especially ascribed status, ownership, rights over property and over people. It traced the way that groups and statuses related to rights over land and cattle, how chiefly lineages held together, what was transferred at marriage, what was the domestic division of labour, and so on. The question of whether persons did or could 'own' things as distinct from 'receiving them only to give them away' did not arise. Even kinship itself has been treated in the Africanist literature as essentially a matter of the rights of some people over others, and how women, children, strangers, and so on were acquired or exchanged between groups to become kin much as cattle or commodities changed hands. There is no doubt that this model of African society as based on the management of rights, claims, and possessions entered the anthropological literature as a result of the interests of colonial authorities in developing a kind of modern justice among native peoples. There is, however, another factor, which has to be taken seriously, and that is the historical background of exploitative trade, including the slave trade, which dominated African social history for some centuries in the western parts of the continent and the Saharan regions, rather longer in the Nile Valley and northern Ethiopia, rather less on the eastern coast. Trade does turn things into commodities, by definition separable from the makers or their purchasers. When human beings are traded, they become, whether in the bodily sense (for a few) or in the conceptual imagination (for a much wider community), commodities. The idea that some persons have rights over others, up to and including ownership, can itself be transmuted into a variety of forms, and this itself is unquestionably a part of the complex pre-colonial history of Africa and the historical context in which anthropologists came to study. This is illustrated well by Charles Piot's accessible ethnography of Kabre villages in northern Togo, where he draws on ideas being developed in places like Melanesia and South America as well as Africa.[29] In questioning the simple equation of 'modernity' with recent one-way change, he traces the historical relation of present-day Kabre practices about gifts, persons, and 'kinship' to the days of the slave trade and the colonial encounter.

There is no doubt that from the beginning of scholarly accounts about the more accessible regions of Africa—say from the mid-nineteenth century—there was already tremendous upheaval, and a political history of population movements and the rise and fall of trade centres and kingdoms which no one could ignore. Populations were often dense, the land productive, and at least in the Nile Valley and coastal regions there was a long-established history of contact. There were local narratives relating to what was recognizably *political history*, and the facts of the outside world's impact could sarcely be screened out. Visions of a primal archaism simply did not hold for Africa (or Europe) in the way they perhaps did for Australasia or the Americas—perhaps there had been too much historical divergence away from intellectually interesting early forms such as envisaged in Allen's 'tetradic' model, or Lévi-Strauss's elementary structures. This might largely account for the conspicuous lack of attention given to African kinship systems in the work of the American evolutionist, Durkheimian, and structuralist schools. It is significant that anthropologists working in Africa gave more attention to the writers who had sought to find the basis of law in oriental societies; Henry Maine's pioneering work on India initiated the comparison of 'status' versus 'contract' as a substantive foundation of social order.[30] The concepts of social status, and role, and the transaction or transmission of rights, duties, and claims between holders of such positions came to be central in much research on African kinship, along with a set of questions about the way that groupings within society were composed and maintained over the long term. *Continuity of groups* and the *legitimate control of resources* were key concerns; and given the prevailing circumstances of political history in Africa, we can accept that these concerns were shared by public spokesmen (and they were mostly men) for the communities under study.

What are the key ideas about kinship and marriage which were formulated in the 'African colonial' period of British social anthropology? They often employed the notion of 'descent' as a backbone to what a kinship system might be. Now the idea of 'descent' in ordinary English becomes ambiguous when applied to all kinds of African kinship systems without further speci-fication, because it can refer to biological continuity, although it is perfectly well understood that the concept can legally have 'social' referents overriding the criterion of 'natural' kinship, as in adoption. In many of the ethnographic studies where 'descent' was employed as a technical term, the key idea was not necessarily biological continuity of bodily substance but 'jural' or cus-tomary legal membership of, or recruitment into, a social group. Where the idea of a common origin and continuity was emphasized, this was often pre-sented as a tribal genealogy, as it is in the Middle East. Groups thus defined were represented in the literature as 'descent groups'. Evans-Pritchard, as one of the key pioneers in this field, was quite clear in his famous studies of the Nuer pastoralists of the southern Sudan that he would follow the usage of the people themselves in distinguishing 'descent' as a political or jural concept distinct from ramifying personal kinship networks. Agnatic, or patrilineal, descent was the idiom in which groups rallied in a political manner, pursuing both conflicts and alliances, and defining collective territorial claims. The network of 'kinship' was called into play in interpersonal contexts or the arrangement of marriages, adoptions, and so on; here, the classification of kin was on different principles from that of agnatic descent. For example, there were four logically balanced categories of kin for every *ego*: those traced through the father's brother, the mother's brother, the father's sister, and the mother's sister. These were metaphorically represented on the model of a cow: relatives of the right hindleg, left hindleg, right foreleg, and left foreleg respectively. When bridewealth was collected in on the groom's side, and dis-tributed on the bride's side, these were the relevant categories, and not the patrilineages of the two parties as such. This is a common source of misun-derstanding about the Nuer, despite the clarity of Evans-Pritchard's accounts, and is a good example of the way in which anthropological discussion in a later period tended to merge notions of kinship in Africa with those of descent.[31] Since that time, in 'ordinary English' and in anthropological writings, 'descent' has slipped towards meaning one variety or another of continuing biological connection with the past and imagined future (see my further discussion in Chapter 10). Where there is no imagination of a corporate past or future, as has been claimed, for example, in relation to

Melanesia, it is certainly inappropriate to represent kinship as a kind of 'descent'.

The minimal use of 'descent' implies the concept of lines of continuity from one generation to another, a tracing which can be, for example, from father to son to son etc., or mother to daughter to daughter. Patrilineal or matrilineal genealogies can be remembered in this way, even where there are no 'descent groups' recruited on this basis. A number of further questions have then to be asked; first, what is the quality, the content, of this transmission from father to son and onwards, or mother to daughter and so on? Is it a matter of the passing on of some bodily characteristics through the physical act of reproduction, or is it simply a matter of laws about the transmission of property? How should a father be defined, that is, as the 'biological'/natural father, or the 'social'/legal father? Does the society in question make a distinction, and if so, how is this related to the laws of marriage? In a system like that of modern Britain, there are residual elements of all these aspects of the patrilineal idiom, for example in the transmission of surnames and parental responsibilities. But British society cannot be said to have patrilineal descent groups (with the possible exception of the royal family). Where there are such groups, it is then very important to ask how the next generations are recruited. Men do not simply give birth to their offspring. Does a patrilineal descent group perpetuate itself by marrying women from outside, or in other words is it an exogamous unit? Or does it seek to perpetuate itself largely through finding wives for its young men from within its own bounds, in other words, does it practise endogamy? In the former case, from a woman's point of view, she experiences a transfer at marriage from her father's group to that of her husband, but there are many variations in the way she (and her children) can continue to relate to her natal group, her children's 'mother's brothers'. In the latter case, a woman's life is likely to continue within the same community in which she was brought up; her uncle and aunt become her father- and mother-in-law, and she assists in arranging a marriage for her children within the same largely endogamous unit. While the official public description of a system like this (which, as I have mentioned, prevails in much of the Middle East) is likely to be in terms of 'patrilineal' descent, fostered over time through a preferred marriage between a boy and his patrilateral parallel cousin, it can readily be seen that because there are so many overlapping links between individuals in such a group it is always possible to trace alternative paths of connection. The links through women may be statistically as important as those through men, and attention to the women's point of view may yield a different perspective.[32]

The idea of a systematic tracing of a line of continuity from a mother to her children and her daughters' children is known as matriliny. As hinted above, this line may be imagined even where there is a public jural structure of patrilineal descent. Where the patrilineal connection is important for economic and political affairs, and for group membership, a matrilineal connection may nevertheless be of personal, moral importance, and even embody ideas of 'natural' or biological transmission.[33] Those societies which have developed a fully-fledged system of the organization of group membership and political economy upon the basis of the matrilineal principle have always been of particular interest to anthropologists, and it is a good idea for every student who finds this odd to study two or three in order to get the hang of things. One of the famous, and still flourishing, examples of a matrilineal society is that of the Ashanti kingdom of Ghana. The anthropologist Meyer Fortes was able to draw on a substantial earlier literature celebrating Ashanti's royal traditions and the conspicuous presence of Queen Mothers, its art, and its religion, and to analyse in sympathetic detail the way that matrilineal practices and values pervaded the whole. As a scholar with a wide range of field experience and also a particular interest in matters psychological and moral, he was able to pinpoint some of the really intriguing aspects of West African matriliny and to convey a sense of how deeply embedded its patterns were in distinctive notions about the human community, gender, and the make-up of the individual person.[34] Lévi-Strauss remarked that some of the best anthropology has been written about matrilineal societies, as they provoke perplexity and fresh thought.[35] In a more pragmatic vein, Robin Fox drew attention to some of the ground-level problems which follow from assuming that 'authority' is everywhere held by males, and that a stable sort of society is likely to combine the principles of co-residence with the harmonious exercise of authority and transmission of rights and duties among its members.[36] Thus, there was (for the functionalists who thought like this) what Audrey Richards identified as the 'matrilineal puzzle' of how a man could exercise authority over his wife and son but at the same time over his sister's son who was his heir, since they were likely to be living in different places. She showed how there were various compromise 'solutions' to this problem of combining continuity of authority with continuity of residence.[37] We could point out today that the logistical problem fades away if we stop thinking of 'authority' as a simple resource always held by males (especially fathers); and if we remember that while a society with patrilineal, patrilocal groups may seem harmonious to the men, and well-integrated to the outsider, it poses many logistical problems and personal dilemmas for the women. The whole 'puzzle' of matriliny arises from the classic scholar's expectation that a man should be 'in control' of his own children and that this will lead to a well-integrated society. As Engels saw long ago, this attitude has its own history, and we can accept in large measure that what he called 'the world-historical defeat of the female sex' has something to do with the rise of private property, capital, and the state.[38]

There are some particularly fascinating ethnographic cases where both patri- and matri-principles have been embraced, and even two overlapping sets of descent groups formed accordingly. Everyone belongs to one of each set, but membership is relevant in distinct spheres—for example, land and houses may be inherited in the first case, and moveable property and religious affiliation in the other. Daryll Forde presented such a system in a kind of 'ethnographic present' for the West African Yakö, while Richard Fardon has shown the variability of the relationship between patri- and matri-filiation over historical periods in parts of West Africa.[39] Yet other kinds of community may claim common 'descent', including some that are content to recruit people through any type of kin link (usually termed 'cognatic' descent groups) and some where the descent of a chiefly house is selected for emphasis and the admixture of ordinary hangers-on is conveniently left out. We would be wise to remember not only the hybridity of any real-life community but also the cross-sexuality of the roots of any individual—Jean-Loup Amselle writes of the 'originary interbreeding' which lies behind all identity.[40] More than one principle is always at work in the forms of sociality: some are working against each other—societies are not always harmonious or well integrated in any simple way. As I have hinted, men and women may not envisage a marriage system in the same way, and it is probably a human universal that those in a position of privilege or dominance are likely to see their opportunities in a more global, co-ordinated pattern or system than those whose opportunities are limited, hemmed in by poverty, remoteness, or entrenched low status. A slave may be spoken of as 'adopted kin' by a host family, but this may not be how it seems to the slave. Kinship is to a large extent a matter of rhetoric, and of its implementation in practice. Bloch has described all kinds of different situations in which 'kinship' terms are applied by both the state-forming Merina, and the forest-dwelling Zafimaniry of Madagascar, and reminded us of how often we too use ideas of brotherhood and the like in an expansive way, as a moral and tactical strategy in the relativities of social life.[41] At the same time, it is possible for tangible structure of a kinship kind to exist, and to be observed in all kinds of ways, without actually being verbalized or celebrated, as Bloch has shown for the presence of comprehensive moieties among the Zafimaniry.[42]

Against the background of the predominantly pragmatic interests of anthropology in the colonial period, we can now recognize a new generation of writing on kinship in Africa able to combine the pragmatic and political with the logical and poetic. At its best it is drawing on elements from British, French-language, and North American traditions in anthropology. The Belgian anthropologist Luc de Heusch combined structuralist and political interpretations for central Africa, while Africanist anthropologists are now attempting to trace the gender dialectics of given places through the history which has shaped them. Richard Fardon has shown for the various Chamba populations of Nigeria and the Cameroon how a historical perspective reveals shifts in the balance of rhetoric as well as advantage as between the mother's and the father's side of social continuity. Present-day oral histories of 'the Chamba' (a geographically and linguistically heterogeneous population spread over a wide area) focus either on the continuity of patri-clans in the context of stories of southward migration and conquest; or on the increasing ritual inclusiveness of settled communities in the north, defining themselves in the shape of matri-clans.[43] I myself presented an Ethiopian study pointing to the pragmatic robustness of what Lévi-Strauss and the alliance theorists had regarded on theoretical grounds as unstable patterns of exchange. Long-term cycles, such as those of ideal generalized exchange, promoted the 'integration' of society, but it was an integration that had more of a diagrammatic than a real-world meaning. Among the Gumuz of the western borders of Ethiopia, there is (or was at the time of my study) a thoroughgoing system of marriage by direct exchange between parties, cast in the idiom of the literal 'exchange of sisters' between men of different groups. This was not a general rule of marriage between two moieties, as no marriage could be repeated in the next generation. There was, rather, a fragmented pattern of overlapping short-term reciprocal ties—'short cycle' reciprocity of a kind puzzling for the structuralists, who could see no overall 'integration' in it. However, the question of integration looks quite different from the point of view of the long-term historical stability of such practices over a region. Among the Gumuz, there is evidence that over time, the overlapping pattern of short-term reciprocal ties not only persisted, but took on an increasingly exclusive and systematic form, in that other forms of marriage were outlawed, and gradually the system came to operate as a barrier against the penetration of the local social economy by outsiders, during and after a period when the Gumuz were subjected to slave-raiding.[44]

Don Donham, working in a part of Ethiopia less disturbed in modern times, has analysed the interpenetration of power and gender in the Maale kingdom. Like the other studies mentioned above, Donham's analysis echoes some of the recent themes in Melanesian anthropology discussed earlier. It rests on a set of questions about how the location and control of exchanges over productive and reproductive capacity is locally understood: but at the same time asks how this understanding relates to what we might see, broadly in a Marxist tradition, to be the more objective reality. Labour in the fields was the key limiting factor in the old Maale system of shifting agriculture (with supplementary activities such as animal rearing and bee-keeping). From a man's point of view, labour was given in tribute to those senior to oneself in a hierarchy which led up to the *kati*, or divine king. There were tributary relations between households, for example, a younger brother would be expected to give labour (and even crops and animals) to an elder brother, the elder brother would give to the subchief, he to the chief, and he to the king. In local rhetoric, there were also balanced exchanges of labour between households, but Donham's painstaking analysis demonstrated that younger brothers were working harder on their elders' fields than vice versa. Women were expected to work not so much for their household or husbands, as in a gendered collaboration with them, by virtue of their own reproductive capacity. They were not given much agency in themselves, however, being seen as recipients of male power, and were even spoken of as the 'earth in which seeds are planted'. They were *given* in marriage by their families, rather than exchanged (as in the Gumuz case) or even married in return for bridewealth. Children would nevertheless 'belong' to their father like the crops to a farmer. The wider relationship of senior to junior men in the political hierarchy was also modelled on this asymmetrical relation of gender, such that proper tribute payments would secure the prosperity and fertility of the giver. The king was seen as the most essentially male figure of all, who actually had males allocated to him in a conventionally transvestite role as 'wives'. As transcendent male, he was the source of all fertility in the kingdom, of subjects, rains, crops, and of child-bearing women. He conducted sacrificial rituals on behalf of the whole kingdom, and its past kings, to ensure this fertility. In parallel, each person who was 'senior' in the hierarchy conducted analogous rituals on behalf of those junior to them. Refusal of tribute or disputes at any level of the hierarchy were liable to incur the risk of infertility. Donham's point is that while the system turned on labour tribute, as well as on biological reproduction which requires as much input from women as from men, the local ideology turned on the idea of the gendered nature of productive powers, something always given and vested in others up the scale of maleness. Success in productivity and procreation was thus made to appear dependent on the 'fertility' bequeathed by others. Marx identified a fetishization of commodities in industrial society; Donham identifies an analogous fetishization of fertility, which like the former, actually screens out the importance and agency of human labour in social relations.[45]

Conclusion

The domain of relations between male and female itself shapes the forms of life in which children are born, brought up, and themselves participate in the further making of generative relations. Here we have to accept, in academic analysis as in everyday life, the entanglement of the social and cultural with the biological. We all know that human sexual encounter engages the mind as well as the body, and is impossible to think of except in contrast with the other kinds of social relation we have outside that encounter. Until the advent of artificially assisted reproduction (to be discussed in Chapter 10), sexuality, however refined and essentialized, even severely constrained, was also the sole source of human life; and its mythical and symbolic association with both life and death remain powerful. Relations between the sexes take up a larger proportion of human reason, emotion, poetry, worry, joy, legal argument, micro- (and occasionally macro-) politics than probably any other field of experience we basically share with the rest of the animal world. This has almost beyond a doubt been the case since the beginning of human history. Anthropologists have long regarded systematic comparison of the rules, regulations, symbolism, and ceremony of the male–female relation and the way these govern the raising of new generations as the core of their discipline. They have returned again and again to the ethnography of kinship and gender as a basic problematic of their field of study. It supplies a certain corrective to today's over-preoccupation with the isolated individual as the locus of all human-scientific inquiry. While accepting the profound importance of the subjective, anthropologists must always keep in mind the relevance of those social patterns in which any given person comes to define their subjectivity;

since it is through very particular patterns of marriage (and of course of a range of other liaisons, also specifically social, defined as extra-marital) that the person exists at all, and through which he or she will contribute to the birth of the next generation. The basic moral puzzle about how far our schemes of 'relatedness' to others are or should be rooted in the fact that we mate with and give birth to each other (whether within or without the conventional regulations) is one of anthropology's distinctive and still fascinating questions. It is now understood that sexuality itself is not simply a natural, biological attribute of individual human beings but highly responsive to social, cultural, and symbolic shaping and expression: part of our 'ceremonial' lives in the sense of that concept I have adopted in this book.

CHAPTER EIGHT

Human Bodies, Social Persons, and Conscious Selves

CAN we imagine such a thing as 'a person' in the abstract? Try. The figure which spontaneously comes to mind must surely have some very specific features—whether male or female, baby or adult, healthy or sick, hopeful or exhausted, happy or angry, Japanese or Irish, dressed or undressed, friend or stranger. Fairly soon, we need to ask not only 'What is a person?'—but in the suggestive phrase of Christina Toren, *who* they are. In criticizing 'natural science' models of the human person, she claims that for her, 'The fundamental question from an anthropological perspective is how do people become who they are?'[1] And yet an artificially generalized notion of the human person, the abstract individual, has been made a cornerstone not only of the experimental human sciences, but of much of the social sciences, as discussed above in Chapter 2. I shall return below to the question of how this has come about, and in Chapter 10 to the relevance of micro-studies of persons to the large-scale operations of today's world and the very important modern political debates about the status of the human person as such.

First we should recognize the fact that much abstract theorizing about 'society' has come to seem stale and lifeless. How can 'society' be thought of, it is asked, as something separate from the warm-blooded, thinking, living people who make it up? Why should we not focus on people as we find them, their consciousness, their feelings, their voices, and how they present themselves to the world? Are there not sides of human life which we have (rightly or wrongly) come to think of as outside 'society' anyway? There is at present a tide of feeling that Durkheimian sociology, for instance, has led to a neglect of 'the individual person' by its emphasis on the objectivity of social forms. And there is a burgeoning literature on 'the self' and a foregrounding of personal experience in the writings of many critics of social science, whether their own or that of those they study. These issues arise from the confrontation of two views of the human person: the question of 'legal' categories and definitions, versus the 'wholeness' of the human condition in an existential or phenomenological sense—often coming down to a question of 'the body' or the personal consciousness. These latter topics captured attention from many anthropologists in the late twentieth century. The sociocentric vision of the Durkheimian tradition in particular has been questioned, and Durkheim's views characterized as a kind of social determinism, a denial of the value of agency and individuality. A slightly hysterical note has sometimes crept into the championing of individual personality, choice, and the autonomy of the self.

However, no one is 'free' of their social context, any more than they can be of the specific language or languages they speak. Is it possible to retain the claims of a 'social science' vision, even in relation to modern human individuality and consumer-style autonomy? This is a core issue for anthropology today. A helpful way of entering our discussion here is to avoid any direct confrontation with Durkheim's ideas, which are often structured around a too-sharp dualistic 'opposition' of society and individual, and to consider instead some writings of Marcel Mauss, his nephew, colleague, and successor. Mauss is justifiably celebrated for his essay *The Gift*, but there are many other works from which we can also draw inspiration.[2] His late essay on the notion of person has recently become well known, but for reasons which will become clear, I shall not take this as my starting point but return to it below.

I. MAUSS'S TRIANGLE: THE ORGANIC, THE PSYCHOLOGICAL, AND THE SOCIAL

In a series of fairly short pieces written in the early 1930s, partly in the context of presenting arguments about the importance of sociology, or ethnology, to an audience of psychologists, Mauss put forward a model of the human condition as triangular; he argued that there are always present the three aspects of human existence: the organic, the psychological, and the social.[3] These are not separable elements to be analysed in isolation, by different sciences. They are three planes or dimensions of human life which meet together in each and every particular human being. Human existence is therefore an empirical 'totality' in which the organic, psychological, and social are co-present, always entailing and shaping each other, and he insisted that the analytical study of humanity should always recognize this. Mauss wrote of his conception as *l'homme total*. This is not easy to translate, because he is not indicating that the individual as such is a self-sufficient entity, let alone that this individual is of the male sex. 'The total man' will not do in English, nor can we satisfactorily work with 'the complete human being'—because of its clash with a very late modern symbolic ideal, to which few of us feel we have attained! The fact that we ourselves may feel 'incomplete' as a human being does not mean that organic, psychological, and social factors have not all contributed to our sense of predicament. In glossing Mauss's concept, therefore, we should avoid the notion of 'completeness' and use a phrase such as 'the totality of the human condition', or the study of 'humanity in its totality'. Today as much as ever, specific human sciences tend to develop tunnel vision, to narrow as they professionalize their special technical ideas in relation to the body or the mind, particularly in connection with the 'measurement' of behaviour or perception, and thus lose touch with the real-life complexity of these things.[4]

In developing his arguments, Mauss first considered how our physical lives, and the seemingly ordinary ways in which we use our bodies in walking, swimming, digging, and so on are shaped by learning and convention. The French way of walking is different from the American; the discipline of marching in various armies is clearly the product of training, but there are less 'consciously' trained ways of sitting, squatting, carrying objects, and so on. When it comes to questions of how the eyes are used in social encounters, how people use their bodies in sexual situations, in giving birth, or in illness, the 'social' aspect is again obvious when you think about it comparatively, but in every cultural tradition much has been internalized as 'natural' bodily behaviour. The same is true, and in tremendously significant ways for history, of the way we work productively in the fields or factories, and some of these points have been developed very effectively by Nathan Schlanger.[5] It is also relevant that we remember the importance of learning through practice in the formation of intellectual habits and its bearing on the formation of domains of knowledge, ordinary or specialist; Maurice Bloch's writings have already been introduced as a useful indicator of current anthropological interest in this field, and I touch on them again below.[6] Returning to Mauss, we can agree that the claims of psychology to explain all action in terms of conscious intention or even unconscious reason are difficult to apply across the board when we recall how much of our behaviour is scarcely thought out at all; much is purely 'responsive' in a given habitual situation. His concept of the totality of the human condition refers not to the individual as such, but to the multi-dimensional character of any human being as a site where organic, psychological, and social planes of existence meet. As a telling example, he points to the way that 'rhythms and symbols bring into play not just the aesthetic or imaginative faculties of a human being but their whole body and whole soul simultaneously'. Much behaviour is comparably responsive; it is not rationally thought out all the time, or intentionally communicative in the way that a psychologist might think of 'intention'. Mauss asks us to consider the mother who gets up when her child cries, the labourer who responds to the tool of his trade as much as he manipulates it, or the herdsman who 'drives' the animal which is actually leading him. These are 'instinctive' acts and reflexes illuminated by 'idea-signs', and through them our material and social life is constituted (an image of the exchange and circulation of the *elements of significant action* which he uses also in the context of the dance, as I have discussed above in Chapter 4). Human beings commune and communicate through such acts and in grasping this, Mauss claims, we may be able to understand 'the mass movement or group movements that constitute social phenomena'.[7]

Mauss went on to argue a much more difficult point, that social convention can directly affect organic existence to the point where a collective expectation of death in certain circumstances can result in a person actually dying, without that event being explicable in terms of the person's own psychological state. Now psychologists and physiologists today are much more sensitive than they were in Mauss's time to factors in the social environment, such as stress, which can have direct organic effects on the body through the switching on of genes which (even in other primate species) release chemicals influencing mood. Matt Ridley explains that the outside world, for example an impending exam, can cause stress resulting in a rise in the hormone cortisol, which switches various genes on, suppressing the immune system. This enables the body to rise to the challenge of 'fight or flight' from danger, but at the same time you are more susceptible to colds and flu around the exam season. Is the conscious brain in charge, or the genes, or the social situation? There are mutually affecting links in all directions. Interestingly, Ridley notes the presence of 'social' pressures resulting in physically evident stress even among low-status monkeys in zoos.[8] These observations seem to confirm Mauss's insight about the direct impact of social phenomena upon the body and psyche, an insight almost prophetic in relation to the later development of the human sciences.

Thus Mauss diverges from the dualistic conception of the human condition which was so central in the work of his mentor, Émile Durkheim: a dualism of individual and society, of material body and spiritual soul, of profane and sacred. Against Durkheim's *homo duplex* he pleads for a more secure grasp of the integrated character, not just of the whole or 'concrete' human being, but of the human condition in its totality. In the life of human beings, the organic, psychological, and social intersect with each other, and no form of human science which is limited to one of these dimensions can be sufficient unto itself. When Mauss claims some exemption for a minority of the educated (and male) elite, who are supposedly able to exercise more conscious self-control over impulsive response than can women and the lower classes, we have to remember the ethos of the time and the fact that these comments were made as part of an oral address to a group of distinguished and no doubt all male clinicians—and perhaps make allowances; his evocation of the 'totality' of human beings nevertheless strikes an important resonance with current issues in anthropology.

Nor is the relevance of his vision limited to social existence thought of in the 'behavioural present'. He points out that the attitudes, or dispositions, of people in relation to the world, built up through education in the broad sense, engage their memory, and their expectations. Such memory and expectation are built into historical phenomena, to the workings of the law, art, and the economy—as is clear when we think of speculation, credit, and even the nature of money. He considers that the study of moral expectation and illusion is particularly fruitful, and that war makes us aware of such things. The reference here is to the First World War, of which Mauss himself had direct experience.[9] His remarks clearly place the dispositions and expectations of people within history. For him the human being is within, not outside, the passage of time and the chain of large historical events, and good ethnography and anthropological analysis should recognize that the specificity of what has happened in the past is generally present as part of expectation at any particular moment (and therefore must enter into any explanation of action). The passage of time also links us to each other in ways we cannot escape; whether considered socially, psychologically, or 'simply' organically. The very concepts of what a person may be are not only internal to that person, but include his or her links with or separation from others. All persons, even in their self-consciousness, are thus *placed* historically.

Bloch has drawn on some of his students' work to illustrate this point. When we consider the enduring community of the Sadah, descendants of the Prophet Mohammed and therefore a religious élite in Yemen, and poor peasant communities of the lowland Philippines, we find a profound difference in the way that self-understanding relates to historical process. The distinctive standing of the Sadah is attributed to past scriptural authority vested in them and maintained partly through patrilineal descent, made exclusive through endogamous marriage. They do not see themselves as changing, but almost as the same people reproducing themselves outside the tides of history. The Philippine peasants' view of the nature of a person is not definitively given at birth in this way, but as in other South-East Asian systems of ideas, negotiated in the course of a life's journey as the past is left behind and the future opens up to more opportunity. Following a complex history of colonization, they see themselves as responsive to changing conditions of history and fashions, adopting foreign ways with ease and negotiating with powerful other peoples they cannot evade.[10] History and memory, Bloch suggests, are internal rather than external to them as persons. In these cases, comparison shows that the very notion of what a person is cannot be generalized; we could add that even a psychologist conducting interviews, or a philosopher reflecting on the human sense of self, would have to recognize that here they are faced with more than the subjective, and that historical study of the very categories in which their subjects think of themselves has to be taken into account.

This point brings us to Marcel Mauss's well-known 1938 essay which is usually known as 'The category of the person' (a fuller rendering of the French would be 'A category of the human mind: the notion of the person, the idea of "myself"').[11] This essay offers a broadly evolutionary story of the way that the modern idea of individual autonomy, moral character, and agency has developed, in the context of *droit et morale*, that is, legal and customarily sanctioned practice. It is suggested that in primeval tribal society there was no such notion embodied in rules, that people were simply carriers of some predefined role or identity, in the way that Pueblo dancers today might endlessly re-enact the spirits of their ancestors, or Kwakiutl might wear the masks of their clans, thus embodying their forebears in material representation according to a timeless blueprint of the social whole. With the Greeks and Romans, things began to change, with the development of explicit rights for citizens; and Western civilization has built on this with the rise of philosophical

FIG. 18. Fonteyn: with mask, 1937. Photo: Sasha/Hulton Archive HG1051/ Getty Images.

writings on individual consciousness and reason and Judaeo-Christian ideas of the individual soul before God. The modern idea of the person, Mauss points out, has come to be something taken for granted; but by considering the ethnographic record we can see how long and complex it is. There are many deep insights in this essay, and it has been defended with some energy by Nick Allen.[12] It is important to note that some criticisms of its apparent relativism and failure to allow for the presence of a subjective sense of self everywhere are not justified. Mauss makes it clear that while we can acknowledge a universally felt sense of self, the publicly celebrated and stylis- tically marked aspects of individual autonomy in the modern West are a quite specific social phenomenon.

We could nevertheless make other criticisms: for the modern idea of personal rights, and those of personal equality which mark today's ideology, have not simply evolved in the rather quiet way that Mauss's essay implies. They have been fought over, starting with various riots of slaves and plebs in the ancient world, passing on to the French revolution (to cut history rather short) and continuing with the suffragette and anti-racist movements of our own times. People have died for the freedoms which Mauss sees enshrined in the modern theory of the person, and those freedoms have been articulated against earlier forms which have come to be seen as oppressive. The 'evolution' of the idea of the person is thus entangled with the dialectics of struggle entailed in the rise of the modern economy and nation-state. A Pueblo or Kwakiutl tribesman, or a Roman slave-soldier, with a grievance against his neighbour, had no access to resources or a legal framework within which to pursue his rights *against personal oppression* as a modern person in a modern country (usually) can. Nor until very recent times could women exert independent economic or legal rights outside the framework of marriage; the argument is now passing on to the rights of children, and even our kin among the higher primates.

What we can certainly take very seriously from Mauss's essay is that the modern category of the person, with all its private rights and self-possession, does indeed have a history. And further, as Mauss himself points out, it is a fragile 'Idea', whose future we cannot predict. From our perspective today, we see the idea in rhetorical form extended across the world to the whole of humanity, while conditions on the ground are sometimes at variance, especially in the absence of basic political security and the rule of law backed by stable government. Western liberalism over the rights of refugees, women, and children in developing countries, some with strong political ideologies of their own, can come up against hard realities. Even 'at home', in the USA and Europe, new claims to individual rights are being pressed not on the basis of the equality of individuals, but on the special interests of minorities, sometimes newly self-defined minorities, as the frameworks spread for recognizing difference based on racial origin, cultural heritage, or gender, and sexual orientation.[13] These were the very kind of criteria which the 'modern' idea of the person, as discussed by Mauss, was supposed to transcend. The new promotion of personal identities in democratic countries, however, takes place within the general protection of citizens by the modern law, and does not leave all social protection to the organization of 'identity' as such. In the turbulent countries of the post-colonial (including post-socialist) world the same basic protection of persons as such is very fragile, and identity politics can become deadly.

We shall return later to this question of 'the modern person' and current formulations of 'identity' in relation to the market and other features of today's global society (Chapter 10). In the rest of the present chapter, I set out briefly some of the pressures which have made 'social' anthropology more aware of the bodily and psychological dynamics of human life, enlivening a former curiosity about norms, customs, and the rules and regulations of society as such. After touching on the recent growth of anthropological interest in 'bodily' matters, I focus on the way that body, society, and person are mutually implicated at the margins of our lives; this has been recognized in classic treatments of death, but is less often appreciated in the circumstances of our conception, gestation, and survival through infancy. I then turn to consider some cross-cultural studies of subjectivity in respect of emotion, consciousness, and intellect—or 'cognitive anthropology'. Ethnographic cases, including some from 'close to home', illustrate the contextuality of our ways of knowing, especially of knowing persons, and provide further illustration of the relevance of the Maussian triangle.

Body: a shift from 'social facts' to the material locus of human existence and experience

In the 1960s, Victor Turner and Mary Douglas were writing about the relation between body and society, revealing ways in which we draw on bodily idioms in representing the social world. Turner showed how bodily substances, such as blood, milk, and excreta, come to signal moral depth in particular sorts of kinship or social relation; and Douglas highlighted our widespread use of bodily motifs in talking about boundaries, strong centres, and vulnerable margins in the context of social relations. Both Turner and Douglas also showed how ideas about illness and healing practices, and thus the sufferings of individual subjects, were underpinned by these fundamental 'collective representations' of the body in society.[14] Godfrey Lienhardt's powerful literary evocation of the personal qualities of Dinka religious experience in his study of 1961 has already been discussed in Chapter 5, and the deep connections of religious and medical phenomena became a focus of his student Jean Buxton's later study set among the nearby Mandari people. In the early 1960s too Merleau-Ponty's influential book *Phenomenology of Perception* was published, and David Pocock was characterizing the key turn in post-war anthropology as a shift from 'function' to 'meaning'. His own first monograph on India had a fairly conventional format dealing with caste and kinship, but his second was entitled *Mind, Body, and Wealth*, and, matching perhaps the general change of direction, endeavoured to convey to the reader what it was actually like to live and grow up in an Indian village permeated by the very bodily concerns of caste purity. Pocock later elaborated upon the whole idea of a 'personal anthropology', contributing directly to some of the 'reflexive' consciousness of today's researchers.[15] By the mid-1980s, the 'anthropology of experience' had become a creative research field, inspired partly by Victor Turner's later work in collaboration with specialists in performance studies and social psychology.[16]

It was the rise of 'women's studies' in anthropology from the early 1970s, however, and its later metamorphosis into the anthropology of gender, that really put the human body, its experience and subjectivity/reflexivity with respect to others onto the research agenda. Kinship diagrams had so little life, and descriptive ethnographies of social structure seemed not only bloodless but blind to the presence of women in a way that suddenly seemed to contradict human realities. Why were women absent from, or silent in, so many works of anthropology spanning the globe? The question then arose as to how far the life experiences of women are common to them as a category; and how far does 'culture' or 'society' subordinate women universally. One of the results of these debates was a recognition that people relate to 'society' in different ways, from more different perspectives and personal experiences than the ethnographic observer or rationalist sociologist might suppose. The life of a man and of a woman, for a start, are not easily reduced to a common denominator. Marx had long ago pointed out the difference between class perspectives; now we could no longer assume consensus across gender perspectives. Feminist scholarship achieved a turn-over in the agenda of the social sciences, and particularly perhaps in anthropology, a subject so dependent upon personal engagement as a method of inquiry (see my discussion of this shift in the previous chapter).

Following a pioneer collection edited by John Blacking on *The Anthropology of the Body*, which included essays on medical topics as well as dance and body language, there has been a flood of books and papers dealing in one way or another with the body in a 'touchy-feely' way. A recent example is Michael Lambek and Andrew Strathern's collection *Bodies and Persons*, deliberately comparing Melanesian and African cases to bring together the best new ideas from people working in these two different regional traditions of ethographic writing. Others have focused on topics such as body-building, diet and food, vegetarianism, meat-eating, physical sexuality, and so on, from a tangible, subjective perspective, as distinct from the formal sociological approaches of an earlier period. For example, in relation to food, there were studies in the 1960s which emphasized social manners and cultural styles of presentation and consumption. We remember Lévi-Strauss's abstract analogies on 'the raw and the cooked'; and Mary Douglas, on what is edible and what is not in a given cultural scheme, and on how to decipher a meal. There were studies of 'cannibalism' as mainly a symbolic idea 'in the mind', rather than a medical reality. However, food is not merely a currency of social etiquette or symbolism. There are few things more 'bodily' than food and drink; but recent work in anthropology and 'cultural studies' has shown how through such material media, and their direct organic effects on the body, people convey social messages and develop their self-image in relation to others. Pat Caplan has drawn together essays by British anthropologists on eating in, eating out, food on holiday, health and heart attacks, wedding cakes, and diet in general as a marker of difference. This flow of studies is matched in America; for example, the in-depth study by Carole Counihan linking the anthropology of food and the body with gender and power and drawing on fieldwork in Sardinia and Florence. The shift from what Mary Douglas called 'implicit meanings' to the very explicit significance of bodily matters can be seen also in the field of illness and healing. Instead of probing for foundational religious explanations and 'symbolically' efficacious ritual treatments, anthropologists came to recognize the realities of bodily conditions and substantive material treatments in illness. A recent example of field-based research on these lines is Maia Green's study of the use of medicines and other substances in rural areas of Tanzania. Both attitudes to, and organic effects of, substances have come to be central in research concerning alcohol, drugs such as cola or *khat*, hallucinogens, and medicines old and new, including self-administered antibiotics. The burgeoning literature in all kinds of medical anthropology reflects this turn from 'theories' of illness towards the material bodily basis of our existence, and the techniques we use to manipulate, improve, or heal the bodies of the sick or enhance our own lives through the use of physical discipline or the ingestion of substances. In China, as Elisabeth Hsu has shown, such techniques and treatments are devoted as much as anything to cosmic harmony, while in the individualistic, consumerist West they are promoted as a means to the deliberate cultivation of the self.[17]

Sexuality is a further aspect of 'bodily' life which has come onto the agenda in recent anthropology. Most pre-1960s ethnography tended to assume one stereotype or another of sexuality in tribal society: either that the customary rules and regulations of family discipline kept sexuality very much within the laws of marriage; or that in 'primitive' societies, there was an extraordinary degree of sexual freedom. Despite its eye-catching title, Malinowski's monograph *The Sexual Life of Savages in Northwest Melanesia* did not really demonstrate the degree of personal sexual freedom it evoked in principle for the matrilineal Trobrianders who were ignorant of physical paternity. Margaret

Mead did claim to have found this kind of freedom in what became the type case of Samoa, where by comparison with the repression and constraints of American teenage life, youths and maidens were at liberty to experiment without fear or guilt. However, interestingly, Mead found the opposite in her study of the formal discipline and parental constraint in Manus, New Guinea. Her work has been criticized for its impressionism and exaggeration, but at least she did attempt to look into the question of sexuality as an aspect of personal and emotional bodily life, over and beyond the formal rules and regulations of marriage and kinship.[18] It was some decades after his original fieldwork that Evans-Pritchard published some fairly intimate vernacular accounts of sexual life, including lesbianism, among the Azande,[19] and anthropologists are only now making sexuality a main focus of their studies (as against noting a few transgressions of customary law, or exceptional ritual acts of a sexual nature).

Recent useful works include a collection on *Sex and Violence* and one on *Dislocating Masculinity*. Angela Hart has studied prostitution, from the clients' point of view, in a Spanish Catholic town, and Heather Montgomery has investigated child prostitution, including the homosexual trade for Western clients, in Thailand, as far as she can from the children's point of view.[20] Both projects attempt to get behind the formal categorizing of the sex trade as illicit and the moral condemnation of those who participate in it, to admit the unrecognized scale of unofficial sexual activity in so many contexts and to understand how people, including children, live within it, partly drawing on the mores of their former home life and partly constructing a new world of justifications. Suzette Heald's studies of masculinity, sexuality, and ritual in East Africa, especially among the Gisu, draw explicitly on the mores of vernacular culture, and also take the story on to their encounter with today's circumstances.[21] Heald has been able to use her ethnographic understanding of African societies to criticize some of the stereotypes of casual 'sexual networking' assumed to be 'traditional' by many of those working with AIDS studies in Africa. She has been able to show how sexual relations in rural societies are hedged around with careful restrictions and prohibitions, being seen not only as a fruitful source of life but also as a dangerous source of death; and that the 'networking' now commonly found in towns is no more a product of traditional cultural values than would be true for towns and cities and migrant populations anywhere. The way in which modern life has shaped private sexuality, and made it an appurtenance of intense personal identity as distinct from being just one aspect of our relations with other people, was investigated by Foucault, and his work has illuminated how closely the intimate side of life is everywhere linked with the public and the political.[22] We should also note that anthropologists have paid fresh attention in recent years to the realities of incest and child sexual abuse. Not so long ago, incest was regarded in anthropology as an imagined construct of behaviour totally incompatible with the rules of exogamy human beings had everywhere constructed. However, a growing public realization of the real possibilities of cruelty within the family, and of the oppression of children by adults in general, has forced anthropologists to rethink this problem. Jean la Fontaine has been able to show that while there is a great deal of fantasy surrounding accusations of satanic ritual abuse of children in Britain, the reality of sexual exploitation is undeniable and at a disturbing level.[23]

Towards mind, feeling, and consciousness

Beyond the body, anthropologists have come to reflect upon the mind. Many consider today that we need to put the conscious individual back in the centre of our inquiries, and not feel shy of moving into fields once monopolized by psychology and philosophy. I believe that the shift from a sociocentric to an egocentric style of anthropology (if you wish) was under way before any of the relevant philosophical writings were being cited by anthropologists, and would probably have taken place without their prompting. However, reference began to be made to the theoretical school we now know as 'phenomenology', to Merleau-Ponty's work mentioned above and to the German predecessors identified and discussed there, Heidegger and Husserl.[24] These philosophers had sought the realities of the world as we know it in our experiencing selves, and in feeling as much as in intellectual perception. Their arguments have resonated with the concerns of many anthropologists in recent years, and have helped shape a wave of new writings concerned with the existential realities of life, of 'being' or 'dwelling' in the world. These writings have drawn attention to the commonalities of human life and the basic organic foundations of existence we share with each other and even with other animal species. They have criticized the division between 'nature' and 'culture' as an obstacle to understanding how the individual melds elements of both together in journeying through his or her own 'lifeworld'. The story of individuals is seen as a process of self-directed growth, and of maturing experience, and of interactions with others gradually creating meaningful patterns over time. A distinguished exponent of this approach is Tim Ingold, who has developed these ideas in several contexts. For example, he has very helpfully criticized the view that our genetic make-up at birth predisposes us in a passive way to respond to and absorb as wholes the various kinds of culture we are exposed to. He has again very constructively emphasized the way in which we learn in a cumulative way, building on skills already acquired through the application of 'educated attention' in environmental contexts of experience and learning throughout our lives.[25]

The appeal of this line of inquiry is strong, and helps overcome much of the stuffy formalism still prominent in both the sociological and the biological sciences. On the social side, however, it bypasses the problem of recognizing the regularities in our mutual interactions and collaborations. A view from self-experience cannot account for the grammar of language, or the choreography of dance, by adding up the sentences we happen to speak or steps we happen to perform. How would an approach from phenomenology begin to describe the enduring historical qualities of Shakespeare? A second serious difficulty is that like all approaches basically starting from individual subjectivity, phenomenology cannot handle differences of scale in social and political life. Is there no essential difference between the encounter of two heads of state, on the one hand, and two fishwives, on the other? Is there no difference between foraging for one's fruit and veg in the forest and apparently doing much the same thing in a supermarket (where everything is physically available but prices are decided by people and financial systems way beyond one's ken)? Is the 'lifeworld' of a peasant in peacetime basically the same when he (or indeed she) becomes a soldier during war? The best sociology has always attempted to keep the 'macro' level in view, to understand its systematicity, and to relate micro-social studies to it. The real challenge for 'experiential' anthropology is to do the same.

A parallel challenge faces those anthropologists who have pondered the sources of our individual consciousness and ways of knowing the world by seeking inspiration from psychologists and philosophers oriented more to the intellect than to the emotions. Even animal consciousness is increasingly understood as discriminating, in respect of environmental intelligence and also coded communication with other creatures of the same or even different species. Is it not essentially in this respect, whether by degree or qualitatively, that human consciousness is distinctive? Is it not a question of our greater capacity than the other animals for deliberate reason, logical thought by a mind operating independently of body, in the tradition of Descartes? The aim of demonstrating rationality and 'intellect' as operating in all human communities was a concern of anthropology up to the middle of the twentieth century, because of the prevalence of stereotypes and even professional theories of 'primitive mind' which denied it to those who had not yet attained a 'civilized' state. Today we accept that while all human beings are capable of 'rationality', this is a very narrow conception in itself of 'reason', and even so, absolutely nobody is ruled by reason alone; intellect and feeling are linked. We have a good deal of ethnography about 'abnormal' states of consciousness, for example, dreaming or trance, identifiable as distinct phenomena out there because of their abnormality; but not very much about the comparative study of 'normal everyday' consciousness. As Anthony Cohen has pointed out, this is something extraordinarily difficult to pinpoint; we lose our focus when we turn it back on itself and try to objectify it, even though the philosophers have written plenty to guide us.[26] Not every cultural tradition has a discourse about 'the mind'; Godfrey Lienhardt pointed out that the Dinka, for example, do not have a term we can translate 'mind'. Some commentators have asked the ultimately absurd question as to whether this means we can simply say that the Dinka do not have minds (echoing the way that early Spanish missionaries wondered whether the indigenous American peoples had souls).[27] It is only very recently that ethnographers have begun to investigate just how people 'think the mind works' or account in possibly other ways, in their own discourse and theory, for feelings or types of consciousness, understanding, and the capacity for decision-making. This kind of ethnography is beginning to show how far such discourse and theory often relates, not to abstractions of a metaphysical or religious kind in isolation, as Cartesian or modernist Christian theory might have predicted, but to ways in which the body-and-psyche is thought to work together as a field of conscious forces both within itself and in relation to others. This is the special field of 'cognitive anthropology' or psychological anthropology.

A pioneering work here was a collection edited by Paul Heelas and Andrew Lock on *Indigenous Psychology*.[28] It has been succeeded by a large literature, extending, for example, from the professional medical anthropological studies of Roland Littlewood to the self-reflecting literary mirror which Nigel Rapport holds up to his own, and his readers' own, forms of and discourses about self-consciousness in *Questions of Consciousness*.[29] Cohen and Rapport, along with the contributors to this last volume, are not looking for the organic basis of animal-comparable consciousness, but seeking to identify what it is that completes that dimension in the making of a human being.

They do not pursue the sense-laden subjectivity of event-awareness to the extent of the phenomenologists we have discussed above. They are similarly concerned with dwelling 'in the world', but that world is more than forests and wildlife, it is a social world inhabited by others who are both like and unlike oneself, which is rather different, because it provides the frame within which we theorize ourselves as agents having certain kinds of (socially conceptualized) consciousness. Christina Toren has investigated the ways that children in Fiji develop a sense of themselves through exploring the social world around them—not just 'the environment' however conceived, but an interactive game-playing world in which they learn not only who other people are but who they are seen to be themselves in the patterns of kinship and social hierarchy.[30] She makes the pointed observation that 'intersubjectivity is the primary condition of human being in the world', and regards as micro-history the way that forms of sociality are transmitted through interaction between the generations. Because the human personality to a degree makes itself through specific micro-historical processes of engagement, 'natural science' models of mind are bound to be inadequate; 'For when we come to consider the ontogeny of any given human being, at any time of life and in any time or place, it becomes clear that the biological, the psychological, and the sociocultural are not discrete functional domains, but fused aspects of a unitary phenomenon—the phenomenon of autopoiesis'—that is, of self-making, something that all animals do, but (borrowing Orwell's words not Toren's) human animals do better than others.[31]

We have today a wide range of studies which would place individual consciousness, action, intention, self-reflection, emotion, and experience at the heart of comparative study. While some of these seek to dislodge the Durkheimian legacy by focusing on the singularity and autonomy of persons everywhere, most also make quite clear that the field of social interaction itself has a singularity and a historical existence and mode of transmission. Several could arguably be woven back into the Durkheimian tradition, especially if we accord Mauss a key role in the transmission of that tradition.

2. THE BEGINNINGS AND ENDINGS OF PERSONS

However free the person may feel themselves to be, this feeling disappears in episodes of illness; and even more sobering to remember, every life has its time limits. At death, and even at birth, the individual in question has very little or no 'agency' or 'rational choice' or autonomous selfhood, certainly no 'ego'. At these bodily margins of life, not only 'identity' but organic existence itself is conferred by others upon oneself. The individual psyche is not so much *conscious of itself*, as *others are conscious of it* in their own way of thinking. This is generally accepted in the sociology of death, but less often in the case of birth, where the complexity of social specifications has not often been considered. What is the nature of 'being in the world' for very early human organisms? They would not exist at all without the intentional and socially directed efforts of others.

Death

It is well known that in the context of death, social definitions come to dominate organic events. There are funerals, inquests, registrations, burial markers, and final memorial rites. Because of its obvious and evident prominence in the social lives of the living, death has received a large amount of attention in anthropology. A classic piece was written by Hertz at more or less the same time as van Gennep's landmark study of rites of passage. Hertz emphasized the way in which death rites marked, in their imagery, a continuing process of collective life within society, even a rebirth, despite organic decay and the loss of a member. Recent important work still draws on these studies.[32] The deeply difficult question of what happens to body, personality, and social position at death, and what is the responsibility of the survivors, permeates modern hi-tech and medicalized society as it has troubled earlier historical periods. Where should we draw the line between personhood and mere organic human matter? For example, there is a new medical definition of 'brain stem death', which can be applied in cases where a human being is being kept alive in a bodily sense, heart and lungs working because of artificial stimulation, but where there is no apparent brain function. When the patient is a potential donor of organs for transplant, the fresher they are the better, hence the pressure on doctors to declare that the patient is brain dead and 'unplug' the apparatus. The definition of death in this situation is controversial, as the patient still looks normal and is breathing. Relatives are consulted for their permission, but however rationally they respond, it is an extremely distressing situation. It also tends to receive a lot of publicity, as death situations do in any case. There are always more death announcements than birth announcements in the papers, and more people present at a funeral or memorial gathering than a birth or child's first birthday. However, it is not only at the end of human life that dilemmas over the organic, social, and 'spiritual' aspects of a person occur.

Physical birth and social beginnings

The new definitions of legal death are nowhere near as controversial as current modern debates over the beginnings of legal personhood. The problem has been heightened by precise and changing forms of both medical technique and of the law. We might at first think that the dilemmas over early personhood are only found in technically advanced conditions, but it is important to recognize that debates of this kind are not peculiar to 'us'. Debates and contested claims over the definition, even recognition, of the beginnings of the human person, while they vary in content, are in some ways mutually resonant across the world, as the ethnographic record sometimes reveals. However, this is a tricky area, being so often the province of women, discreetly dealt with and not at all as accessible to the observer as the rituals of death.

Apart from royal families, birth has always tended to be seen as a pre-social event, a matter of mere biology. However, there is good reason for us to revise this view. First let us consider the *couvade* as practised by the Huaorani of the Amazonian lowlands of Ecuador, and as analysed by Laura Rival.[33] *Couvade* is conventionally understood as a set of taboos or restrictive practices affecting the father of a child during the time that his wife is actually expecting a child, giving birth, and caring for it in infancy. These practices have often been presented as a kind of symbolic mimicking of the biological processes of gestation and the post-natal vulnerability of women. This dualistic approach lends itself to elaboration of body versus spirit, the father bringing the child's spirit into the social world as the mother brings its body forth. Laura Rival emphasizes, by contrast, that at least for the Huaorani, both parents play an active and complementary role in the material and moral aspects of the pro-creative process. For Huaorani, the child is the product of shared substance, of a combination of blood and semen involved in an extended process of growth. Repeated sexual relations assist the development of the foetus, and the role of the father in nourishing the mother during pregnancy is also important. There is no sharp line between biology and society or between the respective relationship of the parents to the child at the moment of birth itself. *Both* parents observe the kind of restrictions conventionally associated with *couvade*, that is perinatal dietary rules and limitations on physical activity. Huaorani men do not *imitate* birth: they take an active part in it, often as midwives. The father will massage the mother's body during labour, he may assist in delivery with his own hands, he cuts the umbilical cord, and assists his mother-in-law with every task. For later births especially, he is in charge. While it is the official father who cuts the cord, other men who have had sexual relations with the mother and thus contributed to the growth of the child may also observe some of the *couvade* taboos. Here we find a multiplicity of links, blurring the line between consanguineal and affinal kin, and between the biological and social aspects of kinship.

The child is welcomed like a guest, fed by its immediate parents, and gradually becomes part of the longhouse-sharing economy, a person in the full sense. The *couvade* observances are the initial way of marking public acceptance of the new life. A non-desired child is not welcomed in this way. The fact of an actual birth is not as significant socially as is the pre- and perinatal acknowledgement conferred by the *couvade*, and without it the child will be buried with the afterbirth. In other words, the social definition of the beginning of personhood, along with social bonding, starts before birth and carries on as a process of co-parenthood afterwards.

This account of the Huaorani case marks a departure. The bodily events of conception, gestation, and birth are often sharply distinguished in anthropological writing from the rituals which mark the naming, and final social identity, of a child. But these events are separate in time, and there is often very little said about what lies in between them. There are abstract theories of the origin of individual human existence, but these rarely meet up with the point at which, in orthodox social theory, society gives a new member a name and a conventional status. Somewhere within this large gap, filled with all sorts of imaginings from myth, science, and religion, a significant sociomoral identification takes place: what Marcel Mauss has called the 'recognition' of an individual child. 'Recognition' is not a public formality of naming or baptism, but a pragmatic and sometimes quite private acceptance, conferring on the embryo, foetus, or infant at the least a provisional understanding of where it has come from and an extension of basic physical care, in order that it may live and grow.[34]

In the historical development of medicine, Western science has typically 'naturalized' the pre-birth space as an area for investigation and experiment, though often in the face of religious counter-views, as illustrated from medieval times up to this very day. Joseph Needham in his wonderful book on the history of embryology ridiculed not only 'the charms and incantations of barbarous midwives'[35] but also the eighteenth-century doctors—of divinity —at the Sorbonne, who recommended intra-uterine baptism by syringe. He claimed that there was no place for ethics in biology.[36] But if ethics were entirely detached from the world of organic life, what on earth would it be about? Ethics and biological life do seem to meet as a matter of practical morality in relation to events, such as childbirth, which demand that the plurality of 'narratives' give way to the singularity of decision. It is still very common for both lay people and specialists in medicine and science to regard the space and time before birth, and even the perinatal time, as a matter of basic biology. 'Society' begins later. Helen Callaway was one of the first anthropologists to criticize these assumptions, but the arguments are still with us.[37]

Early anthropology often reported infanticide and abortion among tribal peoples as merely a matter of good environmental sense, by implication arrogating to the Judaeo-Christian tradition any social predicament or moral sensitivity in relation to the unborn. This picture was often linked in anthropological writing with a portrait of primitive woman as the most pure expression of natural organic fertility, popping behind a tree and giving birth like a cat with kittens.[38] This image of primeval womanhood is, I believe, among the most unjust, and unjustifiable, of all those in the lumber-room of modern anthropology.

In reviewing the (mainly nineteenth-century) literature on infanticide available to him, Westermarck softened the bleak picture of this practice as simply rational population control. Customary expectations were not always 'sufficiently great to silence the voice of parental love'. He gives a long list of exceptions; considers that some authorities have exaggerated the prevalence of the custom, quotes an authority who considers that 'the Australian Black is himself ashamed of it'; that the arrival of whites may in some cases, such as among the Californian Indians, have provoked the practice; and that many peoples and civilizations had compensating forms of adoption for unwanted children. He notes ironically that while the pagan world was indifferent to the sufferings of the exposed infant, the early Christian world came to treat the sinning woman with great cruelty; up to the early nineteenth century infanticide was treated as a capital offence everywhere in Europe.[39]

Among the farming and animal-rearing Chagga who live on the forested slopes of Kilimanjaro in Tanzania, for example, according to a study of 1940, there were elaborate theories of prenatal development, and a series of special feasts during pregnancy which drew in a widening range of relatives. During this time crucial life or death decisions could be made about the expected child. As soon as 'the new life announces itself' (presumably by foetal movement), the woman should inform her mother-in-law that 'If God pleases, I am no more one person but two in my heart'. If she does not, her husband's family will suspect that the child is not theirs. For while Chagga value fertility very highly, this is only within marriage. The concerns of a husband's family were directed to this question, and they would observe the behaviour of the newborn in accepting or rejecting food from them being a sign of legitimacy. They and the local chief were also concerned about 'normality' in the foetus and infant (a long list of bad omens were spoken of). If illegitimacy or abnormality were suspected, there should theoretically be abortion or infanticide; but pressure from the husband's side, or from the chief, was resisted in a whole range of ways by the mother, her brother, and his family, who sought fresh opinions from diviners, etc.; and in a large number of cases, delay itself saved the child. The very passage of time, especially after an infant was delivered, thus served to give substance, we could say, to the idea of mutual 'kinship' with it on at least somebody's part. It is possible to argue that the Chagga engaged in a variety of 'legal', moral, and practical arguments over extending social recognition to the products of human conception which show parallels to those of the modern West.[40]

There is always uncertainty, provisionality, in the imagined space of pre-birth, and what might arrive from it. For the Gusii the newborn is a 'visitor', a 'stranger'. Clothes are not bought in advance—how do you know, women say, you are not going to give birth to a piece of meat or a hyena?[41] Problems of serious deformity, when they present themselves, are not problematic. It is the advance suspicion of abnormality which causes concern. A recent illuminating study of Jamaican beliefs about 'false-belly' syndrome, which leads to the birth of 'witchcraft' babies, fathered by 'duppies' or spirits of the dead, illustrates how a discourse can be used as a cover for pre-emptive abortion of a baby, even when there is no particular reason to assume it is abnormal.[42] Such ambivalences are not the only aspect of worry and silence surrounding fertility. Edwin and Shirley Ardener struggled with the difficulties of investigating the 'facts about fertility' in their first fieldwork in the Cameroons.[43] Rosanne Cecil has written a moving account of the memories of elderly women in Northern Ireland about their experiences of miscarriage, still-birth, and infant death, not normally spoken of at all, and causing distress even in recollection.[44] A woman may defiantly bring up a child even in social circumstances which condemn it, as a recent study of poor women in nineteenth-century Paris, harrassed by the police and having only their own networks for support, shows.[45] The value placed on legitimacy may shift over time, maybe even because of an increasingly positive attitude to the recognition of a child in socially adverse conditions. Or the conditions themselves may shift over time.

Living society with all its unexpected eruptions and illegitimacies and concealments cannot be tidied up as easily as the ideal monumental representation of it through the exemplary dead. But with the passage of time, the contradictory voices and silent bits are soon forgotten and only the public story memorialized. Society inscribes itself, sometimes quite violently, on the organic processes of conception and birth—without which, however, society would not exist. Even the most autonomous of selves and free-willing of psyches comes into the world in a very bodily way, mediated by actions and decisions taken by a range of persons already part of the social matrix into which the new life is to be introduced. We can ask of babies, at birth or even before, not only 'what' they are but 'who' they are. If they are essentially 'nobody', they may become 'no body', and have no future freedoms at all.

3. SOCIAL SHAPING OF THE PRIVATE SELF: ETHNOGRAPHIC CASES

Interrogating some good ethnograpic studies can reveal more than the medical or psychological laboratory or the social theory seminar how connected Mauss's three dimensions of our individual lives are in practice.

Persons and selves at Avatip

An exemplary study by Simon Harrison explores psychological aspects of the notion of the person in its social context among people living at Avatip in New Guinea. Here, the standard received notion of a traditional tribal culture as an integrated whole is criticized. At Avatip, ritual does not celebrate moral consensus. There are rather two separate and to some extent contradictory spheres, the political-ritual arena of male competitive display, and the domestic-personal-moral sphere of egalitarian and mutually supportive interaction. These are in an unstable and equivocal relationship. They correspond, moreover, to two aspects of the person. Constructs of person-hood, Harrison argues, are significant not only for psychological insight, but for sociological analysis also. There are two basic dimensions of selfhood: 'Understanding' (*mawul*) which is based in the liver and which has the capa-city to 'hear' others, and 'Spirit' (*kaiyik*) which 'speaks'. The Understanding is predisposed to 'hear' other people—through comprehension, obedience, pity, desire—which have in common the capacity to identify with others. Without *mawul*, as in senility or insanity, one is 'deaf', according to Avatip people. Spirit is not so much an internal capacity, but an image, a shadow or reflection (and today the same word *kaiyik* is used for a photograph). It can be glossed as 'life force', mischievous and amoral when detached from the Understanding. But when properly attached, *kaiyik* is the source of competit-ive and courageous independent strength, especially in men. It is an 'active voice', assertive, and displayed through male initiatory cults and ceremonial debates. Separable from the organic human being, it is an image expressed and embodied in ritual paraphernalia including masks. For Harrison, the duality of *mawul* and *kaiyik* pervades social relations at Avatip, but it is not a Cartesian division of mind or soul and body, nor a simple Durkheimian one of society and individual. It is embedded in well-defined domains of sociality which do not fit comfortably with one another but are somewhat at odds; Harrison's analysis reveals in multiple ways how the organic, the psycholo-gical, and the social are mutually articulated in Avatip.[46]

Action and meaning: Ilongot

We have come to know the Ilongot through the work of Renato and the late Michelle Rosaldo. Ilongot people are notorious for their reputation as headhunters of the forests of the interior of Luzon, the northernmost island of the Philippines. Through the Rosaldos, however, we come to feel we know them as persons, regardless of their practices which raise the starkest kind of worries about moral, and psychological, relativism. The Rosaldos do not offer simply 'another culture', nor a society shaped ruthlessly by its own rules and regulations. They place 'real persons' at the heart of their analysis, persons who emerge increasingly as variants of ourselves as the Rosaldos learned more of the Ilongot past and their historical conception of their own society and its place in the world.

William Jones was the first Ilongot ethnographer. After a year in the field, he was murdered by the Ilongot in 1909. He was somewhat carried away by the exotic character of the people, which seemed to echo the Wild West of his childhood. The longer historical view is no less important for us to understand. In the pre-Spanish period, that is, pre-1565, it is likely that although there would have been patterns of reciprocal feuding, violence would have not been seen as particularly characteristic of the interior highlands. But since then, the impact of external events has intensified internal violence and established the image of the Ilongot as feared headhunters among the lowland populations. There is some evidence that even the Spanish collected heads.

In 1898, following the Spanish/American war, the United States took the Philippines as a colony, with policing of the margins. The Ilongot withdrew into the hills, fearing 'pacification patrols'. By the 1930s more raiding and killing among the Ilongot themselves was recorded. A period of intense violence resulted from the Japanese invasion of 1941 and the subsequent pursuit of the US forces, who followed the Japanese to the hills in 1945. A third of the Ilongot population was lost at this time. The immediate post-war period was quiet, but the 1950s saw a new intensification of violence; raiding of their lowland neighbours and taking of their heads replaced the former killings among themselves. In about 1955 the fundamentalist US New Tribes Mission began work.

Renato Rosaldo criticizes the static approach to the analysis of society. He began to recognize the way in which the Ilongot spoke of the past in terms of patterns: both in space, as every story involved the tracing of specific movements through the forest; and in time, as periods of headhunting alternated with quiet periods of *pistaim*—not a peculiar native concept, as he first thought, but pidgin for the English 'peacetime'. Different cohorts of men had reached maturity in very different circumstances: some in times of violence, others in times of quiet. These latter sometimes wistfully looked forward to the eruption of violent drama ahead in the future, when they too could prove themselves, achieve their laurels as it were.[47]

It is through this discourse about past and present and future, as much as through the observation of events, that Michelle Rosaldo is able to portray the way the Ilongot understand the inner psyche and how people are shaped by their interactions with each other through history. Headhunting may signal weirdness and crazy bloodlust to outsiders; as it does still to the lowland population, who speak of the Ilongot as though they were an exotic natural species. A popular lowland myth was that an Ilongot youth must give a severed Christian head to the father of his desired bride, and therefore kills when the fire tree blooms and arouses his desire to mate in springtime. This myth was unknown to the Ilongot themselves; for them, headhunting was set within a whole framework of other ideas and activities which valorized not the bloodshed as such but the making of adult men. In their fieldwork of the late 1960s, the Rosaldos found headhunting was still something perfectly familiar, and most young men aspired to taking a head before marriage.

By 1974, however, when they made a return trip to the field, they found that large numbers of people were nominally Christians, and no longer interested in headhunting. Did this mean a real change of heart? Michelle Rosaldo argues on the contrary, that the way Ilongots understood the world, and themselves, had not changed dramatically. Their views of personality, and emotion, and the drive to action, remained much the same, but could now, in a way, accommodate Christianity. What are these fundamental views of the human person, and their shaping by social life and history?

First, within the person is a vital organ, the heart (*rinawa*). The heart is the seat of an energy or 'anger', *liget*, which can be a passionate drive to action, and of knowledge, *beya*, which through careful reflective language can temper action. Hearts can be weighed down and saddened by *liget*. Ilongot said it was not gods, but these heavy feelings that made men want to kill; 'in taking heads they could aspire to "cast off" an "anger" that "weighed down on" and oppressed their saddened "hearts"'. Michelle Rosaldo decided to take such explanations seriously. 'Whereas other anthropologists have been inclined to work "from outside in", first describing a patterned social world and then asking how individuals are "socialized" to work and live within it, I found it more illuminating to begin from the other pole of the analytical dialectic and ask how personal and affective life, itself "socially constructed", is actualized in and orders the shapes of social actions over time. This required an investigation of Ilongot words denoting "energy/anger/passion" and civility, or "knowledge"—and, at the same time, a discovery of local assumptions about the persons, relationships, and events to which such words were characteristically applied.'

Liget is an admirable energy in people, when focused: it drives them to work hard and achieve things. It can grow within people: it responds to confrontation with others, it is touched off by the envy of others, and also by sharp stimulating tastes such as ginger, or chilli. If it is dispersed, especially in a young person, it can cause you to 'run amok' and create senseless violence. But if concentrated, strong and tight like a knot, it can help you to be successful, in hunting, gardening, and killing. Your heart can be weighed down by grief, envy, ambition, but can be lightened by a successful achievement which casts off this weight, and makes your heart light again. The exemplary achievement of this kind is to take a head. We should note that the satisfaction does not come from the actual killing of another person—in fact the fatal blow may come from others who follow up the first spear. The satisfaction, the 'catharsis' and the glory, go to the man who is ceremonially given the privilege of 'tossing' the head to the ground later. To Ilongots, the *liget* that beheaders know is neither good nor bad in itself, it is an energy which can lead in different directions; to wild violence and social chaos (especially when untempered by wisdom and knowledge in adults), or it can spur people on to industry, and to productive relations between old and young, men and women, to success in marrying, and in killing. It is stimulated in the arena of egalitarian competitive relations between young men, and between young women, which is a key to Ilongot life.

As *liget* may grow throughout one's life, so does its complement, *beya*, knowledge or civility. Ilongot babies 'know nothing' and lacking *beya*, they are extremely vulnerable to experiences of disruption and shock. In young persons, thoughtless violence can be excused, since the youngster does not 'know' yet how to control him or herself. Usually 'himself', however; for women have both less *liget* and less *beya* than men. Their hearts are not as 'high' as those of men. It is interesting that the difference is not an inborn one; it is a difference of life experience. Men have more excitement and challenge in their lives; they go off hunting in the forest and meet wild animals; they see foreign people; they participate in raids; all these stimulate the growth of their internal energies. Moreover, they also learn to participate in peace negotiations, in the making of trade exchanges, and the diplomatic use of oratory. All this experience heightens their knowledge and wisdom; and their ability to help control the passions of the young, for example by helping organize a kind of rota whereby the youngsters are allocated turns in the chance to take a head and thus focus the energy within.[48]

As for the Ilongot acceptance of Christianity: they spoke of themselves in 1974 as 'following a new path'. In Christian conversion, they accepted that a new and soothing 'knowledge' was to be introduced to an impassioned heart; and that Christians' passion would therefore be lowered. Competition was to be calmed down generally. On the volleyball court there was rivalry and anger, but not of the intense kind that could only be assuaged by taking a head. Young men were less easily converted than older married men and young women, however; Michelle Rosaldo asked of one man, 'Is he a

Christian?' and got the answer, 'No, he's a bachelor.' The grief caused by the death of relatives always had led to a heavy heart, needing to be lightened somehow, and the Rosaldos analyse the way in which the death of kin often led people to accept Christianity, representing conversion as a way of dealing with this burden, rather than seeking vengeance. Along with the new knowledge of Christian teaching, of course, came opportunities for pursuing trade and wealth, undeniably competitive paths to potential success and thus for exercising the old energies in a new way.[49]

Inuit ideas of intelligence

The cross-cultural validity of intelligence tests is notoriously questionable. A rather different way of asking qestions about 'intelligence' is to take ethnographic accounts seriously, and to recognize its situatedness; it can scarcely operate without specific language and dedicated practices and skills. This point is beautifully illuminated by Nick Gubser's portrayal of the way that the Nunamiut, inland caribou hunters of northern Alaska, deal with ideas of mind and intelligence. They speak of *ishuma*, a capacity located in the head, which develops as life unfolds. A small child has no *ishuma*, but at the age of 4 or 5, the brain solidifies and the child can remember, can think, and can use past experience to solve present problems. *Ishuma* is also (to put it in our dualistic terms) the repository of the emotions. In neurotics, the *ishuma* is distorted—such a person thinks too much, and in illness the *ishuma* may leave the body. In old age, it may be lost, so that the person cannot talk straight or think properly. Knowledge is past cumulative experience available for present application; that is to say, 'intelligence' is not separate from experience and memory, and Nunamiut go on learning from experience throughout life. The ideal of an intelligent person is a keen-eyed and clever hunter, working alone or with one or two companions. As a result of learning the conditions of land, snow, wind, and light, and the habits of the animals, he can eventually outwit them. We might say this is all very understandable, even congruent with folk wisdom elsewhere and even some doctrines in modern psychology. It is in the precise details that the Nunamiut view takes on a highly specific and historically situated character. A very special place is given to eyesight as an organ of intelligence-and-knowledge. In these far northern regions, we must remember, half the year is continuously dark for long periods, and half the year is correspondingly light. Hunting is done in the summer months when the land stretches out to distant horizons, every detail of the landscape can be significant, and people do not like the view to be obscured by fog or forests. The cycle of contrast between light and darkness plays an important part in the symbolism of all the northern peoples as well as their practical lives, and it is not surprising to find that the judgement of the hunter is associated with acuity of eyesight. Moreover, people and even animals who do not see very well are likely to be regarded as stupid. Even in the way that knowledge and truth are talked about, the visual is an important key; the eyes do not lie, and an eyewitness account can be relied upon as true.

The Nunamiut attribute human characteristics such as intelligence to animals in an interesting way. Shrews, voles, mink, muskrat, and lemmings are considered not to see very well, and therefore to be unintelligent. Ermine are thought to be slightly cleverer because they make a living by hunting themselves and killing ptarmigan and other small animals. Similarly the weasel at least knows enough to outrun a rock-thrower and reach its hole. The river otter, however, is much more intelligent than the other small animals, while the beaver is a very intelligent animal and difficult to catch. Only two or three persons were known to have had any luck. The Nunamiut regard the beaver's habit of warning other beavers of danger by slapping the water with their tails as a typical example of the clever way they co-operate with others. The wolf is the most intelligent of all the animals, especially the older wolf who has learned the ways of the human hunter. Foxes are clever too, while hares are rather stupid—people laughed about the inane appearance of a couple of hares sitting on the snow and blinking their big eyes in the bright spring sun. The grizzly bear is a powerful animal known to have acute senses of hearing and smell, but thought to have little visual acuity, and therefore not regarded as clever. If it takes a good look, it can see, but doesn't bother to look around until threatened, when it looks around wildly trying to locate the source of danger, defecates a great deal (to the later amusement of storytellers), and rushes off up a mountain. One of the striking images of Nunamiut zoology to us is their respect for the intelligence of the mountain sheep, greater than that of moose or caribou (the real hunter's quarry). These wild sheep can see extremely well, almost, the Nunamiut say, as if they had telescopes in their eyes. They are constantly looking out for wolves and humans in the plains below. If you look up through your telescope at them, you will see them already looking down at you.[50]

Few of us would pass a Nunamiut intelligence test. The whole 'modernist' project of testing intelligence is predicated on the presence of a psychological capacity, given in our organic make-up, however much cultivated by later education. But the problem is how on earth to define, let alone measure and compare this capacity, without simultaneously using as a yardstick the very skills and type of training which the subject of the study has internalized (or failed to internalize) through education.

Arithmetic indoors and outdoors

The tailoring of our thought processes to our practical lives extends even into the world of the modern shopper. Even literate and numerate people think rather as hunter-gatherers might when they set out from home to get the groceries. Jean Lave has produced a fascinating study of the way that we leave the formal number processing of school mathematics behind when we venture out into the supermarket—and make our decisions according to a whole range of qualitative, rough and ready, proportionate judgements that bypass the rationality of the price-mechanism as managers try to operate it. 'Outdoor' maths entails thinking, rather, in chunks of goods and assemblages of packets of different sizes and how they fit into the shopping as a whole, planned recipes, the pattern of various family likes and dislikes, and the cupboard space at home. Goods chosen for discount by the store may be good 'value for money' but shoppers do not spend much time comparing prices per gram for this and that size packet or discounted item (in the way they would have done in school); they use rules of thumb which make more sense of their overall objective, comparing the value or usefulness of packets as a whole. Moreover, people progress in an accustomed way through the supermarket (as they might have done through the forest in ancient times), looking for the fifty or so items they need each week, scarcely noticing the managers' efforts to entice them to lengthen the list by careful marginal cost calculations and a strategic placing of special buys. Slimming programmes too, in principle, demand mathematical skills of the schoolroom type with the calorie-chart and the food scales; but those who follow them soon adopt rough and ready available props which approximate allowances—a useful old cup filled to the blue line, cutting a particular packet of butter into six pieces you know count more or less as 'small'.[51] We could add that cooking in general often settles down into such routines, dependent on specific old pots and spoons and familiar ovens whose behaviour at specific temperatures we have come to know as a qualitative thing. It is always difficult to transfer your cookery skills from one kitchen to another, or one brand of ingredients to another, let alone one measuring system to another. British people may have given up thinking in pounds, shillings, and pence—but a good number of women over a certain age still think in pounds and ounces.

Conclusion

There is a lot of popular discussion these days of 'the self' and 'identity' and knowledge as something *possessed* personally. But these discussions can take too much for granted from modern ideas about citizenship, individual rights, moral autonomy, and independent minds or souls, something I discuss further in Chapter 10. Examples I have introduced above indicate how careful we have to be with the notion of 'individual identity' except as a legal and linguistic convention within a set of others. People don't exist in isolation, but in the context of the kind of patterned linkage outlined in earlier chapters; 'the person' is not a very good starting point for understanding the basic elements of society, but rather the kinds of connectivity we find between persons. The elemental model of sociality must include more than one; there must be at least a set of dyadic relations. Or even triadic—you and me, as the unit 'we', and a representative of the background against which our existence as a pair is defined. Anthropology recognizes that even the sharpest subjective sense of 'self' is set in highly specific contexts. It is a salutary experience to realize that we have to ask of ourselves, if we are honest, 'What are the connectivities, and conversations, and pre-existing social relations, which brought me into being and within and through which "I" exist?'

An important, and growing field of study and practice, which I have touched on but not had space to develop here, is in the application of anthropological ideas to the question of medical diagnosis and treatment. Bio-medicine treats the organism; psychiatry, the mind; counselling or some such, the effects of social disturbance or deprivation. But in the light of the anthropological effort being made to *see the connections* between these aspects of the human being, the technical work of the doctor or counsellor itself, perhaps especially when over-professionalized, has to be gently questioned. Did the magicians, herbalists, diviners, and witchdoctors of classic ethnography do any better? It is true that some of the key drugs in modern use are derived from plants long known to tribal practitioners, though the modern rush to seek more of them may be based on a romantic illusion. Medical anthropology is a challenging field indeed.

PART IV

*Practice, Production, and Politics
in the Ceremonial Arena*

CHAPTER NINE

The 'Home-Made' Patterns
of Livelihood

A CROSS the world it is the dwelling and local settlement, or set of temporary settlements, that provide a concrete focus for the understanding of lived social space and its resonances for the development of the individual's experience of belonging to a patterned world. A study of the sites of daily working activity is relevant not only to the 'traditional' worlds of subsistence or semi-subsistence production, but also to the life of localities well within the reach of capitalism, state influence, or modern communication networks. Before writing *The Wealth of Nations* in the late eighteenth century, Adam Smith visited a pin factory.[1]

I. PLACE, HOME, AND *HABITUS*

We live upon the surface of the earth (despite illusions of freedom in occasional flight) and this surface has its own shape and texture, including the patterning of land and sea, relief, climate, vegetation, and surface water. These features provide the ecological setting for animal species to find their way of living and to reproduce, the setting in which they have thus evolved. They also provide a base line to our human lives, not only our pragmatic activities, but to our conceptual understandings of the organized qualities of differentiated space, and our orientation within it. However these may vary with patterns of social form and cultural representation (and both of these are spatially articulated), there are primary features such as coasts, valleys, and mountains, around which human significance comes to be woven. Human geographers, such as Vidal de la Blache on the regions of France, and landscape historians such as W. G. Hoskins on the English countryside, have explored in exquisite detail how rural communities have fashioned their field patterns, hedges, wells, routes, and forests, as well as their settlement patterns and vernacular architecture, using materials and tools to hand, in the light of social and cultural priorities of the different historical periods.[2] Within anthropology, there has also been a long-established line of inquiry into how communities use the resources of their environment in specific, locally reasoned, and collectively transmitted ways; Daryll Forde's *Habitat, Economy and Society* illustrates a range of earlier ethnographic descriptions of this kind.[3] More recent work emphasizes not only fundamental rationales, but subjective valuations in the way environments are conceptualized and used through vernacular categories of 'indigenous knowledge' and moral priorities.[4]

For example, Mary Douglas has offered a fascinating account of the Lele of the southern Congo basin, and the way that she found them using their forests and lands. This pattern did not seem very efficient to those in the days of Belgian colonial rule whose job it was to promote rational development.[5] Lele country consists of deep, forested river courses and higher grassy plateaus in between, where the villages are located. They value the forest as the source of all that is fresh, wholesome, cool, and pure. They collect water, firewood, wild fruits and herbs, hunt game and fish there, and generally speak and think of themselves as a hunting people. Clearings are made in the forest for the cultivation of maize and a variety of other crops, a task to which both men and women contribute. However, the forest is regarded primarily as the proper domain of men, has religious and symbolic prestige, and women are frequently prohibited even from entering it. Women's sphere is the drier, hotter grassland, where they tend some palms and bananas, and groundnuts. A few goats might be found in a Lele village, but because things of the grassland are not pure like those of the forest, they are not reared for local consumption but only for passing on in trade exchanges. The separation of forest from village, and the interdependence of the sexes, are themes which run not only through the economic life of the Lele villages but also through their high evaluation of harmony in human relations and their ritual ceremonies and religious ideas. Lele used not to invest heavily of their time and labour in the fields or other productive tasks. As I have mentioned in Chapter 5, their interest in earning cash and seeking the material rewards of modern life came about only when the missionaries managed to loosen the hold of the older generation of men over the arranging of girls' marriages, and thus providing new opportunities to young men and women to marry according to their own wishes and form a new kind of modern household.[6]

Transformations of this kind can sometimes obscure a degree of continuity of spatial forms on the ground. There may be long-lasting built structures of ditches and hedges, fields and clearings, pathways and terraces which provide an infrastructure for future productive activity even where social and technical factors change. There is also the matter of spiritual 'investment' in the forms of the land itself, which can exert influence far into a future beyond any link with former pragmatic land use; Australia is a famous case, but there are others.[7] The 'inscribing' of the frameworks of social life on the land, at one particular period, can produce a historical momentum which can shape and constrain things indefinitely. Think of the British debt to Roman road builders. Simple notions of living and dwelling in a place and investing it with symbolism of the moment are not enough. The historical weight of past lived patterns is sometimes very heavy. Kirsten Hastrup has been able to use sources going back many centuries to trace the way in which ideas of nature and practices devoted to the making of the human landscape have gradually created the Iceland of today, as it exists and as the Icelanders understand it and use it.[8]

Bourdieu pursued the problem of specifying the way in which particular communities worked with their environments (including their 'built environments') in customary patterns, even internalizing these patterns into their bodily techniques and mental outlook, while still struggling to create and produce. He adopted the concept of *habitus* from Mauss, who had used it in writing of the way that the human body is educated within a specific context to move and act effectively.[9] In his *Outline of a Theory of Practice* Bourdieu proffers *habitus* as a working concept to handle 'traditional' rural society and the symbolically resonant productive patterns of its labouring. He developed it as a shorthand for the accustomed round of practised, partly habitual, but actively productive social and cultural life of the Kabyle peasants of the Algerian hills. In a later work Bourdieu applied the idea of *habitus* to the context of industrial society, and I return to this analysis in the next chapter.[10] The term has found wide currency, as it captures in its sense of pattern both environmental constraints and human agency, without allowing a collapse into cosy images of tradition and harmony.

Today, because of a new popular romanticism about tribal life which assumes that all was organic harmony in traditional circumstances, we should be careful not to take it for granted that pre-modern communities simply lived in accordance with nature; we should expect any human occupation to modify the geographical features of a region in specific ways. The 'natural landscape' as we find it today, even in the wildest-seeming places, has been created in part by past human activity. Such activity has moreover, contrary to some current views, not always been detrimental to the conservation of the land and its fertility. In Zambia, the Bemba traditional agricultural system was oriented to 'sustainable' patterns of production until very recent times. A study from the western Sahara shows traditional methods in an even more positive light. The villages of Kissidougou in the savanna landscape of the western Sahara each nestled in a cluster of forest. It used to be assumed that the human population had actually deforested the open spaces in between the 'forest islands'. But it has recently been shown that far from deforesting the region, the methods of cultivation actually helped sustain and even increase the vegetation and tree cover around the villages, through composting, watering, and the encouragement of shade for houses and vegetable plots.[11] Where our visible rural legacy is a 'built environment' of roads, hedges, walls, and ditches it is especially obvious that we are never acting on nature raw, but have worked and reworked our relation to the land up to the present. We still do so as we turn barns into holiday homes, and start re-landscaping the mountains themselves—in national parks like the English Lake District—to match the paintings of a generation ago. To mould the land into our own vision of how it should be is nothing new, however. It is ancient, and has left a residue not only in the ways we use our spade and hoe but in the very ways we use the imagery of the land in the way we speak of other things (consider how English is permeated with phrases such as the 'sunny uplands', the 'moral high ground', getting 'bogged down' in detail, dealing with a 'thorny problem', surviving the 'valley of the shadow', and even constructing ambitious programmes for 'blue skies research').

The trend in anthropological writing about human beings and the environment over several decades has been to complicate the simple dualism of 'nature' and 'culture'. The human domain and its environment are not totally separate, the one acting upon the other in some epic struggle. Current study focuses on the mutual participation of the culturally defined human and his or her 'natural' surroundings.[12] This concern with the responsiveness and vulnerability of human beings to nature is closely in line with 'phenomenology' or an orientation to individually located experience in the social sciences, and overlaps in some ways with literature, even poetry, celebrating place and the qualitative atmosphere of landscape. Paul Carter's literary study of the way that the modern Australian landscape was built up through history draws on explorers' memoirs, settlers' letters home, drawings and imaginings, tracing the translation of hope and dreams into material reality.[13] Anthropologists have moved decisively into this kind of writing; an outstandingly interesting collection of essays by American anthropologists is Feld and Basso's *Senses of Place*.[14] This book claims to take a phenomenological approach to the idea of place, and to argue that abstractions of space in general follow from the experience of place, rather than vice versa. Rather than being simply a part of local understandings and 'local knowledge' to use Geertz's phrase, places are as often as not multiply defined, contested, people as often as not displaced and linked with the places they remember only in their imagination. The book contains several substantial and sparkling ethnographic essays, including one by Charles O. Frake on place and 'sheltered identity' among the English of Norfolk.[15] Another recent collection of essays, by anthropologists based in Britain, is edited by Eric Hirsch and Michael O'Hanlon with the title *The Anthropology of Landscape*, also emphasizing the observer's experience of place.[16] Landscapes are not set out objectively in the way that a geographical realist might expect, but are always from particular angles, in which some elements are foregrounded, others faded into the background. Visual metaphors for our apprehension of the environment are almost inescapable in the Western artistic and aesthetic tradition, a point which has provoked creative anthropologists into imagining other possibilities. For example, Alfred Gell identified a marked tendency in New Guinea languages, specifically in Umeda, to 'phonological iconicity'; that is, to significant evocations of meaning through particular sounds.[17] These include not only obvious examples of onomatopoeia, words like the English 'hiss', 'buzz', or 'crunch'. Seemingly arbitrary words are also made into what the linguists call ideophones, like *sis* for 'mountain', which in Umeda does indeed evoke 'the sound that a mountain makes' or at least 'the shape in articulatory/ acoustic space' made by a mountain. Gell is not a way-out relativist in arguing that Umeda culture is keyed to sound-symbolism; he argues that there are good grounds for accepting an environmental rationale. In a thick forest, one's visual range is limited, and the traveller or hunter concentrates visually on things close by while being aware of things at a distance through hearing or even scent. The Umeda concept of something 'hidden' is not so much something you cannot see, but something near by that is silent. In a forest, from a Western point of view too, you cannot 'see the landscape' and can easily get lost. But Gell's point is more than a straightforward environmental/ perceptive one; the person growing up in Umeda does not face the forest in some state of nature, but is equipped with the sophisticated tools and poetry of the Umeda language, a world which elaborates knowledge in the idiom of hearing in ways comparable to the deeply visual idiom of English. This is a way of knowing about the world we could learn too, but we would learn it best in a forest.

Trees themselves are laden with symbolic suggestion. Laura Rival's striking volume *The Social Life of Trees* brings together anthropological essays both on the 'real-world' importance of trees and forests, and on their evidently universal appeal to the human imagination. They have stimulated ideas about life, about family history, about knowledge of good and evil, of roots and branches as an image of 'structure' in the abstract, about permanence, about shade and coolness and life, about fruitfulness and the origin of things, across the languages and cultural traditions of the world. Tree symbolism varies, but it is not arbitrary nor incapable of translation. However 'imagined', forests are a vital part of the organic surface of the planet on which our survival depends, and modern 'green' politics is based upon the primary aim of forest conservation.[18]

Domestic space: homes, settlements

Innovative and influential studies of the house as a social space were published by Littlejohn on the Temne house in 1960; and by Pierre Bourdieu on the northern Algerian Kabyle house in 1980.[19] House symbolism can be very complex, especially when movement is taken into account, relations between the outside and inside cosmologies, and the perspectives of different members of the household. The Kabyle house is rectangular and divided by a low interior wall into two parts: the larger for human use, upslope; and the smaller one, a stable, on the downslope, though women and children may sleep in a loft above the animals. The fireplace is at the upper end of the main room, the main door on the east side and the weaving loom against the well-lit wall opposite, where honoured guests are seated. Orientations to the east are very important in the male-dominated public external spaces, of the ploughing fields and sacrifical rituals, and the outside as a whole is represented as a male domain against the house, which is a female and private domain. However, there is a contrasting set of homologous polar oppositions within the house, where the upper end is the male domain and associated with 'culture', while the lower end is a female domain associated with 'natural' processes, of animal growth, of sexuality, childbirth and death. The cardinal point symbolism is actually reversed by contrast with the outside world: the inside of the wall facing the main door (though the western wall from an outside point of view) is thought of as the 'east' and the darkened inside of the 'front' (and eastern) wall is thought of as the 'west'. This internal orientation is the symbolic space of the woman, not a mirror image on the same scale, but contained within it. There are asymmetrical links between the two patterns; as the man enters from his external, eastern space, he turns to his right, to the inside daylight on the loom wall and the fire, to the noble space of the internal 'east'. As a part of Bourdieu's ramifying analysis of the internal relations between the parts of the house, he also notes the way in which marriage unites the whole. The main 'master beam', explicitly identified with the master of the house, rests upon a central forked pillar identified with the wife and extends its protection from the male to the female section. The poetic spatial symbolism of the house is not grafted directly onto common-sense geography or architecture. It represents compli-cated gendered perspectives constituting a world within a world; Kabyle say 'Men look at things from outdoors, women look at things from indoors.'[20]

While anthropologists have taken an increasing interest in the material construction of houses and settlements as a touchstone for exploring ideas and symbols, there has been a complementary movement on the part of archaeologists towards the cultural interpretation and lived aspects of the historical material structures they investigate. Ian Hodder, working in Africa, pioneered the idea of symbolic archaeology, and really creative work has been done by people who have come into anthropology from archaeology, such as Henrietta Moore.[21] Archaeologists have always been interested, for example, in rubbish dumps, and she investigated just how and why, as well as where, rubbish was deposited around the Marakwet villages of north-western Kenya. She also showed how a processes of negotiation, especially between men and women, led to the making and remaking of houses and the use-patterns of domestic space as conditions were shifting in Kenya as a whole towards engagement with the modern economy. Social practices in the making of domestic space have also been explored in fascinating ways by Shirley Ardener in relation to the gendering of space, and by Joy Hendry in relation to the sign-ficance of bounding or 'wrapping' of private space in Japanese architecture.[22]

The house as a social form

Lévi-Strauss drew attention (in several of his relatively late writings, mainly in the 1980s) to the way in which an abstract concept of 'the house' as a 'moral person'—or perhaps, to further Anglicize the concept, 'social personage' might be the key organizing principle in cognatic societies without clear lines of descent or alliance. The internal organization of 'the house' on any complex scale represented for Lévi-Strauss the beginning of the exercise of power and the reproduction of power relations on a domestic scale. In a long-term historical sense, this was supposed to be the point where generalized rules about open networks of kinship organization began to break down. The abstract idea of the house as an enduring social form has been taken up and effectively brought into relationship with the more explicit approaches to house architecture and living space in a series of studies edited by Janet Carsten and Stephen Hugh-Jones.[23]

Clearly drawing inspiration from Bourdieu, Hugh-Jones shows how the Tukanoans of north-west Amazonia conceptualize social relations in two materially grounded and complementary ways, each based on a contrasting gendered reading of the space of the house. The Tukanoans build large, high, partitioned longhouses, beautifully decorated on the front. Suspended above the inside space is a palm-leaf box with heirlooms; below this is a wooden trough used to brew beer for feasts. The life of a longhouse, *maloca*, is connected with that of the leader of the group who sponsors its building: when he dies, the 'people of the house' (based around a group of brothers, their wives, and unmarried sisters) either reforms or divides. The longhouse is internally divided by partitions into individual family units, between which there are various tensions. However, while food is produced and cooked at family level, it is served and eaten collectively, in the shared space at the centre. The community may be exogamous, but symmetrical alliance and a preference for close marriage lead to territorial groups which are relatively endogamous. A large *maloca* and its occupants may be known as a 'dance house' after the feasts offered to visiting affines who come to dance in it. The reciprocal pattern of feasting between affinally related and interdependent houses is represented in the ritual context mainly by the visiting men, while the house community itself in this context is associated with women and female activities. The complementary meeting of husband and wife in the individual family compartment is thus nested within a larger series of the conjunction of male and female on the model of marriage, including relations between different *maloca* and extending to the territorial group. In mythology the inclusive image of womb and child extends to the relations between cosmos and humanity. The longhouse itself replicates the pattern of the cosmos in intricate detail, even to the ornaments suspended above which evoke the light of the sun, and the long beer trough below matching the anaconda-canoe in which proto-men and women travelled up the primal river. All these images evoke the inclusiveness of the house, particularly from the women's point of view. However, there is also a male initiation cult from which women are excluded, and in this context the uniqueness of the house group and the ancestry of its clan is emphasized, together with the hierarchy of men within it. The house is thus capable of being represented in more than one way at the same time, even to the point of being seen sometimes as a woman facing to the rear, and as a man facing to the front. Hugh-Jones thinks that the Tukanoan case may well fit with Lévi-Strauss's suggestion that the house may integrate contradictory notions which anthropologists have developed to analyse kinship types, and also that it may have a fetishistic quality serving specifically to mask the contradictions of formal 'alliance'.

Compared with the analytical formulations of structuralism, the grounded level at which forms of 'the house' are treated in this collection reminds us that with or without an elevated recognition of entities such as The House of Windsor, and whether or not there is a class of 'house-societies' analytically distinct from other kinds based on descent or alliance or class, pretty nearly everyone actually lives in a house of some kind along with other people, usually of different age and sex. Houses may be very modest indeed, they may last long or be continually rebuilt, they may be mere seasonal shelters: but they are always constructed in significant patterns, and they are used in distinctly social ways. They provide a way in, for the stranger or the anthropologist, to the life of a community, giving access both to everyday activities and to the real-life setting in which discourse about the more elusive principles of what constitutes matriliny or patriliny, appropriate marriages or shameful liaisons, rank, hierarchy, or gender take place.

Maurice Bloch's account of the house among the Zafimaniry in this volume illustrates how a very humble dwelling may be built as a social space for actual living, part of the *habitus*, but also how it may be set in historical and remembered time beyond that of the unfolding generations, and may come even to signify historical time on a political as distinct from domestic level. Zafimaniry, who live in scattered settlements in the southern forests of

Madagascar, place great significance upon their houses (by comparison with the state-forming Merina people of the north, who according to Bloch have an 'anti-house ideology' and stress rather the tombs of the dead). The Zafimaniry house is the core of the marital relationship, represented as an ideal compatibility between the spouses. In times of relative peace, the creation and maturing of this relationship is a long process. Part of it is the physical construction of a house by the young man, near his parents' house, starting simply with three hearth stones in a wooden frame and three posts. One of these is the 'hot post', made of very hard wood and placed nearest the fire. At this stage, however, the rest of the house is likely to be made of flimsy reed and bamboo mats which let in light and sound. The house has to be blessed before the couple can cook and have sex in it. An elder rubs the posts with taro which has been cooked on the hearth, thus bringing together the parts of the house associated with the man and the women respectively. Taro is a root-crop not only of symbolic but also practical importance to the Zafimaniry. Because it stays in the ground for up to six years and multiplies by itself, it can be relied upon for survival even when, for climatic or political reasons, there are no other crops. The marriage is strengthened over time with the birth of children, and the house acquires 'bones' as the flimsy mats are gradually replaced with vertical wooden planks. The house 'hardens' further with time, as decorative carving is added especially to the posts, doors, and windows. Eventually, as the original couple die off, the house may become respected as a 'holy house' of forebears, as their descendants continue to repair and redecorate it and seek blessings.

In 1947 there was a fierce round of reprisals by the French authorities in Madagascar against an anti-colonial movement. The Zafimaniry were particularly badly affected. The village where Bloch later worked was picked on as having welcomed the rebels, the French rounding up the population and burning the whole village. Many escaped to the forest and hid there for two and a half years before returning. Their return was prompted by the death of the father of the head of the village, whose body, it was felt, should be brought back to the place where the main holy house had once stood. 'He revived for a moment, said a "Hail Mary" and then finally died and was buried.' The people began to come back, but there were problems, including the sickness of the baby son of the village head, until a spirit medium had instructions in a dream. The deceased father recommended that certain leaves should be cooked on the hearth of the holy house, poured on the place where the posts had been, and then fed to the baby. The baby recovered;

the original marriage having been reconstructed, the holy house had been resurrected, and the village was rebuilt. This analysis shows how a focus on the house as a dwelling need not—must not—limit us to an experiential present; and how the smallest element of ritual practice can evoke and reinstate a much wider whole which can survive even physical destruction.[24]

A relational view of 'home'

The notion of 'home' comes most clearly into focus when one is away from it. It is from a distance that the question makes sense as to 'where is your home?' The idea of a centre, and a home-base, is not only an understandable human perspective on space, but it has a pragmatic foundation. It has proved a helpful tool to palaeoanthropologists, who talk of the return of scavengers or hunter-gatherers to a central place, perhaps with a hearth, perhaps a sense of 'home'. One is reminded of sheep and their 'heugh' or home-base on the fell, to which generations of a flock become accustomed. The idea of home can be much more complex than this, however; home is not necessarily one spot, or even one stretch of land. This is partly because we are multiple in our own beginnings, and connections with the past. The vast majority of us have more than one spot we can think of as home, even in a fairly stable society: our maternal or paternal homes, our own marital home, our homes at different times and so on. A further important reason why 'home' is rarely one spot, however, is the frequency of regular migration: repeated movements are found in a large proportion of human communities, especially those movements linked to seasons. There may be an accustomed pattern of seasonal movement between ecological zones, especially for pastoralists; this may be more a kind of network in itself, conceptually of that form, and interlinked with the networks of others. There is a rhythm in the way we use space. Such networks imply differentiation of the idea of belonging to a place; but they do not remove the sense of a spatial coherence, and even within the subjectivity of one person, a sense of a wider whole. Home need not be one spot, but could be a regular circuit or inscribed patterns of movement, as most obviously with the seasonal migrations of some hunting peoples, and of many pastoralists, or fishing and seafaring communities. Marcel Mauss's classic study of the Alaskan Inuit (introduced earlier) explores the spatial polarity of their social life, as they move between the aggregated settlements on the coast, where they remain through the dark winter and can live to some extent from fishing, and the open interior plains of the tundra, where they disperse to hunt caribou in the long, light summer. The spatial rhythm is matched by the seasonal oscillation, to shape what Mauss calls the 'double morphology' of Inuit social organization.[25] This duality of form, an oscillation in space and time, might be missed by some future archaeologist who sees the residue of inland and coastal settlements as evidence for two quite separate tribal communities. But in high latitudes where the winter/summer contrast is strong, as in equatorial regions where there can be extreme swings between wet and dry seasons, the regular movement of human groups, especially those herding animals, itself provides a trajectory which in its own rhythm is 'home'.[26]

Trading, fishing, and seafaring communities may also have a more complex idea of home. Built into their way of life is the need to be mobile, to move especially between resources, suppliers, and markets, and families may well spread themselves over a network of places, making strategic marriages as a part of the extension of trading networks.[27] Where is 'home' for them, at any given point in history? Modern labour migration and urbanization represents a dramatic situation where families and individuals may try to keep up the sense of having two or more homes; this, together with recent work on the place of movement and 'travelling cultures' in general by James Clifford, is discussed further in Chapter 10 on the 'new spaces' of modernity.

Local political space

Space is not merely marked out and lived in, but is one of the prime arenas for politics—so often a struggle, partly ceremonial, over the control of space and place. There are sometimes clearly articulated spatial patterns to rivalry, for example geographically based 'moiety patterns' such as the north/south halves of Shillukland, stretched up and down the White Nile river, or the east/west oppositional patterns thrown up on either side of hill ranges, such as that between the red rose of Lancaster and the white of York. Factionalism and segmentary politics often have a 'grounding', as is clear from Evans-Pritchard's classic analysis of Nuer political relations. Physical space can become social or political space in a very tangible way. Paul Dresch has developed a model of Yemeni tribal politics upon the principle of tribal entities and authorities maintaining their honour and status essentially by being able to protect the space in which dependants and family live. The honour and political standing of sheikhs depends upon their ability to offer protection and security within their territories, to challenge any violation, and also to deal diplomatically with mediators and messengers. Furthermore, spatial forms in Yemen have an extraordinarily stable character over the long term.[28] We might recall here the salience of spatial political forms even among the indigenous hunting and gathering peoples of Australia, where there was a system of inter-tribal 'ambassadors' able to move between political spaces.

There is more to the appreciation of 'political space' than the dramatic confrontation of representative chiefs and kings. At the ground level, every community operates within a framework of provisions concerning access to land, water, and forests, and a system of transmitting these rights from one generation to the next. This set of provisions concerning land tenure and use of resources may belong to a set of customary conventions accepted as self-evidently 'traditional' and assumed timeless, or it may be the result of specific patronage initiated by particular chiefs and kings, or legislation by governments. 'Traditional' tenure can be remarkably resistant to legislative reform, however, as Tim Jenkins's study of the robust forms of transmission of family farms through women in the Pyrenean region of Béarn has shown.[29] The pattern there today is recognizably the one we can trace from the medieval period onwards, right through the rise of the nation-state and the French revolution. The study of land tenure and the social reproduction of rural communities who work the land for a living is still, along with 'kinship and marriage', a basic plank of anthropological study. It may not seem very glamorous or philosophically exciting, but it is within frameworks of this kind, more or less consciously articulated, that human beings have for millennia faced 'the environment' and each other. The question of possession, property, and the social transmission of material goods and rights within specific localities has recently been reconsidered by anthropologists in an important collection ranging from 'traditional' anthropological contexts such as Melanesia and African hunter-gatherers to post-socialist Eastern Europe, inheritance in industrial England and Japan, and the US historical 'frontier' of South Dakota.[30] The application of anthropological insights to these topics reminds us that while it is true that the mass growth of cities and conurbations and the international economy has transformed the way the earth's resources are used, it has only sharpened the importance of our recognizing and attempting to control the nature of social and political rights to and responsibilities for the earth, our shared home.

2. WORK, WEALTH, AND EXCHANGE

Productive labour demands much of the individual body and mind: muscles, labour, concentration; and the deployment of learned skills of every kind. Nobody, however, works very productively on their own; work is a social phenomenon, collaborative in its practice and its purpose, and loaded with rhetorical purposes and values. Adam Smith, Marx, and Durkheim all explored the ways in which work is organized, and to what shared ends. Durkheim's *Division of Labour in Society* sought a middle way between the natural good of the 'free market' envisioned in the tradition of classical economics and the utilitarians, on the one hand, and the fundamental driving forces of history identified by Marx, on the other, as transforming primitive communism into feudalism and thence into capitalism.[31] Durkheim saw the specialization of labour not as a matter of spreading competitive market behaviour, nor as a matter of growing patterns of exploitation of labour by the powerful, ultimately by capitalists. He saw specialization rather as of mutual advantage; as contributing to the overall co-operation and cohesion of society. He identified this kind of cohesion as 'organic', as distinct from the mechanical cohesion, or solidarity, of society where everyone performed the same kind of small-scale subsistence work. The major large-scale example of mutually beneficial occupations in a social economy is usually taken to be Indian caste, in which groups are distinguished mainly according to occupation. Within a specific village, the different households engage with each other in a system of reciprocity known as *jajmani*. This works through a set of overlapping exchange-partnerships between people of different castes, but the same locality. Louis Dumont has argued that in Hindu India, we find the most elaborate (and historically enduring) case of hierarchy known in history.[32] Here, the principle of relative purity in the scale of human life embraces all other pragmatic dimensions of differentiation, including those of wealth and power. The principle is embodied in the status of the Brahman caste, whose life validates the system as a whole. One is born into the caste system, which gives one a very specific location in a vast structure of evident 'inequality', and one lives it in one's body, through the rules of purity concerning food and contact with others, including sexual and marital relations and the engendering of children. Dumont contrasted the Indian case with that of Western systems of power, status, and rank, but allowed also the presence of traces of hierarchy in the West. Gender seems the most obvious

FIG. 19. Building on each other's work: Makonde carving
from East Africa. Photo: Adrian Arbib. Original in author's
possession.

domain to consider, alongside parenthood, but there are perhaps others too.
Very few social scientists today would feel that the Durkheimian contrast of
organic versus mechanical solidarity was appropriate or helpful in analysing
modern societies whether industrial or rural, oriental or Western, large or
small scale, even the internal domestic working relations of a happy household. Anthropologists have increasingly come to see both inequality and
competition in productive and exchange relations everywhere. It may be that
the older question of where collaboration and mutuality lie in productive

and reproductive life has been lost sight of, obscured by a sharper questioning of power and privilege than Durkheim allowed.

The ends of productive labour are, however, less obvious than we might at first assume. On the anthropological side, for example, the temptation is to assume a rather pragmatic view of the purpose of work being to provide for basic needs, with perhaps occasionally extra items produced as surplus to support a few chiefly families or indulge in a few luxury items for status display and strategic exchange. The purpose of work in pre-modern societies is too easily taken to be plain survival, not so much the gratification of social or aesthetic ends in themselves. But an important lesson has to be learned here, that is, we should avoid a simple transfer to all human life of modern 'industrial' ideas about productive labour as distinct from activities in the voluntary or private sphere. The category 'work' and its overtones, as distinct from leisure and fun, is produced and coloured by the circumstances of the rise of industrial capitalism and what Marx saw as the alienation of the whole person from the productive activities in which they were engaged. A collection of essays by anthropologists on 'work', edited by Sandra Wallman, has illustrated just how pervasive the modern theoretical distinction is between paid employment and the rest of life, even though the picture is full of contradictions when looked at closely.[33] A moment's reflection is enough to remind us that vast areas of non-paid activity in urban, industrial society are also hard work and very productive, in a human sense, even if they lie outside the statistics of the economists. Vocational commitment extends beyond paid hours; household and child care is supposed to be a sort of hobby for men and while demanded from women, arguments that it is serious work and should be 'paid' for rarely get a proper hearing; while the arts, supposedly a leisure activity for amateurs, can become a major life commitment for them.

The work/leisure contrast does not fit at all well in rural and traditional contexts where production is for subsistence as well as for the market, where labour is rarely hired from outside the family, and where much activity is accompanied by songs and laughter—if occasionally brawls. The writings of Max Weber have shown how very specific have been the circumstances in which the modern puritan approach to work and economic activity developed in northern Europe (as distinct from the more profligate and luxury-loving Catholic countries of the south). His classic *The Protestant Ethic and the Spirit of Capitalism* explored the matrix of ideas and practices concerning the godliness of work in itself and care over money and time, the intrinsic merit of savings and investment for the future, and the promise of personal salvation in the context of early Calvinism.[34] This striking study, though concerned with a particular religious movement in seventeenth-century northern Europe, illuminates much more widely the importance of social values and religious and cultural attitudes for economic history in general. It also disposes effectively of some of the assumptions made in classical economics and utilitarian theory about rational, profit-motivated, and money-conscious behaviour being a common denominator to human nature in general. Not all human beings and not all societies are like the Calvinists of three centuries ago.

One of the most striking examples of the misplacing of our common assumptions about work is the way in which we have tended to represent the lives of hunters and gatherers, both in the archaeological past and in the modern day. Because they do not have the kind of luxuries that we assume will be the fruits of our labours, we tend to see them as still 'working hard' to obtain the basic survival needs. Marshall Sahlins has very successfully undermined this image of hunting and gathering societies as living on the edge of starvation, individuals grubbing around for a few roots and leaves simply to keep alive.[35] He reverses the hand-to-mouth morality we have often assumed in such conditions, identifying hunters and gatherers rather as the 'original affluent society'. Certainly some hunting groups have been pushed into the least hospitable of environments in the world today, but this is because so much of their former territory has been colonized by others. Even in the harsh conditions of the desert or the tundra, however, they do not systematically scratch and scrape for food all day long, every day: there are difficult times, but then a windfall—a large game animal, or a shoal of fish, or a good rainy season producing plenty of fruits comes along, and they can enjoy abundance for a good while. In former times when the richer natural environments were available to hunters and gatherers, they certainly did not face a daily grind as the condition of their survival.

In an earlier age when anthropologists were mostly innocent of economic theory and analytical concepts, they spoke of 'modes of subsistence' in traditional society, meaning a reliance on fishing, or a combination of agriculture and pastoralism, perhaps even modest production for local markets. Later, a more deliberate use of concepts from political economy and economic theory entered. Debates focused in the 1950s and early 1960s on the relative claims of 'formal' techniques of rational economic analysis as applied to subsistence or peasant economies and 'substantive' accounts, more oriented to the rounded description of economic activity as it was embedded in social relations, linked to presiding structures of authority and clothed with local meaning. In the former, measures of resources and investment of time with respect to maximizing value dominated, while in the latter the emphasis was upon patterns of tribute and the redistribution of wealth, the hierarchy of incommensurable 'spheres of exchange' (such as the distinct sphere of cattle for brides in marriage, or hospitality for work in the fields, or the operation of a kind of rationing by chiefs through limitations on the use of primitive currency). The latter approach lent itself to illuminating studies of the way that cash, and production for markets, could partially enter a subsistence system without undermining it altogether (though there was, in retrospect, a touch of conservative romanticism here, challenged by Barth, who drew attention to the possibilities of entrepreneurial opportunity in such a context).[36]

New perspectives, with a harder political edge and an awareness of historical pressures in the post-colonial world, developed from the 1960s under the growing inspiration of Marxism. The vocabulary of anthropology was reoriented as a result. For example, there was a sharper analytical use of the phrase 'mode of production'. This had already been used in a holistic, descriptive way, for example by Sahlins in his portrayal of the 'domestic mode' of agricultural production, but it came to be applied more strictly to partial aspects of a local economy, entailing a focus on the social relations of producing specific crops or animal herds, and the cultural (or 'ideological') momentum which allowed the system to reproduce itself. Claude Meillassoux, on the basis of his research in West Africa, famously proposed the 'lineage mode of production' as a system in which elders maintained their dominant position over women and junior men through the control not only of herding but also marriage through the giving of cattle in bridewealth.[37] Don Donham's analysis of the ideology of gender and fertility in the operation of production and the transfer of surpluses among the Maale, summarized above in Chapter 7, is a particularly clear example of this kind of analysis of a traditional political economy and the kinds of inequality which it may perpetuate. Donham has also pointed to the shortcomings of those views of the domestic mode of agricultural production which take at face value the principle of reciprocity in working relations between households. These may be represented as mutually balanced; he showed that in practice, they are not necessarily so, and that imbalances with an ideological component may result in the generation of real inequalities.[38] Donham himself has attempted to refresh our understanding of Marxian theory, and apply it more creatively to non-market social economies, by starting from first principles and re-translating from Marx's original German terminology; thus for 'forces of production' and 'relations of production' he experiments with 'productive powers' and 'productive inequalities', which is certainly effective for Maale.[39]

Exchange: a classic theme in anthropology

Production and the social organization of 'work' lie behind the more evidently attractive and often explicitly public ceremonial phenomena of circulation and exchange. Anthropologists have long been intrigued by the prevalence of 'exchange' as a theme in social relations, and whether or not they have always paid attention to the productive labour behind it, they have put forward some striking ideas for the social sciences. We have to start with Mauss's essay on 'The Gift', originally written in French in the 1920s, which uses historical material from Rome and ancient Scandinavia together with Boas's writings on North America and Malinowski's on Melanesia to invest-igate what drives the circulation of material goods, services, and ceremonies in human society and what particular niche the role of money might occupy in the forms that 'exchange' has taken in world history.[40] The essay is sometimes taken to be about 'gift-giving' as a human universal, and how the Trobrianders and so forth give each other gifts just as 'we' do in modern (market-based) society, making friends and influencing people. But this is a shallow understanding of the essay. A rather different reading has been given by John Davis—it is true he has pointed out that middle Britain spends a similar proportion of its resources on 'gifts' as the Trobrianders do, but of course these resources are themselves very different, and so are the transfers in question. The differences are partly concealed by the ambiguities of moral significance in any transfer of items; it is not always clear what is a com-modity, and what a gift, if one moves from the individual intention to a more sociological perspective. Recent studies have emphasized how commodities themselves can acquire a sort of social history, as they pass along a variety of quite different links of barter, gift, and sale over time.[41] Mauss's original study is not of individual human beings and their motivations for giving 'gifts', nor is it about the modern notion of a gift as a sort of optional extra to the standard economic circulation of goods. It is a comparative study of the forms that socio-political economies can take, primarily in the 'archaic' or pre-modern, pre-market-dominated human world. The significance of the study, however, is not merely antiquarian, but an exploration of the sources and emergence of modern market-oriented social forms.

The examples explored by Mauss illustrate not so much the prevalence of 'gifts', but of the underlying principle of *donation* rather than *contract* or *sale* shaping the pre-modern forms of socio-political economy. These by definition were not based upon the general circulation of money, its penetration of the sphere of labour and its use as an instrument for investment towards the accumulation of socially powerful financial capital. The original French of Mauss's title uses the term *le don*, a concept closer perhaps to 'donation' or 'benefaction' or 'wealth transfer' than it is to the English 'gift', better captured in the French *le cadeau*. The latter evokes a box of chocolates, a silk blouse—a luxury to mark a special occasion. The principle identified by Mauss as driving the pre-monetary social economy is that of *an enduring pattern of material circulation by donation*: not a scattering of one-off presents, but of sustained and directed transfer, material and non-material, maybe voluntary from one point of view, but obligatory from another, that is from the point of view of such transfers being part of an enduring collective pattern into which any given person's activities are likely to be caught up.[42] Hence, the competitive feast-giving of the Pacific American 'potlach', reaching extraordinary levels of the competitive destruction of property in the late nineteenth century (a time of inflated wealth from lucrative trading in the region and a reduced population); and hence the elaborate ceremonials of the *kula*, in which the Trobriand islanders took to ornate canoes to pass on specific goods and valuables clockwise and counter-clockwise in exchange with a circle of neighbouring islands. Such exchanges were not just 'gifts', but at one and the same time the bartering of useful goods, the maintenance of diplomatic relations, the negotiation of hierarchies and status within and between clans or islands, and the ceremonial celebration of a shared, wider political community.

This insight into the massive social relations of the transfer and deployment of goods and valuables in pre-modern forms of social economy has direct implications for feudal and later industrialized society too, having intimate relations with the workings of both. Consider first the medieval monasteries and the role of their charitable benefactions in the history of the early modern economy. Ilana Silber, who has explored this theme, has also studied the role of major charitable giving in the United States, not always in the sense of 'alms to the needy' but in the building up of civic life and high culture in the major cities. In both cases we are a world away from birthday extras and even, arguably, capitalism in the strict sense.[43] The seriousness of philanthropic transfers of wealth in America reminds us that investment in

the major institutions of the modern economy, quite apart from the continuing efforts of interested governments to control and shape that economy,
is the outcome of desires beyond those a rational computer could figure out.
Mauss himself argues that economic rationalism grew out of wider social
forms, historically, and while his analysis does not go nearly as far as Marx's,
he paints a picture of human misery under capitalism. Towards the end of
The Gift he made a number of positive observations about liberal reform and
the provision of social benefits in modern factories and workshops.[44] We
shall return to the imaginary world of the 'Free Market' in Chapter 10 below;
but for now, in the context of this discussion of the way anthropologists
have approached the study of exchange, let us consider some real arenas of
exchange, including markets, on the ground. Do they work according to
'market principles' any more than hunters and gatherers rationalize their use
of time in the interests of survival, or subsistence farmers maximize the way
they draw on the labour of family and neighbours? Tim Jenkins has drawn a
portrait of a French rural farmers' market which shows how flawed is the version of the 'economic man' who shows up there; and Marc Augé has drawn a
hilarious picture (from the economist's point of view) of a truffle market in
the same country—riddled through with game-playing and social exchange
of a ceremonial rather than a calculating kind.[45]

Exchange, equality and inequality

What is a 'fair exchange? This is an ideal commonly thought to be realistic
in market-oriented societies, where the principle is accepted that a fair price
can be arrived at by agreement between the parties. However, at a theoretical
level, and in policy-making by businesses and governments, it is recognized
to be more problematic. In Marxist theory, the notion of a fair exchange
is regarded as a deceptive illusion, especially when it comes to capitalism.
The foundational exchange of wages for human labour is at bottom an unfair
exchange, the employer inevitably benefiting more than the worker, and
cumulatively so as capital accrues and more workers can be employed more
exploitatively, losing control over the product of their labour and losing
touch with the basic human liberties and dignities they once had. The
extreme case of human alienation is of course slavery; is there a fair price for
a whole human being in any circumstances? Meillassoux has demonstrated
how even in the most apparently benign circumstances of the lives of slaves
in a prosperous host society, there is always behind this scenario a chain of

events going back to an original 'deracination' of the person or his or her ancestors from home and from kin, followed perhaps by a series of trading deals which repeat that severance.[46] Although a certain kind of liberty and socially embedded fairnesses were left behind, 'freedom' and 'equality' become explicit goals to be struggled for. We might not think so today, but then the freedoms which are celebrated in modern democratic countries have emerged from historical conditions in which great oppression flourished. Moses Finley has shown how the very notion of 'freedom' came to be spelled out in the specific provisions of agreements over manumission or emancipation from slavery in the ancient world, and the same principle is matched in later periods.[47] The French revolution, the struggle against slavery in the United States, and the foundation of the League of Nations and United Nations after world wars all generated most magnificent statements of human rights and freedoms, freedoms which had not needed to be spelled out before. All these freedoms have concerned the individual's rights in relation to a wider regime of social and political practice which has been condemned as unjust. The language of rights and freedoms has gained a wide currency in recent decades, being taken up by the women's movement, by minority cultural groupings, and by Western foreign policy makers and the media in an international context. The specifics have not always kept up with the power of the rhetoric, however, and the passionate condemnation of perceived 'inequality' can lead to unexpected outcomes.

However, even in the circumstances of humble traditional and local communities, the questions of fair exchange and the difficulty of creating freedom and equality are recognized and reflected upon. Egalitarian relations and fair exchanges have to be struggled for even in hunter-gatherer communities, where equality seems to be a given condition of social life, as James Woodburn has shown. It would be a mistake to assume it a 'natural' or unproblematic given. Woodburn has shown for the Hadza of Tanzania how complex the instituting and maintenance of egalitarian social relations can be, quite as awkward a balance between ideal and practice as in modern socialist societies.[48] Generally in subsistence societies, the inevitable delays in completing what are notionally 'fair exchanges' notoriously lead to manifest indebtedness, inequality, patronage, and even institutions of pawnship or bond-slavery which may seem charitable and fair to those involved at the time. This can happen particularly when natural or man-made disasters reduce an individual or a population to destitution. Children today are given away or sold by their parents in circumstances of war or famine, in the hope that this way they may survive or even have a better life. James Brooks has revealed the scale of inter-group 'adoption' and slavery in the history of the American South-West.[49] There is, in other words, a darker side to 'exchange', present as much in pre-modern as in modern circumstances. As Mauss pointed out, the word 'gift' in German can mean poison.

The very process of exchange, based perhaps on existing difference between the parties, reinscribes that difference as it proceeds. Whether such reinscribing of difference necessarily creates inequalities is a real problem for anthropologists, especially those, for example, working in Melanesia where relations between persons emerge from the very flow of material things, including bodily exchange between the sexes and the generations. In the absence of a cash economy, of course, there cannot be a clear line between gifts and commodities of the kind that characterize a market economy, and so a person in Melanesia cannot so obviously become a commodity in the way that an ancient Roman debtor or people raided from the fringes of the upper Nile could. 'Inequality' is a matter of degree and context, just as 'equality' has to be, as Marilyn Strathern and Richard Fardon have respectively argued.[50] The overwhelming interest of anthropologists in 'exchange' has sometimes led to assumptions that all social life operates on this basis, and there have been warning voices. Not all status and power or wealth is earned by giving things away; things can be deliberately kept back, autonomy can be pursued as an ideal, and reciprocity (in the simple sense) refused. Pierre Clastres is a long-standing critic of 'exchangeism' as an unthinking way of analysing social and especially political relations. He has applied a model, rather, of the local pursuit of self-sufficiency across lowland South American communities as a way of understanding their interrelations. Pressures towards endogamy have been discussed above in Chapter 7. Other refusals are more familiar; for example, the life commitments of hermits and monks in various religious traditions, or the refusal of captitalist 'interest' on money in Islam.

From Mauss's highlighting of the Maori 'spirit of the gift' *hau* onwards, it has been clear that moral and religious phenomena are mixed in with the 'economic' sphere. People are playing complex symbolic games over wealth, giving, trading, or conserving wealth, even refusing to participate in life's normal give-and-take—games which are not only rooted in the immediate material world but refer to an invisible world too. Religious alms, gods in the market place, all remind us of Weber's insight into the Calvinistic drive behind early modern capitalism, of Marx's view of religion as a clouding of the people's insight into the true conditions of their oppression. The social anthropologist has to be sensitive to the invisible, to realize that no act of production or of transfer is self-evidently what people might say it is at the time, but part of implicit processes which invite analysis of a more abstract kind. These processes are never mechanically given in human nature or in the laws of the market or of historical determinism: they demand a consideration of the specific ways in which materiality of production and circulation relates to cultural evaluation and to moral or religious action in given encounters. It is in such social and symbolic negotiation over the material conditions of our existence that we can begin to diagnose fundamental liberties or injustices, modern or pre-modern, and expose them to debate.

CHAPTER TEN

Towards Large-Scale Modern Forms

I T is true that anthropologists have tended to concentrate on the small-scale, relatively face-to-face phenomena of social relations, rather than on the abstract workings of capitalism, government, or global cultural movements. At the same time it is equally true that there is a 'human' scale, and a ceremonial character, to the way these phenomena work too—though the relationship between power, politics, personal participation, and ceremony in modern, large-scale forms is admittedly not the same as in the more coherent local context of classic anthropological research. However, anthropologists, as I suggested in my early chapters, are in fact extremely curious about hidden principles and connections and can be quite creative when they look at large-scale systems. Many today are involved in revealing the layers of complexity involved in local/regional/world connections. Some still study at the 'village' level, but a growing number are investigating the dispersed networks of refugees, transnational migrants, or international entrepreneurs, and a few are going for central institutions of the global power structure such as the European Parliament or the BBC. Modern, large-scale, and urban society has typically been assumed to be amorphous, just a mass of anonymous individuals who show up as statistics in social trends. Taking a different tack, this chapter is presented as a wake-up argument about the qualitatively patterned nature of activity in large-scale modern society and the way we are all vulnerable to, and often co-opted by, these patterns.

I. THE NEW SPACES: COMMUNICATIONS, CITIES, AND POPULAR CULTURE

First, we need to remember some basic facts about the expansion of the world's population. About ten thousand years ago, before the neolithic revolution and intensive agriculture got under way, estimates suggest there were between one and ten million people in the whole world. By AD 1500 there were probably between 425 and 540 million; and by 1900, between 1,550m and 1,762m. By 1950 we numbered 2,555m and by the year 2000, 6,079m. Estimates for 2050 stand at 9,079m, but the good news is that the annual rate of increase has been falling since 1970, and this trend is expected to continue.[1] Numbers used to be controlled by ecology, disease, and war. With material improvements in production and standard of living, we have tended initially to experience great increases in population because of higher levels of infant survival, medical treatments, and greater life-span. Industrialization and urbanization has then tended to produce what is known as the 'demographic transition', in which marriage tends to be later and birth rates are limited deliberately by families, so the rate of overall growth slows down. A growing proportion of the world's population is now concentrated in cities, where the demographic transition is setting in, but large rural areas of the developing world are still experiencing the initial modern phase of accelerated growth.

Social implications of scale and movement

Behind the growth of the world's population is the extraordinary development of the technologies of production, circulation, and communication, from the railways and the telegraph on, which have played such an important role in defining what we mean by the modern era and the nature of its contrast with the past (a theme recently explored by Ruth Finnegan). These technical advances have enabled not only the growth of the population but its mobility and its tendency to increasing concentration. David Harvey has shown how the relations between places are very responsive to all kinds of technical change. Modern communications in themselves affect the spatial relations between capital investment and labour, on the national scale and globally. Recent decades have seen increasingly powerful concentrations of financial investment and decision-making; while in one sense there are flows of money and information across the globe, these flows are clearly structured

—they do not reach everywhere, and it is possible to argue that the global economy has in itself deepened inequalities on a world scale.[2]

Some of the sharpest evidence of difference, including economic inequality, is found in the great city concentrations. It was sometimes assumed that urbanization produced an anonymous mass of individuals, interacting with each other in the terms of impartial rules of the market and of citizenship. If at all, people were defined essentially by their type of work in the productive economy, capitalist or socialist. There can be no doubt of the dominance of the economic frame in modern life, however organized by technology and commerce, and however analysed according to status, or class, or participation; but all the major sociologists have sought to look beyond it, to understand the relationship between that frame and the political institutions and cultural and social lives of the people who live with it, and within it. There is an extensive literature on the way that class and status are entwined with the history of art and high culture generally, from Veblen's classic work on elites and their conspicuous consumption to Bourdieu's sharp analysis of the sociology of sophisticated 'taste and culture' in a modern nation such as France.[3] High culture has perhaps always depended on patronage, if not always that of the Church or private noble families, then at least today national committees able to dispense grants. Music offers some wonderful examples of cultural expression as a part of class and power, even international politics—see, for example, the recent book *Imperialism and Music*.[4] In the sections that follow, I depart from the usual canons to focus on selected examples of the way that distinctively anthropological analysis has been able to illuminate, first, aspects of popular (rather than élite) culture, including sports and tourism, and second, the 'ceremonial' life of cities.

Arenas of popular culture: sport

A conventional view of the history of art, music, and sports is that they were once rooted in the specialized domain of religion and ritual, and have only in the course of recent centuries come to have a secular or mass character. However, if we take sports as a clear example, as Huizinga's *Homo Ludens* demonstrated, there is plenty of evidence from ethnography and history that many sports have been plainly 'secular' as far back as we can trace.[5] Nevertheless they can be infused with symbolism and collective energy even in the most mundane modern circumstances. A pioneering anthropological study of British rural society showed how a whole village became entrammelled in

FIG. 20. Rhythms of industrial life (weekday): L. S. Lowry, *Coming from the Mill*, 1930 (oil). The L. S. Lowry Collection, City of Salford.

FIG. 21. Rhythms of industrial life (weekend): L. S. Lowry, *Bandstand, Peel Park, Salford*, 1925 (pencil). The L. S. Lowry Collection, City of Salford.

FIG. 22. Choreography of a late imperial afternoon: The Sudan Club [British members only], Khartoum, 1952. Photo: Bert Hardy/Picture Post collection, Hulton Archive HQ5956/Getty Images.

FIG. 23. Nationalism embodied: members of the Czechoslovakian Nationalist Organization participating in a mass gymnastic exhibition at the open-air stadium in Prague, c.1935. Hulton Archive JM1612/Getty Images.

the complex projects and passions of organized football.[6] A recent collection offers a fascinating range of studies in this vein. In his introductory chapter to *Sport, Identity and Ethnicity*, Jeremy MacClancy argues the need to incorporate the study of sport into that of social life as a whole.[7] Previously regarded by social scientists as marginal to the real business of society, as Saturday afternoons are popularly seen as a non-serious extra to the working week, sport should be recognized for the central phenomenon it is in modern life. It has long been associated with ideas of character building, and the image of persons and communities, even nations and empires, especially in competition and mutual celebration. Today it is big business, especially for the media and tourist industries, a major political arena for nations, and for the creation of national and gender images. The various sports are means whereby bodies are trained, identities are made, and contested, and control over them is a direct political concern of both élites and proletariats. Sport does not merely reflect society from the margins, it is an integral part of society, and through it one may reflect on society itself, its morals and politics and the expression of character. MacClancy's collection offers studies of Turkish wrestling (rural, local, personal) and its contrast with football (national, modernized through media), female bull-fighting in Spain, Asian cricket in Britain, and football strikes in Zimbabwe. Metamorphoses of the Venice Regatta, between ritual and sport, are traced in history, as are the transformations of polo from an 'anarchic tribal game' of the Himalayas (like its cousin the Afghan *buzkashi*). From Assam, a survivor of this apparently ancient royal game was reinvented as a British regimental sport in Hurlingham and reintroduced to colonial India in the mid-nineteenth century, now professionally cultivated by the military elite and sponsored by the Ministry of Tourism and Culture, its annual tournament at Shandur attended by top brass and VIPs flown in by helicopter, its 'history' documented in tourist brochures and its spectacle broadcast over satellite TV. MacClancy makes the point that 'any particular sport is not intrinsically associated with a particular set of meanings or social values. . . . Rather, a sport is an embodied practice in which meanings are generated, and whose representation and interpretation are open to contest'.[8] In these respects, it is parallel with other ceremonial genres discussed in this book, as well as sharing the attributes of internally self-referential rules about space, time, a sense of sequenced action within an anticipated or designed event, and of formal relations between participants. There is always a choreographical 'grammar' to a game or sport: a formality of turn-taking, or of competitive opposition, of complementary combination of actions by the

FIG. 24. The sport of kings: camel racing for Elizabeth II and Philip, Duke of Edinburgh, during visit to the Sudan, 1965. Photo: Terry Fincher/Express collection, Hulton Archive JC7909/Gett Images.

participants, and often of consciously designed presentation to an informed audience. A sport or game is not always like the Durkheimian 'church' gathering: it does not always constitute some kind of totality—though we might have to think carefully about the Olympic Games or national games where anthems like 'God Save the Queen' are sung. Most games are self-referential and complete in themselves, standing as a 'part' rather than a 'whole' to the wider social life, though with other leisure activities often occupying a specific place in the overall rhythms of work, politics, and religion.

Travel: a ceremonial revival

Celebratory travel has recently become a mass activity, from having been a rather esoteric taste of the élite classes of the Romantic period. In James Clifford's book *Routes* we are shown how pervasive is the modern idea of 'travelling' and of culture as a kind of exploration, a kind of theatre-going, with the rest of the world, rural or urban, as a stage offering performances for the regular pilgrim or tourist. The tourist trade has seen many changes in demographic, class, gender, and specialist emphasis, but there is no denying the rise of restless patterns of *movement* in the modern world. The anthropology of tourism is booming, with studies being published of the hard work and expense, as well as fun and pleasure, involved in the treks not only to Canyons and Waterfalls but around Important Archaeology, Stately Homes and Gardens, and Museums. 'Culture' itself has now become commoditized as an object for the tourist's curiosity, as brochures advertising holidays in Kenya or even Scotland reveal.[9] Museums have become living, hands-on scenarios, along with a flowering of newly recognized local authenticities, and historical personalities. Stage performances are literally part of tourism too: from the seaside music hall or pantomime we have moved on to regional traditions of acting in tourist areas; you can visit the annual season of the Santa Fe Opera as well as the extraordinary panorama of the Grand Canyon while on holiday in the American South-West; or in the more modest setting of the English Lake District you can see plays of the world in Keswick's brand-new Theatre by the Lake, promoted as productions staged 'against the magnificent scenery of Derwentwater'.

Marc Augé has proclaimed the era of postmodern 'non-spaces', 'non-places'. Attributing to Baudelaire's *Tableaux Parisiens* a very lucid modernity—the city seen as a working unity of old and new against the eternal skies—he insists that 'supermodernity' has replaced this clarity with shifts of gaze and the dissolution of coherent relations between individuals.[10] Augé speaks of an 'excess' of space, and events, of journeys and movements and transitional, anonymous places. But his opposition between the old and the supermodern is too polarized; there were journeys in the old days too, and even anonymous places and identities—think, for example, of soldiers, sailors, slaves. As for today's non-places: they are real in their own way, and encompassed by 'real' places. You don't live all the time in an airport or supermarket—you go there for a purpose, and come back home. The air traveller (and I read Augé's book on a transatlantic plane) may be in a kind of supermodern space, rather different from the pre-modern space of the medieval French village below, but is the difference really not better thought of as degree rather than kind? What Augé does not realize about supermodern non-places as 'transit' is that they do not exist on their own in a vacuum; they exist, for actual people and for social collectivities, between quite concrete formations. They are reminiscent of the liminal or in-between stage of the familiar model of rites of passage. He scoffs at the idea of a 'Durkheimian' analysis of the Paris airport lounge, but forgets the hugs and tears and present-giving at either end of the journey, beyond the security gates. Air passengers are closed off from normal space because of modern nationalism—they are in neither one country nor the other, legally—and they behave, temporarily, in very constrained and standardized ways. Very few people indeed (though it does happen occasionally) slip off into permanent limbo between national spaces and classifications.

The non-spaces in fact do not exist in a self-encompassing vacuum: they depend upon the existence of nations, and cities, and capital concentrations in very specific spots, such as New York and Silicon Valley. Non-space may be a phenomenological subjective experience; but objectively this illusion depends on the work being done very much 'on the ground'.

The public life of cities: ceremonial form and action

Let us return to cities: What has anthropology said about urban life? Urban life used to be contrasted in every way with the rural scene, as anonymous, work-dominated, and oppressive. The first field explorations in urban anthropology were mainly concerned with small groups, often of the poor, or rural migrants, mainly in new cities of the colonial territories though there were a few pioneering studies in Britain and the USA too.[11] A linked theme was the reconstitution of the older tribal identities into new ethnic formations among immigrants in industrial urban conditions, partly as a result of the conditions of organized labour and trade unions. The study of urban elites such as trading groups has followed, along with the attempt to portray the overall social shape of towns and cities in historical perspective. Ulf Hannerz has made a useful distinction between anthropology *in* the city, and *of* the city, noting—with reference to Erving Goffman—the stage-like quality of the city's layout and the theatrical character of much city life.[12] Here we are returning perhaps to an older theme. It is not always remembered that Durkheim's teacher was Fustel de Coulanges, whose seminal work on 'the ancient city' and the way its forms provided a setting for social life was a foundational text in Evans-Pritchard's teaching of anthropology.[13] Contemplating the character of a whole town or city also reminds us of the ceremonial significance of the patterned urban space, its linked potential for political display and action, its calendar of community performances, and its role as regional showcase—as I shall illustrate below with the example of Santa Fe.

Towns and cities may wax and wane in importance. Bath, for example, as an urban centre, has not remained the same social world over the centuries

FIG. 25. New traffic in old streets: Bath, 2000. The Roman baths (encircled) are still a centre of attraction in the ancient heart of the city, itself re-patterned over time. Getmapping plc.

from the Roman period, through its eighteenth-century elegance to its present-day traffic congestion and busyness; but its persistence as a focal nucleus in the built landscape over such long periods is remarkable. All towns are literally historical residues and demonstrate in a concrete way their own past and the often lasting circulatory pattern of their activities. They are material entities in a way that nations are not; nations are a legal supposition, not a set of buildings and inherited significant spaces. Many towns and cities are older than today's nations, older than languages and modern forms of culture. Some in Britain, for example, have been settled and lived in without a break for a couple of millennia—from long before the Anglo-Saxons arrived to launch the beginnings of English; the Romans built their towns and roads in a Celtic land. The revelations of archaeology show us the material remains of Pompeii, into which we can so easily insert ourselves and imagine our lives as householders, merchants, or charioteers—even dancers. The material remains left by rural communities are never so condensed or homey-feeling as those of cities. Nor can special monuments or dramatic burial sites offer the same sense of belonging; they are remote, sacred, strange, whereas the humble pavements and counters and ruts and potholes of Pompeii's backstreets have a powerful familiarity. Cities connect us to the past more tangibly than nations, language, or images of the cultural life of hunters or cultivators can do. There are Roman toilets in Carlisle, very earthy reminders which evoke the lived realities of the past in our imagination more directly than the more celebrated glories of antiquity.

Ancient traditions of city-building prompt us to reflect on two more general points. First is the prominent role played by complexes of buildings which have had a religious or ceremonial function. Second is the way that such core complexes appear to relate to the regions around them. In his magisterial study of the evidence of the earliest traditions of city building, with particular reference to the Shang dynasty of North China in the second half of the second millennium BC, Paul Wheatley has emphasized these points and argued that they are the key to understanding the very genesis of cities.[14] He criticizes standard sociological definitions of the city and of urbanism, from Max Weber to Louis Wirth, definitions which have tended to rely on descriptive features of the modern form—concentrated populations, market activities, specialized occupations, or governmental roles, as diagnostic of the city everywhere. Surveying the character of early focal settlements of obvious distinction and regional eminence, especially from China, the Middle East, the Yoruba kingdoms, and Central and South America, Wheatley prefers to emphasize the way these core settlements served as ceremonial centres, with temples, royal tombs, monuments for the gods, and so forth. Such sites were often focal points for a wider region, and could attract other functions, including exchange, though not necessarily in the first place the modern kind of market exchange. He argues that they could become in themselves pivotal points from which the qualities of surrounding regional space, its cosmological bearings and its social life, are generated. In innumerable cases, this has been the early story of many of our modern cities today, obscured as it may be by the overwhelming secular and material considerations of economy, housing, government, and traffic plans. Wheatley finds the geographers' theories of 'central place' and the hierarchy of such places in the definition of regions at encompassing levels more helpful than the sociologists' rough-and-ready empiricism.

We could point also to Geertz's conception of an 'exemplary centre', developed especially for traditional kingdoms (see the next chapter), but relevant to an essentially *relational* view of the city and those outside who look to it, who take their bearings from it. The city is an exemplary centre in multiple ways: whether ancient or modern, it is the place for demonstrating public opinion, fashion, and style to a wider public. Even on the TV, reporters stand outside significant buildings to interview the street population, and through the media, street life, street fashion, and 'street-wise' behaviour spread everywhere. Exemplification works the other way too, as images of the countryside and the notion of 'remote areas' become intensified among city-dwellers themselves. However, while the displays of Scottish sports or the Welsh Eisteddfod, tribal dancing in African beach resorts, or cultural heritage museums in the North American native reservations entrance the city traveller, it is in the public life of cities that we find ceremonial enactments at their most condensed, and most political, and most potentially dramatic— even sometimes literally explosive. Ancient Rome had its battles and riots as well as imperial displays, and the modern city fosters excited congregations in a no less compelling way.

Santa Fe showcase: ceremonial competition on a frontier

I have mentioned the city of Sante Fe in New Mexico, and I would now like to present it as a prime exemplar of several of the themes developed in this and some earlier chapters. This city, since 1848 firmly incorporated in the United States but previously a northern frontier garrison town of Mexico, means

FIG. 26. Fiesta parade, Santa Fe, c.1935. Photo: T. Harman Parkhurst, courtesy Museum of New Mexico (11849).

many different things to different people. It has a very dense concentration of 'symbolic' activities per square mile—most of them in the single square mile of the city centre. Here is a shared physical stage for the celebrations of a variety of different traditions and local communities. These share a peaceful present but a chequered and occasionally very violent past, which also, on many occasions, took the form of *performance* around the central Plaza. Santa Fe today must surely draw as many tourists per head of the local population as any town of its size in the world. It has already attracted several anthropologists, who have tended to emphasize the successful blending of elements. My own summary will try to trace something of the continuing competition over the city's ceremonial space and even ritual elements, the historical fault lines beneath the extraordinary efforts of each community, or faction, to triumph in the competitive (and today lucrative) game of ceremonial excess.

A student of Victor Turner, Ronald Grimes moved the anthropological study of rituals firmly from the traditional tribal context to the city, in his study of public ceremonial and drama in Santa Fe. The annual calendar of festivals and performances is highly elaborate, each of the three 'cultural groupings' in the city identified today (the Native Americans, the Hispanics, and the Anglos) contributing their share and often reflecting ironically off each other's traditions. Turner in his introduction suggested that contradictions need not be an issue in the 'metalanguage' of public performances, which are not just a reflection of reality but 'the very means by which a city reflects upon its own growth'.[15] Deirdre Evans-Pritchard, who has also presented us with an intricate and vivid study of Santa Fe, emphasizes the way that the external demands of tourism now strongly influence current formations of ethnicity, authenticity, cultural production, and the politics of competition for commercial space in the Plaza. She writes that the city 'attracts hundreds of thousands of tourists each year because of its picturesque plaza, its historic role as a Spanish imperial capital, its nearby Indian pueblos, its wealth of museums, and its cultural events—and its ski slopes. It has an image as an Old World haven where one can meet the American Other, the unassimilated Native American culture.'[16] The city authorities have now granted representatives of the latter the right to occupy the whole length of the portal of the Palace of Governors (centre stage, as it were, facing the Plaza) on a daily basis, selling jewellery and crafts in native costume. Who is actually an Anglo, a Hispanic, or a Native American can be very complicated because of the region's past;[17] but the modern categories are clear in the language of ceremony and the theoretical rights to symbolic space in the city.

Grimes does not dwell much on history, but offers an analysis suggesting the overall coherence of Santa Fe's annual rituals under the presiding presence of the Catholic Church. Dominant here are the crowning of the Marian image of La Conquistadora, by a papal representative from Rome, proclaiming her rule over the domains of her 'metaphorical kingdom' of New Mexico, and the Corpus Christi processions with the statue through the city. He is clear that 'cultural systems often contain contradictions' but also that 'public rituals can mask them'. He emphasizes how the spatial form and focus of the three ceremonial traditions of the city come together in one place; the central Plaza, more in the manner of Old World cities than New. We could ask, however, whether this physical coming together is to some extent an illusion of integration. The Plaza has always been a site of contested dominance, competing style, and new ideas. If you wished to make a statement or mount a demonstration in this city you would use the Plaza, even today. The public rituals, events, and parades may borrow from each other and even attempt their own synthesis, but they approach from different angles. They each retain a specific cycle of dates, while using the same central place; they intersect, rather than blend together. Richard Murphy has used the image of a Cubist painting to portray the socio-cultural life of another frontier town, Lahore, which used to be largely Hindu and built in Indian architectural style but following the partitition between India and Pakistan has become predominantly Muslim, while pulled also towards Western modernity.[18] Santa Fe is today, thankfully, much less fraught politically than Lahore, but I find this image of different planes or perspectives from the past cutting across or even through each other in one place more helpful in understanding Santa Fe than the image of one great ceremonial whole. This is not always obvious to tourists, towards whom Santa Fe presents a harmonious all-season package of world entertainment and successive events of local culture. Let us fill in some of the longer story.[19]

In 1595 the Spanish adventurer Juan de Oñate moved northwards from the silver-mining territories of Mexico. He settled in the northern Rio Grande valley, but faced severe local resistance from the Pueblo dwellers and put them down with great brutality. Some at Acoma had a foot cut off. Following Oñate's resignation, the Spanish crown nevertheless decided to found a colony, establishing the capital at Santa Fe in 1610. It was built according to the Laws of the Indies, essentially as a garrison town with the Governor's Palace facing the central plaza. The Franciscans followed with nearly fifty mission complexes at Native American pueblos in the region (including

Acoma—pictured earlier, in Fig. 2), but unfortunately the seventeenth century saw famine, warfare, and epidemics. In 1680 the region was overrun by a
series of attacks on isolated missions and ranches which became known as
the Pueblo Revolt. Tano- and Tewa-speaking groups, totalling about 1,500
people, occupied the town of Santa Fe. It was transformed into a communal
Pueblo-style village of three- and four-storey dwellings around two fortified
plazas with a ceremonial *kiva* or ritual shrine at the centre of each.

In 1692 the Spanish returned, led by Diego de Vargas. After a brief siege, he
forced the Pueblo Indians to erect a cross in their main plaza; he knelt and
kissed it, and required the Pueblo leaders to do the same. These events are
known locally today as 'the peaceful reconquest of Santa Fe'. The following
year, however, de Vargas returned and attacked. The result was catastrophic:
some native Americans committed suicide (including the Pueblo leader,
'Governor José'), some were executed, some fled, hundreds were sentenced to
ten years' servitude. The violence is not often recalled in later symbolism and
ceremony—rather the contrary. As early as 1712 the Spanish authorities had
resolved that there should be on 14 September (twenty years after the 'peaceful' reconquest) a Fiesta, with Mass and a procession through the main Plaza,
in honour of the Exaltation of the Holy Cross. The first map was made in 1766,
showing church and government to the east and north of the main Plaza,
itself a civic space where the mounted militia drilled and where fiestas and
markets were held. Santa Fe was an important frontier garrison but a drain on
the royal treasury, its elite exporting only sheep, wool, pine nuts, and Indian
slaves to the mines. When Mexican independence came in 1821, the struggle
had weakened central government and its links to the provinces; but in the
same year the opening of the 'Santa Fe Trail', the alternative trade route from
the US side, led to a new prosperity. The Plaza blossomed into a mercantile
centre. The new trade had led to much intermarriage and co-operation
between the Spanish-speaking élite and American traders, with political
implications. When Santa Fe was occupied during the 1846 US–Mexican
War, volunteers from the Army of the West brought a sixty-foot pole from
the mountains; when they reached the Plaza, they planted that pole at its
centre. A few days later, the Stars and Stripes was run up this makeshift
flagpole. The historian Chris Wilson comments, 'Governor General Diego
de Vargas, who forced Pueblo leaders to kneel before a cross erected in the
Plaza in 1692, would have understood.'[20] In 1848 the US formally annexed
New Mexico and California, enabling trade to pass right through to Mexico
and the Pacific Coast.

In the latter half of the nineteenth century the influx of Anglo-American investors and professionals led to the effective appropriation of lands worked by the Mexican population. The Plaza was turned into a park with trees and paths, from 1862. Walkways converged on a central point, marked by a bandstand in 1866, and replaced in 1867 with an obelisk commemorating the American (and Mexican and Pueblo) dead of the Civil and Indian wars. A branch railway arrived in 1880. A deliberate campaign to try and attract business to Santa Fe, including tourist business, had started in the 1890s, but commentators were already noting the clash between the demands for modernization and the dangers it posed to 'the haloed glow of romance that broods with its benign wings over the antique walls of this ancient city'.[21] The turn of the century saw the importance already of illustrators, photographers, and early archaeologists, in developing the picturesque. From 1907, calendars showing Pueblo or Navajo (rather than Spanish) scenes were in wide circulation; and in 1909, the Museum of New Mexico was founded. By the time statehood was granted in 1912, 'Anglo-Saxon' dominance and attitudes of superiority were provoking the Mexican elite to emphasize their 'Castilian' and therefore aristocratic Spanish ancestry, while the 'Anglos' were praising the Pueblo Indians as a purer and, therefore, more industrious and moral people.[22]

The museum crowd meanwhile were devoting themselves to the promotion of Santa Fe's heritage, adding costumed historical parades with a distinctly elite and solemn Spanish flavour to the Church processions. A plan was devised in 1912 for the restoration of the old city, with the promotion of a local Santa Fe style by the joint Museum of New Mexico–School of American Archaeology. The main mover was Edgar Lee Hewett, later said to be 'more interested in cultivating the popular fascination with the Southwest than in scientific scholarship', and succeeding despite the suspicions of heavyweight academic anthropologists such as Franz Boas.[23] He quickly embarked on the restoration of the Palace of the Governors, as well as promoting the archaeology of the elegantly patterned cliff dwellings and valley settlements left by the shadowy predecessors of the modern Pueblo peoples. Nationally there was the City Beautiful campaign (part of the Arts and Crafts movement); Santa Fe was the smallest US city in the movement, and the only one to break with the classicist norm and go for a 'local revival style'. A romantically inclined art colony soon emerged in Santa Fe, and by the 1920s tourism was booming.

It was not long before the new American immigrants, led by social activists and members of the art colony, sponsored a 'counter Fiesta'. The programme

ɪɢ. 27. Zozobra burning, Santa Fe Fiesta, *c*.1942. Courtesy Museum of New Mexico (47328).

of free events for the people at large was called 'Pasatiempo' (pastime, amusement), and since its initiation in 1924 this populist and irreverent September
festival, immediately dubbed the 'Hysterical Pageant' with tongue-in-cheek
parodies and pop icons, has never looked back.[24] People began to call it the
'grand carnival'. By 1926, local artists had fabricated a giant figure they named
Zozobra, whose burning has ever since provided a striking and sombre note
(Grimes suggests that it evokes 'primal awe and fear' at the festival)[25]—and
were calling for the removal of 'the earnest, autocratic, tee-totaling Hewett'
as museum director. The Catholic-Spanish festivals and the neo-pagan Fiesta
span the summer season today, and counterpoint each other in many ironical
echoes. The question of 'ethnic' and cultural representation at each event,
the choice of who is to play the de Vargas figure, and who the Fiesta Queen
(sharply counterpointing La Conquistadora) now occupies the local politics of
the city, along with the commercial spaces opened up for the arts and crafts
of the Indian market, the summer and winter Spanish markets, the opening
of the ski season (which should coincide with Thanksgiving), Christmas with
its heavy garlands of Pueblo mythological figures, American flags, and the

late summer season of satirical melodrama (a legacy of the art colony). There have been rows over the commercialization of the church festivals; the statue of La Conquistadora has been stolen; questions were raised in 1998 by Native Americans as to whether the city should be celebrating the 400th anniversary of the Spanish conquest. Someone made this time the occasion to sever the left foot of the mounted statue of the Spanish conqueror Oñate, as he had once severed the feet of prisoners from Acoma. The statue, located near San Juan, has now been repaired, but its presence is not advertised and only determined visitors can find it. The city itself, however, has now become a world platform: every year you can see Shakespeare in Santa Fe, or go to the world-class Santa Fe Opera—a few years ago you could see Jonathan Miller's *Magic Flute* in Santa Fe, itself transposed to a luxury hotel in 1930s Europe: as if the city itself were not sufficient as a theatrical spectacle. Thanks to the power of the tourist magic, it has become a stage on which the world can come to see itself, if care is taken in selecting the appropriate dates. The Plaza, first taken over by local conquest from the Spaniards, and celebrated as a crucial religious centre by the Pueblo peoples, only to be reconquered by Spaniards and then US forces, is now draped with shops, stalls, and street vendors offering Hopi silver, Acoma pots, Zuni fetishes, and Navajo rugs. How local are the locals (a loaded question as Deirdre Evans-Pritchard's essay shows)? Many families take part in a whole range of Santa Fe's ceremonial activities, whether Indian, Hispanic, or even Anglo. The date cycles are distinctive and separate; the 'representations' and collective memories are too. Ironical commentaries can be exchanged. A few years ago came the latest innovation, in Albuquerque's South Valley, of a rival Hispanic ceremony of burning the figure of a man, to rival Santa Fe's Zozobra. What we could almost dub the 'Santa Fe potlach' of continually inflating, competitive, and partially destructive, feasting thus goes on. The public ceremonial of Santa Fe has more faces, and more historical shadows, than Grimes conveys.

Conclusion: from France, to Trinidad, to Notting Hill

The pastimes and fashions of elites can, notoriously, filter down. But the culture of the people has its own character, or rather mix of character. Popular culture in the world of modernity and the city is by no means an easy concept, for it draws on so many sources: from imitating, or sometimes burlesquing, generations of the elite forms, to recreating rural folk festivals and inventing streetwise humour. When Abner Cohen turned his attention from

West Africa to the streets of London, he captured something of the special magic of the Notting Hill Festival, a transformation of the lenten Trinidad Carnival, which itself incorporated elements from the former elite French practice of creole dramas on the island. In London, the festival is no longer a Trinidadian event but a generally Afro-Caribbean one, and even arguably a London event as such. It is not only in cities and immigrant communities where ceremony and ritual are now becoming very visible to anthropologists of the modern world; there is a growing literature on the surge of interest in local rituals across Europe, for example, on museums and the heritage industry everywhere; on the increasing elaboration of Christmas in various parts of the world and so forth.[26] Danny Miller has argued that the idea of consumption itself, with all the house decoration, food preparation, and shopping that goes into it, is a kind of ritual, imbued with morality and symbolism, even religious overtones, though some may still feel the need for an anchor in the basic facts of capitalism and the way it tends to promote inequalities. The consumer is king as long as he—or more usually she—has a full purse, but not everyone involved in the production of the goods we see in the supermarket has this power.

The conditions of modern life were once conventionally understood as a steady progression of rational improvement towards a uniform sameness in the standard of living. This perspective once seemed to make anthropology redundant, but modern—postmodern if you wish—conditions have not ful-filled this gloomy promise. It could be argued that the world is witnessing a revival of the singular and the ceremonial, a new recognition of the power of the grand collective gesture as a mode of action. We are acknowledging the drama and variety of human life, we rarely appeal to the rationality of 'our western civilization', we see a new vitality in popular culture across the world. All this is particularly clear in the field of those activities apparently outside 'work' in the serious sense for the ordinary person—entertainment, sport, fashion, the artistic effort put into making homes and gardens, amateur the-atricals, and so on. It could be argued that the economy itself is oriented to the ceremonial to a remarkable degree. All these fields are domains of invest-ment and many people's working wage depends upon production for them. Even today's economist needs to understand these areas which are core to the anthropologist's long-standing concern with value, symbol, and participation. Technical advances in print production, not to mention the electronic media, have widened the participation of people across the world in cultural activities which were once typically very local events or 'luxuries' of the privileged.

2. THE MODERN PERSON AND 'THE MARKET'

We have shown above in Chapter 9 how we have to qualify our understanding of what a market in the literal sense is—that is, a market place, gatherings on market days, the judgements made over price and exchangeability: is it a phenomenon for which the economists can fully account? We have suggested, rather, that it is a social phenomenon full of ceremony, transmitted form, and public sentiment, a patterned form of activity into which individual human beings try to fit themselves, rather than it being (as the utilitarians like Barth would have it) the outcome of directed conscious purposeful activity by human actors as born entrepreneurs. If this, rather than rational commodity exchange, is the nature of the concrete 'market-place', then how far can utility effectively serve as a metaphor for that wider abstraction of 'The Market' supposed to drive modern life? Marx built his explanatory system from the starting point that the apparent 'fairness' of the concrete market-place was a false basis for understanding the structural exchanges of general capitalism: primarily the fundamentally 'unfair' exchange of wages for labour. Despite his demonstration, which many cynical capitalists would admit contained some truth, the rhetoric and justifications of capitalism continue to propagate the notion of the fairness of market principles, the automatic good of wealth accumulation, and the moral exemplar of the entrepreneur.

To illustrate these points, I will draw on some of the arguments in a collection of recent papers edited by James Carrier on the question of what the idea of 'The Market' might mean in what I would like to label 'vernacular' contexts.[27] The collection is devoted to modifying our received view of the dominant place of the 'Free Market' in shaping the social forms of capitalist society. Carrier himself suggests that market principles, deriving from classical economics and utilitarian theory, do not dictate the way that even businesses operate, let alone ordinary people. We can best understand this ironic situation by thinking of 'The Market' as a cultural artefact, a level of public language or discourse, which circulates freely and is employed by all but does not bear a direct relationship to what we do. Nor do its principles explain the distribution of wealth or other basic aspects of the societies we live in. It can become pure ideology, and anti-State ideology at that, as shown in Susan Love-Brown's chapter on the American anarcho-capitalists who seek salvation from imposed government through self-reliance and the defence of individual property-owning.[28] Carrier studies the fortunes of a different sort of American, a certain Mr Hawken, supplier of garden tools and furniture in California, whose ups and downs we know about because he wrote his auto-biography.[29] Through his writing emerges a very different entrepreneurial 'self' from that presupposed by Adam Smith in *The Wealth of Nations* or by subsequent latter-day market theorists. Hawken sees himself as a 'free' indi-vidual, and as an innovator, but his motivation is not so much to make money —it is to live the satisfying life of a good human being. He recommends others to treat employees and customers as though they were friends; he keeps his word, even in impersonal commercial situations; he almost regrets the need to be dealing with money, a polluting substance. 'The Market' from which he so clearly distances himself at least in his autobiographical musings eventually drives him out of business. But he comes from a long lineage, perhaps including the nineteenth-century Quaker business families, even the seventeenth-century Calvinists. The lineage itself is surviving the Market quite well.

Malcolm Chapman and Peter Buckley show on the basis of their detailed research among some British technical firms that decisions are almost never made on the basis of cold rational calculation: numerical evidence of prices, profits, forecasts are always accompanied by a verbal counterpoint drawing on personal gut-feeling, memories, and loyalty to a firm as such.[30] The line between buying in components, say, or making them yourself is rarely calcu-lated on the basis of the economic science of 'transaction costs', but on the a priori assumption that it is important above all that the company itself should survive. 'Companies have identities, just as do clans or countries . . . Managers invest moral virtue in the integrity of the classification with which they are familiar. Threats to it, and anomalies within it, generate sentiments straight out of *Purity and Danger* (Douglas 1966)'.[31] Joel Kahn's contribution to the book traces the way in which the principles of the Market, and an anti-Market social critique, have long coexisted in the West and indeed may entail one another.[32] The vehement modern Islamic social critique of the Market may be seen as accompanying the world-wide expansion of that Market, at least of the market as an important level of public language, and to be a recent extension of an older argument that continues to be a part of Western society.

Carrier's persuasive argument that we think of 'The Market' as a kind of public language helps us to see why we are all now speaking of ourselves as consumers (we are customers on the British railways, rather than passengers;

FIG. 28. Symbols through and through: carved figures on the front of a Seattle store, *c.*1930. Pho
by Smith; RAI 4158. Courtesy of the Royal Anthropological Institute of Great Britain and Ireland.

politicians design their policies with the supposed demands of voters in mind; etc.). Does this mean that we really have been turned into a consumer-led society, or simply that we have a new way of pretending this? The idea that one's identity is now best seen as expressing itself in the consumer field has been promoted in very plausible ways. Danny Miller's arguments are capturing attention here—for example, on the way that personal choice leads to the celebration of display and commodification in the ultra-modern circumstances of historically uprooted and resettled populations like some in the Caribbean, how the Western middle classes are embracing the capitalists' very image of self through shopping and consumption, and how modernity combines a project of living in the 'ephemeral present' with a specially fostered nostalgia for the past.[33]

However, we are not quite in a situation where all is defined by the consumer—there are still butchers, bakers, and not a few candlestick makers on the productive side. While much of today's research focuses on consumption, identities in the industrialized countries are still linked today, as they were in classic sociology, to people's place in the productive system. As Bourdieu has shown so vividly, the sign-laden practices of industrial society can be looked at in a surprisingly similar kind of way to those of agricultural peasants (see above, Chapter 9). He applies the *habitus* idea to industrial society—'Habitus are generative principles of distinct and distinctive practices—what the worker eats, and especially the way he eats it, the sport he practices and the way he practices it . . . different from the industrial owner's corresponding activities. But habitus are also classificatory schemes, principles of classification, principles of vision and division, different tastes.'[34] He explains that these principles and differences 'become symbolic differences and constitute a veritable language . . . In fact, the main idea is that to exist within a social space, to occupy a point or to be an individual within a social space, is to differ, to be different.' This 'language' in which I set myself off from others, and give significance to our differences, is not, however, an arbitrary one, but one anchored in the economic structure. 'The social world embraces me like a point. But this point is a point of view, the principle of a view adopted from a point located in social space, a perspective which is defined, in its form and contents, by the objective position from which it is adopted.'[35] Bourdieu notes that we all spend a lot of time playing with the signs and significations of who we are in the system (and no doubt a lot of these games involve our stepping to and fro across the line separating the image of producer from that of consumer). What we can all agree on is the powerful rhetoric of individuality and choice in the 'modern' world, whatever that rhetoric may gloss over with reference to one's 'objective position'.

What has happened to the notion of the person?

If pre-modern society allocated name, status, and character to the individual person, how far can we say that the 'modern' person has escaped similar constraints of social form? Following my earlier discussion in Chapter 8, Mauss's triangular model of the person as the site where the organic, the psychological, and social intersect is surely equally applicable, though these may be rather different in content and interrelation. Mauss's later essay on the 'concept of the person' is at heart an examination of where that difference lies, and one of the key aspects of the difference (echoing his work on 'the gift') is shown to be in the way that the modern person relates to things.[36] In Roman times a profound distinction was made between the law of persons, of things, and of actions. 'Ownership' was developed over things, exchanges and debts were articulated in a newly lucid way, and while the primitive form of identities could be likened to the wearing of inherited insignia in a masquerade, 'ownership' among the Romans came to encompass the idea of individually 'owning' the mask (originally *persona*) or name through which one had spoken. The *persona* came to be synonymous with the true nature of the individual; only the slave was excluded from this right, as a slave has no personality, not owning even his or (especially) her own body, let alone goods. In ancient German law, again following Mauss, a free man was distinguished from the slave in the idiom of his being the proprietor of his own body. We should emphasize the further point, though Mauss does not, that a slave by definition has been reduced to the property of someone else, and is essentially not a person because he or she can be bought and sold as a commodity. It is in this extreme context that ideas of personal and political freedom have often come to be articulated in history, sometimes through violent political action.[37] Modern times have also seen claims to freedoms other than those of equal citizenship emerging from the ranks of those whose personal standing has come in some way to seem less than full, often on bodily grounds, such as gender, disability, sexual orientation. In addition, the idea of personal worth as measurable in terms of proprietory rights over one's own body has suddenly become very prominent in our 'postmodern' times. We worry about rights over bodies after death, before birth, gifts and even sales of body parts by the living, rights to bodily sexual gratification without responsibility to others, and to manipulation of the physical elements of one's own body for purposes of 'artificial' reproduction. Now, finally, the large questions of who has rights to the knowledge and control of genes have become central debates. Personal freedom is today more than an imagined ideal of liberty, equality, and fraternity within a community of like citizens. Rhetorically, it is now teetering on the brink of claiming absolute personal autonomy among some wealthier circles of the advanced countries. This is some way from the ideas of intellectual and moral autonomy that Mauss emphasized in his famous essay on the historical emergence of the modern concept of the person, and the self, but then he did also remark that the 'Idea' itself was fragile, and that we could not predict what would happen to it. It seems that the idea has been stretched almost to absurd limits in some parts of the world, before it has effectively reached many other parts at all. The current global mismatch between privilege and misery with respect to personal freedoms is very sobering.

We could say the same of the rush to identify everything important about people as being in their genes. In the days before genes were heard of, ideas of blood and race and instinct and sexual difference were often promoted as explanations of, and even justifications for, social action, but we look back with great unease on what has been done in the name of biological science (eugenics, state-sponsored racism, and the like). We have today not only new science, but new lay and popular understandings and expectations of science which are helping to shape applications in practice. Questions of ethics and the law are raised not so much directly by the technical possibilities of the new genetics, but by public expectations of the uses to which they can be put. In the developed countries the context of these expectations is a new faith in biological science as a way of divining the truth about the human condition, whether considered collectively or individually. The image of the organic has come to dominate public discourse about what social relations, human origins, personal and group identities actually are. It is not easy to analyse such a shift in the general perception of human realities when you are living in the middle of it. It is nevertheless important to keep an analytical distance, because what is happening in the new technical field, especially about reproduction, is more than just scientific advance, it is propelled by ideas about society, and specifically increasingly powerful ideas about the primary moral significance of biological connection.

It has been argued that Western views of the field of kinship and family have long presupposed that biological relations are somehow the 'real' bedrock upon which 'artificial' connections are built in different ways by legal fictions, and by the remarkable variety of strange-sounding social arrangements reported by ethnographers. What used to be understood as a biological connection was of course the always bodily, palpable business of sex, pregnancy, and lactation. It is not only in the West that this kind of contrast, as between, say, 'natural' and adoped children, can be found. The Nuer famously distinguish between social fatherhood, and 'natural' links with children conceived outside marriage (as the Romans distinguished between *pater* and *genitor*). There was a time when 'natural' children were hushed up in the interests of the legitimate family; but along with the rise of women's rights the basis of such legitimacy has been eroded in many ways. At the same time the spread of contraception and even the acceptance of abortion in certain circumstances has reinforced the idea that all children actually born are presumed wanted. There is a more open and liberal attitude towards children born outside wedlock, one-parent families are now common, and the stigma of illegitimacy has almost disappeared. The rights of adopted children to seek out their 'real' parents are being advocated widely, and legally secured in many countries. These changes have appeared to reinforce, in mainstream Western society, the idea that *real* parenthood and kinship is justifiably founded in 'natural' connection.

This is the context in which the new genetic sciences have been popularly welcomed: but they have introduced a totally new idea about 'natural' kinship, which is less and less to do with sexuality, and even pregnancy, but rather with the abstract though very enticing idea of microscopic genes and reproductive cells. The diagnostic and forensic use of DNA tests to establish the underlying causes of illness and the basis of 'real' individual identity are proving extremely attractive to the public. While corporations are rushing to law to patent commercially valuable genes, a poet and casino waitress from Bristol recently declared her wish to become the first person to patent herself, that is her own genes.[38] Into this scenario the possibilities of the new reproductive technologies (NRTs) have made a dramatic entrance. Assistance to couples with techniques of artificial insemination with the husband's sperm (AIH) were first supplemented by the discreet use of donor sperm (AID), supporting the older social forms. However, there has been increasing emphasis on the choice of donor, and concern about his anonymity. In several Western countries, along with unashamed acknowledgement of 'natural' kinship in other contexts, there have been growing demands that AID children, like adopted children, should have the right to find out and even make contact with their 'real' father. In the context of surrogacy, where a woman may give birth to a child for another woman, or for a couple, having received either donated sperm or a donated embryo fertilized *in vitro*, the complications escalate. Questions arise as to what is a real mother, the genetic or the carrying mother. In the UK at least, there has been a shift of popular opinion towards the genetic definition. The law as it stands treats the woman *who gives birth* as the parent, though arguments have been successfully put by couples who have provided an embryo for implantation that they should both be registered as the parents. A recent case involved a commissioning couple A and another couple B, who agreed that Mrs B would be implanted with couple A's embryo. Everything went according to plan, including the handing over of the baby to Mr and Mrs A, until the birth had to be registered. Mrs B was named as the mother, since she had given birth to the child, and Mr B as the father, as her husband. Eventually Mr A succeeded in changing the registration to himself as the natural father, and much later at a second court hearing, Mrs A won her argument to be the legal mother, on the grounds of her genetic parenthood. Commercial surrogacy, for money, is still outlawed in the UK, though available in the USA. A key technique which facilitates the NRTs today is that of freezing gametes and embryos: the act of freezing in itself establishes a degree of control, of ownership of the elements of reproduction, even after the donor's death, which has never been possible before; nor is it anything to do with facilitating 'what is only natural'. Today's farmer knows very well that these techniques are far from 'nature'.

The technical possibilities of the NRTs are giving a new momentum to the popular Western understanding of the right to reproduce oneself, and even one's social kind. Infertility is seen as a medical, treatable condition, rather than a 'natural' condition to be accepted. Many patients turn up for treatment, prepared to accept anything that science can offer, and push against the law to get what they want. Increasingly sophisticated techniques for managing the in-vitro fertilization of egg and sperm, and even 'testing' the resulting embryos for defects, or even for positive qualities, raise disturbing problems concerning our 'possessiveness' over having our very own genetic children. This attitude has grown with the possibility of separating sexuality completely from reproduction. Sexual relations have always been the context of new birth; whatever the particular circumstances, sexuality has always meant some hybridity in the life of the self and in the generation of new selves, while dispensing with sexuality in the making of new life seems to promise containment, control, circumscription, of self in relation to others.

Is the trend towards emphasizing a genetic naturalism in the definition of kin, and the pursuit of human reproduction on this basis, found everywhere in the world where the NRTs are coming in to use? The answer is complicated. Outside the ultra-modern movement in the Western secular mainstream, there are in fact enclaves where different views prevail. The ultimate expected feat of the NRTs is of course cloning, and nobody as far as I am aware has defined this as natural in any way. It is a technique known to belong to the 'artificial' side of producing farm animals. Around Christmas 2002 the news was announced by the Raelian cult based in the USA that they had succeeded in cloning a baby (though proof of this fact was still being awaited many months later). The almost universal reaction was that this was either dangerously unnatural, or against God, or both. Quite apart from technical difficulty, medical problems, and a high failure rate, many considered that cloning adversely affects the dignity and rights of the child. Here, I would like to add a major reservation from the social side. In normal births, any child has a multiplicity of links to build on in later life; parents and ramifying networks on both sides of the family, a broad base of social connection from which to launch into life. By definition, a clone has only one parent, and will be socially incomplete in this sense even if well cared for. Advertisements in the USA offer the chance of cloning pets, favourite dogs or cats, so they will be born again; this illustrates well the syndrome of the commissioning party as owner or patron, and the erasing of any autonomy, or 'otherness', in the created being. Mary Warnock has argued that even if medically safe, there would still be objections to cloning because of one person having so much control over another. The young clone would have a permanently skewed, contingent relationship to its 'parent', and would relate to other kin only through that dependent link.[39] This would overdetermine that young person's social identity and undermine his or her humanity, if we accept my argument that our capacity for multiple engagement is a normal and liberating aspect of that humanity. It is arguably an erosion of the human rights of a person to be born into a permanently asymmetrical relation to one other person, a relationship which can scarcely be kept secret, and nor should modern morality expect it to be. Despite genetic identity, the parent and clone are not equal like twins, because the clone is forever in a secondary, dependent relationship and can never attain normal social adulthood. This ultimate process for the reproduction of an individual ignores the fact that children throughout history have been born and brought up in contexts of partnership and social patterns of reciprocity, of give and take between the parties and over the generations. Cloning is a material celebration of the most extreme kind of individualism we can imagine: it is very interesting that the first claims to have achieved it have been made by a new age religious cult proclaiming what most would regard as totally false claims to human transcendence over science.[40] This anomalous act of creation is taking to its absurd limits what Paul Heelas has referred to as the sacralization of the individual—something that Durkheim himself had predicted in a general way.[41] Here is a religious enclave within Western hi-tech society which is transparently using the NRTs to try and embody *their ideals of social form* in a distinctive way.

Reflections on what is happening in other religious enclaves, or in different parts of the world, illustrate the same point. Among the Mormons in Utah, AIH is strongly encouraged when couples face fertility problems, but because of Mormon views on sexual purity and the biological definition of continuing family lines, AID is a difficult issue and the religious authorities have spent many years pondering what clear guidance to offer. Bob Simpson has shown how people in Sinhalese Buddhist families in Sri Lanka, partly in reponse to state calls for larger families, have eagerly sought help through the NRTs. Drawing on a deep historical level of ideas about marriage, including former polyandry, they are very comfortable with the idea of donor sperm from a brother of the infertile husband. The idea of joint fatherhood as in certain homosexual partnerships in the West is read in a rather different way. The social partnership and joint fatherhood of two men still echoes former normal arrangements over the maintenance of family farming estates, but this was not based on personal sexual orientation at all—it was a pragmatic working family form involving a set of brothers who shared a wife. In the clinic of today, Sri Lankans do not seek anonymous sperm donors, but often propose bringing in a brother.[42] A detailed study of the use of NRTs in Israel further illuminates the socio-cultural and even political ways in which the manipulation of 'nature' is shaping the very body of the people. Susan Kahn shows us several levels on which discourse and practice concerning the new techniques operates: at the level of the state, families are encouraged to have children; this includes full entitlement by Jewish women, not only married but single or divorced women, to seek assistance with conception and childbearing. The national policy reflects ancient Jewish principles about the very continuity of the people through women, a classic case of matriliny (which used to be combined with a high degree of endogamy), and while Rabbinical law debates the pros and cons of single mothers, their use of the NRTs as such has not been condemned. However, there is a concern over incestuous relations in religious law, any offspring of which are abominations. Therefore, the religious authorities are concerned to restrict the numbers of Jewish sperm donations, in case there should be involuntary marriages between half-kin in the next generation. An ideal solution for clinics (and for women, who often prefer tall and light-coloured children) can therefore be to use sperm from non-Jewish donors, such as German and Scandinavian kibbutz volunteers.[43] Cases such as these show clearly how the NRTs are being drawn into very different modern discourses about the reproduction not just of human beings but of social and cultural forms, some of them ancient and very 'anthropological' looking. These cases should alert us to the discourse of the mainstream West too: how 'natural' indeed are the social forms now being pursued through the rhetoric of naturalness?

CHAPTER ELEVEN

From Local to Global Peace and War

I. THEATRES OF ORDER AND OF VIOLENCE— AND THE NEED FOR HISTORY

Questions about 'human nature': aggressive or peaceful?

THERE have been many older anthropologies which have assumed competition and combativeness, even aggression, in human beings as a part of our evolutionary inheritance, but as natural tendencies which we have learned to control better as civilization has matured.[1] There was a common view in the nineteenth century that warfare was a means whereby societies and nations had created human history itself in their struggles with each other. The original museum collections made by General Pitt Rivers consisted of weapons assembled for this reason, to illustrate the long fights for survival and the role that military technology had played in history. This endeavour matched Herbert Spencer's vision of the principles of social evolution as a story of healthy competition between nations.

But is history driven by essentially inevitable tendencies to aggression? The problem remains even if we try to reverse the premiss: to suggest that human beings are 'by nature' peaceful creatures, and that it is only the stresses of social life, especially in its modern forms, which produce violence. A very interesting collection of studies entitled *Societies at Peace* attempted to draw together some ethnographic examples of 'peaceful societies', as a criticism of the premiss of natural human aggressiveness. In their introduction, Signe Howell and Roy Willis ask: 'If aggression and violence are part and parcel of what it means to be human, then why is it that there exist societies where aggressive or violent behaviour is conspicuous by its absence?'[2] They asked their contributors to consider human beings as meaning-makers, rather than as biological primates, especially in the domain of local concepts of human nature, inner states, child-rearing, social interaction and control, and the handling of deviant social behaviour. Howell and Willis remind us of Ashley Montagu's writings on peaceful coexistence,[3] and the more recent work of Michael Carrithers,[4] pointing to our innate 'sociality', as a positive and peaceful capacity. They criticize the reification of aggression as a discrete category, pointing out that warfare does not always equal individual aggressive behaviour, and that 'behaviour' anyway is full of ambivalent significances. Clayton Robarchek contributes a helpful essay on the way that images of 'Man' as either aggressive or peaceful by nature, as famously portrayed in the writings of Hobbes and Rousseau respectively, have provided the main axis of debate in Western history about violence and peace in the evolution of society. He notes how ethnographers can easily fall into stereotyping; the Semai Senoi of the hilly forests of Malaysia have been placed alternately on one side or the other of the divide. They have been portrayed as 'quintessential noble savages' by ethnographers who have focused on 'Senoi Dream theory', and as 'raging bloodthirsty killers' by proponents of instinctive human aggression.[5] This kind of essentializing is obviously not helpful; but it sells ethnography, and a now notorious case comes from the Amazonian lowlands.

The Yanomamo of the Venezuelan interior became famous in the 1960s as an exemplar of violence embedded in a pattern of community behaviour almost to the point of its naturalization.[6] For many, they have come to stand for humankind in its 'primeval' state, and most certainly a Hobbesian version of this imagined state. With deep irony, as well as tragic revelation, it is the Western scientific establishment which now stands accused of carrying raw violence and exploitation to the Yanomamo, at the same time reading its own obsessions with individual male competition into their cultural world.[7] The ongoing row about the work of anthropologists and other scientists among the Yanomamo has become a debate about the ethics of anthropology as a whole, has entered the world's newspapers and TV, and can be followed on the internet. The popularity, or notoriety, of the case is not surprising in view of the way that the original ethnographers of the people strove to set up the Yanomamo as an extraordinary exemplar of humankind's essentially violent nature in the first place.[8] The focus of the best-selling book *The Fierce People*, according to the editors of the series in which it appears, is upon the Yanomamo as 'a product of long-term sociocultural evolution without intervention from outside alien populations and life ways . . . The behaviors and norms of people who are very different from us become, though shocking and disturbing at times, real and comprehensible when placed into anthropological perspective.' The ethnographer, Napoleon Chagnon, clearly relishes the sense of difference as such (his first day in the field illustrated what his teachers had meant by 'culture shock') and he indulges right away in a visual image of the Yanomamo character: 'I looked up and gasped when I saw a dozen burly, naked, sweaty, hideous men staring at us down the shafts of their drawn arrows! Immense wads of green tobacco were stuck between their lower teeth . . . and strands of dark-green slime dripped or hung from their nostrils.'[9] These images were vividly presented in a series of related films.

The Yanomamo have become a standard character in anthropology's dramatis personae, and the 'cultural' cipher for a predisposition to violence in several broader debates. Marvin Harris in his *Cannibals and Kings* refers to them in the context of the argument that protein deficiency leads to violence, offering among others the following memorable comment, which must have found its way into numberless unthinking essays and examination answers: 'War is the ultimate expression of the Yanomamo lifestyle.'[10] In a very different context, arguing for the need to take tolerance as far as one can in anthropology, Elvin Hatch uses the Yanomamo to illustrate the dilemmas of the relativist who supposedly has to approve their behaviour.[11]

At this point, let me embark on the critique of such naturalistic stereotyping that will run through the rest of this chapter. We have to set the events, experiences, and reports of significant violence into their historical context. It is relevant to note how recent critics have revised our understanding of the patterns of violence that have been described for the Yanomamo. Far from being the result of long-term 'socio-cultural evolution', they have been shown by Brian Ferguson to be the recent product of colonization and other external historical impacts upon the Amazon basin. Together with Neil Whitehead, Ferguson edited *War in the Tribal Zone*, the outcome of one of the major conferences of the mid-1980s on the general topic of violence and anthropology, one which, however, sought to historicize the evidence.[12] His chapter there contains elements of his later book *Yanomami Warfare*, 1995. The general lessons that we can take from this body of work relate to the ambivalences of the kind of peace achieved through imperial conquest. Whether we are looking at the frontier of the Roman empire in North Africa, the modern imperial extension of the Portuguese empire into Amazonia, or

British rule in India, the actual making of a border may guarantee a kind of peace on one side, but it actually stimulates feuding and warlike activities among the populations on the far side. They may become each other's rivals for imperial favour, they may find trade goods seduce them away from subsistence production, and it may be that the spread of metal objects provides a new source of weaponry even in quite distant regions beyond empire.

Historical circumstances on the frontiers of empire have contributed to many of our standard images of wild and violent tribes. The Nuer were presented as warlike from as early as the mid-nineteenth century; but travellers' reports were based mainly on what their non-Nuer guides—government 'friendlies'—were telling them.[13] The beautiful and intricate ethnographic analyses by Renato and Michelle Rosaldo of personhood and social life among the 'head-hunting' Ilongot of the hilly forests of the Philippines, introduced in Chapter 8 above, also illustrate how external stereotypes have been influential in imperial history there too; and how internal memory and images of violence in such regions are rather more complex than might be thought, drawing in part on these external perceptions.

Alan Campbell makes some very pertinent contributions to this theme in his concluding essay to *Societies at Peace*. He sees the use of descriptive or diagnostic terms, such as aggressive or peaceful, for whole societies as problematic and as concealing complexity. He warns against the binarism of such labels; instead of saying the Yanomamo are aggressive, and some other group not, we should ask something along the lines of 'How do these people deal with certain basic human predicaments?' He discusses the notion of basic plots in literature, and wonders whether this approach could be used in human life, along with a critical evaluation of who is doing the telling. The main question will then be, 'What is the historical predicament of the people who are described?', and 'What is the nature of their relations with others?' In frontier Brazil there are stereotypes of 'wild' and 'tame' Indians. First contact in these regions was in 1500. From the variations in the descriptions of Indian groups coming from the frontier since then, Campbell suggests that the wild cannibal character was attributed to those attempting to fight back at any given place or time; and the tame image was repeatedly applied to those groups who had experienced violence in the past and were anxious to escape it again, or were afraid of dying out through disease. 'They hope that this particular contact with outsiders will protect them and give them a chance. It's hard to be a warrior people when there's only thirty of you left and when there's nowhere to go.'[14]

Violence and gender: again, naturalistic assumptions and the historical lesson

There is a widespread assumption that men are more violent than women; that the cultivation of masculinity inevitably glorifies violence. In David Riches's collection, *The Anthropology of Violence*, at least three of the papers deal with violence as competitive masculinity—in the contexts of the Spanish bullfight, Japanese films, and football hooliganism.[15] But is masculinity always associated with violence in the same kind of way? Is it innate or cultivated? Violence is not of course an exclusively male preserve. It is true that women do take part in war—for example, village women were fighters in traditional Ethiopia, and killers in the recent Rwandan genocide. National armies in many countries now recruit women soldiers on a professional basis. However, in traditional or modern circumstances, the war situation tends to sharpen gender difference and can become a brutal celebration of the masculinity/power nexus, as when soldiers go on rampages of killing and rape. Acts of violence bordering on 'ritual' are here not just symbolizing the war, they are the war. But not all wars are the same; and not all forms of male—or female—aggression are the same. Even this side of our behaviour which seems so easily to lend itself to 'human science' types of explanation, can seem more complicated when put into historical perspective.[16]

An illuminating study of how multiple levels of 'causation' feed into masculine homicidal action is Suzette Heald's investigation of the roots of violence among the Gisu of Uganda. Heald asked herself why this rural community in the early 1970s (before the country was engulfed by civil wars) had a rate of homicide almost equivalent to that of Mexico City. In tackling her answer on a number of different levels, including external colonial images of the violence of the Gisu, increasing population pressure on land and rivalry between fathers and sons over inheritance, the imposition and then withdrawal of colonial administrative institutions and courts, Heald chooses to emphasize the ceremonial cultivation of the masculine personality. Gisu men underwent, and many still undergo, a rite of circumcision as young adults. This rite is both physically and psychologically traumatic, but for Gisu it focuses the 'anger' within men's bodies in a socially controlled way so that they become effective warriors in defence of their people and their land, regardless of whether or not there is a rational war to fight at any given time. Heald traces the way in which historical processes led to the rise of mafia-style 'protection' gangs, vigilantes known as *bamajonisi* ('emergency') who saw their role as the maintenance of law and order. Although this preceded the formation of local people's militias or liberation movements of the kind which later came to dominate the politics of many parts of North-East Africa, and of course accepting that detailed circumstances differ from place to place, the story Heald has to tell has widespread echoes.[17]

The exemplary centre: theatres of ceremony, power, and violence

The actual conduct of hostilities has always had a deeply ceremonial character, in the deployment of force in trained, carefully choreographed and often visibly displayed collective manoeuvres which threaten, or carry out, military action. Declarations of war are made not so much in ordinary language as through symbolic gesture, such as 'throwing down the gauntlet'— and are sometimes known from the very absence of language, as when a letter requesting troop withdrawals is ignored. Military training itself, with its formal ranking, hierarchies of command, rituals of personal achievement, and disciplined use of weapons, is almost the clearest example of the conjunction of ceremony and power that we have. No wars in history reflect the inborn aggressiveness of human nature in the raw sense, but the way they are commemorated in words, in actions, and in art suggests how vulnerable we all are to the celebration of power, aggression, and resistance.

The military example reminds us of the frequent presence of violence, or the shadow of violence, at the heart of ceremony. Political, religious, and life-cycle rituals often entail frightening displays of weapons or symbolic strength; blood sacrifice; or the bodily marking of initiates. René Girard has explored the underlying theme of violence behind kingship and the sacred in general, and Luc de Heusch has shown the entanglements of kingly power over the wild, as well as over human life and death, in his survey of sacrifice in Africa. Bloch has also developed an argument about the transformations between life and death which pervade religious and kingly ritual, and drawn out the connection with the image of the hunter and his prey.[18] These studies evoke worlds in which you cannot separate 'real' power and domination from its 'symbolic' expression and ritual enactment. There are resonances even with the conduct of empire; Felix Padel has revealed the ironies behind the way that the British, in the early nineteenth century, endeavoured to stamp out the practice of human sacrifice among kings and chiefs in the Kond Hills—they did it in part by punitive execution and a public display

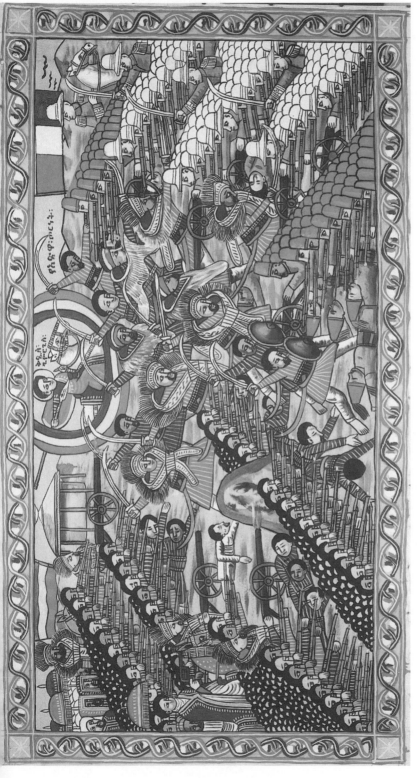

Fɪɢ. 29. War's glory: *The Battle of Adowa, 1896*. The victorious Ethiopians advance against Italian-led troops, encouraged by their Emperor Menelik II (top left), the Empress Taiytu (left), and a vision of St George (in a rainbow matching the green, yellow, and red of their national flag). Oil painting anon., c.1965, Addis Ababa. Photo: Oxford Photographic Services (2498). Original in author's possession.

of the bodies. Claims to power can very commonly be recast into claims to the ultimate right to control life and death.[19]

According to Geertz's essentially 'cultural' if historically located study of a non-Western non-modern polity, the Balinese state in the nineteenth century did not represent a systematic concentration of power, nor a methodical form of government. It was oriented rather 'toward spectacle, toward ceremony, toward the public dramatization of the ruling obsessions of Balinese culture: social inequality and status pride'. It was a 'theatre state' in which the kings and princes were the impresarios, the priests the directors, and the peasants the supporting cast, stage crew, and audience. The great ceremonial occasions, mobilizing vast wealth and vast numbers of people (and, we might note, considerable violence), were 'not means to political ends' but ends in themselves. They were what the state was for. The Balinese idea of sovereignty rested on what Geertz calls 'the doctrine of the exemplary centre'. The complex of court-and-capital, *negara*, was both a microcosm of the supernatural order and the material embodiment of political order. The ritual life of the court, and the life of the court generally, provided a timeless model according to which worldly status was ordered and people should seek to pattern their lives. Legitimation was provided by myths of early conquests and the establishment of early capitals; since the high period of Balinese civilization (as it is remembered) there has been dispersal, fragmentation, and decline, but at every level in the loose pyramid of courtly centres as recorded for Bali in the nineteenth century the original paradigm was being re-expressed—not so much as a celebration of history, but as a direct striving after the authentic re-creation of a truly exemplary centre.[20] The argument emphasizes distinction from, and inapplicability of, Western political theory and ideas of power and the state. How could such mainstream theory anyway encompass the royal cremation and practices of suttee? The royal women go voluntarily to a spectacular death; however, the theatre, many would say today, and ordinary Balinese might even have said then, obscures the human realities of what is going on. What kind of realities should we be aware of, in cases like this of the Balinese theatre state?

Bali's troubled past has been emphasized by Leo Howe. He notes that 'culturalism is not enough' to understand peace and warfare. Bali is indeed 'peaceful' in some ways, with notions of the emotional equilibrium of individuals, but (in addition to the theatrical violence of royal ritual, discussed above) we have to face historical facts. In the nineteenth century there were wars between Balinese kingdoms; Balinese slaves were considered good mercenaries by the Dutch military; in the Dutch war against the Balinese in 1848, the latter lost 2,000 dead; there were later phenomena of mass suicides in front of advancing Dutch armies. In the modern political violence of 1965–6 there was appalling carnage, estimates of the numbers killed being as high as 100,000. This was a hierarchical society in which lords and nobles used to exercise occasionally brutal power, and preside over small wars between rival kingdoms. The fact that high castes as well as low held views about tranquillity and order as ideals did not later prevent them from having their eyes gouged out and their hands chopped off. In addition, however, to the kinds of conflict involving differences of rank and power, there are typical kinds of kin relationships in which there can be violence. These include relationships between a mother and her son's wife; and between co-resident brothers. A mother-in-law can even coerce her daughter-in-law into a truly subordinate role, symbolized in a 'nasty, private ritual' in which the girl prostrates herself on the ground and the mother-in-law treads on her head. Howe's account, developed further in his monograph on Bali, reminds us of the way that external events, especially of colonial conquest, can affect the internal patterns of violence in a society.[21]

Divine kings, religious holism, and the motif of ritual transcendence

In his classic writings on divine kingship, Frazer did not separate the political from the symbolic. They were intertwined, almost 'the same thing'. A. M. Hocart, in the inter-war period, also developed an analytical concept of the nature of kingship as a complex of ritual and administrative elements in authority, essentially dependent on each other in a schematic whole (with a sacred origin) to which the wider domains of social organization were assimilated.[22] However, mid-twentieth-century anthropology, especially in the colonial context, did heroically attempt a separation: for example, Evans-Pritchard did so in distinguishing between the idea of the Shilluk divine king *reigning*, as a figurehead, from his *ruling*, as a political power, over his people. The king 'symbolically' transcended the division in the kingdom. British social anthropology in the colonial period typically thought of politics in terms of good administration. Much of its mainstream literature is founded upon a premiss of order, in the intellectual, symbolic, legal, and practical fields; the very concept of 'society' has been taken for granted as the art of living together despite our instincts for anarchy. Historians were the ones who faced the facts of economics, technology, institutionalized violence, competitive wars between states and the forces of revolution; anthropologists tended to celebrate the arts and achievements of cultural tradition and consensus politics within nations or the smaller scale patterns of stateless societies. Shared ideals, values, and rituals were celebrated as the locus of a social world, in the face of material factors which might be tearing it apart. Where local conflict could not be ignored, analysis tended to seek some overarching social dialectic which *contained* such violence, for example the rules of the feud and the conventional means of re-establishing a state of peace and order.[23] For Radcliffe-Brown, the function of kingship, in the absence of police and army, was to act as a symbolic sanction on the social order as a whole. In these and other theories of the mid-twentieth century, anthropology's business was essentially to study the principles of that order and the role of ritual in keeping the peace. Things today look different.

Hindu India is another classic site where integrative theory has held sway: those who follow Louis Dumont, for example, insist that status in the encompassing hierarchies of caste purity cannot be equated with the Western political science concept of status, itself translatable into worldly power.[24] Since the end of colonial empire and the rise of nationalism across the world since the 1960s, anthropologists have been asking themselves whether they have been too preoccupied with 'merely' cultural and religious aspects of social life and failed to see the realities of wealth and power and the destructive aspects of social action. Looking for the 'realities' of domination, political tension, and the social workings of power has become a priority in research and analysis only relatively recently. Today it has become very tempting to anthropologists to try and deal head-on with the pressing questions of violence, disorder, displacement, and peace-making efforts which lead the agenda of current events in so many parts of the post-colonial, post-Cold War world. But the frameworks of political reason which are often brought to the modern negotiating table, themselves laden with the rhetorics of democracy and economic freedoms and the individual morality of world figures, do not always lead to straightforward solutions or even to the understanding of deeply entrenched situations. We should not be afraid to counter the shallowness of much modern political-science textbook reason by invoking, as we used to, our passion for rich symbolic understandings and the potency of ritual and rhetoric. Political power, or even 'domination' as the Marxists say, is rarely a straightforward matter of the imposition of the social peace or the direct 'command' of resources or people, as we have seen in the case of the Maale kingdom described above in Chapter 7.

Dramas of resistance and opposition: the 'ceremonial' weapons of the weak

Those in humble positions in society, untrained perhaps in public affairs, cannot often use language persuasively, but they can use ceremonial action, often in very explicit ways (what James Scott has called 'weapons of the weak').[25] Explicit use of 'non-violence' in a ceremonial way against power has a long and interesting history. Not only in Hindu India has the enactment of non-violence had a high profile, but there is the recently studied case of the non-violent, anti-colonial movement among Muslim Pakistani Pashtuns on the Afghan border in the late 1940s, described by Mukulika Banerjee.[26] This is a part of the world stereotyped by others (and often by locals) as almost instinctively violent. A reviewer commented that this case study, from a region now feared as a hotbed of terrorism, is important because to conceive of alternative futures, alternative pasts must be remembered.[27]

The anthropological literature is full of analyses of the ways in which the weak or marginal can influence the actions of the strong. I. M. Lewis has illustrated how the marginalized may evoke fear among their superiors through their supposed possession of ritual powers such as the evil eye, magic techniques, and so on.[28] Shirley Ardener has traced the long history in West Africa of the women's way of demonstrating disapproval to authority—by stripping or turning around to reveal their bottoms en masse—a specialism also of the Moonie cult. [29] I have already introduced the subversive aspects of the East African Beni-Ngoma marching, and of slave and refugee dances, in Chapter 4. From the authorities' point of view, in all these sorts of cases, 'You can't speak to these people, you don't know what's in their minds.'

Language, memory, rationalizing violence

Violent action is not always self-explanatory at the time, but rationalized later in language and memory. Michael O'Hanlon once found himself, his wife, and a friend caught up in a dramatic battle in New Guinea.[30] It had all the signs of a very traditional Wahgi affair, with spears and colourful gear, though it was in part a provocation to the police. However, he found it very difficult to get any 'explanation' of what was going on, and even at the time the experience (which was a little fearful as the spears flew fairly close and it was not clear which way the action would turn) had a dream-like quality.

There were no actual deaths, and raw violence or physical aggression did not seem to be the main thing at issue. It was only much later, in a different place, with a different group of Wahgi whom he knew better, that O'Hanlon had conversations about ancient battles which began to give him some idea of the nature of the event he had actually seen. Reflection and recollection through language gave a variety of hints as to what was 'really' going on, though the whole, we might say, was more than the sum of these accounts, and more related to the nature of ceremonial demonstration than to any rational theory of the causes of conflict.

We are now a long way from Hobbes and Rousseau, and their imaginings of the 'nature' of human beings or society. We are back in a more manageable world of events set in specific space, economic and political relations, and time sequence, and recorded, even perhaps 'imaged', through written texts and photographs which have their own specific history. Violence is present in the imagining of past and future, in musings and dreams and fictional representation of all peoples, as much as in their actions, or non-actions, and a proper anthropology must include these dimensions.

Theatres of peace and peace-making

I have shown how deeply 'ceremonial' are the projects of violence and war, and also many strategies of the politically weak. Peace-making is also 'ceremonial' in character, but in addition to that requires the careful use of language on many levels besides the obviously ceremonial in order to transcend the actions of violence. The role of language is dominant in peace, as the role of wordless but deeply significant action is dominant in war. In addition to the multiple ordinary conversations between individuals in power, out of power, and even across the lines of conflict, rhetoric is inherent to peace-making; appeals are made to higher authorities and gods, to ideals and hopes, honour and dignity has to be restored and offence forgiven or somehow wiped out by the power of words. Mediators are brought in, not so much for their capacity for action as for speech, and for their command of a wider audience than merely the combatants. Treaties have to be worded most carefully, and signed by all parties.

The composition of feuds typically involves oratory and lavish gestures of conciliation; peace-making involves speeches by intermediaries—such as the famous leopard-skin chief of the Nuer—as well as by the parties; and the procedure in courts depends firmly upon language. Here it is useful to recall the philosopher J. L. Austin's discussion of how language itself can be a social act; on 'doing things with words'. The strength of linguistic rhetoric in politics has been emphasized by Bloch. He has shown how oratory, ritual, and authority come together in the theatre of managing political relations, sometimes bordering on religious discourse.[31] Language, plain and theatrical, is of the essence in systems of law and justice. Sir Henry Maine's *Ancient Law*, dealing with the contrast between status and contract by reference to Asian as well as historical European examples, is only one of the works by legally trained scholars in the nineteenth century which helped to lay the foundations for comparative sociology and social anthropology. Lawyers' sense of what a society is depends very much upon language, not only in the formulation of rules and regulations and judgements, but also in the rhetorical use of abstract moral concepts such as justice and fairness in the settlement of disputes. What concepts of this kind were there in preliterate polities? The 'jural' approach to social structure, which characterized much anthropology in the colonial period (as discussed in Chapter 7), did seek to go beyond the principles of customary law in order to understand better the social processes of dispute settlement and the way that moral rhetoric pervaded these processes. Max Gluckman's work in Zambia yielded both detailed social analysis of the judicial process among the Lozi rulers of Barotseland, and also philosophical writings on the comparability of human ideas about justice and 'the reasonable man' behind the way that debate took place and judgements formed.[32] The operations of 'ordinary' language here were clearly the very stuff from which agreement and co-operation were being re-negotiated in society. Ritual proclamations on their own are a very brittle form of peace-making; but always an effective contribution to hostilities.

Peace and order do not exist 'naturally' in society: like war, they have to be made. I have argued so far in this chapter that, while peace-making requires a good deal of ordinary language, feeding into the symbolic formalities, the conduct of aggressive action and war is deeply imbued with sheer ceremony of a kind which can gather its own momentum, provoke its mirror-image in retaliation, and remain remarkably resistant to the persuasions of 'reason' and language. I have suggested we reject any dualism of nature versus society or culture, and seek to engage a more historical perspective that can reveal how these 'alternatives' are not opposed for all time but overlap and realign themselves in shifting ways with the changing scale of events in history.

2. STATES, 'NATIONS', AND THE STRUGGLES
OF THE PEOPLE

We are all enmeshed in a set of socio-political (and ceremonially celebrated) structures we are so used to we tend to take them for granted and forget their salience: our own 'sovereign' nation-state, and others in the global arena. Of course this is by no means a static form—many regions of the world show states in flux, realigning their alliances and hostilities, even merging and dividing. But the concept and material existence of states is a clear one: based on a notion of exclusive, bounded sovereignty founded in the industrial age of Western Europe in the nineteenth century and borrowed, echoed, reduplicated across the world since. Nation-states have their own governments, capital cities, flags, anthems, airlines, and a large degree of autonomy in the control of resources and the making of laws. They also have (with a few exceptions which prove the importance of the rule) very clear boundaries on the ground, and a clear relationship (normally) to their population: people either are, or are not, citizens of a given country, according to specified criteria. This framework of nation-states and citizens, whatever else may be said about it, is the primary matrix of 'modern' society. It remains so, moreover, in the face of the spread of international finance and 'global markets', communications up to and including the World Wide Web, the weakening and collapse of states in certain areas and the rise of transnational communities. Sovereign governments, however their sovereignty may be challenged and undermined in practice from within and without, are still the key institutions in the way the world system works. We suspect these days that faceless international capitalists are bypassing and buying off governments behind the scenes; but this scenario may be exaggerated and governments can play their own game. Whether that is always in the interests of their own citizens is another matter.

The contradiction between the idea of the 'nation' as a historically connected body of people who share the essentials of a moral community, and the 'State' as a rational ordered framework for the disinterested planning and administration of the life of its individual citizens, was clear from the very beginning. To simplify dreadfully, the ideal notion of the modern 'nation-state' brings together the old German romantic image of the spirit of a people historically formed on the land together, and the Enlightenment rationalism of post-revolutionary French social planning for equal citizens. One might reflect also on the endlessly shifting counterpoints between the United Kingdom as a State and the 'peoples' or 'nations' who contest its structure while defining themselves and their collective political rights with varying degrees of clarity and seriousness. No country combines the two ideals in perfect harmony. They are uncomfortably yoked in almost every case. In particular, notions of romantic local nationalism tend to proliferate, and foster regional movements for special status within the State, even sometimes struggles for independence and the formation of a separate State. In the second half of the twentieth century we have seen the spawning of dozens of new States 'freed' first from the territorial embrace of former European empires and more recently from that of the Soviet Union. Each is struggling with the contradictions of State and 'nation' in one way or another.

Partly because of the built-in mismatch between the concept of 'a people' and the sovereign governmental framework of a State, many movements of regional or social disaffection within States or across the borders of States have fostered particular embodiments of the idea of the rights of *a people* as such to special recognition. This phenomenon in today's language is glossed as 'ethnicity', as in such terms as 'ethnic consciousness', 'ethnic pride', 'ethnic hatred'. The word has older roots, *ethnos* deriving from an ancient Greek context where its sense was not very different from some modern uses of 'race', as in a phrase such as 'this continent is inhabited by several races'. It is not separable from the idea of a biologically connected community, sharing 'blood' as the Greeks themselves were a people of one blood.[33] However, the term has had a chequered and ambivalent history, and was adopted into the social sciences more or less enthusiastically from the 1960s *as an alternative* to biologically based racial categories or primordial renderings of 'tribe'. Fredrik Barth and Abner Cohen emphasized for anthropology its situational and variable nature, and Edwin Ardener the roots of 'ethnic' classification in language patterns of the powerful which bore no necessary relation to the signified. It has become very clear that in the discourse of the nation-state system, it is through the eyes of a dominant self-defining national civilization that groups are distinguished as 'ethnic' whether they like it or not, whether they have mobilized themselves as a community or not. In modern Britain, journalists have even come to use 'ethnic' to mean straight racial appearance, as in newspaper reports which mention that at a certain meeting 'there were quite a few people of ethnic background in the room', or that there was a need for 'white and ethnic' communities to be encouraged to live in the same areas. The implication is clear, that in modern

British discourse 'ethnic' has become a straight racial alternative to being 'white', whatever that might mean.

Discussions of 'ethnic identity' have thus been transformed from the 1960s when Barth and Cohen could emphasize its optional, voluntary nature, as something belonging to a shared public language you could mobilize with your fellows, or manipulate as you crossed one nominal boundary or another. Ethnic identity is spoken and written of today as something 'given' in your background, which you have internalized, or at least have the right to internalize. This trend has gone further in the United States than in Europe.[34] It signifies part of the wider internalization of gender and other characteristics as something individually possessed, rather than being part of the available language through which you participate in the social world. 'Ethnicity' is now commonly taken to be an attribute of individuals who are personally in themselves Kosovan, or Hindu, or Black British, regardless of their social milieu or aspirations. In defining 'ethnic groups', it is rarely considered in journalistic or bureaucratic contexts whether such groups even define themselves as a distinct community, let alone perpetuate themselves by intermarriage or by other means. Where there are distinct such groups, enduring through endogamy, shared diet, occupation, and style of life, commentators are not always comfortable with the application of the term; is a Hindu local caste community, for example, in India or East Africa or Britain, an 'ethnic group'? If they had a quarrel with another caste, would this be an 'ethnic conflict'? And if not, why not? And why, if there is a fight at the other end of town, and a newscaster asks the reporter on the spot what it's about, and the reporter answers that 'ethnic conflict' has erupted, what kind of explanation is that?

Marcus Banks has untangled many of these ambivalences in the modern notion of the 'ethnic'. His commentary in 1996 made it clear why the anthropologist should treat 'ethnicity', along with the history of nations and nationalism which has spawned it, as a phenomenon of modern discourse to be studied critically in its context of use, rather than as a neutral term of social science corresponding to some given condition of the human world.[35] He and Richard Fardon have both come very close to suggesting that we abandon the term altogether,[36] and I believe the arguments for rejecting it as a term of general description or analysis are now overwhelming. However, we cannot abandon the 'concept' of the nation-state. It is not merely a 'matter of opinion'—though vital to the success of the mix are the opinions and the perceptions of the dominant about their identity as against others whose difference they are pleased to name. At least with regard to the 'State' component, it is a 'concept' of a very different order. States exist in concrete ways and impinge on the lives of people.

It is important to recognize how much writing now exists by anthropologists (and anthropologically sensitive political scientists) on the nation-state, nationalism, and its counterpoints of region, minority peoples, and 'ethnicity'. Ernest Gellner's general guide provides a strong historical background;[37] Benedict Anderson's emphasis on the way that modern forms of literacy and print journalism have paved the way for the conception of a wider national community in which one can feel a participant has proved very useful.[38]

But even before these major contributions, nationalism had come to demand the attention of anthropologists as a direct result of the challenge to European empire especially in India and then Africa. Even Malinowski had expressed sympathy with African nationalist aspirations in the 1930s, and tried to rally the liberal or even radical feelings of other anthropologists.[39] One of the factors which provoked a real change in anthropology in the 1960s (see the discussion in Part I) was the 'end of empire', and one of the criticisms which anthropologists were obliged to recognize was their seeming neglect of the context of colonial rule and its effects on the people they commonly studied. This context went beyond the direct presence of colonial officials, missionaries, traders, police, even the effects of national boundaries set up by colonial powers. There were indirect consequences from the very establishment of the 'colonial peace' on formerly turbulent areas, and the provocation of disturbance elsewhere where there had been relative peace—such as on the edges of imperial territory, or the border zones of competing colonial powers. Anthropologists of the period from the 1930s to 1950s were not in fact so naive as to simply arrive in a village and describe what was there as timeless tradition: there are outstanding examples of research into the local effects of labour migration, and economic change, and the rise of urban communities.[40] It cannot be denied, however, that at this time anthropologists rarely took a longer historical view of the community they were studying, or a wider political view of their reshaping by the conditions of colonial rule, and they never actually focused squarely on colonialism and its ideology, or missionaries, or national or city life as such.

All this began to change, together with the rise of a new interest in using the methods and insights of anthropological research in the regions of the historical civilizations—India had long been represented on the anthropological agenda, but a new generation of researchers began to work in the Middle East, in the mainstream communities of the Far East, and in (mainly remote and rural) areas of North America, Europe, and Britain. The focus still tended to be on specific locales, but their relation to the wider regional and national situation and to the historical background was increasingly visible. It was really from the margins that 'nations' and 'nationalism' began to appear in anthropological study: very good examples are provided by the work of some of Edwin Ardener's students, including Malcolm Chapman, Sharon Macdonald, and Tamara Kohn on the somewhat infectious phenomenon of 'Scottishness' and the way in which it has grown in an ironic, oxymoronic way with the increasing political and literary clout of Englishness. Maryon McDonald's work on the Breton regional movement drew parallels with the Scottish work and showed how fully a part of national politics, even to the point of challenging the nation-state as such, regional difference could become.[41] To understand the Bretons, and the way a regional 'heritage' could become a vehicle for argument about the nation-state as such, was in fact to study France. Anthropology has since focused on many regional movements across the world, and often this has reflected in crucial ways on questions about the character of nations and nationalism.

A few studies began to appear in the 1970s and 1980s of whole nations as such, including their internal diversity, their search for ways of managing this in a workable political system, and the way that elite groups tend to arise and establish, partly through cultural means, a hegemony of power. John Davis has analysed Libya in this way, Don Donham Ethiopia, Paul Dresch Yemen, and Bourdieu has provided a very sophisticated analysis of France, even comparing it with Japan.[42] Other scholars have taken the framework of colonial empire, or the history of a nation-state, fully into account as a part of their analysis of the society and culture of a particular locality and how it has become what it is—outstanding examples would include the work of Jean Comaroff on the Tshidi of South Africa, and Michael Herzfeld on the central mountain villages of Crete.[43] As always, it is the historians who have pointed the way in dealing with whole nations, changes of government, revolutions, and so forth, and they have given us some powerful models of the role of ceremonial in these contexts and as a part of these processes. Of outstanding importance are Eric Hobsbawm and Terence Ranger's trailblazing book *The Invention of Tradition* and also Paul Connerton's *How Societies Remember*, which show how authority can everywhere manipulate the notions of ceremony and tradition, and mount newly designed ritual performances, in its own interests.[44] The kinds of modern state theatre presented in Victorian India, in Nazi Germany, or Soviet Russia, may be exceptional in their imagery of raw power but they have many echoes too. The military parades of annual national days remind us very directly of the profoundly ceremonial character of military action itself. Anthropologists have tended to focus more on local public ceremonies in modern national contexts, but to see them in increasingly political ways; there are several good examples in a recent collection edited by David Parkin.[45] However, anthropologists are developing ways of handling the phenomena of national culture, especially perhaps in the case of Japan, where Roger Goodman has explored aspects of education, art, and popular culture in relation to national tradition. Work on the Middle East inevitably follows the trace and shadow of national and international conflict. Here an exemplary study is Michael Gilsenan's portrayal of the threads of fear and threat which run today through even the ordinary lives and deaths of all persons in the Lebanon, colouring the sense of who people are, signalled in the subtle shifts of gaze, the jokes and silences, the towering scenery of damaged multi-storeys, with an uneasy, televisual theatricality peculiarly of our times.[46]

State borders

A recent book reaffirms the centrality of States as the key political framework within and against which those self-defining nations and other-defined 'ethnicities' emerge and fade as players on the stage. The collection edited by Thomas Wilson and Hastings Donnan does this by devoting attention to communities living on international frontiers.[47] They caution us that globalization and postmodern rhetoric about freedom to escape the old categories and boundaries have not abolished the existence of States. They remind us that the currently fashionable politics of identity, gender, ethnicity, and transnationalism in which people merge in and out of the old rigid frameworks, combining and recombining in new and liberating ways ignores the continuing existence of real boundaries on the ground and their constraining power. Those who really do cross boundaries, who participate in more than one cultural world, who live as far away as it may seem possible to get from the centres of authority, sometimes know more of the power of States and their contradictory relationship to the lives of people and communities than those more sheltered. We could remind ourselves that in the spacious heartlands of the United States, the dream of building oneself and one's community (and perhaps throwing off the dead hand of government) is a strong one, and news from the rest of the world drifts in and out of the public consciousness without demanding much attention. Even in Europe, the momentum towards economic and political co-operation is tending to minimize the distinction between States and the significance of boundaries on the ground. However, at the Mexican border, the US is more conscious of itself as a State with problematic neighbours;[48] and since Spain joined the European Union in 1992, the points where it adjoins Morocco have become explosively sensitive as the contact zone between Europe and Africa. As Europe's internal borders have faded, the Spanish enclaves and islands of the north Moroccan coast have been transformed as a result of pressure from would-be immigrants and reinforced as a barrier of 'fortress Europe'.[49]

However, as several chapters in Wilson and Donnan's collection discuss, international frontiers need not be politically contested or diplomatically problematic for them to be of deep social, cultural, symbolic, and imaginative significance for borderland communities and indeed beyond. Martin Stokes, for example, contributes an essay on the way that 'globalization' especially in the form of media transmissions of songs and music across frontiers con-tradicts nationalism, with special reference to the Hatay province of southern Turkey.[50] This province extends in a peninsula-like way along the Mediter-ranean coast into Syria, has had a complex past, and Syrian nationalists have not yet given up their claims to it. The province has a large Arabic-speaking population, and an 'Arabic'-sounding dialect of Turkish. Incoming Turks who come for business or employment in local government or the military are ill at ease, especially with the prevalence of a form of popular culture known as Arabesk. This is primarily a musical form, but also associated by Turkish critics with 'an all-embracing kitsch anti-culture which stretches from films and other low-brow pleasures associated with squatter-town life, to corruption, cynicism and sleaze in party politics'; a visitor noted with dis-approval pictures of a transsexual Arabesk star.[51] 'The South' in general has a mythical dimension for Turks, evoking hybridity and 'oriental' chaos and undermining the national struggle to modernity. Hatay signifies 'the South' for the rest of Turkey, as a late annexation even seeming to contest the patri-archal masculinity of the act of making the original boundaries of modern Turkey. The high sobbing lyrics of Arabesk song construct a subject torn by unrequited longings and the memory of violence and rejection. Stokes explores the resonance of these allegorical sentiments with the experience of immigrants who move from the south to the big cities and back to their homeland in the Hatay, where everyday relations between Arabs and Turks are affected by the pervasive presence of the border and the overwhelming significance of national definitions and citizenship. Arabesk provides a cultural space within which other things can be imagined—we might add, a theatre of the political imagination.

Revolutions, wars, and displacements

Occasionally, an anthropologist has been able to witness the effects on people of major revolutionary or violent events of the kind which have helped to make the modern world what it is. These may carry with them a momentum of intent which looks to future rather than present justification, and change profoundly the way in which people see themselves and speak of themselves as placed in time, as they look back and forward in different ways. This kind of change is often traced to its seeds in the French Revolution, when as Lyotard has noted (specifically for the French, but the resonance is wider), all that the French now celebrate as philosophy, literature, and politics began under the sign of a crime, the killing of a good king who was the incarnation of legitimacy.

Don Donham draws on this observation and on other aspects of the French, Russian, and Chinese revolutions to give resonance to his account of the seemingly extraordinary patterns of the impact of the Ethiopian socialist revolution of 1974 upon the rural people of the south of the country, specifically those of the former 'divine kingdom' of Maale.[52] Revolutionaries dug up and burned the royal relics with tremendous theatrical effect, under the approving gaze of the local educated, if conservatively Christian, elite. When evangelical Christian missionaries had arrived from North America to Maale in the 1930s, despite their anti-modernist stand at home, they spread a new conviction of the need to prepare for the future, through education and modern forms of living. A vanguard was thus prepared, unknowingly and ironically, who would abandon their traditional allegiances and respect for the *ancien régime*, the line of divine kings and traditionalist supporters. It was this same vanguard of young Christian men who escorted the revolutionary Marxist student cadres to the villages in 1975, and encouraged them to desecrate the royal remains. Their presence facilitated the later penetration of the socialist state into Maale affairs, even though the peasantry had become disaffected with the revolution itself. Indeed international events had combined by 1977 to thrust Ethiopia into the front line of the Cold War, very much a puppet of the Soviet Union. The Marxist language of the rival factions of the young intelligentsia in the capital, Addis Ababa, was taken over by the fierce in-fighting of the military regime, and vicious killings spread through the towns and spilled over into the countryside. By the early 1980s, the regime had accommodated itself more to the older model of Ethiopian nation-hood, embracing Amharic civilization and the Orthodox Church leadership, while evangelical Christian churches had themselves become identified as American-backed enemies of the state and the revolution. Even in Maale, there were armed struggles between the peasant associations and those Christians who wished to hang on to their church. By 1991, the socialist regime in Addis Ababa collapsed; and later in Maale, traditionalists reburied the bones of the old king in a ritually appropriate way and reinstalled a successor.

The human suffering entailed in the aftermath of the Ethiopian revolution has been documented in some detail along with the mass military mobiliza-tion of citizens, the deaths and refugee movements caused as a result of inter-nal factional terror and as a result of the rise of several armed opposition movements. The Ethiopian case is not of course alone: the armed strife, gra-tuitous killings, and human displacement caused either directly by the Cold War or by its aftermath and the disintegration of States are unfortunately now found across the globe. Many of the areas affected have been the sort of places in which anthropologists have worked, and some are 'classic' areas. Nuerland in the southern Sudan is a prime example: the choreography of factionalism as described by Evans-Pritchard has become caught up in an international arena of conflict, partly overlapping with that of the Ethiopian struggle already mentioned, but primarily with the internal wasting conflict of the Sudan, now immensely worsened by the opening up of important oilfields. Throughout the late 1970s and 1980s Nuer groups straddled the active Cold War frontier between the Sudan and Ethiopia; their territory and politics are now mixed up in the rapidly shifting relations of the West with Islamic regimes. It is scarcely surprising that there has been serious internal conflict between Nuer groups, but the political space of the pressures feeding these conflicts is vastly wider than in the 1930s, and anthropology is obliged to become aware of the 'macro-scale' behind even very local events.[53]

Even where a researcher is not personally caught up in a war zone or does not choose to study one, the current world scene (not to mention some involvements close to home) has obliged them to think hard about questions of violent change, physical violence itself, war, military activity as such,

ɔ. 30. Still hopeful: Southern Sudanese guerrillas, 1971. Photo: John Downing/Express collection, ɪlton Archive JF2400/Getty Images.

resistance, death, flight, and the implications of life for uprooted people and communities. Current conditions of violence and warfare in the world, escalating locally and generally in some frightening ways, are seemingly less explicable than in the days of imperial expansion, or the Second World War, or even the Cold War. In practice, and in their substantive research, anthropologists are increasingly documenting the processes and consequences of warfare and violence, but we have the sense of a failure of theory. Anthropologists go *as reporters and consultants* into professional fields, finding employment, for example, with development charities, human rights organizations, and the media. Partly because of this there is a 'new ethnography' of displacement, dislocation, war and violence and suffering. A few, like Valentine Daniel, Richard Werbner, or Liisa Malkki, have written directly on these questions as a result of their first-hand intensive research in affected areas. The current situation has also stimulated a new growth industry in what used to be called 'applied anthropology', as young people seek to work with international development and relief organizations, making investigations and writing reports about conditions on the ground among refugees or the dispossessed generally. The best of this work is innovative and striking, and is already beginning to have an influence on the way that mainstream anthropology constructs its research and teaching agendas. At the same time there is a feeling of a great gap between this new 'ethnography of disorder' and the standard, or classic literature of our subject, and maybe the social sciences in general. How are we to place the new and often close-up descriptions and visual images of violence, how are we to handle them in the academic context? We are also beginning to recognize that violence and displacement is actually not a new phenomenon; it is an old one, but it has been remarkably 'silent' in a lot of earlier anthropological literature. Disorder and suffering have only recently become a focus of attention and this recognition is fuelling some important writing and modifying the underlying social science presumptions of a tendency towards order in human life—that is, order as a kind of agreement to keep the peace.[54]

The question of gender in the context of violent situations illuminates some of these problems. War and violence are gendered social phenomena in some obvious ways we are conscious of, but also in less obvious ways. The prosecution of war itself is largely perceived as a masculine project, often at the level of the state itself, as Melissa Leach has demonstrated for West Africa.[55] It is inevitable that the masculinity of war becomes a bodily as well as an imaginary matter; women can be captured, raped, enslaved, and so on, not just as a consequence of war but as a mode whereby the war itself is carried out. Roland Littlewood has written on the widespread phenomenon of military rape, and there have been reports of large-scale sexual attacks on women in the context of the civil wars in Somalia and over its borders in Kenya.[56] On the whole, it is true that men fight and women stay at home, or merely play a supportive role. However, women were active fighters in the 'old days' in Ethiopia, and are so in modern Eritrea and Israel. In the 1994 genocide in Rwanda, many women took part, not only in organizing things but in actual killings, to the surprise of Western observers.[57] What is conservatively assumed in Western gender discourse to be the quiet and submissive role of women in 'traditional societies', an assumption which seems to justify the efforts of international agencies to raise women's consciousness and status in life, does not always fit the situation. Moreover, if we look at history, we find that women in situations of general violence, including war, are by no means contained or defined only by the placid images of peacetime. War can open up practice and attitudes in this respect; the Second World War in particular famously did this for women. Not only on the battlefield, but behind the lines in agriculture, factory production, transport, and trade, opportunities expanded for women and gave them a new-found degree of freedom. This is matched in the current wars of Africa, for example, even in the refugee camps where women have to take on responsibilities they may never have had before, and as in the Second World War case, women often face a dilemma when peace returns and they are expected to go back to the kitchen sink. The 'gender awareness' programmes of the rehabilitation and development agencies do not always recognize that women's capacities for independent action in situations of war and its aftermath are stretched to the limit, that they would actually prefer to have their menfolk back as partners in the household rather than be lectured on the need for meetings about women's rights by youngsters from the aid agencies.

In the face of recurring waves of news about human disasters, the impulse among anthropologists, and indeed many others in the 'ivory tower', has been to rush out and offer help, to visit the distressed, starving, and displaced, and make reports for Oxfam and the UN on their condition—especially, in the case of anthropologists, their cultural background and needs, and increasingly to provide a platform for their own voices to be heard. These worthy motivations have inspired some ground-breaking accounts which are helping to shift the journalistic as well as the scholarly lens towards the human interest level, to turn 'the refugees', for example, into real individual people.

The problem is that this focus of human sympathy, reinforced by the visual impact of television and newspaper pictures, can move so close that we lose touch with the wider situation and the possibility of analysing it. The result can be a 'naturalizing' of the causes of disasters—people are displaced and hungry almost as though they had been hit by a natural disaster like a flood or an earthquake, even when the context is one which their own government, or even their own local liberation movement, has positively helped to create. David Keen has explored the interlocking interests of government policy makers, soldiers, merchants, and investors in *maintaining* the famine of the late 1980s in Bahr-el-Ghazal Province of the southern Sudan, and this case study has wide resonance.[58] Alex de Waal, in his 1997 book *Famine Crimes*, has shown with chilling clarity how the well-meaning activities of workers in the humanitarian and aid organizations have themselves become institutionally entangled with the very political structures which have created and are keeping wars and famines going. He argues that the best guarantee against famine is the political accountability of governments to their own people; in India the long struggles by the people against famine forged a new understanding in the early twentieth century that it was a *duty of government* to prevent such loss of life, and the Famine Codes of 1901–7 laid down practical principles which have been of proved value since. In Africa in the last generation this has rarely been achieved; states have themselves been weakened, and the pervasive presence of humanitarian aid has helped remove the moral and political initiative from the affected communities. De Waal's insights derive in part from his original research in Darfur in the mid-1980s as a doctoral student in anthropology. Here he saw at first hand the actual effects of a sudden inflow of aid into a region which was just on the point of beginning to recover from a period of drought and hunger. By drawing people away from their home areas, by concentrating them in camps where infectious diseases could easily spread, and by undercutting the local grain markets, aid was arguably an obstacle to the economic rehabilitation of the region and the reinstatement of a system of collaborative social production. De Waal extends his critique in *Famine Crimes* to the power of the current 'humanitarian international' in the messy politics of the post-Cold War, its complicity with the leading political and military interests of the rich world, and the hollowness of its rhetorical claims to act in the name of morality and human rights. These may be large-scale phenomena, but in their implementation and effects on others, not to mention the anger that Western domination can provoke, perhaps especially through ceremonial and verbal humiliation, they are the arena within which individuals act.[59]

Those questions which focus on 'human nature' rather than history have tended to place the roots of violence in the make-up of the individual human being, rather than in the make-up of the social world. We should find a way of asking questions which arise from a different discourse from that of the standard human sciences, that of a historical anthropology, which does not see social forms, economy, technology, language, and ceremony as added onto the 'nature' of human beings but as primary human phenomena in themselves. These questions, which can be contrasted with the 'naturalistic' type, seek contextualization and the analysis of those very phenomena as such in the making of events.

PART V

Concluding Essay

CHAPTER TWELVE

Anthropology as a Human Science: Conversations with History and Religion

> A certain capacity for critical self-reflection belongs to the way the human animal belongs to its world . . . this is . . . constitutive of the way that humans, as opposed to beavers or beehive hairdos, are actually inserted into their environs. That they are able, within limits, to make something of what makes them, is the very index of their historicity, a mode of being possible only to a labouring, linguistic creature.
>
> Terry Eagleton[1]

THE human capacity for productive labour, and for language (our old self-images as 'the Toolmaker' and the 'Speechmaker' respectively) are still robust ways of summing up our nature as a species. But Terry Eagleton's interesting comments in the quotation above also draw our attention to the way that humans (with these capacities) are 'actually inserted into their environs'. We must then ask, what are those environs? Eagleton clearly has more in mind than surrounding forests. He is referring implicitly to *social environs*, to the context of collective human life within which we grow up and acquire physical habits, language, an ear for music, an eye for art, and so on, all those things which complete our humanity. As Clifford Geertz remarked recently, 'Words, images, gestures, body-marks, and terminologies, stories, rites, customs, harangues, melodies, and conversations, are not mere vehicles of feelings lodged elsewhere, so many reflections, symptoms, and transpirations. They are the locus and machinery of the thing itself.'[2] Apart from a few biological hardliners, anthropologists and others are willing to accept the social articulation of these phenomena of shared human life and their historicity—the way they are passed on to successive generations, and also transmitted over geographical space. But what systematic understanding do we have of these 'social environs'?

Anthropologists do share a hunch that there is more of a systematic character to the underlying formats of social life than meets the eye, or can be described in everyday language by individual participants. A range of bold explanatory schemes have drawn and held the attention of anthropologists, who worry over them like the proverbial dog with a bone, applying, testing, and re-analysing them critically in the light of ethnography, mostly from outside the modern West where most 'grand' theories originated. We could point to the fascination exerted by classic figures such as Marx on political economy and the drive behind history, Freud on the inner compulsions of the psyche, Darwin on the evolution of the forms of life through competitive selection. All these (and others) have their champions today. Does anthropology, specifically social or socio-cultural anthropology, have anything to offer alongside or in counterpoint to these?

It is difficult to spell out what a general anthropological theory might be, as the discipline has many internally competing and well-articulated views, but this does not mean that anthropologists do not fundamentally share a common, if rather fuzzy, vision. In this book I have tried to put into words what that vision is, referring to a wide range of work representing today's senior influential figures, as well as my own contemporaries, and a rising generation of younger scholars. I have also appealed to the analytical legacy of Durkheim, Mauss, Lévi-Strauss, Evans-Pritchard, Victor Turner, Pierre Bourdieu, and Alfred Gell. In trying to bring the anthropological shared vision into focus I have found it helpful to draw on some illuminating writings by scholars in neighbouring fields, such as Wittgenstein in philosophy, Collingwood who combined philosophy and archaeology, Suzanne Langer who moved philosophical thinking into the forms of feeling, David Harvey who has reinvented the concept of socio-geographical space, and Merlin Donald, an experimental psychologist who liberated himself from the laboratory. I have also relied very much on background reading in history and current events, especially the efforts of historians and political scientists to understand the turbulence of past and current events in Africa, in formulating my argument (though I have not often quoted from specific sources). The converging relationship between anthropology and history is now widely accepted, and the question mainly in people's minds these days asks what is the difference between these disciplines, if any? Part of my aim has been to show the integral links between them, but also to maintain the distinctiveness of the anthropological stance: which does still seek to consider ourselves as a species, to accept the validity of scientific methods in understanding our nature and history, but at the same time to see as clearly as possible what is the reach of each particular method and what are its limitations, given the socially rooted drive to action and representation which marks our distinctiveness. We have made our history and repeatedly try to make ourselves conscious of it, as Eagleton suggests; scientific theories and methods are in a very important way a part of that effort, as are religious beliefs or literature.

In my effort to specify more clearly the foundations of anthropology, in the chapters above I have drawn on the work of predecessors and contemporaries to focus upon the ubiquitous presence of *ceremonially significant forms of practice* on the model of the game, or the dance, or the drama. Marc Augé has written of our 'staging of the world' and of the concept of 'ceremonial community', which can be adapted from an immediate setting to one which images wider spaces and times; such extendability of scale is vital to our understanding the 'ludic' aspect of action in history.[3] The diversities of language, productive labour, religion, peace and war, and whatever we might mean variously by 'culture' are always set in *strategically significant* motion, sometimes in competition or conflict with each other. They are rarely invented from scratch, but are grafted upon the past, sometimes reinforcing and sometimes contradicting each other. If we limit our study to cultural phenomena in the conventional sense of expressed values and attitudes, or styles in music, literature, art, or perhaps especially religion—in which so much ceremonial creativity is drawn together—we may over-emphasize their abstract differences at the expense of understanding their historical connections. We may also run the risk of accepting a self-defining ideology, especially an exclusive religion, as a totalizing definition of all it embraces. Proponents of such faiths may indeed wish to create a total world in their image, something especially noticeable in the modern era, but this can become a divisive political claim, a flag-waving exercise which can lead to confrontation.

Are there special problems for anthropology in the exclusivity claimed by some of the champions of Religion? How far should the study of religion in society constitute a separate field, and how far should it take its place among other social phenomena? Why does social science have difficulty, sometimes, in being accepted by one or another body of religious opinion? A related

question asks how can we deal, as human scientists, with the apparent relativity of truths, whether we are ourselves religious believers or not? 'Religion'
is indeed often set apart even in the softer social sciences, sometimes as
though the topic itself were so esoteric as to be marginal to the mainstream
interests of sociologists and even anthropologists. To leave the study of religion to specialists, however, is to impoverish our conception of social life
by leaving everything else, by default, essentially 'secular'. To separate out
a domain of the religious is to assume a *generalized* dichotomy between the
sacred and the profane, in the Durkheimian way, the kind of dichotomy
which can stultify our comparative insights into the quality of human life
because it is modelled essentially upon Judaeo-Christianity, a 'world religion'
defined by the disciplines of scripture and the structuring of time and space
according to specific divine authority.

The view taken here is that the separation of the study of religion from that
of society in general flows from an unthinking modernist assumption, and
actually *creates* problems for anthropology, because it assumes a more banal
and utilitarian character to everyday life than is the case. It also tends to leave
the anthropological study of art or poetry or music, in the West once part
of the sphere of the Church, but now more a part and parcel of everyday life
than we often recognize, somewhat stranded. The roots of this problem can
be found in the development of the science-led modern world-view, dating
mainly from the late nineteenth century. From that time we can trace the
tendency to oppose the concepts of science and religion, and specifically to
oppose the idea of reason and utility in the explanation of social life to the
idea of 'blind faith' or religious belief as entailing a suspension of reason.
Richard Dawkins's series of lucid arguments on this theme are an excellent
example of this view of the need for modern people to see with the eyes of
clear reason through the rosy illusions of religious faith.[4] My arguments have
been rather against this current, in that I have hinted that utility and rational
self- or group-interest have been a specialization out of more morally complex cultural and social patterns, and should not be opposed to them as different, or somehow more basic. Altruism, in this view, is not to be explained
by a logical twist to genetic compulsion or rational choice theory; altruism in
any system of social relations, taken as a whole, is as real as self-interest in the
way that one may join with others in the choreographies of real life.

As with other troubling questions, there are advantages here in looking at
the past of our discipline. In the second part of Chapter 5 I traced the way that
anthropology shifted, between the 1880s and the 1980s, away from debates

about 'primitive' religion to explore the religious side of life anywhere and everywhere, including (and perhaps especially) heartlands of the dominant world religions. From being primarily a naturalistic quest, the anthropological study of religion has become a more historicized, critical, and self-reflexive inquiry, as it has moved from a discipline focused only on what Christendom defined as the pagan world of darkness beyond its domain to a direct concern with the way in which Christian or Islamic practice and belief itself, for example, forms a part of social life in specific contexts of the 'heartland'. This shift towards a historical rather than a naturalistic mode of inquiry is particularly clear in the way that anthropology has studied religion, but it has happened in the way the discipline as a whole has developed. A historical method of inquiry does not mean that 'science' is excluded; on the contrary, by insisting that inquiry in the realm of the human involves engaging like forms of consciousness and essentially translatable kinds of cultural expression, as the historian normally does, the concept of a 'human science' is more securely founded.

There are those who would passionately endorse the continuing need for anthropology to keep its scientific, or at least systematic comparative, ambitions in view, and have defended the ambition of anthropology to be a generalizing science.[5] How can this be linked with history? Anthropology is not primarily understood to be concerned with principles of change and agency, or with the contrasts in thought and value between one period and another, as history is. And yet the way in which history can retain a 'generalizing' and objective aim, while admittedly exploring the subjectivities of the past through those of the present, gives us in anthropology a model we could emulate. Collingwood's writings here offer us inspiration: as a philosopher and archaeological historian, he insisted on the connection between knowledge of others and knowledge of self. While social anthropology has been seen at times in the past as a kind of natural science of social forms, it has today come closer to being a kind of historical inquiry in Collingwood's sense and shares the philosophical character of that kind of investigation into the linked and overlapping ways that human beings have lived, and thought, and continue to do so today. People do not simply 'behave'. They act and speak with each other in the frame of complex patterns of practice and meaning that articulate both memory and expectation, while being themselves grounded in history. For this reason there cannot be a 'non-social' anthropology, a human science which sets aside the kind of 'sociality' we find celebrated in the humanities, in poetry, religion, or music.

Most academic disciplines in the humanities are library-based. They rest upon the existence of written sources whether outside or within their own tradition (even where some laboratory work or statistical number-crunching is required, as in some kinds of archaeology or sociology). Language in its written forms, whether past or present, is the locus of their understandings. The pursuit of anthropology as I have outlined it here also rests to a very large extent upon the phenomena of language, but because of its entanglements with living people and ongoing events takes a broader view of what those phenomena are in the human world. It is sensitive to the fact that languages are not only 'writeable' but exist as living means of general sociality and communication, and that the spoken forms ultimately encompass the written, as one has to be taught how to read any text—at whatever level. It is also conscious of the layers of metaphor, irony, concealment, and self-reference in living language, which may fade from any written version though it can be put back in by an imaginative reader or a creative actor (see Chapter 4 above). Anthropology is also seeing increasingly how language is imbricated in 'nonverbal' forms of communication, such as the bodily modes of gesture, and the arts of music, or visual images.

Anthropology has pioneered the method of the direct study of human life, through personal immersion in fieldwork. However, while this promises a lot, it can only ever be a minor part of what the scholar does. Anthropology works in practice most of the time on written texts, whether ethnographies from across the world, theoretical treatises, or the kind of documentation of a region which is the stuff of research alongside fieldwork, and it has to try to re-imagine the living context in which those human beings encapsulated into texts lived and interacted, using language and other modes of expression among themselves. When an anthropologist does this, it is very close to the method of the historian. Fieldwork in fact occupies only a fraction of the lifetime of an anthropologist; even though imaginatively inspiring throughout a career, it cannot measure up to the time spent by anthropologists mulling over written texts, and in effect working as historians do.

In another sense too there is affinity with history. In the technical sciences, theories can suddenly be displaced and seem irrelevant to current thinking and research. In the humanities, the ideas of past scholars are not so easily dumped. Because we can make allowances for their time and context, because we can re-enter the debates to which they saw themselves as contributing, we can see the parallels with other, even modern (and postmodern) formulations of similar debates and see where our own vote might be placed. By applying a kind of ethnographic sympathy, we can learn much from the scholarly ideas of the past. Most writers hope after all that their work will be discussed and recycled in the thought and practice of others, not simply catalogued by the librarian and physically tucked away in a corner cupboard. 'Listening' to the past of our subject is not all a sorting out of dead metaphors; we can frequently recognize fresh relevance in what earlier writers have been saying, and use their insights as a guide. In the chapters above, the ideas of Mauss and Collingwood from the first part of the twentieth century, and those of Evans-Pritchard from the middle period, have been drawn into the presentation for this reason. All three could be regarded as engaged in the quest to make scholarly exploration of the forms of thought and social life more systematic. None sought to reduce the complexity of human phenomena to some simple model or to proclaim, prematurely, some 'scientific' way of reaching general explanatory principles or final truths.

There is a difference between the very 'modern' notion of a totally true statement, or belief, on the analogy of a mathematical equation, and the more accommodating idea of pragmatic agreement in the making of our lives together with others, where the edges of accepted truth are a little compromised, a little fuzzy, a little more emotional perhaps than the propositions of logic or mathematics, belonging to the spoken rather than the written word, to intuition and 'resonance' rather than to proof. The sharper senses of proof and truth often appear to be validated through writing, literacy, and the accumulation of authoritative texts. But they are impossible to disentangle, in practice, from their interpretation, from the personal words of priest, teacher, or judge. The anthropologist needs to see clearly how textual authority operates in life, and how closely this may approach the more obvious 'oral' forms of spoken and enacted wisdom. In Douglas Johnson's study of the Nuer prophets, he draws on Collingwood's insight that the prophet, like the artist, reveals to people what is in their own hearts. During their time, the prophets may not speak very lucidly; but in their words, or in the songs they may inspire, successive generations see true insights into their own predicaments.[6] This is rather different from the literally spelled-out certainties of modern fundamentalism, where there is little space for alternative readings, little political room for social accommodation and a tendency to demonize the opposition.[7] Truths anchored in the written word tend to partner modern forms of commoditized knowledge: and of political authority and the discipline of persons. Such truths aim to eliminate ambiguity and provisionality, insisting on the mono-meanings of words, signs, and actions. There always was a certain 'multiplicity' in mythical-ritual/religious systems, and the way that people lived with them; what has modernity done to this? We are faced with literal signification not only in language but in art, as in the monuments and purposefully constructed ceremonies of nationalism. We are also confronted with increasingly strong demands for allegiance in religious communities, and increasingly sharp categories of personal identity (recall the former apartheid state of South Africa, and also the Rwanda of the early 1990s). There is a creeping essentialization of personal ethnicity even in the official world of the UK census and employment monitoring, not to mention the situation in the USA.

Anthony Giddens, asked as a sociologist to comment on the future of anthropology, has suggested that while anthropology may face problems, it is not alone—the other social sciences are facing similar problems because of the great transformations which have affected all our lives over the last few years. He suggests that some of the newly relevant aspects of social life come from the older agenda of anthropology itself: for example, ethnicity, ritual, and religion. Anthropology's past 'contains ideas that either remain as important as ever they were, or have actually become more significant today'.[8] He recommends that anthropology reinvent itself. Postmodernism, he points out, is not the answer—it is too close to post-structuralism, which is a 'defective theory of meaning and therefore of representation', relying as it does on abstract and detached signifiers rather than the context of practical experience and the production of knowledge by everyone in that context. He suggests that a 'rekindling of the anthropological imagination' is needed —presumably in a larger community than just that of the anthropologists— ready to uncover and contest unjust systems of domination.[9] This observation, I hope, will strike a chord with a younger generation of students in the human sciences in the widest sense, to whom the torch is now being passed at a difficult and dangerous time in the world's history.

Let us recall Collingwood's view of philosophical inquiry, which itself looks into those systems of ideas-and-action which have prevailed in history; in this sense history is a metaphysical investigation, for it seeks to compare, reflexively, the presuppositions of one such system with those of another.[10] There is no extra-historical domain in which pure categories exist for philosophical contemplation. Part of our self-awareness must include a recognition of the historical formation of those ideas on which we act, and their relation to other forms. The fieldwork encounter is more than an engagement of individuals, however empathic. It is a lens through which we should seek to focus on those *historical formations of sociality* outside which human beings and their behaviour cannot be isolated for study. The Trobriand Islanders and the Australian Aborigines are among those 'remoter' peoples who do not appear in standard history books, but have exercised the imagination of every anthropology student through the texts of anthropological literature. Even the professional anthropologist is not required to have visited all such peoples personally in order to work the relevant literature into a new critical synthesis. An assessment of the literature itself is a part of an anthropologist's training, and normally precedes field experience. This necessary study of written texts is a real point of correspondence with the work of historians, and not very different from their exercise of empathy in re-analysing, and re-enacting in their imagination, the life of the ancient Greeks or Romans or allowing them to defamiliarize our own.

There have been bold, important claims in recent years that different kinds of anthropology should be, or are being, generated from within 'other' historical and civilizational contexts. A question which is heard more and more often asks whether there can be an Islamic anthropology, a Japanese or African anthropology (and so on presumably *ad infinitum*). Critical viewpoints are certainly opening up through the regional spread of professional anthropology, as they did from the 1970s on with respect to feminist perspectives. All these new kinds of writing question the privilege accorded to, or claimed by, standard English-language anthropology (much less so with, say, French or Italian anthropology) with its imperialistic outlook and Western biases. The question of 'alternative' anthropologies must be welcomed, in my view, especially as a way of *extending the global conversation* which anthropology has always aimed to explore. The image of 'the West' which is used as a target of criticism in some of the new 'alternative' perspectives is itself under deconstruction by anthropologists, as some are probing the façade of decency, democracy, and liberal values which the West presents to the world.[11] Cross-currents are the name of the game: a revealing study by Rebecca Karl shows how it was partly through the performance of newly shaped satirical forms of traditional opera relating to Western countries and the Boer war that China first began to form a notion of the wider modern world in the early twentieth century and its own place within that world.[12]

Conscious more now than ever before of history, past and recent, and processes of change and movement, we are alive to contemporary political events in a way that I believe is new to anthropology. We once overvalued the credulity and religiosity of the pagan worlds and now we wonder whether we have all been over-sanguine about the rationality of the world's so-called 'civilized'. Evans-Pritchard showed how rational and intelligible, and translatable, the pagans were; and now we are beginning to accept what creatures of feeling we moderns—or postmoderns or whatever—are, and how difficult it is to translate even among ourselves. Anthropology was once called a child of the Enlightenment. Now we are faced with a kind of counter-Enlightenment in the waves of new religious activity found even in the most technically sophisticated parts of the world, religious fundamentalism in various alarming varieties, emotive politics, and impulsive expressions of cultural certainty. There are serious games afoot, and the need for clear and moderating language—in the human sciences as in the world we share—has never been greater.

Notes

PART I

Chapter One

1 Matt Ridley, *Genome: The Autobiography of a Species in 23 Chapters* (New York: HarperCollins, 1999), 151.

2 N. J. Allen, 'The field and the desk: choices and linkages', in P. Dresch, W. James, and D. Parkin (eds.), *Anthropologists in a Wider World: Essays on Field Research* (Oxford & New York: Berghahn, 2000).

3 Marcel Mauss's development of the idea of morphology as a material, spatial, temporal, and demographic foundation for holistic social analysis is reflected in the lucid case study he prepared with Henri Beuchat, *Seasonal Variations of the Eskimo: A Study in Social Morphology* [1904–5] (London: Routledge & Kegan Paul, 1979). The translator, James J. Fox, offers an extended commentary on the concept, and its relation to other aspects of Mauss's work, in his Foreword (esp. 3–10).

4 Edwin W. Ardener, '"Behaviour": a social anthropological criticism' [1973], in *The Voice of Prophecy: And Other Essays*, ed. M. Chapman (Oxford: Blackwell, 1989), 105–6; 'The new anthropology and its critics' [1971], ibid. 48.

5 Ludwig Wittgenstein, 'Remarks on Frazer's *Golden Bough*', in James Klagge and Alfred Nordmann (eds.), *Philosophical Occasions 1912–1951* (Indianapolis & Cambridge: Hackett, 1993), 129. This text is further discussed in Chapter 6. James G. Frazer, *The Golden Bough: A Study in Magic and Religion*, abridged edn. in one volume [1922] (London: Macmillan, 1960).

6 Wittgenstein, 'Remarks on Frazer', 129. Other commentators who have drawn attention to this striking image and its context include Rush Rhees, 'Introductory note' to the first English translation, 'Remarks on Frazer's "Golden Bough"', *The Human World*, 3 (1971), 18–28; Jacques Bouveresse, *L'Animal Cérémoniel: Wittgenstein et l'Anthropologie*, Collection *Le Bruit du Temps* (Paris: Éditions l'Âge d'Homme, 1982); R. Needham, 'Remarks on Wittgenstein and ritual', in *Exemplars* (Berkeley & Los Angeles: University of California Press, 1985), 154–5, 174–7; Elizabeth F. Collins, 'A ceremonial animal', *Journal of Ritual Studies*, 10 (1996), 59–84; Frank Cioffi, *Wittgenstein on Freud and Frazer* (Cambridge: Cambridge University Press, 1998), esp. ch. 3; Brian Clack, *Wittgenstein, Frazer and Religion* (London/New York: Macmillan/St Martin's Press, 1999), esp. 148–54; Philippe Corbier de Lara, 'L'Homme Rituel: Wittgenstein, Sociologie et Anthropologie', Ph.D. thesis (Sorbonne IV, 2000).

7 Needham, 'Remarks on Wittgenstein', 177.

8 R. G. Collingwood, *An Essay on Philosophical Method* (Oxford: Clarendon Press, 1933), ch. 3.

9 Georgina Born, *Rationalizing Culture: IRCAM, Boulez, and the Institutionalization of the Musical Avant-Garde* (Berkeley: University of California Press, 1995). Mukulika Banerjee, *The Pathan Unarmed: Opposition and Memory in the Khudai Khidmatgar Movement*, World Anthropology (Oxford/Santa Fe, N. Mex.: James Currey/School of American Research Press, 2000). Sarah Franklin, *Embodied Progress: A Cultural Account of Assisted Conception* (London & New York: Routledge, 1997).

10 Jeremy MacClancy (ed.), *Exotic No More: Anthropology on the Front Lines* (Chicago & London: University of Chicago Press, 2002).

11 Steven Feld, *Sound and Sentiment: Birds, Weeping, Poetics, and Song in Kaluli Expression*, 2nd edn. (Philadelphia: University of Pennsylvania Press, 1990). Alfred Gell, 'The language of the forest: landscape and phonological iconism in Umeda', in M. O'Hanlon and E. Hirsch (eds.), *The Anthropology of Landscape: Perspectives on Place and Space* (Oxford: Clarendon Press, 1995).

12 Akira Okazaki, 'Recapturing the Shadow: Dream Consciousness, Healing and Civil War in the Borderlands between Northern and Southern Sudan', The Evans-Pritchard Lectures, 1999, All Souls College, Oxford.

13 Laura Rival, 'Androgynous parents and guest children: the Huaorani *couvade*', *JRAI* (NS), 4 (1998), 619–42.

14 Barker's comments were made in a radio interview. See Eileen Barker, *The Making of a Moonie: Choice or Brainwashing?* (Oxford: Blackwell, 1984), and Kirsten Hastrup, *Studying Action: Anthropology in the Company of Shakespeare* (Copenhagen: Museum Tusculanum Press, 2003). For further reading on the shift of anthropology towards the familiar and personal, see Anthony Jackson (ed.), *Anthropology at Home*, ASA Monograph 25 (London & New York: Tavistock, 1986); Judith Okely and Helen Callaway (eds.), *Anthropology and Autobiography*, ASA Monograph 29 (London & New York: Routledge, 1992); Sharon Macdonald, *Reimagining Culture: Histories, Identities and the Gaelic Renaissance* (Oxford & New York: Berg, 1997).

15 Good starting points on the history of anthropology would include R. G. Lienhardt, *Social Anthropology* (London: Oxford University Press, 1964); George Stocking, *Victorian Anthropology* (New York: Free Press, 1987); James Urry, *Before Social Anthropology: Essays on the History of British Anthropology* (Reading: Harwood, 1993); Alan Barnard, *History and Theory in Anthropology* (Cambridge: Cambridge University Press, 2000).

16 See Wendy James, 'E. E. Evans-Pritchard, 1902–73', in *International Encyclopedia of the Social and Behavioral Sciences* (Kidlington: Elsevier, 2001).

17 My terminology here is minimal. Clear guidance on the early history of humankind can be found in Robert Foley, *Humans Before Humanity: An Evolutionary Perspective* (Oxford: Blackwell, 1995), and Steven Mithen, *The Prehistory of the Mind:*

A Search for the Origins of Art, Religion and Science (London: Thames & Hudson, 1996), who explains the Early/Modern distinction at p. 130. See also Chris Stringer and Clive Gamble, *In Search of the Neanderthals* (London: Thames & Hudson, 1993).

18 Chris Stringer and R. McKie, *African Exodus: The Origins of Modern Humanity* (London: Jonathan Cape, 1996).

19 Kenelm O. L. Burridge, *Encountering Aborigines: A Case Study. Anthropology and the Australian Aboriginal* (New York, Toronto & Oxford: Pergamon Press, 1973).

20 Émile Durkheim, *The Elementary Forms of Religious Life* [1912], trans. Karen E. Fields (New York: Free Press, 1995), pp. xix–xx.

21 Wendy James and N. J. Allen (eds.), *Marcel Mauss: A Centenary Tribute* (Oxford & New York: Berghahn, 1998).

22 Maurice Godelier, *Perspectives in Marxist Anthropology* (Cambridge: Cambridge University Press, 1977); Maurice Bloch, *Marxism and Anthropology* (Oxford: Oxford University Press, 1983); Michael Taussig, *The Devil and Commodity Fetishism in South America* (Chapel Hill, NC: University of North Carolina Press, 1980).

23 For an overview of these developments up to the mid-1980s, see Henrietta L. Moore, *Feminism and Anthropology* (Cambridge: Polity Press, 1988), and for a recent set of reflective essays see her *A Passion for Difference: Essays in Anthropology and Gender* (Cambridge: Polity Press, 1994).

24 See, for example, Michael O'Hanlon and Robert L. Welsch (eds.), *Hunting the Gatherers: Ethnographic Collectors, Agents and Agency in Melanesia, 1870s–1930s* (Oxford & New York: Berghahn, 2000).

25 Kenelm O. L. Burridge, *Someone, No One: An Essay on Individuality* (Princeton: Princeton University Press, 1979); Louis Dumont, *Essays on Individualism* (Chicago: University of Chicago Press, 1986). These issues are further discussed in Chapters 8 and 13.

Chapter Two

1 Bronislaw Malinowski, *Argonauts of the Western Pacific* (London: Routledge & Kegan Paul, 1922); this case study was given a key theoretical place in Marcel Mauss, *The Gift: The Form and Reason for Exchange in Archaic Societies* [1925], trans. W. D. Halls, foreword by Mary Douglas (London: Routledge, 1990).

2 B. Malinowski, *The Sexual Life of Savages in North-western Melanesia* (London: Routledge & Kegan Paul, 1929); discussed in Edmund E. Leach, 'Virgin birth', in *Genesis as Myth and Other Essays* (London: Jonathan Cape, 1969). Later debates are summarized in Sarah Franklin, *Embodied Progress: A Cultural Account of Assisted Conception* (London & New York: Routledge, 1997), ch. 1.

3 Edward E. Evans-Pritchard, *Witchcraft, Oracles, and Magic among the Azande* (Oxford: Clarendon Press, 1937). For a flavour of the later debates, see Bryan Wilson (ed.), *Rationality* (Oxford: Blackwell, 1970).

4 Founding texts include Lionel Tiger and Robin Fox, *The Imperial Animal* (New York: Holt, Rinehart & Winston, 1971; 2nd rev. edn., New Brunswick, NJ: Transaction Publishers, 1998); Edmund O. Wilson, *On Human Nature* (Cambridge, Mass., & London: Harvard University Press, 1978).

5 Richard Dawkins, *The Selfish Gene* (Oxford: Oxford University Press, 1978), preface.

6 Louise Barret, Robin Dunbar, and John Lycett, *Human Evolutionary Psychology* (Basingstoke & New York: Palgrave, 2002), 137–8.

7 Dawkins, *Selfish Gene*, p. x.

8 Hilary Callan, *Ethology and Society: Towards an Anthropological View* (Oxford: Clarendon Press, 1970).

9 Dawkins, *Selfish Gene*, 206–10.

10 Misia Landau, *Narratives of Human Evolution* (New Haven & London: Yale University Press, 1991).

11 Bryan Sykes, *The Seven Daughters of Eve* [2001] (London: Corgi/Random House, 2002).

12 Ibid. 251–63.

13 Steve Jones, *Y: The Descent of Men* (London: Little, Brown, 2002).

14 For a passionate broadside, see S. Rose, R. C. Lewontin, and L. J. Kamin, *Not in our Genes: Biology, Ideology and Human Nature* [1984] (Harmondsworth: Penguin, 1990). For sustained scientific criticism of a range of reductive approaches to the human sciences, including some kinds of evolutionary genetics, see Stephen Jay Gould's *The Mismeasure of Man*, revised and expanded edition of 1996 (Harmondsworth: Penguin, 1997). See also Justine Burley's edited volume *The Genetic Revolution and Human Rights*, the Oxford Amnesty Lectures 1998 (Oxford: Oxford University Press, 1999). For a set of recent sober research studies in the field which do not go for the 'human rights headlines', see Sue T. Parker, J. Langer, and M. L. McKinney (eds.), *Biology, Brains, and Behavior: The Evolution of Human Development* (Santa Fe, N. Mex./Oxford: SAR Press/James Currey, 2000).

15 Martin Daly and Margo Wilson, *The Truth About Cinderella: A Darwinian View of Parental Love* (London: Weidenfeld & Nicolson, 1998). This attractively presented little book is one of a series 'Darwinism Today' edited by Helena Cronin and Oliver Curry. The quotation is from the series blurb on the cover.

16 Ibid. 8.

17 The social and historical significance of dowry or bridewealth systems, in combination with patterns of land tenure and inheritance, especially in the contrasting of the European and Indian regions, on the one hand, and Africa on the other, has been examined in detail by Jack Goody. See, for example, his *Production and Reproduction: A Comparative Study of the Domestic Domain* (Cambridge University Press, 1976). Stepfamilies are given careful comparative attention throughout this study.

18 An overview is given in Steven Mithen, *The Prehistory of the Mind: A Search for the Origins of Art, Religion and Science* (Phoenix Paperback, 1998; orig. pub. London: Thames & Hudson, 1996). See also Jane Goodall, *The Chimpanzees of Gombe: Patterns of Behaviour* (Cambridge, Mass.: Harvard University Press, 1986). For recent research discussions, see Barbara King (ed.), *The Origins of Language: What Nonhuman Primates Can Tell Us* (Santa Fe, N. Mex./Oxford: SAR Press/James Currey, 2000).

19 Matt Ridley, *Genome: The Autobiography of a Species in 23 Chapters* (New York: HarperCollins, 1999), 16–18, 219–30, 301–13.

20 Robert Foley, *Humans before Humanity: An Evolutionary Perspective* (Oxford: Blackwell, 1995).

21 Robin I. M. Dunbar, *Grooming, Gossip, and the Evolution of Language* (London: Faber & Faber, 1996); 'The social brain hypothesis', *Evolutionary Anthropology*, 6 (1998), 178–90; 'On the origin of the human mind', in P. Carruthers and A. Chamberlain (eds.), *Evolution and the Human Mind: Modularity, Language and Meta-Cognition* (Cambridge: Cambridge University Press, 2000). For a synthesis of much current scientific research in this field see Louise Barrett, Robin Dunbar, and John Lycett, *Human Evolutionary Psychology* (Basingstoke & New York: Palgrave, 2002).

22 W. G. Runciman, *The Social Animal* (London: HarperCollins, 1998).

23 Mithen, *The Prehistory of the Mind*, 36 ff.

24 Ibid. 171 ff.

25 Merlin Donald, *Origins of the Modern Mind: Three Stages in the Evolution of Culture and Cognition* (Cambridge, Mass.: Harvard University Press, 1991); *A Mind so Rare: The Evolution of Human Consciousness* (New York & London: Norton, 2001).

26 Donald, *A Mind so Rare*, 10–12.

27 Ibid. 75–6.

28 Ibid. 200–2.

29 Ibid. 260 ff.

30 Ibid. 253–4.

31 Ibid. 266–7.

32 Ibid. 269.

33 Barrett *et al.*, *Human Evolutionary Psychology*, 171–234.

34 Chris D. Knight, *Blood Relations: Menstruation and the Origins of Culture* (New Haven: Yale University Press, 1991); 'Sex and language as pretend-play', in R. Dunbar, C. Knight, and C. Power (eds.), *The Evolution of Culture* (Edinburgh: Edinburgh University Press, 1999). Compare also two other articles in the same volume: Camilla Power, '"Beauty Magic": the origins of art', and Ian Watts, 'The origin of symbolic culture'.

35 Foley, *Humans before Humanity*, 201.

36 Useful background reading would include F. R. Leavis (ed.), *Mill on Bentham and Coleridge* (London: Chatto & Windus, 1950); J. C. C. Smart and B. Williams (eds.), *Utilitarianism: For and Against* (Cambridge: Cambridge University Press, 1973); Mary

Warnock (ed.), *Utilitarianism* (selected readings, including J. S. Mill's 1859 essay *On Liberty*, 126–83) (London: Collins/Fontana, 1962).

37 The approach is clearly set out in Fredrik Barth, *Models of Social Organization* (London: Occasional Paper of the RAI, 1966).

38 Fredrik Barth, 'Segmentary lineages and the theory of games' (London: Occasional Paper of the RAI, 1959). E. E. Evans-Pritchard, *The Nuer: A Description of the Modes of Livelihood and Political Institutions of a Nilotic People* (Oxford: Clarendon Press, 1940).

39 Fredrik Barth, *Political Leadership among the Swat Pathans* (London: Athlone, 1959), 1–2.

40 Barth, *Models of Social Organization*, 1.

41 For a fuller critical review of Barth's key ideas, see Wendy James, 'Illusions of freedom: a note on Barth's individuals', *JASO* 4 (1973), 155–67.

42 Mill, in Warnock, *Utilitarianism*, 54.

43 Diego Gambetta (ed.), *Trust: Making and Breaking Co-operative Relations* (Oxford: Blackwell, 1988); *The Sicilian Mafia: The Business of Private Protection* (Cambridge, Mass.: Harvard University Press, 1993).

44 Anthony Giddens, *The Third Way* (Cambridge: Cambridge University Press, 1998). For a critical view, see Alex Callinicos, *Against the Third Way: An Anti-Capitalist Critique* (Cambridge: Polity Press, 2001).

45 Mary Douglas, 'Introduction' to Mauss, *The Gift*, p. xv.

46 Edward B. Tylor, *Primitive Culture* (London: John Murray, 2 vols., 1871); *Anthropology* (London: 1881); Melville J. Herskovits, 'The culture areas of Africa', *Africa*, 3 (1930), 59–77.

47 Ruth Benedict, *Patterns of Culture* (London: Routledge & Kegan Paul, 1935). A later study of Japanese culture became almost as famous: *The Crysanthemum and the Sword* (Boston: Houghton Mifflin, 1946).

48 Margaret Mead, *Coming of Age in Samoa: A Psychological Study of Primitive Youth for Western Civilisation* (New York: Morrow, 1928). *Growing up in New Guinea: A Comparative Study of Primitive Education* (London: Routledge, 1931); *Sex and Temperament in Three Primitive Societies* (London: Routledge, 1935).

49 Some of Clifford Geertz's most influential essays, such as 'Religion as a cultural system' are included in *The Interpretation of Cultures* (New York: Basic Books, 1973). Talal Asad has offered a significant critique in *Genealogies of Religion: Discipline and Reasons of Power in Christianity and Islam* (Baltimore & London: Johns Hopkins University Press, 1993), ch. 1.

50 James Clifford and G. E. Marcus, *Writing Culture: The Poetics and Politics of Ethnography* (Berkeley: University of California Press, 1986).

51 Edward Said, *Orientalism* (London: Routledge & Kegan Paul, 1978).

52 See, for example, the papers collected in Richard Fardon (ed.), *Localizing Strategies: Regional Traditions of Ethnographic Writing* (Washington/Edinburgh:

Smithsonian/Scottish Academic Press, 1990); and in Allison James, A. Dawson, and J. Hockey (eds.), *After Writing Culture: Epistemology and Praxis in Contemporary Anthropology*, ASA Monograph 34 (London & New York: Routledge, 1997); and Tim Ingold (ed.), *Key Debates in Anthropology* (London & New York: Routledge, 1996).

53 See, for example, George E. Marcus (ed.), *Critical Anthropology Now* (Santa Fe, N. Mex./Oxford: School of American Research Press/James Currey, 1999); Susanna M. Hoffman and Anthony Oliver-Smith (eds.), *Catastrophe and Culture: The Anthropology of Disaster* (Santa Fe, N. Mex./Oxford: School of American Research Press/James Currey, 2002).

54 Elenore Smith Bowen [pseudonym used by Laura Bohannan], *Return to Laughter* (London: Gollancz, 1956); Nigel Barley, *The Innocent Anthropologist: Notes from a Mud Hut* (Harmondsworth: Penguin, 1983); Amitav Ghosh, *In an Antique Land* [1992] (Penguin Books/Granta, 1994).

55 Barbara Pym, *Less Than Angels* (London: Jonathan Cape, 1955); Frank Parkin, *Krippendorf's Tribe* (New York: Atheneum, 1986; first published in the UK, 1985); Dan Davin, *Brides of Price* (London: Robert Hale, 1972).

56 See, for example, David Price, 'Interlopers and invited guests: on anthropology's witting and unwitting links to intelligence agencies', *Anthropology Today*, 18/6 (2002), 16–21.

57 Peter Winch, *The Idea of a Social Science, and its Relation to Philosophy* (London: Routledge & Kegan Paul, 1958).

58 Ibid. 3, 23, 34, 121 ff., 133.

59 Karl Marx, *Pre-Capitalist Economic Formations*, trans. Jack Cohen, introd. Eric Hobsbawm (London: Lawrence & Wishart, 1964). Max Weber, *The Agrarian Sociology of Ancient Civilizations* [1909], trans. R. I. Frank (London & New York: Verso, 1998). *The Theory of Social and Economic Organization*, trans. A. M. Henderson and Talcott Parsons [1947] (New York/London: The Free Press/Collier-Macmillan, 1964).

60 For a set of essays evaluating his ideas by anthropologists who knew him closely, see Raymond Firth (ed.), *Man and Culture: An Evaluation of the Work of Bronislaw Malinowski* (London: Routledge & Kegan Paul, 1957).

61 A. R. Radcliffe-Brown, *Structure and Function in Primitive Society* (London: Cohen & West, 1952). For a recent reassessment see Adam Kuper (ed.), *The Social Anthropology of Radcliffe-Brown* (London: Routledge, 1977).

62 Arnold van Gennep, *The Rites of Passage* [1909], trans. Monika B. Vizedom and Gabrielle L. Caffee (London: Routledge & Kegan Paul, 1960).

63 See Evans-Pritchard's chapter on Lévy-Bruhl in his *Theories of Primitive Religion* (Oxford: Clarendon Press, 1965); and Rodney Needham, *Belief, Language and Experience* (Oxford: Blackwell, 1972).

64 Marcel Mauss and Henri Hubert, *Sacrifice: Its Nature and Function* [1899], trans. W. D. Halls (London: Cohen & West, 1964); Émile Durkheim and Marcel Mauss, *Primitive Classification* [1903], trans. R. Needham (London: Cohen & West, 1963);

Marcel Mauss in collaboration with Henri Beuchat, *Seasonal Variations of the Eskimo: A Study in Social Morphology* [1904–5], trans. James J. Fox (London: Routledge & Kegan Paul, 1979); Henri Hubert, *Essay on Time: A Brief Study of the Representation of Time in Religion and Magic* [1905], trans. R. Parkin and J. Redding (Oxford & New York: Berghahn, 1999); Marcel Mauss (with Henri Hubert), *A General Theory of Magic* [1904], trans. R. Brain (London: Routledge & Kegan Paul, 1972); Marcel Mauss, *Sociology and Psychology: Essays by Marcel Mauss*, trans. B. Brewster (London: Routledge & Kegan Paul, 1979); Marcel Mauss, *The Gift: The Form and Reason for Exchange in Archaic Societies* [1925], trans. W. D. Halls, foreword by Mary Douglas (London: Routledge, 1990).

65 Key texts and ideas are discussed below, with reference to myth in Chapter 5 and to kinship in Chapter 7.

66 Edmund R. Leach, *Rethinking Anthropology* (London: Athlone, 1961). Leach's monograph *Political Systems of Highland Burma* (London: Bell, 1954), illustrates his effort to move away from the comparison of small-scale tribal systems as distinct types and towards the analysis of changing social relations over time and space.

67 Evans-Pritchard specifically evoked R. G. Collingwood's vision of what 'history' could be in sketching his own ambitions for social anthropology, and also followed Collingwood's example in drawing up a new academic lineage for his disciplinary field as he saw it (see particularly his lectures on anthropological 'ancestors' in *Theories of Primitive Religion*, 1965 and *A History of Anthropological Thought*, 1981).

68 E. E. Evans-Pritchard, *Witchcraft, Oracles, and Magic among the Azande* (Oxford: Clarendon Press, 1937). An abridged paperback edition was published in 1976.

69 E. E. Evans-Pritchard, *The Nuer: A Description of the Modes of Livelihood and Political Institutions of a Nilotic People* (Oxford: Clarendon Press, 1940).

70 Mauss, *Seasonal Variations of the Eskimo.*

71 Louis Dumont, 'Preface to the French edition of E. E. Evans-Pritchard's *The Nuer*', trans. M. and J. Douglas, in J. H. M. Beattie and R. G. Lienhardt (eds.), *Studies in Social Anthropology: Essays in Memory of E. E. Evans-Pritchard by his Former Oxford Colleagues* (Oxford: Clarendon Press, 1975).

72 E. E. Evans-Pritchard, *Kinship and Marriage among the Nuer*, 1951; *Nuer Religion*, 1956; both Oxford, Clarendon Press. The secondary debates flourished in American and British anthropology for some decades until fresh field research began to re-position 'the Nuer' within anthropology. See, for example, Douglas H. Johnson, *Nuer Prophets: A History of Prophecy from the Upper Nile in the Nineteenth and Twentieth Centuries* (Oxford: Clarendon Press, 1994); and Sharon Hutchinson, *Nuer Dilemmas: Coping with Money, War and the State* (Berkeley & Los Angeles: University of Calfornia Press, 1996).

73 Tom O. Beidelman (ed.), *The Translation of Culture* (London: Tavistock, 1971). Cf. E. E. Evans-Pritchard, *The Sanusi of Cyrenaica* (Oxford: Clarendon Press, 1949).

74 A special session re-evaluating the Manchester school and the relevance of the extended case study method was held at the 2002 meetings of the European Association of Social Anthropologists in Copenhagen.

75 Wendy James, 'The anthropologist as reluctant imperialist', in T. Asad (ed.), *Anthropology and the Colonial Encounter* (London: Ithaca Press, 1973).

PART II

Chapter Three

1 In these paragraphs I am closely following N. J. Allen, *Categories and Classifications: Maussian Essays on the Social* (Oxford & New York: Berghahn, 2000), ch. 5.

2 Stephen W. Hawking, *A Brief History of Time: From the Big Bang to Black Holes* (New York & London: Bantam Press, 1988). This book was enthusiastically received and discussed. The CD Rom issued to illustrate it offers some short but spectacular colour movie clips of the expanding universe, protons and neutrons, black holes, etc., all very helpful to the imagination, with an occasional glimpse of God in the background (Stephen W. Hawking, *A Brief History of Time*, Focus Multimedia Ltd., UK).

3 É. Durkheim and M. Mauss, *Primitive Classification* [1903], trans. R. Needham (London: Cohen & West, 1963).

4 R. G. Collingwood, *An Autobiography* (Oxford: Clarendon Press, 1939); *An Essay on Metaphysics* (Oxford: Clarendon Press, 1940).

5 R. G. Collingwood, *The Idea of Nature* (Oxford: Clarendon Press, 1945).

6 Maurice Bloch, *How We Think They Think: Anthropological Approaches to Cognition, Memory, and Literacy* (Oxford & Boulder, Colo.: Westview Press, 1998), pp. vii–viii.

7 Ibid. 5–7.

8 Ibid. 14–17, 25.

9 Ibid. 54–63.

10 Allen, *Categories and Classifications*. Ferdinand de Saussure first articulated the powerful analytical contrast between *la langue* and *la parole*: while the latter was the always-changing flow of speech, the former constituted both the co-present or 'horizontal' relations between elements in a sentence and the 'absent' or 'vertical' relations implied as alternative possibilities, such as the substitution of 'cat' for 'dog' in a sentence, or the past for the present tense in a verb. The *parole* kind of relations constitute the 'syntagmatic' plane, and *la langue* the 'paradigmatic' plane, of language.

11 Durkheim and Mauss, *Primitive Classification*, Parts I–IV.

12 For a comprehensive overview, see N. J. Allen, 'Hinduism, structuralism and Dumézil', in E. C. Polomé (ed.), *Miscellanea Indo-Europea*, J. of Indo-European Studies Monograph no. 33 (Washington: Institute for the Study of Man, 1999).

13 Robert Hertz, 'The pre-eminence of the right hand: a study in religious polarity' [1907], in *Death and the Right Hand*, trans. R. and C. Needham (London: Cohen & West, 1960).

14 Claude Lévi-Strauss, *Structural Anthropology* [1958], trans. C. Jacobson and B. G. Schopf (London: Allen Lane, 1963); *Tristes Tropiques* [1955] (Harmondsworth: Penguin, 1976).

15 Louis Dumont, *Homo Hierachicus* (Chicago: University of Chicago Press, 1966).

16 Marcel Granet, 'Right and left in China', trans R. Needham, in R. Needham (ed.), *Right and Left: Essays on Dual Symbolic Classification* (Chicago & London: University of Chicago Press, 1973), 45, 53.

17 Mary Douglas, *Purity and Danger* (London: Routledge & Kegan Paul, 1966). Franz Steiner, *Taboo* [1958], reissued with editorial introduction by J. Adler and R. Fardon (Oxford & New York: Berghahn, 2000).

18 Mary Douglas, *The Lele of Kasai* (London: Oxford University Press, 1963). *Purity and Danger: An Analysis of Concepts of Pollution and Taboo* (London: Routledge & Kegan Paul, 1966).

19 Douglas, *Purity and Danger*, ch. 1.

20 Victor W. Turner, *The Forest of Symbols* (Ithaca, NY: Cornell University Press, 1967); *The Ritual Process: Structure and Anti-Structure* (Chicago: Aldine, 1969); *Dramas, Fields, and Metaphors: Symbolic Action in Human Society* (Ithaca, NY: Cornell University Press, 1974); *From Ritual to Theatre: The Human Seriousness of Play* (New York: Performing Arts Journal Press, 1982).

21 See chapters on 'Ndembu colour symbolism' and 'Muchona the hornet' in Turner, *The Forest of Symbols*.

22 See, for example, Charles O. Frake, *Language and Cultural Description* (Stanford: Stanford University Press, 1980); and Roy Ellen, *The Cultural Relations of Classification: An Analysis of Nuaulu Animal Categories from Central Seram* (Cambridge; Cambridge University Press, 1993).

23 The standard text arguing a broad historical process behind the development of colour terms is Brent Berlin and Paul Kay, *Basic Color Terms: Their Universality and Evolution* (Berkeley and Los Angeles: University of California Press, 1970). An updated version of the theory may be found in C. L. Hardin and Luisa Maffi (eds.), *Color Categories in Thought and Language* (Cambridge: Cambridge University Press, 1997).

24 Collingwood, *Essay on Metaphysics*, 195.

25 David Turton, 'There's no such beast: cattle and colour naming among the Mursi', *Man*, 15 (1980), 320–38.

26 Jean Buxton, *Religion and Healing in Mandari* (Oxford: Clarendon Press, 1975).

27 Further information on Uduk colour terms may be found in W. James, *The Listening Ebony: Moral Knowledge, Religion and Power among the Uduk of Sudan* (Oxford: Clarendon Press [1988]; reissued in paperback with new preface, 1999). See esp. pp. 28–9.

28 A recent major study is Barbara Bender, *Stonehenge: Making Space (Materializing Culture)* (Oxford & New York: Berg, 1988). On Cumbria, a good local source is J. Waterhouse, *The Stone Circles of Cumbria* (Southampton: Phillimore 1985).

29 Elizabeth Watson, 'Capturing a local elite: the Konso honeymoon', in W. James, D. L. Donham, E. Kurimoto, and A. Triulzi (eds.), *Remapping Ethiopia: Socialism and After* (Oxford/Athens, Oh.: James Currey/Ohio University Press, 2002).

30 Johannes Fabian, *Time and the Other: How Anthropology Makes its Object* (New York: Columbia University Press 1983); *Time and the Work of Anthropology: Critical Essays* (Reading: Harwood Academic Publishers, 1991).

31 Henri Hubert, *Essay on Time: A Brief Study of the Representation of Time in Religion and Magic* [1905], trans. R. Parkin and J. Redding (Oxford: Durkheim Press; Oxford/New York: Berghahn Books, 1999). Robert Hertz, 'A contribution to the study of the collective representation of death' [1907], in his *Death and the Right Hand*, trans. R. and C. Needham (London: Cohen & West, 1960).

32 E. E. Evans-Pritchard, *The Nuer: A Description of the Modes of Livelihood and Political Institutions of a Nilotic People* (Oxford: Clarendon Press, 1940), ch. 5. David Turton and C. Ruggles, 'Agreeing to disagree: The measurement of duration in a southwestern Ethiopian community', *Current Anthropology*, 19 (1978), 585–600.

33 E. R. Leach, 'Two essays on time', in *Rethinking Anthropology* (London: Athlone, 1961). R. Needham, 'Percussion and transition', *Man*, NS 2 (1967), 606–25.

34 Wendy James and David Mills (eds.), 'The Qualities of Time: Temporal Dimensions of Social Form and Human Experience', in preparation.

35 Alfred Gell, *The Anthropology of Time: Cultural Constructions of Temporal Maps and Images* (London & Providence, RI: Berg, 1992).

36 Ibid. 315–17.

37 Max Weber, *The Protestant Ethic and the Spirit of Capitalism* (1904, trans. 1958); Marshall Sahlins, *Stone Age Economics* (London: Tavistock, 1974).

38 Michael Cole, John Gay, Joseph A. Glick, and D. W. Sharp, *The Cultural Context of Learning and Thinking: An Exploration in Experimental Anthropology* (London: Methuen, 1971).

39 John H. R. Davis, *Times and Identities* (Inaugural Lecture) (Oxford: Oxford University Press, 1991); 'Tense in ethnography: some practical considerations', in Judith Okely and Helen Callaway (eds.), *Anthropology and Autobiography* (London & New York: Routledge, 1992).

40 J. Butterfield (ed.), *The Arguments of Time* (Oxford/New York: Oxford University Press for the British Academy, 1999).

41 Mary Warnock, *Imagination and Time* (Oxford: Blackwell, 1994).

Chapter Four

1 W. H. McNeill, *Keeping Together in Time: Dance and Drill in Human History* (Cambridge, Mass.: Harvard University Press, 1995). Vernon Reynolds, *Budongo: A Forest and its Chimpanzees* (London: Methuen, 1965), 133–5.

2 Drid Williams, 'Deep structures of the dance', in *Yearbook of Symbolic Anthropology*, 1 (1978), 211–30. Judith L. Hanna, *To Dance is Human: A Theory of Nonverbal Communication* [1979] (Chicago: University of Chicago Press, 1987). Cf. Alfred Gell, 'Dance structures', *J. of Human Movement Studies*, 5 (1979), 18–31.

3 Maurice Bloch, 'Symbols, song, dance and features of articulation: is religion an extreme form of traditional authority?' [1974], in M. Bloch, *Ritual, History and Power: Selected Papers in Anthropology* (London: Athlone, 1989). See esp. 21, 35–8; quotation from 37.

4 A. R. Radcliffe-Brown, *The Andaman Islanders* (Cambridge: Cambridge University Press, 1922).

5 E. E. Evans-Pritchard, 'The Dance', *Africa*, 1 (1928), 446–62.

6 Ibid. 446.

7 Ibid. 451.

8 Ibid. 460–2.

9 Clyde Mitchell, *The Kalela Dance* (Manchester: Manchester University Press, 1956).

10 T. O. Ranger, *Dance and Society in Eastern Africa 1890–1970: The Beni Ngoma* (Berkeley & Los Angeles: University of California Press, 1975).

11 Paul Spencer (ed.), *Society and the Dance: The Social Anthropology of Process and Performance* (Cambridge: Cambridge University Press, 1985).

12 Alfred Gell, 'Style and meaning in Umeda dance', in P. Spencer (ed.), *Society and the Dance*.

13 Jane K. Cowan, *Dance and the Body Politic in Northern Greece* (Princeton: Princeton University Press, 1990), p. xxi.

14 Ibid., p. xii.

15 Ibid. 20.

16 Ibid. 23.

17 Ibid. 141.

18 K. Hazzard-Gordon, 'Dancing under the lash: sociocultural disruption, continuity, and synthesis', in K. W. Asante (ed.), *African Dance: An Artistic, Historical and Philosophical Enquiry* (Trenton, NJ, & Asmara, Eritrea: Africa World Press, 1996).

19 Ibid. 121.

20 Ibid.

21 Ibid. 112.

22 Ibid. 113.

23 Ibid. 114.

24 G. Baumann, *National Integration and Local Integrity: The Miri of the Nuba Mountains in the Sudan* (Oxford: Clarendon Press, 1987).

25 Background on Uduk myth and ritual may be found in Wendy James, *'Kwanim Pa: The Making of the Uduk People. An Ethnographic Study of Survival in the Sudan–Ethiopian Borderlands* (Oxford: Clarendon Press, 1979) and in its sequel, *The Listening Ebony: Moral Knowledge, Religion, and Power among the Uduk of Sudan* (Oxford: Clarendon Press, 1988, reissued with new preface, 1999). A fuller comparative discussion of the motif of the circular dance may be found in W. James, 'Reforming the circle: fragments of the social history of a vernacular African dance form', *Journal of African Cultural Studies* (Special Issue: *Festschrift* for T. O. Ranger, ed. J. Lonsdale), 13 (2000), 140–52.

26 See, for example, Pierre Bourdieu, *The Logic of Practice* [1980], trans. Richard Nice (Cambridge: Polity Press, 1990), 34.

27 N. J. Allen, 'A dance of relatives', *JASO* (1982), 139–46. Cf. comments on music and rhythm in N. J. Allen, *Categories and Classifications: Maussian Essays on the Social* (Oxford & New York: Berghahn, 2000), 86–7.

28 Émile Durkheim, *The Elementary Forms of Religious Life*, trans. Karen E. Fields (New York: Free Press, 1995), 217–18.

29 Marcel Mauss, *Sociology and Psychology: Essays by Marcel Mauss*, trans. B. Brewster (London: Routledge & Kegan Paul, 1979), 21–2.

30 R. G. Collingwood, *The Principles of Art* (Oxford: Clarendon Press, 1938).

31 Ibid. 242.

32 Ibid. 243–4.

33 Ibid. 246.

34 Ibid. 247–8.

35 J. Huizinga, *Homo Ludens* [1938] (New York: Paladin, 1970). Cf. Iona and Peter Opie, *Children's Games in Street and Playground* (Oxford: Clarendon Press, 1969).

36 Ibid. 188–9, 66; introd. by George Steiner, 9–16, esp. at 14, 15, 16.

37 Suzanne K. Langer, *Philosophy in a New Key* (Cambridge, Mass.: Harvard University Press, 1942).

38 Susan K. Langer, *Feeling and Form: A Theory of Art* (London: Routledge & Kegan Paul, 1953).

39 Ibid. 174.

40 Ibid. 175–6.

41 Ibid. 177–8.

42 Ibid. 187.

43 Ibid. 196.

44 Ibid. 197.

45 Ibid. 204.

46 Kariamu Welsh Asante, *African Dance: An Artistic, Historical and Philosophical Enquiry* (Trenton, NJ, & Asmara, Eritrea: Africa World Press, 1996).

47 See, for example, John Blacking, *How Musical is Man?*, 2nd edn. (London: Faber & Faber, 1976); 'Movement, dance, music, and the Venda girls' initiation cycle', in Spencer, *Society and the Dance*.

48 Peter A. Lienhardt (ed. and trans.), *The Medicine Man: Swifa Ya Nguvumali*, by Hasani bin Ismail, Oxford Library of African Literature (Oxford: Clarendon Press, 1968).

49 A. Seeger, *Why Suya Sing: A Musical Anthropology of an Amazonian People* (Cambridge: Cambridge University Press, 1987).

50 Martin Stokes (ed.), *Ethnicity, Identity and Music: The Musical Construction of Place* (Oxford & New York: Berg, 1994).

51 Martin Stokes, *The Arabesk Debate: Music and Musicians in Modern Turkey* (Oxford: Clarendon Press, 1992).

52 Stokes, introduction to *Ethnicity, Identity and Music*, 8–9.

53 Gregory F. Barz and Timothy J. Cooley (eds.), *Shadows in the Field: New Perspectives for Fieldwork in Ethnomusicology* (Oxford & New York: Oxford University Press, 1997).

54 Penelope Gouk (ed.), *Musical Healing in Cultural Contexts* (Aldershot & Brookfield, Vt.: Ashgate, 2000).

55 Ruth Finnegan, *The Hidden Musicians: Music Making in an English Town* (Cambridge: Cambridge University Press, 1990).

56 C. Lévi-Strauss, *The Raw and the Cooked: Introduction to a Science of Mythology 1* [1964], trans. J. and D. Weightman (London: Jonathan Cape, 1970).

57 James C. Faris, *Nuba Personal Art* (London: Duckworth, 1972).

58 See, for example, Anthony Forge, *Primitive Art and Society* (London: Oxford University Press, 1973).

59 See, for example, the essays in Jeremy Coote and Anthony Shelton (eds.), *Anthropology, Art, and Aesthetics* (Oxford: Clarendon Press, 1992); and also Tim Ingold (ed.), *Key Debates in Anthropology* (London & New York: Routledge, 1996), 249 ff.

60 James C. Faris, *Navajo and Photography: A Critical History of the Representation of an American People* (Albuquerque, N. Mex.: University of New Mexico Press, 1996).

61 Anna Grimshaw, *The Ethnographer's Eye: Ways of Seeing in Modern Anthropology* (Cambridge: Cambridge University Press, 2001). Cf. Peter Crawford and David Turton (eds.), *Film as Ethnography* (Manchester: Manchester University Press, 1992).

62 Clare Harris, *In the Image of Tibet: Tibetan Painting after 1959* (London: Reaktion Books, 1999).

63 Marcus Banks and Howard Morphy (eds.), *Rethinking Visual Anthropology* (New Haven & London: Yale University Press, 1997). See particularly the chapters by David MacDougall ('The visual in anthropology'), Georgina Born ('Computer software as a medium'), Felicia Hughes-Freeland ('Balinese on television'), and Dolores Martinez ('Burlesquing knowledge: Japanese quiz shows').

64 A. Gell, *Art and Agency: An Anthropological Theory* (Oxford: Clarendon Press, 1998).

65 Collingwood, *The Principles of Art*, 55.

66 Gell, *Art and Agency*, 94–5.

67 Ibid. Quotations at 257, 258. Cf. Alfred Gell, 'The technology of enchantment', in Coote and Shelton (eds.), *Anthropology, Art, and Aesthetics*.

Chapter Five

1 A classic study is Maurice Halbwachs, *On Collective Memory* [1950], ed. Lewis A. Coser (Chicago: University of Chicago Press, 1992).

2 P. A. Lienhardt, 'The interpretation of rumour', in J. H. M. Beattie and R. G. Lienhardt (eds.), *Studies in Social Anthropology: Essays in Memory of E. E. Evans-Pritchard by his Former Oxford Colleagues* (Oxford: Clarendon Press, 1975).

3 Ibid. 130–1.

4 R. Borofsky, *Making History: Pukapukan and Anthropological Constructions of Knowledge* (Cambridge: Cambridge University Press, 1987).

5 Ibid. 15.

6 Ibid. 18–28.

7 Ibid., chs. 4 and 5.

8 Kirsten Hastrup, *Studying Action: Anthropology in the Company of Shakespeare* (Copenhagen: Museum Tusculanum Press, 2003).

9 C. Lévi-Strauss, 'The structural study of myth', in *Structural Anthropology*, vol. i [1958] (London: Allen Lane, 1963); *The Raw and the Cooked: Introduction to a Science of Mythology 1* [1964], trans. J. and D. Weightman (London; Jonathan Cape, 1970) and further volumes in this series; 'The story of Asdiwal', in *Structural Anthropology*, vol. ii [1973] (London: Allen Lane, 1977), esp. 152–8.

10 David Parkin, 'Ritual as spatial direction and bodily division', in Daniel de Coppet (ed.), *Understanding Rituals*, European Association of Social Anthropologists series (London & New York: Routledge, 1990).

11 Caroline Humphrey and James Laidlaw, *The Archetypal Actions of Ritual: A Theory of Ritual Illustrated by the Jain Rite of Worship* (Oxford: Clarendon Press, 1994).

12 M. Bloch, 'Preface' to *Ritual, History and Power: Selected Papers in Anthropology* (London: Athlone, 1989).

13 M. Bloch, 'The ritual of the royal bath in Madagascar: the dissolution of death, birth and fertility into authority', in *Ritual, History and Power*.

14 M. Bloch, *From Blessing to Violence: History and Ideology in the Circumcision Ritual of the Merina of Madagascar* (Cambridge: Cambridge University Press, 1986).

15 Michael Lambek, *The Weight of the Past: Living with History in Mahajanga, Madagascar* (New York & Basingstoke: Palgrave Macmillan, 2002).

16 Paul Connerton, *How Societies Remember* (Cambridge: Cambridge University Press, 1989).

17 Quoted in R. Monk, *Ludwig Wittgenstein: The Duty of Genius* (New York: The Free Press, 1990), 305.

18 E. F. Collins, 'A ceremonial animal', *Journal of Ritual Studies*, 10 (1996), 59–84, esp. 68, 72.

19 H. Fingarette, *Confucius: The Secular as Sacred* (New York: Harper, 1972), 14.

20 Ludwig Wittgenstein, *Remarks on Frazer's* Golden Bough [MS 1931]; I refer to the English version in James Klagge and Alfred Nordmann (eds.), *Philosophical Occasions 1912–1951* (Indianapolis & Cambridge: Hackett, 1993), 115–55. Specific quotes at 125, 119, 121, 123, 125, 127, 129, 133, 139, 143, 147, 151. For Frazer's own account of the Beltane, or Mayday festivals sometimes represented as a sacrificial rite devoted to Baal, see James G. Frazer, *The Golden Bough: A Study in Magic and Religion*, abridged edn. in one volume [1922] (London: Macmillan, 1960), 808–14, 854–5.

21 An influential analysis on these lines can be found in Ioan M. Lewis, *Ecstatic Religion: An Anthropological Study of Spirit Possession and Shamanism* (Harmondsworth: Penguin, 1971).

22 Janice Boddy, *Wombs and Alien Spirits: Women, Men, and the Zar Cult in Northern Sudan* (Madison: University of Wisconsin Press, 1989).

23 Janice Boddy, 'Managing tradition: "superstition" and the making of national identity among Sudanese women refugees', in Wendy James (ed.), *The Pursuit of Certainty: Religious and Cultural Formulations* (London & New York: Routledge, 1995), see esp. 30–4.

24 E. E. Evans-Pritchard, *Theories of Primitive Religion* (Oxford: Clarendon Press, 1965); Fiona Bowie, *The Anthropology of Religion: An Introduction* (Oxford & New York: Blackwell, 1999); Michael Lambek, *A Reader in the Anthropology of Religion* (Oxford & New York: Blackwell, 2002).

25 Edward B. Tylor, *Primitive Culture* [1871] (New York: Harper & Row, 1958).

26 James G. Frazer, *The Golden Bough* [from 1890; 12 vols.], ed. George Stocking (Harmondsworth: Penguin, 1996). Abridged edn. noted above.

27 The best available account in English of Dumézil's ideas is C. Scott Littleton, *New Comparative Mythology: Anthropological Assessment of the Theories of Georges Dumézil*, 3rd edn. (Berkeley & Los Angeles: University of California Press, 1982).

28 The Folk Lore Society, and its journal *Folklore*, flourished in Britain from the late nineteenth century onwards.

29 Chris Knight, 'Totemism', in Alan Barnard and Jonathan Spencer (eds.), *Encyclopaedia of Social and Cultural Anthropology* (London & New York: Routledge, 1996). There are several other terms which were adopted into anthropological jargon from indigenous languages. 'Fetish' was a West African word that not only entered popular English with a certain deprecatory overtone but in the form of 'fetishism' acquired almost scientific respectability in some of the debates about what came first

and what came later in human history. A favourite general term for the spiritual power of persons or things was the Austronesian word *mana*, introduced along with *tabu* by R. R. Marett, an archaeologist and armchair anthropologist who helped institutionalize social anthropology at Oxford. *Mana* never made it into popular English, but taboo from *tabu* certainly did; and a modern case which is increasingly attractive to young people and to those interested in the New Age religions is *shaman, shamanism*, from Siberia (probably the Tungus language).

30 W. S. F. Pickering has argued that Durkheim's whole image of what a religion was carried rather churchy, Christian overtones, in contrast to Mauss's image of religion, which was rather more imbued with Jewish overtones (see W. S. F. Pickering, 'Mauss's Jewish background: a biographical essay', in W. James and N. J. Allen (eds.), *Marcel Mauss: A Centenary Tribute* (Oxford & New York: Berghahn, 1998).

31 Edmund R. Leach, *Genesis as Myth and other Essays* (London: Jonathan Cape, 1969).

32 A recent example is Mary Douglas, *Leviticus as Literature* (Oxford: Clarendon Press, 1999).

33 Daryll Forde (ed.), *African Worlds: Studies in the Cosmological Ideas and Social Values of African Peoples* (London: Oxford University Press for the International African Institute, 1954). Reissued with a new introduction by Wendy James (Hamburg/Oxford: Lit Verlag/James Currey, 1999).

34 Henri Hubert and Marcel Mauss, *Sacrifice: Its Nature and Function* [1898], trans. W. D. Halls (London: Cohen & West, 1964); E. E. Evans-Pritchard, *Nuer Religion* (Oxford: Clarendon Press, 1956), ch. 8.

35 Michael F. C. Bourdillon and Meyer Fortes (eds.), *Sacrifice* (London: Academic Press for the RAI, 1980).

36 Paul Dresch, *Tribes, Government, and History in Yemen* (Oxford: Clarendon Press, 1989), 50–1, 72 n. 15.

37 R. Needham, *Belief, Language and Experience* (Oxford: Blackwell, 1972).

38 Malcolm Ruel, *Belief, Ritual and the Securing of Life: Reflexive Essays on a Bantu Religion* (Leiden: Brill, 1997), 9–12.

39 Sally F. Moore and Barbara G. Myerhoff (eds.), *Secular Ritual* (Amsterdam: Van Gorcum, 1977). Cf. Daniel de Coppet (ed.), *Understanding Rituals* (London & New York: Routledge, 1992).

40 Talal Asad, 'Toward a genealogy of the concept of ritual', in *Genealogies of Religion: Discipline and Reasons of Power in Christianity and Islam* (Baltimore & London: Johns Hopkins University Press, 1993).

41 Roy A. Rappaport, *Ritual and Religion in the Making of Humanity* (Cambridge: Cambridge University Press, 1999).

42 Humphrey and Laidlaw, The *Archetypal Actions of Ritual*, esp. chs. 4, 11.

43 Daniel Miller, *A Theory of Shopping* (Cambridge: Polity Press, 1998)

44 Evans-Pritchard, 'Religion and the anthropologists', in *Essays in Social Anthropology* (London: Faber & Faber, 1962).

45 E. E. Evans-Pritchard, *Nuer Religion* (Oxford: Clarendon Press, 1956).

46 R. G. Lienhardt, *Divinity and Experience: The Religion of the Dinka* (Oxford: Clarendon Press, 1961).

47 Douglas H. Johnson, *Nuer Prophets: A History of Prophecy from the Upper Nile in the Nineteenth and Twentieth Centuries* (Oxford: Clarendon Press, 1994).

48 I. M. Lewis, *A Pastoral Democracy: A Study of Pastoralism and Politics among the Northern Somali of the Horn of Africa* (London: Oxford University Press, 1961).

49 A preliminary account of this displacement can be found in the preface to the paperback edition of W. James, *The Listening Ebony: Moral Knowledge, Religion, and Power among the Uduk of Sudan* [1988] (Oxford: Clarendon Press, 1999).

50 W. Robertson Smith, *Lectures on the Religion of the Semites* (Edinburgh: Adam and Charles Black, 1889).

51 Max Weber's study, *The Protestant Ethic and the Spirit of Capitalism* [1904–5], trans. Talcott Parsons (London & New York: Routledge, 1992) continues to be very influential in anthropological studies of religion; as do his general writings on the kinds of authority in society. Asad's *Genealogies of Religion* illustrates the way that Weber and Marx have provided new vistas for the anthropology of religion. Compare also Jean Comaroff, *Body of Power: Spirit of Resistance: The Culture and History of a South African People* (Chicago: University of Chicago Press, 1985), and John and Jean Comaroff, *Of Revelation and Revolution: Christianity, Colonialism and Consciousness in South Africa*, 2 vols. (Chicago: University of Chicago Press, 1991 and 1997).

52 For example, see John Campbell, *Honour, Family and Patronage: A Study of Institutions and Moral Values in a Greek Mountain Community* (Oxford: Clarendon Press, 1964).

53 Mary Douglas, *The Lele of Kasai* (London: Oxford University Press 1963); see the final chapter.

54 John Davis (ed.), *Religious Organization and Religious Experience*, ASA Monograph 21 (London: Academic Press, 1982).

55 Clifford Geertz, *The Religion of Java* (Glencoe, Ill.: The Free Press, 1960); Abner Cohen, *Custom and Politics in Urban Africa: A Study of Hausa Migrants in Yoruba Towns* (London: Routledge, 1969); Ahmed Al-Shahi (ed.), *The Diversity of the Muslim Community* (London: Ithaca, 1987).

56 Michael Lambek, *Knowledge and Practice in Mayotte: Local Discourses of Islam, Sorcery, and Spirit Possession* (Toronto: Toronto University Press, 1993).

57 M. Gilsenan, *Recognizing Islam: Religion and Society in the Modern Middle East* (London: Croom Helm, 1982).

58 Roger Just, 'Anti-clericalism and national identity: attitudes towards the Orthodox Church in Greece', in W. James and D. H. Johnson (eds.), *Vernacular*

Christianity: Essays in the Social Anthropology of Religion, Presented to Godfrey Lienhardt (Oxford/New York: JASO/Lilian Barber Press, 1988).

59 Lawrence J. Taylor, *Occasions of Faith: An Anthropology of Irish Catholics* [1995] (Dublin: Lilliput Press, 1997). John Eade and Michael J. Sallnow (eds.), *Contesting the Sacred: The Anthropology of Christian Pilgrimage* [1991] (Urbana & Chicago: University of Illinois Press, 2000). Cf. Richard P. Werbner, *Ritual Passage, Sacred Journey: The Process and Organization of Religious Movements* (Manchester/Washington: Manchester University Press/Smithsonian Press, 1989).

60 In my own work on religion among the Uduk, I decided to incorporate a chapter on the effects of the evangelical Sudan Interior Mission into the heart of the book, rather than tack it on as an extra. See Wendy James, 'The Sudan Interior Mission and "Arumgimis": Expecting Christ', ch. 4 of *The Listening Ebony.*

61 Pascal Boyer, *Tradition as Truth and Communication: A Cognitive Description of Traditional Discourse* (Cambridge: Cambridge University Press, 1990); *The Naturalness of Religious Ideas: A Cognitive Theory of Religion* (Berkeley & Los Angeles: University of California Press, 1994).

62 Dan Sperber, *Rethinking Symbolism* (Cambridge: Cambridge University Press, 1975). Harvey Whitehouse, *Arguments and Icons* (Oxford: Oxford University Press, 2000), and (ed.), *The Debated Mind: Evolutionary Psychology versus Ethnography* (Oxford & New York: Berg, 2001).

63 F. Barth, *Nomads of South Persia: The Basseri Tribe of the Khamseh Confederacy* (Oslo/London: Universitetsforlaget/Allen & Unwin, 1964), 135–53.

PART III

Chapter Six

1 Frances Morphy, 'Language and moiety: sociolectal variation in a Yu:lngu language of North-East Arnhem Land', *Canberra Anthropology*, 1 (1977), 51–60.

2 Oliver Sacks, *Seeing Voices: A Journey into the World of the Deaf* [1989] (London: Pan Books, 1990). Sacks discusses the Martha's Vineyard case at 32–6; my quotation is from 35. The original account is Nora Ellen Groce, *Everyone Here Spoke Sign Language: Hereditary Deafness on Martha's Vineyard* (Cambridge, Mass., & London: Harvard University Press, 1985).

3 A substantial and well-illustrated survey was published by Col. Garrick Mallery, 'Sign Language among American Indians: Compared with that among other peoples and deaf-mutes', in the first *Report of the Bureau of Ethnology* to the Smithsonian Institution, 1879–80 (Washington: Government Publications Office, 1881), 263–552.

4 David Dalby, *The Linguasphere: From Person to Planet* (Hebron, Wales: Linguasphere Press, 1998); cf. *Guardian* (22 July 1997), 5.

5 Recent comprehensive guides to the field include William A. Foley, *Anthropological Linguistics: An Introduction* (Oxford & Malden, Mass.: Blackwell, 1997), which takes a broadly scientific approach; and Alessandro Duranti, *Linguistic Anthropology: A Reader* (Malden, Mass. & Oxford: Blackwell, 2001), with a more 'humanities' perspective. The older compendium, Dell Hymes (ed.), *Language in Culture and Society: A Reader in Linguistic Anthropology* (New York: Harper & Row, 1964) is still useful.

6 Andrew Dalby, *Language in Danger: How Language Loss Threatens our Future* (London: Allen Lane, The Penguin Press, 2002), 24–7.

7 For background, see Foley, *Anthropological Linguistics*, and Duranti, *Linguistic Anthropology*.

8 See, for example, E. W. Ardener, 'Introduction' to the edited volume *Social Anthropology and Language*, ASA Monograph 10 (London: Tavistock, 1971). David Robey (ed.), *Structuralism: An Introduction*, Wolfson College Lectures, 1972 (Oxford: Clarendon Press, 1973).

9 These points happen to be interesting for my own work. The wide range of exploded and imploded sounds in Uduk, for example, while appearing to constitute a lot of 'extra phonemes' by comparison with related languages, required only one further dimension of minimal contrast to be added by linguists to the set which was already in place for comparative linguistics. More recently, on the basis of word-comparison, Uduk has been accorded a particularly 'ancient lineage' in the Nilo-Saharan family, reflecting more directly the probable features of the prototypical language from which all its branches have developed historically. We might well speculate on the socio-historical interest of this example of the conservation of complexity at the level of lexicon as well as at the level of phonemic structure. Christopher Ehret, *A Historical-Comparative Reconstruction of Nilo-Saharan* (Cologne: Rüdiger Koppe Verlag, 2001), esp. 8–9.

10 The fullest application of the method by Lévi-Strauss was to the oral narratives of myth, as mentioned in the previous chapter; and Edmund Leach extended the method to the written materials of scripture and to various coded systems of communication such as traffic lights. See his *Genesis as Myth and Other Essays* (London: Cape, 1969), and *Culture and Communication: The Logic by which Symbols are Connected* (Cambridge: Cambridge University Press, 1976).

11 Noam Chomsky, *Syntactic Structures* (The Hague: Mouton, 1957), *Language and Mind* (New York: Harcourt, Brace & World, 1968). Cf. John Lyons, *Chomsky* (London: Fontana/Collins, 1970).

12 Émile Durkheim, *The Rules of Sociological Method* [1895], trans. S. A. Solovay and J. H. Mueller (New York: The Free Press, 1964); *Suicide: A Study in Sociology* [1897], trans. J. A. Spaulding and G. Simpson (London: Routledge & Kegan Paul, 1952).

13 A good example is Michel Foucault's *The History of Sexuality*, vol. i: *The Use of Pleasure* (Harmondsworth: Penguin, 1988).

14 P. Bourdieu, *Homo Academicus* [1984], trans. P. Collins (Cambridge: Polity Press, 1988).

15 Jack Goody, *The Interface between the Written and the Oral* (Cambridge: Cambridge University Press, 1987); Ernest Gellner, *Nations and Nationalism* (Oxford: Blackwell, 1983). Benedict Anderson, *Imagined Communities: Reflections on the Origin and Spread of Nationalism* (London & New York: Verso, 1983). T. Asad, 'Strong and weak languages', in J. Clifford and G. E. Marcus (eds.), *Writing Culture* (Berkeley & Los Angeles: University of California Press, 1986).

16 Jack Goody, *The Myth of the Bagre* (Oxford: Clarendon Press, 1972).

17 Examples would include Ian Cunnison, *History on the Luapula: An Essay on the Historical Notions of a Central African Tribe* (London: Oxford University Press, 1951); Elizabeth Tonkin, *Narrating our Pasts: The Social Construction of Oral History* (Cambridge: Cambridge University Press, 1992); Kirsten Hastrup (ed.), *Other Histories* (London & New York: Routledge, 1992); for a radical treatment of vernacular texts, see Jean Lydall and Ivo Strecker, *The Hamar of Southern Ethiopia*, 3 vols. (Hohenschaftlarn: Klaus Renner Verlag, 1979).

18 See, for example, the series Oxford Library of African Literature.

19 Jan Vansina, *Oral Tradition* (London: Routledge & Kegan Paul, 1965); *Oral Tradition as History* (London/Madison: James Currey/University of Wisconsin Press, 1985).

20 Wendy James, 'The names of fear: history, memory and the ethnography of feeling among Uduk refugees', *JRAI* (NS), 3 (1997), 115–31, at 129–31.

21 C. Lévi-Strauss, *The Savage Mind* [1962] (London: Weidenfeld & Nicolson, 1966).

22 D. Zeitlyn, 'Reconstructing kinship or the pragmatics of kin talk', *Man* 28 (1993), 199–224.

23 G. C. Fiumara, *The Other Side of Language: A Philosophy of Listening* (London: Routledge, 1990).

24 Michael Herzfeld, *The Poetics of Manhood: Contest and Identity in a Cretan Mountain Village* (Princeton: Princeton University Press, 1985); *Anthropology Through the Looking Glass: Critical Ethnography in the Margins of Europe* (Cambridge: Cambridge University Press, 1987).

25 C. W. Watson and J. Hendry (eds.), *An Anthropology of Indirect Communication*, ASA Monographs 37 (London & New York: Routledge, 2001).

26 Karin Barber, *I Could Speak until Tomorrow: Oriki, Women and the Past in a Yoruba Town* (Edinburgh: Edinburgh University Press for the International African Institute, 1991).

27 Ibid. 221, 224–30.

28 Ibid. 87, 105 ff., 111–12.

29 Ibid. 265–6.

30 Ibid. 25.

31 Ibid. 8.

32 Ibid. 2, 3.

33 Terry Eagleton, *The Illusions of Postmodernism* (Oxford: Blackwell, 1996), 72–3.

Chapter Seven

1 For general overviews, see Robin Fox, *Kinship and Marriage* (Harmondsworth: Penguin, 1967) and Robert Parkin, *Kinship: An Introduction to Basic Concepts* (Oxford & Malden, Mass.: Blackwell, 1997).

2 Key works include Michelle Rosaldo and Louise Lamphere (eds.), *Woman, Culture and Society* (Stanford: Stanford University Press, 1974); Shirley G. Ardener (ed.), *Perceiving Women* (London/New York: Dent-Malaby/Halstead, 1975); and (ed.), *Defining Females: The Nature of Women in Society* [1978], 2nd edn. (Oxford & New York: Berg, 1993); Emily Martin, *The Woman in the Body* (Boston: Beacon Press, 1987); Carol MacCormack and Marilyn Strathern (eds.), *Nature, Culture and Gender* (Cambridge: Cambridge University Press, 1980); Sherry Ortner and H. Whitehead (eds.), *Sexual Meanings: The Cultural Construction of Gender and Sexuality* (Cambridge: Cambridge University Press, 1981); Henrietta Moore, *Feminism and Anthropology* (Cambridge: Polity Press, 1988); Marilyn Strathern, *The Gender of the Gift: Problems with Women and Problems with Society in Melanesia* (Berkeley & Los Angeles: University of California Press, 1988); Henrietta Moore, *A Passion for Difference* (Cambridge: Polity Press, 1994).

3 A. R. Radcliffe-Brown, 'Introduction', to A. R. Radcliffe-Brown and Daryll Forde (eds.), *African Systems of Kinship and Marriage* (London: Oxford University Press for the International African Institute, 1950), 15.

4 E. R. Leach, *Rethinking Anthropology* (London: Athlone, 1961).

5 Suzette Heald, *Manhood and Morality: Sex, Violence and Ritual in Gisu Society* (London & New York: Routledge, 1999), ch. 7.

6 N. J. Allen, 'The prehistory of Dravidian-type terminologies', in M. Godelier, T. R. Trautmann, and F. E. Tjon Die Fat (eds.), *Transformations of Kinship* (Washington & London: Smithsonian Institution Press, 1998).

7 Claude Lévi-Strauss, 'Structural analysis in linguistics and anthropology', chapter 2 in *Structural Anthropology* [1958], trans. C. Jacobson and B. G. Schoepf (New York: Basic Books, 1963); and 'Reflections on the atom of kinship', chapter 7 in *Structural Anthropology*, vol. ii [1973], trans. M. Layton (London: Allen Lane, 1977).

8 Compare A. R. Radcliffe-Brown, 'The mother's brother in South Africa', in *Structure and Function in Primitive Society* (London: Cohen & West, 1952); with C. Lévi-Strauss, *The Elementary Structures of Kinship* [1949], trans. R. Needham (London: Eyre & Spottiswoode, 1969).

9 E. R. Leach, *Political Systems of Highland Burma: A Study of Kachin Social Structure* (London: Bell, 1954); R. H. Barnes, *Kédang: The Collective Thought of an Eastern Indonesian People* (Oxford: Clarendon Press, 1974).

10 Rodney Needham, *Structure and Sentiment* (Chicago: University of Chicago Press, 1962).

11 E. B. Tylor, 'On a method of investigating the development of institutions: applied to laws of marriage and descent', *Journal of the Anthropological Institute*, 18 (1889), 245–69.

12 John F. McLennan, *Primitive Marriage: An Inquiry into the Original of the Form of Capture in Marriage Ceremonies* (Edinburgh: Black, 1865). R. H. Barnes, 'Marriage by capture', *JRAI* 5 (1999), 57–73. Sigmund Freud, *Totem and Taboo: Resemblances between the Psychic Lives of Savages and Neurotics* [1919] (Harmondsworth: Penguin, 1938).

13 M. Godelier, 'Afterword', in Godelier *et al.*, *Transformations of Kinship*, 408–12.

14 L. H. Morgan, *Systems of Consanguinity and Affinity of the Human Family* (Washington: Smithsonian Institution, 1871); *Ancient Society* (New York: Henry Holt, 1877).

15 Godelier *et al.*, *Transformations of Kinship* (1998), introduction.

16 Ibid., esp. 5–6.

17 K. O. L. Burridge, 'Friendship in Tangu', *Oceania*, 27 (1957), 177–89.

18 Strathern, *The Gender of the Gift*. Cf. A. Gell, 'Strathernograms, or the semiotics of mixed metaphors', in E. Hirsch (ed.), *The Art of Anthropology: Essays and Diagrams* (London: Athlone, 1999).

19 For example, see Nicholas Thomas, *Marquesan Societies: Inequality and Political Transformation in Eastern Polynesia* (Oxford: Clarendon Press, 1990); Peter Gow, *Of Mixed Blood: Kinship and History in Peruvian Amazonia* (Oxford: Clarendon Press, 1991).

20 C. Lévi-Strauss, 'The Bear and the Barber', Henry Myers Memorial Lecture, 1962, *JRAI* 93 (1963), 1–11. Similarly daring juxtapositions are made in Lévi-Strauss's *The Savage Mind* (a bald rendering of the more subtle 'la pensée sauvage') [1962] (London: Weidenfeld & Nicolson, 1966).

21 Janet Carsten, *The Heat of the Hearth: The Process of Kinship in a Malay Fishing Community* (Oxford: Clarendon Press, 1997); Janet Carsten (ed.), *Cultures of Relatedness: New Approaches to the Study of Kinship* (Cambridge: Cambridge University Press, 2000).

22 Pierre Clastres, *Archeology of Violence* [1980], trans. J. Herman (New York: Semiotext(e), 1994).

23 Pierre Bourdieu, *Outline of a Theory of Practice* [1972] (Cambridge: Cambridge University Press, 1977), esp. the case study of parallel cousin marriage, 30–58.

24 Paul Dresch, 'Totality, exchange, and Islam in the Middle East', in Wendy James and N. J. Allen (eds.), *Marcel Mauss: A Centenary Tribute* (Oxford & New York: Berghahn, 1998), 127.

25 See, for example, the collection edited by Richard Fardon, *Localizing Strategies: Regional Traditions of Ethnographic Writing* (Edinburgh/Washington: Scottish Academic Press/Smithsonian Institution Press, 1990), especially the chapters on Africa.

26 W. James, 'The anthropologist as reluctant imperialist', in Talal Asad (ed.), *Anthropology and the Colonial Encounter* (London: Ithaca, 1973).

27 See Radcliffe-Brown and Forde, *African Systems of Kinship and Marriage*.

28 Max Gluckman, *The Judicial Process among the Barotse of Northern Rhodesia (Zambia)* [1955], 2nd edn. (Manchester: Manchester University Press, 1973); and *The Ideas in Barotse Jurisprudence* (New Haven: Yale University Press, 1965).

29 Charles Piot, *Remotely Global: Village Modernity in West Africa* (Chicago: University of Chicago Press, 1999).

30 Henry Maine, *Ancient Law* (London: 1871).

31 E. E. Evans-Pritchard, *Kinship and Marriage among the Nuer* (Oxford: Clarendon Press, 1951); introd. by W. James to the paperback edn. (1990), pp. ix–xxii.

32 Bourdieu, *Outline of a Theory of Practice*, 41–3.

33 W. James, 'Matrifocus on African women', in Shirley Ardener, *Defining Females*.

34 Meyer Fortes, 'Kinship and marriage among the Ashanti', in Radcliffe-Brown and Forde, *African Systems of Kinship and Marriage*.

35 Lévi-Strauss, *The Elementary Structures of Kinship*, 117.

36 Fox, *Kinship and Marriage*, ch. 1.

37 Audrey I. Richards, 'Some types of family structure amongst the Central Bantu', in Radcliffe-Brown and Forde, *African Systems of Kinship and Marriage*.

38 Friedrich Engels, *Origin of the Family, Private Property and the State*, 4th edn. (London: Lawrence & Wishart, 1891), 58–9.

39 Daryll Forde, 'Double descent among the Yakö', in *African Systems of Kinship and Marriage*. Richard Fardon, *Raiders and Refugees: Trends in Chamba Political Development 1750–1950* (Washington & London: Smithsonian Institution Press, 1988).

40 Jean-Loup Amselle, *Mestizo Logics: Anthropology of Identity in Africa and Elsewhere*, trans. Claudia Royal (Stanford, Calif.: Stanford University Press, 1998).

41 M. Bloch, 'The moral and tactical use of kinship terms', *Man* (NS), 6 (1971), 79–87.

42 M. Bloch, 'What goes without saying: the conceptualization of Zafimaniry society', in *How We Think They Think: Anthropological Approaches to Cognition, Memory, and Literacy* (Oxford & Boulder, Colo.: Westview Press, 1998).

43 Richard Fardon, *Raiders and Refugees*; cf. also the sequel, *Between God, the Dead and the Wild* (Edinburgh: Edinburgh University Press, 1991).

44 W. James, 'Lifelines: sister-exchange marriage among the Gumuz', in D. L. Donham and W. James (eds.), *The Southern Marches of Imperial Ethiopia: Essays in History and Social Anthropology* (Cambridge: Cambridge University Press, 1986; reissued in paperback with a new preface, Oxford/Athens, Oh.: James Currey/Ohio University Press, 2001).

45 Donald L. Donham, *History, Power, Ideology: Central Issues in Marxism and Anthropology* (Cambridge: Cambridge University Press, 1990), 94–123.

Chapter Eight

1 C. Toren, 'The child in mind', in H. Whitehouse (ed.), *The Debated Mind: Evolutionary Psychology versus Ethnography* (Oxford & New York: Berg, 2001).

2 The most recent translation of the famous essay on exchange is *The Gift: The Form and Reason for Exchange in Archaic Societies*, trans. W. D. Halls, foreword by Mary Douglas (London: Routledge, 1990). For a set of recent essays on Mauss, see W. James and N. J. Allen (eds.), *Marcel Mauss: A Centenary Tribute* (Oxford: Berghahn, 1999).

3 M. Mauss, 'Body techniques' and other chapters in *Sociology and Psychology: Essays by Marcel Mauss*, trans. B. Brewster (London: Routledge & Kegan Paul, 1979).

4 Powerful criticism of misleading scientism in the understanding of human phenomena can be found in the writings of Stephen Jay Gould, for example his *The Mismeasure of Man*, revised and expanded edition (Harmondsworth: Penguin, 1997).

5 N. Schlanger, 'The study of techniques as an ideological challenge: technology, nation, and humanity in the work of Marcel Mauss', in W. James and N. J. Allen (eds.), *Marcel Mauss: A Centenary Tribute*.

6 See, for example, M. E. F. Bloch, *How We Think They Think: Anthropological Approaches to Cognition, Memory, and Literacy* (Oxford & Boulder, Colo.: Westview Press, 1998).

7 Mauss, *Sociology and Psychology*, 27.

8 M. Ridley, *Genome: The Autobiography of a Species in 23 Chapters* (New York: HarperCollins, 1999), 149–52.

9 Mauss, *Sociology and Psychology*, 29–31.

10 Bloch, *How We Think They Think*, ch. 5, referring to the work of G. vom Bruck and F. Cannell.

11 M. Mauss, 'Une catégorie de l'esprit humaine: la notion de personne, celle de "moi"'. Originally a lecture for the Royal Anthropological Institute and published in the *JRAI* 1938; translated first by Brewster in *Sociology and Psychology*, and then again by W. D. Halls in M. Carrithers, S. Collins, and S. Lukes (eds.), *The Category of the Person: Anthropology, Philosophy, History* (Cambridge: Cambridge University Press, 1985).

12 N. J. Allen, *Categories and Classifications: Maussian Reflections on the Social* (Oxford & New York: Berghahn, 2000). See particularly ch. 1.

13 For an insight into this trend see Paul Dresch's ethnographic sketch of an American university campus, 'Race, culture, and—?' in W. James (ed.), *The Pursuit of Certainty: Religious and Cultural Formulations* (London New York: Routledge, 1995).

14 See, for example, V. W. Turner, *The Forest of Symbols: Aspects of Ndembu Ritual* (Ithaca, NY: Cornell University Press, 1967) and *The Drums of Affliction* (London: Oxford University Press for the International African Institute, 1968); M. Douglas, *Purity and Danger: An Analysis of Concepts of Pollution and Taboo* (London: Routledge

& Kegan Paul, 1966); *Natural Symbols: Explorations in Cosmology* (London: Barrie and Rockliff/Cresset Press; 2nd revised edn., Harmondsworth: Pelican, 1973).

15 R. G. Lienhardt, *Divinity and Experience: The Religion of the Dinka* (Oxford: Clarendon Press, 1961); J. C. Buxton, *Religion and Healing in Mandari* (Oxford: Clarendon Press, 1975); M. Merleau-Ponty, *Phenomenology of Perception*, trans. C. Smith (London and Henley: Routledge & Kegan Paul, 1962). D. F. Pocock, *Social Anthropology* (London: Sheed & Ward, 1961), *Kanbi and Patidar* (Oxford: Clarendon Press, 1972), *Mind, Body, and Wealth: A Study of Belief and Practice in an Indian Village* (Oxford: Basil Blackwell, 1973), *Understanding Social Anthropology* (Teach Yourself Books, London: Hodder & Stoughton, 1975).

16 A key publication, which in itself helped revitalize collaboration between British 'social' and American 'cultural' anthropology, was *The Anthropology of Experience*, edited by Victor Turner and E. M. Bruner, with an epilogue by Clifford Geertz (Urbana and Chicago: University of Illinois Press, 1986).

17 J. Blacking (ed.), *The Anthropology of the Body* (London: Academic Press, 1974). M. Lambek and A. Strathern (eds.), *Bodies and Persons: Comparative Perspectives from Africa and Melanesia* (Cambridge: Cambridge University Press, 1998). M. Douglas, 'Deciphering a meal', *Daedalus*, 101 (1972), 61–82; P. Caplan (ed.), *Food, Health and Identity* (London & New York: Routledge, 1997). C. M. Counihan, *The Anthropology of Food and the Body: Gender, Meaning, and Power* (London & New York: Routledge, 1999). M. Green, *Priests, Witches and Power: Popular Christianity in S. Tanzania* (Cambridge: Cambridge University Press, 2003). Elisabeth Hsu, *The Transmission of Chinese Medicine* (Cambridge: Cambridge University Press, 1999).

18 B. Malinowski, *The Sexual Life of Savages in Northwest Melanesia* (London: Routledge & Kegal Paul, 1922). M. Mead, *Coming of Age in Samoa: A Psychological Study of Primitive Youth for Western Civilisation* (New York: Morrow, 1928); *Growing Up in New Guinea: A Comparative Study of Primitive Education* (London: Routledge, 1931); D. Freeman, *Margaret Mead and Samoa: The Making and Unmaking of an Anthropological Myth* (Cambridge, Mass.: Harvard University Press, 1983); I. Brady (ed.), 'Speaking in the name of the real: Freeman and Mead on Samoa', *American Anthropologist*, 85 (1983), 908–47.

19 E. E. Evans-Pritchard (ed.), *Man and Woman among the Azande* (London: Faber & Faber, 1974).

20 P. Harvey and P. Gow (eds.), *Sex and Violence: Issues in Representation and Experience* (London & New York: Routledge, 1994); A. Cornwall and N. Lindisfarne (eds.), *Dislocating Masculinity: Comparative Ethnographies* (London & New York: Routledge, 1994); see the chapter by A. Hart 'Missing masculinity? Prostitutes' clients in Alicante, Spain' in the latter. H. Montgomery, *Modern Babylon? Prostituting Children in Thailand* (Oxford & New York: Berghahn, 2001).

21 S. Heald, *Manhood and Morality: Sex, Violence and Ritual in Gisu Society* (London & New York: Routledge, 1999). See esp. ch. 8.

22 M. Foucault, *The Care of the Self*, The History of Sexuality, 3 [1984], trans. R. Hurley (London: Allen Lane/Penguin, 1986).

23 Jean S. La Fontaine, *Speak of the Devil: Tales of Satanic Abuse in Contemporary England* (Cambridge: Cambridge University Press, 1998).

24 Merleau-Ponty, 'Preface' to *Phenomenology*.

25 See, for example, T. Ingold, *Evolution and Social Life* (Cambridge: Cambridge University Press, 1986); 'Building, dwelling, living: how animals and people make themselves at home in the world', in M. Strathern (ed.), *Shifting Contexts: Transformations in Anthropological Knowledge* (London: Routledge, 1995); 'From the transmission of representations to the education of attention', in H. Whitehouse (ed.), *The Debated Mind*.

26 A. P. Cohen, *Self-Consciousness: An Alternative Anthropology of Identity* (London & New York: Routledge, 1994). On trance and transcendental knowledge, see the classic account of C. Castaneda, *The Teachings of Don Juan: A Yaqui Way of Knowledge* [1968] (Harmondsworth: Penguin, 1976); on dreaming, see, for example, C. Jedrej and R. Shaw, *Dreaming, Religion and Society in Africa* (Leiden/New York: Brill, 1992).

27 Lienhardt, *Divinity and Experience*; 'Some African notions of the person', in M. Carrithers, S. Collins, and S. Lukes (eds.), *The Category of the Person*.

28 P. Heelas and A. Lock, *Indigenous Psychology* (London: Academic Press, 1982).

29 Roland Littlewood, *Pathology and Identity: The Work of Mother Earth in Trinidad* (Cambridge: Cambridge University Press, 1993); A. P. Cohen and N. Rapport (eds.), *Questions of Consciousness*, ASA Monograph 25 (London & New York: Routledge, 1995).

30 C. Toren, *Making Sense of Hierarchy: Cognition as Social Process in Fiji* (London: Athlone, 1990).

31 C. Toren, 'The child in mind', in Whitehouse (ed.), *The Debated Mind*; quotations at pp. 159, 156.

32 A. van Gennep, *The Rites of Passage*, [1909], trans. Monika B. Vizedom and Gabrielle L. Caffee (London: Routledge & Kegan Paul, 1960); R. Hertz, 'On the collective representation of death', in *Death and the Right Hand* [1907], trans. R. and C. Needham (London: Cohen & West, 1960). Compare M. Bloch, *Placing the Dead* (London: Seminar Press, 1971), J. P. Parry, *Death in Banaras* (Cambridge: Cambridge University Press, 1994), and M. Bloch and J. P. Parry (eds.), *Death and the Regeneration of Life* (Cambridge: Cambridge University Press, 1982). See also the more subjective approach in N. Scheper-Hughes, *Death without Weeping: The Violence of Everyday Life in Brazil* (Berkeley: University of California Press, 1992).

33 Laura Rival, 'Androgynous parents and guest children: the Huaorani *couvade*', *JRAI* (NS), 4 (1998), 619–42.

34 The account which follows is drawn partly from W. James, 'Placing the unborn: on the social recognition of new life', *Anthropology and Medicine*, 7 (2000), 169–89.

35 J. Needham, *A History of Embryology*, 2nd edn. (Cambridge: Cambridge University Press, 1959), 232.

36 Needham, *Embryology*, 235–6.

37 H. Callaway, '"The most essentially female function of all": giving birth', in S. Ardener (ed.), *Defining Females: The Nature of Women in Society* (London: Croom Helm, 1978; new edn. in the series Cross-Cultural Perspectives on Women, vol. 4, Oxford/Providence, NY: Berg, 1993).

38 T. Cosslett, *Women Writing Childbirth: Modern Discourses of Motherhood* (Manchester: Manchester University Press, 1994). See esp. ch. 1, 'Natural childbirth and the "primitive woman"', 9–46.

39 E. Westermarck, *The Origin and Development of the Moral Ideas*, 2 vols. (London: Macmillan, 1906), 401–13.

40 O. F. Raum, *Chaga Childhood: A Description of Indigenous Education in an East African Tribe* (London: Oxford University Press for the International African Institute, 1940). Reprinted with new introduction by Sally Falk Moore (Hamburg & Oxford: Lit Verlag and James Currey, 1996). Specific reference is made here to 77 and 165–6.

41 R. A. LeVine *et al.*, *Child Care and Culture: Lessons from Africa* (Cambridge: Cambridge University Press, 1994), 126–7.

42 E. J. Sobo, 'Cultural explanations for pregnancy loss in rural Jamaica', in R. Cecil (ed.), *The Anthropology of Pregnancy Loss: Comparative Studies in Miscarriage, Stillbirth and Neonatal Death* (Oxford: Berg, 1996).

43 E. W. Ardener, S. Ardener, and W. A. Warmington, *Plantation and Village in the Cameroons* (Oxford: Oxford University Press, 1960); E. W. Ardener, *Divorce and Fertility, an African Study* (Oxford: Oxford University Press, 1962); 'Bakweri Fertility and Marriage', in S. Ardener (ed.), *Kingdom on Mount Cameroon: Studies in the History of the Cameroon Coast, 1500–1970* (Oxford/Providence, RI: Berghahn Books, 1996).

44 R. Cecil, 'Memories of pregnancy loss: recollections of pregnant women in Northern Ireland', in *The Anthropology of Pregnancy Loss*.

45 R. G. Fuchs and L. P. Moch, 'Invisible cultures: poor women's networks and reproductive strategies in nineteenth-century Paris', in S. Greenhalgh (ed.), *Situating Fertility: Anthropology and Demographic Inquiry* (Cambridge: Cambridge University Press, 1995).

46 S. Harrison, 'Concepts of the person in Avatip religious thought', *Man*, 20 (1985), 115–30.

47 Renato Rosaldo, *Ilongot Headhunting 1883–1974: A Study in Society and History* (Stanford, Calif.: Stanford University Press, 1980); for references in the paragraphs which follow, see esp. 2–6, 13–14, 17–18, 35, 38–40, 48 ff., 274.

48 Michelle K. Rosaldo, *Knowledge and Passion: Notions of Self and Society among the Ilongot* (Cambridge: Cambridge University Press, 1980); see esp. 18–20, 26, 36, 38 ff., 63.

49 M. Rosaldo, *Knowledge and Passion*, 38, 52–3, 82, 158, 273 n. 9; R. Rosaldo, *Ilongot Headhunting*, 286–8.

50 Nicholas J. Gubser, *The Nunamiut Eskimos: Hunters of Caribou* (New Haven & London: Yale University Press, 1965). Particular reference is made here to 211–12, 221–7, 242–88.

51 J. Lave, *Cognition in Practice: Mind, Mathematics and Culture in Everyday Life* (Cambridge: Cambridge University Press, 1988).

PART IV

Chapter Nine

1 Adam Smith, *An Inquiry into the Nature and Causes of the Wealth of Nations* (1776).

2 Paul Vidal de la Blache, *Tableau de la Géographie de la France* [1903] (Paris: Librairie Jules Tallandier, 1979). W. G. Hoskins, *The Making of the English Landscape* (London: Hodder & Stoughton, 1957).

3 Daryll Forde, *Habitat, Economy and Society: A Geographical Introduction to Ethnology* (London: Methuen, 1934).

4 Roy Ellen, *Environment, Subsistence and System: The Ecology of Small-Scale Social Formations* (Cambridge: Cambridge University Press, 1982).

5 Mary Douglas, *The Lele of the Kasai* (London: Oxford University Press, 1963).

6 Ibid., last chapter.

7 Anthropologists have emphasized how the past is inscribed into the present landscape and indeed today's politics for native communities in Australia. See, for example, Howard Morphy, *Ancestral Connections: Art and an Aboriginal System of Knowledge* (Chicago: University of Chicago Press, 1991).

8 Kirsten Hastrup, *A Place Apart: An Anthropological Study of the Icelandic World* (Oxford: Clarendon Press, 1998).

9 M. Mauss, 'Body techniques', in *Sociology and Psychology: Essays by Marcel Mauss*, trans. B. Brewster (London: Routledge & Kegan Paul, 1979), 101.

10 P. Bourdieu, *Outline of a Theory of Practice* (Cambridge: Cambridge University Press, 1977), and *Distinction: A Social Critique of the Judgement of Taste* [1979], (Cambridge, Mass.: Harvard University Press, 1985).

11 Henrietta Moore and Megan Vaughan, *Cutting down Trees: Gender, Nutrition and Agricultural Change in Northern Province, Zambia 1890–1990* (Oxford/Portsmouth, NH: James Currey/Heinemann, 1994); and James Fairhead and Melissa Leach, *Misreading the African Landscape: Society and Ecology in a Forest-Savanna Mosaic* (Cambridge: Cambridge University Press, 1996).

12 Tim Ingold, *Evolution and Social Life* (Cambridge: Cambridge University Press, 1986). See also the collection edited by P. Descola and G. Palsson, *Nature and Society: Anthropological Perspectives* (London/New York: Routledge, 1996).

13 P. Carter, *The Road to Botany Bay: An Exploration of Landscape and History* (Chicago: University of Chicago Press, 1989).

14 Steven Feld and Keith Basso (eds.), *Senses of Place* [1996] (Santa Fe, N. Mex./Oxford: School of American Research Press/James Currey, 1999).

15 Charles O. Frake, 'Pleasant places, past times, and sheltered identity in rural East Norfolk', in Feld and Basso, *Senses of Place*.

16 Eric Hirsch and M. O'Hanlon (eds.), *The Anthropology of Landscape* (Oxford: Clarendon Press, 1995).

17 A. Gell, 'The language of the forest: landscape and phonological iconism in Umeda', in Hirsch and O'Hanlon, *The Anthropology of Landscape*.

18 L. Rival (ed.), *The Social Life of Trees: Anthropological Perspectives on Tree Symbolism* (Oxford & New York: Berg, 1998). Maurice Bloch's interesting chapter in this volume is entitled 'Why trees, too, are good to think with: towards an anthropology of the meaning of life'.

19 J. Littlejohn, 'The Temne house' [1960], in J. Middleton (ed.), *Myth and Cosmos: Readings in Mythology and Symbolism* (New York: American Museum of Natural History, 1967); P. Bourdieu, 'The Kabyle house or the world reversed', appendix to *The Logic of Practice* [1980] (Cambridge: Polity Press, 1990), 271–83.

20 Ibid. 282.

21 Ian Hodder, *Symbols in Action* (Cambridge: Cambridge University Press, 1982); Henrietta L. Moore, *Space, Text, and Gender: An Anthropological Study of the Marakwet of Kenya* (Cambridge: Cambridge University Press, 1986).

22 S. G. Ardener (ed.), *Women and Space* [1981], revised edn. (Oxford & Providence, RI: Berg, 1993); Joy Hendry, *Wrapping Culture: Politeness, Presentation, and Power in Japan and Other Societies* (Oxford: Clarendon Press, 1993).

23 Janet Carsten and Stephen Hugh-Jones (eds.), *About the House: Lévi-Strauss and Beyond* (Cambridge: Cambridge University Press, 1995). Detailed references to Lévi-Strauss's writings are made in the introduction. I have borrowed my form of words in this paragraph from a spontaneous conference comment by Peter Gow.

24 M. Bloch, 'The resurrection of the house among the Zafimaniry of Madagascar', in Carsten and Hugh-Jones, *About the House*. See esp. 71, 75, 83.

25 Marcel Mauss in collaboration with Henri Beuchat, *Seasonal Variations of the Eskimo: A Study in Social Morphology* [1904–5], trans. James J. Fox (London: Routledge & Kegan Paul, 1979).

26 A recent and interesting example is David Sneath, *Changing Inner Mongolia: Pastoral Mongolian Society and the Chinese State* (Oxford: Clarendon Press, 2000).

27 John Davis, *Libyan Politics: Tribe and Revolution* (London: I. B. Tauris, 1987).

28 Paul Dresch, *Tribes, Government, and History in Yemen* (Oxford: Clarendon Press, 1989).

29 Tim Jenkins, research in progress.

30 Chris M. Hann (ed.), *Property Relations: Renewing the Anthropological Tradition* (Cambridge: Cambridge University Press, 1998).

31 Émile Durkheim, *The Division of Labour in Society* [1893], trans. G. Simpson (New York: Macmillan, 1933).

32 L. Dumont, *Homo Hierarchicus* (Chicago: University of Chicago Press, 1966).

33 Sandra Wallman, *The Social Anthropology of Work*, ASA Monograph 19 (London: Academic Press, 1979).

34 Weber, *The Protestant Ethic and the Spirit of Capitalism* [1904–5], trans. Talcott Parsons (London & New York: Routledge, 1992).

35 Sahlins, *Stone Age Economics* (London: Tavistock, 1974).

36 Raymond Firth, *Themes in Economic Anthropology*, ASA Monograph 6 (London: Tavistock, 1967); see particularly in this volume, M. Douglas on 'Primitive Rationing' and F. Barth on 'Economic Spheres in Darfur'.

37 Claude Meillassoux, *Maidens, Meal and Money: Capitalism and the Domestic Community* [1975] (Cambridge: Cambridge University Press, 1981).

38 Donald L. Donham, *History, Power, Ideology: Central Issues in Marxism and Anthropology* (Cambridge: Cambridge University Press, 1990).

39 Ibid. 58–66.

40 Marcel Mauss, *The Gift: The Form and Reason for Exchange in Archaic Societies* [1925], trans. W. D. Halls, foreword by Mary Douglas (London: Routledge, 1990).

41 Arjun Appadurai (ed.), *The Social Life of Things: Commodities in Cultural Perspective* (Cambridge: Cambridge University Press, 1986).

42 A lucid guide to these themes is given in John Davis, *Exchange* (Buckingham: Open University Press, 1992).

43 Ilana Silber, 'Modern philanthropy: reassessing the viability of a Maussian perspective', in W. James and N. J. Allen (eds.), *Marcel Mauss: A Centenary Tribute* (Oxford & New York: Berghahn, 1998).

44 Mauss, *The Gift*, 66–8, 77.

45 T. Jenkins, 'Fieldwork and the perception of everyday life', *Man*, 29 (1994), 433–55. Marc Augé gives a lively account of a thesis by Michèle de la Pradelle on the ritual character of the Carpentras truffle market in his *An Anthropology for Contemporaneous Worlds* [1994], trans. Amy Jacobs (Stanford: Stanford University Press, 1999), 71–6.

46 Claude Meillassoux, *The Anthropology of Slavery: The Womb of Iron and Gold* [1986], trans. A. Dasnois (Chicago: University of Chicago Press, 1991). Cf. James L. Watson (ed.), *Asian and African Systems of Slavery* (Oxford: Blackwell, 1980). Léonie Archer (ed.), *Slavery and Other Forms of Unfree Labour* (London & New York: Routledge, 1988).

47 M. Finley, 'Slavery', *International Encyclopaedia of the Social Sciences*, vol. 14 (New York, 1968), 307–13.

48 James Woodburn, 'Egalitarian societies', *Man*, 17 (1982), 431–51; Chris M. Hann (ed.), *Socialism: Ideals, Ideologies and Local Practice*, ASA Monograph 31 (London: Routledge, 1993).

49 James Brooks, *Captives and Cousins: Slavery, Kinship and Community in the Southwest Borderlands* (Chapel Hill & London: University of North Carolina Press, 2002).

50 Marilyn Strathern (ed.), *Dealing with Inequality: Analysing Gender Relations in Melanesia and Beyond* (Cambridge: Cambridge University Press, 1987); Richard Fardon, 'Malinowski's precedent: the imagination of equality', *Man* (NS), 25 (1990), 569–87.

Chapter Ten

1 US Bureau of the Census, International Data Base.

2 Ruth Finnegan, *Communicating: The Multiple Modes of Human Interconnection* (London & New York: Routledge, 2002). David Harvey, *The Condition of Postmodernity: An Enquiry into the Origins of Cultural Change* (Oxford: Blackwell, 1989); *Spaces of Hope* (Berkeley & Los Angeles: University of California Press, 2000).

3 Pierre Bourdieu, *Distinction: A Social Critique of the Judgement of Taste* [1979] (Cambridge, Mass.: Harvard University Press, 1985).

4 Jeffrey Richards, *Imperialism and Music: Britain 1876–1953* (Manchester: Manchester University Press, 2001).

5 J. Huizinga, *Homo Ludens* [1938] (New York: Paladin, 1970).

6 Ronald Frankenberg, *Village on the Border: A Social Study of Religion, Politics and Football in a North Wales Community* (London: Cohen & West, 1957).

7 Jeremy MacClancy (ed.), *Sport, Identity and Ethnicity* (Oxford & New York: Berg, 1996).

8 Ibid. 5. Chapters of the book touched on here are as follows: ' "Strong as a Turk": power, performance and representation in Turkish wrestling' (M. Stokes), 'Female bullfighting, gender stereotyping and the state' (J. MacClancy), ' "Our blood is green": cricket, identity, and social empowerment among British Pakistanis' (P. Werbner), 'Players, workers, protestors: social change and soccer in colonial Zimbabwe' (O. Stuart), 'The Venice Regatta: from ritual to sport' (L. Sciama), 'Indigenous polo and the politics of regional identity in northern Pakistan' (P. Parkes).

9 James Clifford, *Routes: Travel and Translation in the Late Twentieth Century* (Cambridge, Mass., & London: Harvard University Press, 1997). An illuminating collection is Simone Abram, Jacqueline Waldren, and Donald Macleod (eds.), *Tourists and Tourism: Identifying with People and Places* (London & New York: Berg, 1997).

10 Marc Augé, *Non-Places: Introduction to an Anthropology of Supermodernity* [1992], trans. J. Howe (London: Verso, 1995), 76, 87–93, 110.

11 Pioneering studies in the industrial towns of South Africa and the Zambian Copperbelt include A. L. Epstein, *Politics in an Urban African Community* (Manchester: Manchester University Press, 1958); Philip Mayer, *Townsmen or Tribesmen: Conservatism and the Process of Urbanization in a South African City* (London: Oxford University Press, 1961); J. C. Mitchell, *Social Networks in Urban Situations* (Manchester: Manchester University Press for Institute of Social Resources, University of Zambia, 1969). See also Jean La Fontaine, *City Politics: A Study of Léopoldville, 1962–63* (Cambridge: Cambridge University Press, 1970); R. S. Lynd and H. M. Lynd, *Middletown: A Study in American Culture* (New York & London: Harcourt Brace & Constable, 1929).

12 Ulf Hannerz, *Exploring the City: Inquiries Toward an Urban Anthropology* (New York: Columbia University Press, 1980), esp. 202–41. Erving Goffman is best known for *The Presentation of Self in Everyday Life* (New York: Doubleday/Anchor Books, 1959).

13 Fustel de Coulanges, *The Ancient City* [1864], trans. W. Small (Boston/New York, 1882). Cf. a pioneering modern anthropological study of urban form: Eva Krapf-Askari [later Eva Gillies], *Yoruba Towns and Cities: An Enquiry into the Nature of Urban Social Phenomena* (Oxford: Clarendon Press, 1969).

14 Paul Wheatley, *The Pivot of the Four Quarters: A Preliminary Enquiry into the Origins and Character of the Ancient Chinese City* (Edinburgh: Edinburgh University Press, 1971).

15 Ronald Grimes, *Symbol & Conquest: Public Ritual and Drama in Santa Fe* (New York: Cornell, 1976). See Victor Turner, 'Introduction', 9–10.

16 Deirdre Evans-Pritchard, 'The Portal Case: authenticity, tourism, traditions and the law', *Journal of American Folklore*, 100 (1987), 287–96.

17 See James Brooks, *Captives and Cousins: Slavery, Kinship, and Community in the Southwest Borderlands* (Chapel Hill & London: University of North Carolina Press, 2002).

18 R. Murphy, 'Space, class and rhetoric in Lahore', D.Phil, thesis, Oxford 1996.

19 My account follows Chris Wilson, *The Myth of Santa Fe: Creating a Modern Regional Tradition* (Albuquerque: University of New Mexico Press, 1997).

20 Ibid. 46.

21 Ibid. 79.

22 Ibid. 50.

23 Ibid. 118.

24 Ibid. 211.

25 Grimes, *Symbol and Conquest*, 210.

26 Jeremy Boissevain (ed.), *Revitalizing European Rituals* (London: Routledge, 1992). Daniel Miller (ed.), *Unwrapping Christmas* (Oxford: Clarendon Press, 1993).

27 James G. Carrier (ed.), *Meanings of the Market: The Free Market in Western Culture* (Oxford & New York: Berg, 1997).

28 Susan Love-Brown, 'The free market as salvation from government: the anarcho-capitalist view', in Carrier, *Meanings of the Market*.

29 James G. Carrier, 'Mr Smith, meet Mr Hawken', in Carrier, *Meanings of the Market*.

30 Malcolm Chapman and Peter J. Buckley, 'Markets, transaction costs, economists and social anthropologists', in Carrier, *Meanings of the Market*.

31 Ibid. 239.

32 Joel S. Kahn, 'Demons, commodities and the history of anthropology', in Carrier, *Meanings of the Market*.

33 Daniel Miller, *Modernity: An Ethnographic Approach: Dualism and Mass Consumption in Trinidad* (Oxford & Providence, RI: Berg, 1994).

34 Pierre Bourdieu, *Distinction*, 8.

35 Ibid. 8–9, 13.

36 Marcel Mauss, 'Une catégorie de l'esprit humaine: la notion de personne, celle de "moi"'. Originally a lecture for the Royal Anthropological Institute and published in the *JRAI* 1938; translated first by Brewster in *Sociology and Psychology*, and then again by W. D. Halls in M. Carrithers, S. Collins, and S. Lukes (eds.), *The Category of the Person: Anthropology, Philosophy, History* (Cambridge: Cambridge University Press, 1985).

37 For a very perceptive analysis of this, see M. Finley, 'Slavery', *International Encyclopaedia of the Social Sciences*, vol. 14 (New York, 1968).

38 *Guardian* (29 Feb. 2000).

39 Mary Warnock, *Making Babies: Is there a Right to have Children?* (Oxford: Oxford University Press, 2002), 97 ff.

40 Raelian cult reports. See the website www.rael.org. Updated assessments will no doubt appear regularly in both the scientific and the popular press.

41 Paul Heelas, *The New Age Movement: Religion, Culture and Society in the Age of Postmodernity* (Oxford & New York: Blackwell, 1996).

42 B. Simpson, 'Localising a brave new world: new reproductive technologies and the politics of fertility in Sri Lanka', in M. Unnithan-Kumar (ed.), *Human Reproduction, Medical Technologies and Health* (Oxford & New York: Berghahn, 2003).

43 Susan M. Kahn, *Reproducing Jews: A Cultural Account of Assisted Conception in Israel* (Durham, NC: Duke University Press, 2000), esp. chs. 3, 6.

Chapter Eleven

1 See, for example, Lionel Tiger and Robin Fox, *The Imperial Animal* [1971], with a new introduction by the authors (New Brunswick & London: Transaction Publishers, 1998).

2 Signe Howell and Roy Willis, *Societies at Peace: Anthropological Perspectives* (London & New York: Routledge, 1989), p. vii.

3 Ashley Montagu, *The Nature of Human Aggression* (Oxford: Oxford University Press, 1976).

4 M. Carrithers, 'Sociality, not aggression, is the key human trait', in Howell and Willis, *Societies at Peace*.

5 Clayton A. Robarchek, 'Hobbesian and Rousseauan images of man: autonomy and individualism in a peaceful society', in Howell and Willis, *Societies at Peace*, 32, 34–5.

6 Napoleon A. Chagnon, *Yanomamö: The Fierce People* [1968], 3rd edn. (New York: Holt, Rinehart & Winston, 1983).

7 Patrick Tierney, *Darkness in El Dorado: How Scientists and Journalists Devastated the Amazon* (New York & London: W. W. Norton, 2000).

8 For a discussion of the place of the Yanomamo and other 'tribal exemplars' in the teaching and dissemination of anthropology, see W. James, 'Type-casting: anthropology's *dramatis personae*', in Jeremy MacClancy and Chris McDonaugh (eds.), *Popularizing Anthropology* (London & New York: Routledge, 1996).

9 Chagnon, *The Fierce People*, 9–10.

10 Marvin Harris, *Cows, Pigs, Wars and Witches: The Riddles of Culture* (London: Hutchinson, 1975), 48, 68, 72.

11 Elvin Hatch, *Culture and Morality: The Relativity of Values in Anthropology* (New York: Columbia University Press, 1973), 92–3.

12 Brian Ferguson, and Neil Whitehead (eds.), *War in the Tribal Zone: Expanding States and Indigenous Warfare* [1992], with new preface (Santa Fe, N. Mex./Oxford: SAR Press/James Currey, 2001).

13 Douglas H. Johnson, 'The fighting Nuer: primary sources and the origins of a stereotype', *Africa*, 51 (1981), 508–27.

14 Alan Campbell, 'Peace', in Howell and Willis, *Societies at Peace*, 214–15, 221–3.

15 David Riches (ed.), *The Anthropology of Violence* (Oxford: Blackwell, 1986).

16 See, for example, the studies in G. Aijmer and J. Abbink (eds.), *Meanings of Violence: A Cross-Cultural Perspective* (Oxford & New York: Berg, 2000).

17 Suzette Heald, *Controlling Anger: The Anthropology of Gisu Violence* [1989] (Oxford/Athens, Oh.: James Currey/Ohio University Press, 1998).

18 René Girard, *Violence and the Sacred* [1972] (Baltimore: Johns Hopkins University Press, 1977). Luc de Heusch, *Sacrifice in Africa: A Structuralist Approach* (Bloomington: Indiana University Press, 1985). Maurice Bloch, *Prey into Hunter: The Politics of Religious Experience*, the Lewis Henry Morgan Lectures, 1984 (Cambridge: Cambridge University Press, 1992).

19 Felix Padel, *The Sacrifice of Human Being: British Rule and the Konds of Orissa* (Delhi: Oxford University Press, 1995).

20 Clifford Geertz, *Negara: The Theatre State in Nineteenth-Century Bali* (Princeton: Princeton University Press, 1980), 13–15, 18.

21 Leo E. A. Howe, 'Peace and violence in Bali: culture and social organization', in Howell and Willis, *Societies at Peace*, 107, 108, 111; *Hinduism and Hierarchy in Bali*, World Anthropology (Oxford/Santa Fe, N. Mex.: James Currey/School of American Research Press, 2002).

22 A. M. Hocart, *Kings and Councillors: An Essay in the Comparative Anatomy of Human Society* [1936], ed. R. Needham (Chicago & London: University of Chicago Press, 1970).

23 The *locus classicus* is E. E. Evans-Pritchard, *The Nuer* (Oxford: Clarendon Press, 1940); cf. Max Gluckman, *Order and Rebellion in Tribal Africa* (London: Cohen & West, 1963).

24 Louis Dumont, *Homo Hierarchicus* (Chicago: University of Chicago Press, 1966).

25 James Scott, *Domination and the Arts of Resistance: Hidden Transcripts* (New Haven: Yale University Press, 1990).

26 Mukulika Banerjee, *The Pathan Unarmed: Opposition and Memory in the Khudai Khidmatgar Movement*, World Anthropology (Oxford/Santa Fe, N. Mex.: James Currey/School of American Research Press, 2000).

27 Review by Sunil Khilnani, 'The frontier Gandhi?', *Times Literary Supplement* (2 Nov. 2001), 28.

28 I. M. Lewis, *Ecstatic Religion* (Harmondsworth: Penguin, 1971).

29 Shirley Ardener, 'Sexual insult and female militancy' [1973], in S. G. Ardener (ed.), *Perceiving Women* (London/New York: Dent-Malaby/Halsted, 1975).

30 Michael O'Hanlon, 'A view from afar: memories of New Guinea Highland warfare', in P. Dresch, W. James, and D. Parkin (eds.), *Anthropologists in a Wider World: Essays on Field Research* (Oxford & New York: Berghahn, 2000).

31 J. L. Austin, *How to Do Things with Words* [1962], ed. J. O. Urmson and Marina Sbisa (Oxford: Oxford University Press, 1975). For further reading on this theme, see Ralph Grillo (ed.), *Social Anthropology and the Politics of Language* (London & New York: Routledge, 1990). See particularly Michael Gilsenan's contribution to this volume on 'Word of Honour'. See also Maurice Bloch, 'Symbols, song, dance and features of articulation: Is religion an extreme form of traditional authority?' [1974], in his collected essays, *Ritual, History and Power: Selected Papers in Anthropology* (London: Athlone, 1989); and also his edited volume *Political Language and Oratory in Traditional Society* (London & New York: Academic Press, 1975).

32 Henry S. Maine, *Ancient Law: Its Connection with the Early History of Society and its Relation to Modern Ideas* [1861] (London: Routledge, 1913). Max Gluckman, *The Judicial Process among the Barotse of Northern Rhodesia* (Manchester: Manchester University Press for the Rhodes-Livingstone Institute, 1955); *The Ideas in Barotse Jurisprudence* (Manchester: Manchester University Press, 1972); *Politics, Law and Ritual in Tribal Society* (Oxford: Blackwell, 1965).

33 Roger Just, 'Triumph of the ethnos', in Elizabeth Tonkin, Maryon McDonald, and Malcolm Chapman (eds.), *History and Ethnicity*, ASA Monograph 27 (London & New York: Routledge, 1989).

34 Paul Dresch, 'Race, culture, and—what?' in W. James (ed.), *The Pursuit of Certainty: Religious and Cultural Formulations* (London & New York: Routledge, 1995).

35 Marcus Banks, *Ethnicity: Anthropological Constructions* (London & New York: Routledge, 1996).

36 Richard Fardon, 'African ethnogenesis', in Ladislav Holy (ed.), *Comparative Anthropology* (Oxford: Blackwell, 1987).

37 Ernest Gellner, *Nations and Nationalism* (Oxford: Blackwell, 1983).

38 Benedict Anderson, *Imagined Communities: Reflections on the Origin and Spread of Nationalism* (London & New York: Verso, 1983).

39 Wendy James, 'The anthropologist as reluctant imperialist', in Talal Asad (ed.), *Anthropology and the Colonial Encounter* (London: Ithaca, 1973).

40 For example, Audrey I. Richards, *Land, Labour and Diet in Northern Rhodesia: An Economic Study of the Bemba Tribe* (London: Oxford University Press, 1939).

41 Maryon McDonald, *We are not French! Language, Culture, and Identity in Brittany* (London: Routledge, 1989). Tonkin *et al.*, *History and Ethnicity*.

42 John Davis, *Libyan Politics: Tribe and Revolution* (London: I. B. Tauris, 1987); Donald L. Donham, 'Old Abyssinia and the new Ethiopian empire: themes in social history', ch. 1 in D. L. Donham and W. James (eds.), *The Southern Marches of Imperial Ethiopia: Essays in Social Anthropology and History* [1986], reissued with new preface (Oxford/Athens, Oh.: James Currey/Ohio University Press, 2002); Paul Dresch, *Tribes, Government, and History in Yemen* (Oxford: Clarendon Press, 1989); Pierre Bourdieu, *Distinction: A Social Critique of the Judgement of Taste* [1979] (Cambridge, Mass.: Harvard University Press, 1985).

43 Jean Comaroff, *Body of Power, Spirit of Resistance: The Culture and History of a South African People* (Chicago: University of Chicago Press, 1985); Michael Herzfeld, *The Poetics of Manhood: Contest and Identity in a Cretan Mountain Village* (Princeton: Princeton University Press, 1985).

44 Eric J. Hobsbawm and T. O. Ranger, *The Invention of Tradition* (Cambridge: Cambridge University Press, 1983); Paul Connerton, *How Societies Remember* (Cambridge: Cambridge University Press, 1989).

45 David Parkin (ed.), *The Politics of Cultural Performance* (Oxford & New York: Berghahn, 1996).

46 Roger Goodman, *Japan's 'International Youth': The Emergence of a New Class of Schoolchildren* (Oxford: Clarendon Press, 1993). Michael Gilsenan, *Lords of the Lebanese Marches: Violence and Narrative in an Arab Society* (London & New York: I. B. Tauris, 1996).

47 Thomas M. Wilson and Hastings Donnan (eds.), *Border Identities: Nation and State at International Frontiers* (Cambridge: Cambridge University Press, 1998). See especially the editors' introductory chapter.

48 Michael Kearney, 'Transnationalism in California and Mexico at the end of empire', in Wilson and Donnan, *Border Identities*.

49 Henk Driessen, 'The "New Immigration" and the transformation of the European-African frontier', in Wilson and Donnan, *Border Identities*.

50 Martin Stokes, 'Imagining "the South": hybridity, heterotopias and Arabesk on the Turkish-Syrian border', in Wilson and Donnan, *Border Identities*.

51 Ibid. 265–7.

52 What follows is summarized from Donald L. Donham, *Marxist Modern: An Ethnographic History of the Ethiopian Revolution* (Berkeley & Los Angeles/Oxford: University of California Press/James Currey, 1999).

53 For a historical treatment and chronology up to 2002, see Douglas H. Johnson, *The Root Causes of Sudan's Civil Wars* (Oxford/Bloomington: James Currey/Indiana University Press, 2002), esp. ch. 7. Recent anthropological work on the effects of the Sudanese civil war on the Nuer includes Sharon Hutchinson, *Nuer Dilemmas: Coping with Money, War, and the State* (Berkeley & Los Angeles: University of Calfornia Press, 1996).

54 For example, see E. Valentine Daniel, *Charred Lullabies: Chapters in an Anthropography of Violence* (Princeton: Princeton University Press, 1997); Richard Werbner, *Tears of the Dead* (Edinburgh: Edinburgh University Press for the International African Institute, 1991); Liisa H. Malkki, *Purity and Exile: Violence, Memory and National Cosmology among Hutu Refugees in Tanzania* (Chicago: University of Chicago Press, 1995); Paul Richards, *Fighting for the Rain Forest: War, Youth and Resources in Sierra Leone* (Oxford/Portsmouth NH: James Currey/Heinemann, 1996); Susanna M. Hoffman and Anthony Oliver-Smith (eds.), *Catastrophe and Culture: The Anthropology of Disaster* (Santa Fe, N. Mex./Oxford: School of American Research Press/James Currey, 2002).

55 Melissa Leach, 'New shapes to shift: war, parks and the hunting person in modern West Africa', *JRAI* 6 (2000), 577–95.

56 Roland Littlewood, 'Military Rape', *Anthropology Today*, 13/2 (1997), 7–16.

57 African Rights: *Rwanda: Not so Innocent. When Women Become Killers* (London: African Rights, 1995).

58 David Keen, *The Benefits of Famine: A Political Economy of Famine and Relief in Southwestern Sudan, 1983–1989* (Princeton: Princeton University Press, 1994).

59 Alex de Waal, *Famine that Kills: Darfur, Sudan, 1984–1985* (Oxford: Clarendon Press, 1989); *Famine Crimes: Politics and the Disaster Relief Industry in Africa* (Oxford/Bloomington: James Currey/Indiana University Press, 1997), 12–16.

PART V

Chapter Twelve

1 Terry Eagleton, *The Illusions of Postmodernism* (Oxford: Blackwell, 1996), 36.

2 Clifford Geertz, 'Culture, mind, brain / brain, mind, culture' [1999], in his collected essays, *Available Light: Anthropological Reflections on Philosophical Topics* (Princeton & Oxford: Princeton University Press, 2000), 208.

3 Marc Augé, *An Anthropology for Contemporaneous Worlds*, trans. Amy Jacobs (Stanford: Stanford University Press, 1999), 64, 63.

4 For example, Richard Dawkins, *The Blind Watchmaker* (London: Longman, 1986).

5 See the contributions of Keith Hart and others in Tim Ingold (ed.), *Key Debates in Anthropology* (London & New York: Routledge, 1996), esp. the 1988 debate, 15–54.

6 Douglas H. Johnson, *Nuer Prophets: A History of Prophecy from the Upper Nile in the Nineteenth and Twentieth Centuries* (Oxford: Clarendon Press, 1994).

7 For anthropological commentaries, see, for example, Lionel Caplan (ed.), *Studies in Religious Fundamentalism* (London: Macmillan, 1987); Wendy James (ed.), *The Pursuit of Certainty: Religious and Cultural Formulations* (London & New York: Routledge, 1995).

8 Anthony Giddens, 'Epilogue' to Cris Shore and Akbar Ahmed (eds.), *The Future of Anthropology: Its Relevance to the Contemporary World* (London: Athlone, 1995), 275.

9 Ibid. 276–7.

10 R. G. Collingwood, *An Essay on Metaphysics* (Oxford: Clarendon Press, 1940). *The Idea of History* (Oxford: Clarendon Press, 1946).

11 James G. Carrier (ed.), *Occidentalism: Images of the West* (Oxford: Clarendon Press, 1995).

12 Rebecca E. Karl, *Staging the World: Chinese Nationalism at the Turn of the Twentieth Century* (Durham, NC, & London: Duke University Press, 2002).

Select Bibliography

I. SOME FOUNDATIONAL TEXTS

ASAD, TALAL (ed.), *Anthropology and the Colonial Encounter* (London: Ithaca Press, 1973).

BARTH, FREDRIK, *Political Leadership among the Swat Pathans* (London: Athlone, 1959).

BENEDICT, RUTH, *Patterns of Culture* (London: Routledge & Kegan Paul, 1935).

BOURDIEU, PIERRE, *Outline of a Theory of Practice* (Cambridge: Cambridge University Press, 1977).

CALLAN, HILARY, *Ethology and Society: Towards an Anthropological View* (Oxford: Clarendon Press, 1970).

COHEN, ABNER, *Custom and Politics in Urban Africa: A Study of Hausa Migrants in Yoruba Towns* (London: Routledge, 1969).

DOUGLAS, MARY, *Purity and Danger: An Analysis of Concepts of Pollution and Taboo* (London: Routledge & Kegan Paul, 1966).

DUMONT, LOUIS, *Homo Hierarchicus* (Chicago: University of Chicago Press, 1966).

DURKHEIM, ÉMILE, *The Elementary Forms of Religious Life* [1912], trans. Karen E. Fields (New York: Free Press, 1995).

—— and MAUSS, MARCEL, *Primitive Classification* [1903], trans. R. Needham (London: Cohen & West, 1963).

EVANS-PRITCHARD, EDWARD E., *Witchcraft, Oracles, and Magic among the Azande* (Oxford: Clarendon Press, 1937). Abridged edition issued in 1976.

—— *The Nuer: A Description of the Modes of Livelihood and Political Institutions of a Nilotic People* (Oxford: Clarendon Press, 1940).

—— *The Sanusi of Cyrenaica* (Oxford: Clarendon Press, 1949).

—— *Kinship and Marriage among the Nuer* (Oxford: Clarendon Press, 1951).

—— *Social Anthropology* (London: Allen & Unwin, 1951).

—— *Nuer Religion* (Oxford: Clarendon Press, 1956).

—— *Essays in Social Anthropology* (London: Faber & Faber, 1962).

—— *Theories of Primitive Religion* (Oxford: Clarendon Press, 1965).

FIRTH, RAYMOND (ed.), *Themes in Economic Anthropology*, ASA Monograph 6 (London: Tavistock, 1967).

FORDE, DARYLL, *Habitat, Economy and Society: A Geographical Introduction to Ethnology* (London: Methuen, 1934).

FORTES, MEYER, and EVANS-PRITCHARD, E. E. (eds.), *African Political Systems* (London: Oxford University Press, 1940).

FOX, R., *Kinship and Marriage* (Harmondsworth: Penguin, 1967).

FRAZER, JAMES G., *The Golden Bough: A Study in Magic and Religion*, abridged edn. in one volume [1922] (London: Macmillan 1960).

—— *The Golden Bough* [from 1890; 12 vols.], ed. George Stocking (Harmondsworth: Penguin, 1996).

GEERTZ, CLIFFORD, *The Interpretation of Cultures* (New York: Basic Books, 1973).

GLUCKMAN, MAX, *Politics, Law and Ritual in Tribal Society* (Oxford: Blackwell, 1965).

GOODY, JACK, *Production and Reproduction: A Comparative Study of the Domestic Domain* (Cambridge: Cambridge University Press, 1976).

HERTZ, ROBERT, *Death and the Right Hand* [1909], trans. R. and C. Needham (London: Cohen & West, 1960).

HUBERT, HENRI, *Essay on Time: A Brief Study of the Representation of Time in Religion and Magic*, [1905], trans. R. Parkin and J. Redding (Oxford: Durkheim Press; Oxford/New York: Berghahn Books, 1999).

LEACH, EDMUND R., *Political Systems of Highland Burma: A Study of Kachin Social Structure* (London: Bell, 1954).

—— *Rethinking Anthropology* (London: Athlone Press, 1961).

LÉVI-STRAUSS, CLAUDE, *The Elementary Structures of Kinship* [1949], trans. R. Needham (London: Eyre & Spottiswoode, 1969).

—— *Structural Anthropology* [1958], trans. C. Jacobson and B. G. Schopf (London: Allen Lane, 1963).

—— *The Savage Mind* [1962] (London: Weidenfeld & Nicolson, 1966).

LIENHARDT, R. G., *Divinity and Experience: The Religion of the Dinka* (Oxford: Clarendon Press, 1961).

MALINOWSKI, B., *Argonauts of the Western Pacific* (London: Routledge & Kegan Paul, 1922).

MAUSS, MARCEL, *The Gift: The Form and Reason for Exchange in Archaic Societies* [1925], trans. W. D. Halls, foreword by Mary Douglas (London: Routledge, 1990).

—— *Sociology and Psychology: Essays by Marcel Mauss*, trans. B. Brewster (London: Routledge & Kegan Paul, 1979).

MEAD, MARGARET, *Coming of Age in Samoa: A Psychological Study of Primitive Youth for Western Civilisation* (New York: Morrow, 1928).

NEEDHAM, RODNEY (ed.), *Rethinking Kinship and Marriage*, ASA Monograph 11 (London: Tavistock, 1971).

—— (ed.), *Right and Left: Essays on Dual Symbolic Classification* (Chicago & London: University of Chicago Press, 1973).

RADCLIFFE-BROWN, A. R., *Structure and Function in Primitive Society* (London: Cohen & West, 1952).

TURNER, VICTOR W., *The Forest of Symbols: Aspects of Ndembu Ritual* (Ithaca, NY: Cornell University Press, 1967).

—— *Dramas, Fields, and Metaphors: Symbolic Action in Human Society* (Ithaca, NY: Cornell University Press, 1974).

VAN GENNEP, ARNOLD, *The Rites of Passage* [1909], trans. Monika B. Vizedom and Gabrielle L. Caffee (London: Routledge & Kegan Paul, 1960).

2. RECENT INNOVATORY WORKS

ABU-LUGHOD, LILA, *Veiled Sentiments: Honor and Poetry in a Bedouin Society* (Berkeley: University of California Press, 1986).

APPADURAI, ARJUN (ed.), *The Social Life of Things: Commodities in Cultural Perspective* (Cambridge: Cambridge University Press, 1986).

ARDENER, EDWIN W., *The Voice of Prophecy and Other Essays*, ed. Malcolm Chapman (Oxford & New York: Blackwell, 1989).

—— (ed.), *Social Anthropology and Language*, ASA Monograph 10 (London: Tavistock, 1971).

ARDENER, SHIRLEY (ed.), *Defining Females: The Nature of Women in Society* (London: Croom Helm, 1978; new edn. in the series Cross-Cultural Perspectives on Women, vol. 4, Oxford & New York: Berg, 1993).

ASAD, TALAL, *The Genealogies of Religion: Discipline and Reasons of Power in Christianity and Islam* (Baltimore & London: Johns Hopkins University Press, 1993).

BANERJEE, MUKULIKA, *The Pathan Unarmed: Opposition and Memory in the Khudai Khidmatgar Movement*, World Anthropology (Oxford/Santa Fe, N. Mex.: James Currey/School of American Research Press, 2000).

BANKS, MARCUS, *Organizing Jainism in India and England* (Oxford: Clarendon Press, 1992).

—— and MORPHY, HOWARD (eds.), *Rethinking Visual Anthropology* (New Haven & London: Yale University Press, 1997).

BARBER, KARIN, *I Could Speak until Tomorrow: Oriki, Women and the Past in a Yoruba Town* (Edinburgh: Edinburgh University Press for the International African Institute, 1991).

BLOCH, MAURICE, *Ritual, History and Power: Selected Papers in Anthropology* (London: Athlone Press, 1989).

—— *How We Think They Think: Anthropological Approaches to Cognition, Memory, and Literacy* (Oxford & Boulder, Colo.: Westview Press, 1998).

—— *Prey into Hunter: The Politics of Religious Experience*, the Lewis Henry Morgan Lectures, 1984 (Cambridge: Cambridge University Press, 1992).

—— and PARRY, JONATHAN P. (eds.), *Death and the Regeneration of Life* (Cambridge: Cambridge University Press, 1982).

BODDY, JANICE, *Wombs and Alien Spirits: Women, Men and the* Zar *Cult in Northern Sudan* (Madison: University of Wisconsin Press, 1989).

BORN, GEORGINA, *Rationalizing Culture: IRCAM, Boulez, and the Institutionalization of the Musical Avant-Garde* (Berkeley: University of California Press, 1995).

BOROFSKY, ROBERT, *Making History: Pukapukan and Anthropological Constructions of Knowledge* (Cambridge: Cambridge University Press, 1987).

BOURDIEU, PIERRE, *Distinction: A Social Critique of the Judgement of Taste* [1979] (Cambridge, Mass.: Harvard University Press, 1985).

BROOKS, JAMES F., *Captives and Cousins: Slavery, Kinship, and Community in the Southwest Borderlands* (Chapel Hill, NC, & London: University of North Carolina Press, 2002).

CARRIER, JAMES G. (ed.), *Meanings of the Market: The Free Market in Western Culture* (Oxford & New York: Berg, 1997).

—— (ed.), *Occidentalism: Images of the West* (Oxford: Clarendon Press, 1995).

CARRITHERS, MICHAEL, COLLINS, STEPHEN, and LUKES, STEVEN (eds.), *The Category of the Person: Anthropology, Philosophy, History* (Cambridge: Cambridge University Press, 1985).

CARSTEN, JANET, and HUGH-JONES, STEPHEN (eds.), *About the House: Lévi-Strauss and Beyond* (Cambridge: Cambridge University Press, 1995).

CLIFFORD, JAMES, *Routes: Travel and Translation in the Late Twentieth Century* (Cambridge, Mass., & London: Harvard University Press, 1997).

—— and MARCUS, G. E. (eds.), *Writing Culture: The Poetics and Politics of Ethnography* (Berkeley & Los Angeles: University of California Press, 1986).

COHEN, ABNER, *The Politics of Elite Culture: Explorations in the Dramaturgy of Power in a Modern African Society* (Berkeley: University of California Press, 1981).

COHEN, ANTHONY P., *Self-Consciousness: An Alternative Anthropology of Identity* (London & New York: Routledge, 1994).

CORNWALL, ANDREA, and LINDISFARNE, NANCY (eds.), *Dislocating Masculinity: Comparative Ethnographies* (London & New York: Routledge, 1994).

COWAN, JANE K., *Dance and the Body Politic in Northern Greece* (Princeton: Princeton University Press, 1990).

CRAWFORD, PETER IAN, and TURTON, DAVID, *Film as Ethnography* (Manchester & New York: Manchester University Press, 1992).

DAVIS, JOHN H. R. (ed.), *Religious Organization and Religious Experience*, ASA Monograph 21 (London: Academic Press, 1982).

DE WAAL, A., *Famine Crimes: Politics and the Disaster Relief Industry in Africa* (Oxford/ Bloomington & Indianapolis: James Currey/Indiana University Press, 1997).

DONHAM, DONALD L., *History, Power, Ideology: Central Issues in Marxism and Anthropology* (Cambridge: Cambridge University Press, 1990).

—— *Marxist Modern: An Ethnographic History of the Ethiopian Revolution* (Berkeley & Los Angeles/Oxford: University of California Press/James Currey, 1999).

DRESCH, PAUL K., JAMES, WENDY, and PARKIN, DAVID (eds.), *Anthropologists in a Wider World: Essays on Field Research* (Oxford & New York: Berghahn, 2000).

FABIAN, JOHANNES, *Time and the Other: How Anthropology Makes its Object* (New York: Columbia University Press, 1983).

—— *Time and the Work of Anthropology: Critical Essays* (Reading: Harwood Academic Publishers, 1991).

FARDON, RICHARD (ed.), *Localizing Strategies: Regional Traditions of Ethnographic Writing* (Washington/Edinburgh: Smithsonian/Scottish Academic Press, 1990).

FELD, STEVEN, *Sound and Sentiment: Birds, Weeping, Poetics, and Song in Kaluli Expression*, 2nd edn. (Philadelphia: University of Pennsylvania Press, 1990).

—— and BASSO, KEITH (eds.), *Senses of Place* (Santa Fe, N. Mex./Oxford: School of American Research Press/James Currey, 1999).

FERGUSON, R. BRIAN, and WHITEHEAD, NEIL L. (eds.), *War in the Tribal Zone: Expanding States and Indigenous Warfare,* revised edn. (Santa Fe, N. Mex./Oxford: School of American Research Press/James Currey, 2001).

FINNEGAN, RUTH, *The Hidden Musicians: Music Making in an English Town* (Cambridge: Cambridge University Press, 1990).

FRANKLIN, SARAH, *Embodied Progress: A Cultural Account of Assisted Conception* (London & New York: Routledge, 1997).

GELL, A., *The Anthropology of Time: Cultural Constructions of Temporal Maps and Images* (Oxford & Providence, RI: Berg, 1992).

—— *Art and Agency: An Anthropological Theory* (Oxford: Clarendon Press, 1998).

GILSENAN, MICHAEL, *Recognizing Islam: Religion and Society in the Modern Middle East* (London: Croom Helm, 1982).

—— *Lords of the Lebanese Marches: Violence and Narrative in an Arab Society* (London & New York: I. B. Tauris, 1996).

GLEDHILL, JOHN, *Power and its Disguises: Anthropological Perspectives on Politics* (London & Boulder, Colo.: Pluto Press, 1994).

GOODMAN, ROGER, *Japan's 'International Youth': The Emergence of a New Class of Schoolchildren* (Oxford: Oxford University Press, 1990).

HANN, CHRIS M. (ed.), *Property Relations: Renewing the Anthropological Tradition* (Cambridge: Cambridge University Press, 1998).

HARRIS, CLARE, *In the Image of Tibet: Tibetan Visual Culture after 1959* (London: Reaktion Books, 1999).

HASTRUP, KIRSTEN, *A Place Apart: An Anthropological Study of the Icelandic World* (Oxford: Clarendon Press, 1998).

HEALD, SUZETTE, *Controlling Anger: The Anthropology of Gisu Violence* [1989] (Oxford/ Athens, Oh.: James Currey/Ohio University Press, 1998).

—— *Manhood and Morality: Sex, Violence and Ritual in Gisu Society* (London & New York: Routledge, 1999).

HEELAS, PAUL, *The New Age Movement: Religion, Culture and Society in the Age of Postmodernity* (Oxford: Blackwell, 1996).

—— and LOCK, A., *Indigenous Psychology* (London: Academic Press, 1982).

HENDRY, JOY, *Wrapping Culture: Politeness, Presentation, and Power in Japan and Other Societies* (Oxford: Clarendon Press, 1993).

HOWELL, SIGNE, and WILLIS, ROY (eds.), *Societies at Peace: Anthropological Perspectives* (London & New York: Routledge, 1989).

HSU, ELISABETH, *The Transmission of Chinese Medicine* (Cambridge: Cambridge University Press, 1999).

HUGHES-FREELAND, FELICIA (ed.), *Ritual, Performance, Media*, ASA Monograph 35 (London & New York: Routledge, 1998).

HUMPHREY, CAROLINE, *Karl Marx Collective: Economy, Society and Religion in a Siberian Collective Farm* (Cambridge: Cambridge University Press, 1983).

—— and LAIDLAW, JAMES, *The Archetypal Actions of Ritual: A Theory of Ritual Illustrated by the Jain Rite of Worship* (Oxford: Clarendon Press, 1994).

HUTCHINSON, SHARON E., *Nuer Dilemmas: Coping with Money, War, and the State* (Berkeley & Los Angeles: University of California Press, 1996).

INGOLD, TIM, *Evolution and Social Life* (Cambridge: Cambridge University Press, 1986).

JAMES, WENDY, *The Listening Ebony: Moral Knowledge, Religion, and Power among the Uduk of Sudan* (Oxford: Clarendon Press, 1988). Reissued in paperback with new preface, 1999.

—— (ed.), *The Pursuit of Certainty: Religious and Cultural Formulations* (London & New York: Routledge, 1995).

KAHN, SUSAN M., *Reproducing Jews: A Cultural Account of Assisted Conception in Israel* (Durham, NC: Duke University Press, 2000).

KAPFERER, BRUCE, *A Celebration of Demons* (Bloomington: Indiana University Press, 1983).

LAMBEK, MICHAEL, *Knowledge and Practice in Mayotte: Local Discourses of Islam, Sorcery, and Spirit Possession* (Toronto: Toronto University Press, 1993).

—— *The Weight of the Past: Living with History in Mahajanga, Madagascar* (New York & Basingstoke: Palgrave Macmillan, 2002).

MACCLANCY, JEREMY, *Consuming Culture* (London: Chapmans, 1992).

—— (ed.), *Sport, Identity and Ethnicity* (Oxford & New York: Berg, 1996).

—— (ed.), *Exotic No More: Anthropology on the Front Lines* (Chicago & London: University of Chicago Press, 2002).

MCDONALD, MARYON, *We are not French! Language, Culture, and Identity in Brittany* (London: Routledge, 1989).

MEILLASSOUX, CLAUDE, *Maidens, Meal and Money: Capitalism and the Domestic Community* [1975] (Cambridge: Cambridge University Press, 1981).

MILLER, DANIEL (ed.), *Unwrapping Christmas* (Oxford: Clarendon Press, 1993).

MOORE, HENRIETTA, *Feminism and Anthropology* (Cambridge: Polity Press, 1988).

Moore, Henrietta, *A Passion for Difference: Essays in Anthropology and Gender* (Cambridge: Polity Press, 1994).

Morphy, Howard, *Ancestral Connections: Art and an Aboriginal System of Knowledge* (Chicago: University of Chicago Press, 1991).

O'Hanlon, Michael, and Hirsch, Eric (eds.), *The Anthropology of Landscape: Perspectives on Place and Space* (Oxford: Clarendon Press, 1995).

Parkin, David J. (ed.), *Semantic Anthropology*, ASA Monograph 22 (London: Academic Press, 1982).

—— *Sacred Void: Spatial Images of Work and Ritual among the Giriama of Kenya* (Cambridge: Cambridge University Press, 1991).

Parry, Jonathan P., *Death in Banaras* (Cambridge: Cambridge University Press, 1994).

Rival, Laura (ed.), *The Social Life of Trees: Anthropological Perspectives on Tree Symbolism* (Oxford & New York: Berg, 1998).

Rosaldo, Michelle K., *Knowledge and Passion: Notions of Self and Society among the Ilongot* (Cambridge: Cambridge University Press, 1980).

Scheper-Hughes, Nancy, *Death without Weeping: The Violence of Everyday Life in Brazil* (Berkeley: University of California Press, 1992).

Simpson, Bob, *Changing Families: An Ethnographic Approach to Divorce and Separation* (Oxford & New York: Berg, 1998).

Sperber, Dan, *On Anthropological Knowledge* (Cambridge: Cambridge University Press, 1985).

Stokes, Martin, *Ethnicity, Identity and Music: The Musical Construction of Place* (Oxford & New York: Berg, 1994).

Strathern, Marilyn, *The Gender of the Gift: Problems with Women and Problems with Society in Melanesia* (Berkeley & Los Angeles: University of California Press, 1988).

—— *After Nature: English Kinship in the Late Twentieth Century* (Cambridge: Cambridge University Press, 1992).

Thomas, Nicholas, *In Oceania: Visions, Artifacts, Histories* (Durham, NC: Duke University Press, 1997).

Tremayne, Soraya (ed.), *Managing Reproductive Life: Cross-Cultural Themes in Fertility and Sexuality* (Oxford & New York: Berghahn, 2001).

Watson, C. W., and Hendry, Joy (eds.), *An Anthropology of Indirect Communication*, ASA Monograph 37 (London & New York: Routledge, 2001).

Webber, Jonathan (ed.), *Jewish Identities in the New Europe* (The Littman Library of Jewish Civilization, 1994).

Whitehouse, Harvey, *Arguments and Icons: Divergent Modes of Religiosity* (Oxford: Oxford University Press, 2000).

—— (ed.), *The Debated Mind: Evolutionary Psychology versus Ethnography* (Oxford & New York: Berg, 2001).

Wilson, T. M., and Donnan, Hastings (eds.), *Border Identities: Nation and State at International Frontiers* (Cambridge: Cambridge University Press, 1998).

3. INFLUENTIAL WORKS IN NEIGHBOURING FIELDS OF THE HUMAN SCIENCES AND PHILOSOPHY

ANDERSON, BENEDICT, *Imagined Communities: Reflections on the Origin and Spread of Nationalism* (London & New York: Verso, 1983).

COLLINGWOOD, R. G., *The Principles of Art* (Oxford: Clarendon Press, 1938).

—— *An Autobiography* (Oxford: Clarendon Press, 1939).

—— *An Essay on Metaphysics* (Oxford: Clarendon Press, 1940). Later edn. with addit. material, 1998.

—— *The Idea of History* (Oxford: Clarendon Press, 1946). Later edn. with addit. material, 1993.

CONNERTON, PAUL, *How Societies Remember* (Cambridge: Cambridge University Press, 1989).

DONALD, MERLIN, *A Mind so Rare: The Evolution of Human Consciousness* (New York & London: Norton, 2001).

DUNBAR, ROBIN, *Grooming, Gossip, and the Evolution of Language* (London: Faber & Faber, 1996).

—— KNIGHT, C., and POWER, C. (eds.), *The Evolution of Culture* (Edinburgh: Edinburgh University Press, 1999).

EAGLETON, TERRY, *The Illusions of Postmodernism* (Oxford: Blackwell, 1996).

FOLEY, ROBERT, *Humans before Humanity: An Evolutionary Perspective* (Oxford: Blackwell, 1995).

FIUMARA, G. C., *The Other Side of Language: A Philosophy of Listening* (London: Routledge, 1990).

GOULD, STEPHEN JAY, *The Mismeasure of Man*, revised and expanded edn. (Harmondsworth: Penguin, 1997).

GREENHALGH, SUSAN (ed.), *Situating Fertility: Anthropology and Demographic Inquiry* (Cambridge: Cambridge University Press, 1995).

HARVEY, DAVID, *The Condition of Postmodernity: An Enquiry into the Origins of Cultural Change* (Oxford: Blackwell, 1989).

—— *Spaces of Hope* (Berkeley & Los Angeles: University of California Press, 2000).

HOBSBAWM, ERIC J., and RANGER, T. O. (eds.), *The Invention of Tradition* (Cambridge: Cambridge University Press, 1983).

HUIZINGA, J., *Homo Ludens* [1938] (New York: Paladin, 1970).

JOHNSON, DOUGLAS H., *Nuer Prophets: A History of Prophecy from the Upper Nile in the Nineteenth and Twentieth Centuries* (Oxford: Clarendon Press, 1994).

LANGER, SUSANNE K., *Philosophy in a New Key* (Cambridge, Mass.: Harvard University Press, 1942).

—— *Feeling and Form: A Theory of Art* (London: Routledge & Kegan Paul, 1953).

LAVE, JEAN, *Cognition in Practice: Mind, Mathematics and Culture in Everyday Life* (Cambridge: Cambridge University Press, 1988).

MARX, KARL, *Pre-Capitalist Economic Formations*, trans. Jack Cohen, introd. Eric Hobsbawm (London: Lawrence & Wishart, 1964).

MERLEAU-PONTY, M., *Phenomenology of Perception*, trans. C. Smith (London and Henley: Routledge & Kegan Paul, 1962).

MITHEN, STEPHEN, *The Prehistory of the Mind: A Search for the Origins of Art, Religion and Science* (Phoenix Paperback, 1998; orig. pub. London: Thames & Hudson, 1996).

RIDLEY, MATT, *Genome: The Autobiography of a Species in 23 Chapters* (New York: HarperCollins, 1999).

SACKS, OLIVER, *Seeing Voices: A Journey into the World of the Deaf* (Berkeley & Los Angeles: University of California Press, 1989; London: Pan Books, 1990).

SAID, EDWARD, *Orientalism* (London: Routledge & Kegan Paul, 1978).

STEINER, GEORGE, *After Babel: Aspects of Language and Translation* (London: Oxford University Press, 1975).

THOMAS, KEITH, *Religion and the Decline of Magic* (London: Weidenfeld & Nicolson, 1971).

WARNOCK, M., *Imagination and Time* (Oxford: Blackwell, 1994).

—— *Making Babies: Is there a Right to have Children?* (Oxford: Oxford University Press, 2002).

WINCH, P., *The Idea of a Social Science, and its Relation to Philosophy* (London: Routledge & Kegan Paul, 1958).

Index

Note: chapter page numbers are **emboldened**

Abbink, Jon 341
Aborigines, Australian xx, 13–14, 305
  classifications and categories 58, 139
  dance 85, 107, 121
  kinship and marriage 160, 167, 168, 172
  livelihood 215, 225, 335
  persons 200
abortion 200, 201, 264
Abram, Simone 338
Abu–Lughod, Lila 149
Acoma Pueblo (New Mexico) 59, 60, 252,
    253, 256
acting/enactment 10–11, 29–32, 103–5,
    106–7, 117–18, 245
  see also drama
action, qualities of xxi, 7–8, 11, 14, 17, 21,
    50, 55–6, 100, 110–12, 114, 184, 205–6
Addis Ababa 290
Adler, J. 316
adoption 173, 200, 264
Adowa, battle of 275
aesthetics 96–9, 155
affinity/in–lawship 161
Afghanistan 9, 170, 243
Africa xvii–xviii, 11
  classifications and categories 57, 62,
    63, 64; giving shape to time 68, 69, 70,
    71
  dance 76–8, 82–3, 93–7
  grand theory 19; culture 37, 40;
    genetics 24, 27, 31, 32; social science
    46–7, 49, 170–9
  history and religion 298, 303–4, 305
  kinship and marriage 159, 160, 167,
    169–79

livelihood 227, 234; home 214–16,
    218–19, 224, 225
  modern forms 243, 245, 249
  as origin of humanity 12, 27, 31
  peace and war 271–5 *passim*, 279–81;
    and states 284, 285, 290–4
  persons 190, 191, 192, 200–1
  ritual: as drama 103–4, 115; religion 123,
    125–33 *passim*, 135
  speech 143, 149–54
African Americans 80–1
Agaw (Ethiopia) 115
agency 97–9, 124–5; and structure 35–6
aggression, *see* violence
agnatic descent *see* patriliny
agriculture/farming 13, 37, 167, 214, 216,
    229–30
aid, humanitarian 293–4
Aijmer, G. 341
air travel 213, 245–6
Akatawa 101–3
Alaska *see* Inuit, Nunamiut
Algeria 215, 218–19
Allen, Nicholas J. 4
  classifications 53–4, 61, 307, 309, 315, 316;
    see also tetradic theory
  'dance of relatives' 84–5, 159–60, 319
  kinship and marriage 159–60, 163, 164,
    165, 172, 328
  persons 187, 331
Al-Shahi, Ahmed 133, 324
altruism 20, 300
  see also gift-giving
Amazon 10, 93, 198–9, 220–1, 271
American Anthropological Association 38

American Sign Language (ASL) 141
Americas, *see* Latin America; Native
    Americans; North America
Amharic 68, 290
Amselle, Jean-Loup 176, 330
anarcho-capitalists 258–9
Anderson, Benedict 146, 285, 327, 343
animals:
    animal/human divide 6, 21–2, 25, 32,
        142, 179, 194
    animal behaviour 21, 23
    classification 57–8, 62
    comparisons with 21, 22
    consciousness 194
    domain 57
    intelligent 208–9
    pangolin as anomalous 62
    prohibited for food 62–3
    representations of 83, 96
    rights 188
    sacrifice 57–8, 123
    see also masks; primates
L'Année Sociologique xix, 14, 42, 122, 167
anthropology
    as an academic subject 9, 11–12, 14–17,
        128
    applied 49–50, 189, 291–2
    cognitive 195, 202–10
    as a craft xviii
    cultural, *see* social anthropology
    early 163–4, 172, 281, 329, 330, 342
    general theory of 298
    and history 18, 49
    as a human science **297–306**
    visual 95–9
    see also colonialism; ethnography;
        social anthropology
'Apollonian' style 37
Appadurai, Arjun 337
Arabesk 288
Arabs 149, 289
    Arabic language 82, 129–30, 135
    see also Islam; Middle East
Arbib, Adrian ii, 66, 227
archaeology 11, 12, 15, 31–3, 65–7, 254, 298
    see also Collingwood

archive of social memory 101
Arctic 45, 47
    see also Inuit
Ardener, Edwin 4–5, 157, 201, 283, 286, 307,
        326, 334
Ardener, Shirley 157, 201, 210, 219, 279, 328,
        334, 336, 342
Aristotle xx, 53, 110
Arnhem Land 139
art 16, 29, 32, 36, 59, 78, 300, 302
    and dance 86–9, 98–9
    ethnography as 36–40
    grand theory 30, 32
    painting 86, 88, 97
    production and ways of seeing 95–9
    rock paintings 32
    see also dance; literature; music
artefacts, living things made into 57–8
artificial insemination (AIH and AID) 263,
        264–5, 267
Asad, Talal 124, 146, 312, 323, 324, 327
Asante, Kariamu Welsh 92, 318, 319
Asdiwal 107
Ashanti (Ghana) 175
Asia 4, 9, 12–13, 31, 286
    see also East Asia; South Asia; South-
        East Asia
Association of Social Anthropologists of
        the UK and the Commonwealth
        (ASA) xviii
asymmetrical exchange 161–2
asymmetrical time 71
atom of kinship 160–1, 162
Augé, Marc 233, 245–6, 299, 337, 338,
        345
Austen, Jane 24
Austin, J. L. 281, 342
Australia 12, 31, 217
    see also Aborigines
Austronesian languages 143
authority, language within and against
        154–5
Avatip (New Guinea) 202–3
Avebury 67
Azande (Zande people; central Africa) 19,
        46–7

dance 76–7
language 49, 129
persons 192
reasoning 19
ritual and religion 46–7, 125, 126

Baal (Mayday festival, Northumberland)
   113; *see also* Beltane
Bahrain 101
Bahr-el-Ghazal 293
Bakhtin, Mikhail xx, 146, 158
Baktaman (New Guinea) 35
Bali 97, 276–7
Banerjee, Mukulika 9, 308, 342
Banks, Marcus 97, 284, 320, 343
Bantu languages 143
Barber, Karin ix
  on *oriki* 149–54, 327
Barker, Eileen 10, 308
Barley, Nigel 39, 313
Barnard, Alan 308
Barnes, R. H. 162, 328, 329
Barotseland 171, 281
Barret, Louise 310, 311
Barth, Fredrik ix, 33–6, 38, 312
  holistic structures rejected 33–5
  livelihood 230, 337
  modern forms 258
  peace and war 283–4
  ritual 35, 136, 325
Barz, Gregory 94, 320
Basseri (Iran) 136
Basso, Keith 217, 336
Bath 246–8
Baumann, Gerd 82, 319
Béarn (Pyrenees) 225
Beattie, John xvii, xxiii, 314
Bedouin 48, 125
'behaviour', meaning of 4–5, 7
Beidelman, Tom O. 314
Belgium: colonialism 77, 214
Beltane 112, 322 (Scottish Mayday festival;
  see also Baal)
Bemba (Zambia) 216
Bender, Barbara 317
Benedict, Ruth 37, 75, 312

Beni-Ngoma (marching dance, East
  Africa) 77, 78, 279
Berlin, Brent 63, 316
Bernstein, R. J. xxiii
Beuchat, Henri 45, 47, 307, 314, 336
Bible 19, 62
  and kinship and marriage 107, 119,
    122–3, 126
  as source and inspiration 122–5, 126
bilingualism 139, 143
biology xix, xxiii, 11, 19, 43
  see also body; genetics
birth 10, 264–8
  assisted *see* NRTs
  illegitimacy 201, 202, 264
  and medicine 199–200
  prevented *see* abortion
  rites 45
  and social beginnings 183, 189, 194,
    198–202, 266, 297
  of sons desired 116
Blacking, John 93, 190, 320, 332
Bloch, Maurice 309
  classifications and categories 56–8, 70, 315
  dance 75, 318
  kinship and marriage 176–7, 330
  livelihood 221–2, 336
  peace and war 274, 281, 341, 342
  persons 183, 186, 331, 333
  ritual 108–9, 135, 321
Boas, Franz 37, 43, 231, 254
Boddy, Janice ix, 114, 115–18, 133, 169, 322
body 5, 11, 107, 120
  beginnings and endings *see* birth; death
  disabled 262
  language 78, 86, 88, 302
  metaphor 158
  owned by other *see* slavery
  perceptions of 189–93; food 190–1;
    illness and healing 183, 189, 191;
    'natural' behaviour 183, 184–5;
    women's 190
  rights over 262–3
  techniques du corps xviii; *see also under*
    Mauss
  see also dance; sight; sexuality

Bohannan, Laura 39, 313
Boissevain, Jeremy 339
book as ritual's original meaning 124
Born, Georgina 9, 308, 320
Borofsky, Robert 101–2, 321
Bourdieu, Pierre
    dance 79, 319
    history and religion 298
    kinship and marriage 169–70, 329, 330
    livelihood 215, 218, 219, 335, 336
    modern forms 239, 261, 338
    peace and war 286, 343
    ritual 110
    speech 146, 327
Bourdillon, Michael 323
Bouveresse, Jacques 307
Bowie, Fiona 119, 322
Boyer, Pascal 134–5, 325
Brady, I. 332
Brain, R. 314
brain size and structure 26–9
Brazil 93, 272
Bretons 286
bride/bridewealth see under marriage
Britain 304
    art and music 94, 96
    'British social anthropology', formation
        of 42–6
    classifications and categories 65–7
    colonialism 9, 49, 77, 113, 173; modern
        forms 242, 244; peace and war 272,
        274–5, 277–8, 287; 'ethnic' in 283–4
    grand theory 19, 24–5, 35, 49; culture
        36, 39, 40
    key questions 7, 11, 15, 16
    kinship and marriage 170, 174, 177
    livelihood 214, 215, 216–17, 225, 231
    modern forms 237, 239; market and
        person 257, 265; new spaces 240–9
        passim
    peace and war 272, 277–8, 283–4, 286,
        287
    persons 191
    ritual 101, 112–13, 121, 127
    Romans in 7, 248
    speech 141, 142

Brooks, James F. 235, 338, 339
Bruner, E. M. 332
Buckley, Peter 259, 340
Buddhism 135, 267
buildings
    religious 65–7, 248–9, 252–3
    see also house/home
built landscape see cities
bullfighting 273, 338
Burley, Justine 310
Burma 162
Burridge, Kenelm O. L. 165, 309, 329
Butterfield, J. 317
Buxton, Jean 64, 189, 316, 332

Calarco, Joe 104
Callan, Hilary 20–1, 310
Callaway, Helen 200, 308, 334
Callinicos, Alex 312
Calvinism 229, 235–6, 259
Cameroon 177, 201
Campbell, Alan 272, 341
Campbell, John 324
Canada 117–18
    see also North America
Cannell, F. 331
capitalism xxi, 168, 226, 228, 233, 237–9,
        246, 257ff
Caplan, Lionel 345
Caplan, Pat 191
Carlisle 248
Carrier, James 258, 259–60, 339, 345
Carrithers, M. 270, 340
Carruthers, P. 311
Carsten, Janet 169, 220, 329, 336
Carter, Paul 217, 336
Castaneda, C. 333
caste system 116, 168, 189, 226, 284
category, categories of understanding xx,
        56, 253
    see also classifications
Catholicism 222, 228
    modern forms 252–3, 255–6
    ritual 122, 125, 132
Cecil, Rosanne 201, 334
Celts 93, 98

Central Africa 62, 63, 96, 132, 214–15
  see also Azande
Central America see Latin America
centre, concept of 59, 67
  'central place' theory 248–9
  'exemplary centre' 249, 276
ceremony xix, xx, xxi, 33
  'ceremonial animal', humanity as
    xix–xx, 6–7, 17, 33, 299, 307
  ceremonial action, gesture 7, 14, 17, 114,
    257
  ceremonial significance of cities 246ff
  exchange, competition and
    consumption 107, 232, 251
  general aspect of human life and social
    practice xxi, 7, 100, 111, 136, 180,
    199–202, 300
  'grammar' of ceremony 92
  and power, large scale forms 224, 237
  'ceremonial arena' 213–94 see also
    livelihood; modern forms
  peace and war 274–6
  and violence 205–7, 279
  and the making of people see birth;
    kinship; persons; speech
  pattern see grand theory; key questions
  shape and rhythm see classifications;
    dance; drama; music; ritual
Chagga (Tanzania) 200–1
Chagnon, Napoleon 271, 341
Chamba (Nigeria and Cameroon) 177
Chamberlain, A. 311
Chapman, Malcolm 93, 259, 286, 340, 342
charity see philanthropy
children
  abused 24–5, 193
  adoption 173, 200, 264
  and cultural values 34–5, 196
  death of 200–1, 264
  games, play-acting 29, 87
  language acquisition 30, 57
  loss of parents 24
  'recognition' of (Mauss) 199–202
  rights of 9, 188
  sold in famines 234–5
  see also birth

China 191, 248, 289, 305
  classifications and categories 53, 60–1
Chomsky, Noam 145, 326
choreography xx, 5, 75ff, 91, 101
  of games and sports 243–4
  of kinship and marriage 156, 163
  as metaphor for social form in
    movement 8, 75, 91, 98, 300
  possible choreographies imagined, 101
  see also dance
Christianity xxii, 62, 222, 300–1
  attitude to 'pagans' 19, 119, 120–1
  livelihood and 228–9, 235–6
  missionary conversions 131–2, 204–5
  Orthodox 68, 290
  peace and war 289–90
  peculiarity of 'belief' 123
  persons and 187, 200, 204–7
  ritual 107, 119–25 passim, 128–9, 131–3,
    135
  work and exchange 228–9, 235–6
  see also Bible; Catholicism; Protestants
Christmas 255, 257, 266
  impossible to escape 71
chromosomes see genetics
Cinderella 24
Cioffi, Frank 307
circle, metaphor 161–2
circle dances 77, 80, 83, 84–5, 319
circumcision 109, 273
  female 116
cities 8, 91, 141, 202, 285, 339
  dance in 77, 96
  and drama 246; see also Santa Fe
  livelihood 224, 225
  modern forms 238–9, 245–6, 249–57
  public life 246–9
  regions around 248–9
  ritual 117–18
  see also popular culture, urban life
civilization, concept of 12, 14, 17, 23,
    118–19, 306
Clack, Brian 307
class and status 185
  and art/high culture 239
  and consumption 261, 269

class and status (*cont'd*)
  élites 239, 243, 244
  and music 93
classical music and nationalism 93–4
classifications and categories 53–73, 315–17
  cognition and culture 56–8
  primitive 58–61
  space, giving shape to 65–7
  things not fitting 62–3
  time, giving shape to 68–73
  see also colour; dualism; tetradic
    categories
Clastres, Pierre 169, 235, 329
Clifford, James 38, 224, 244–5, 312, 338
clocks 71, 72–3
cloning 264, 265, 266–7
codes 45
  communication (traffic lights) 145, 326
  see also signification
cognition 44, 56, 135
  cognitive anthropology 189, 195, 202–10
  cognitive psychology 56–7
  and culture 29, 30, 56–8
Cohen, Abner 133, 256–7, 324
Cohen, Anthony 195–6, 283–4, 333
Cohen, Sara 93
Cold War 289–90, 291, 294
Cole, Michael 317
collective representations *see*
  representation
Collingwood, R. G. xxii, xviii, 7
  classifications 55, 64, 314, 315, 316
  dance 86–7, 88, 90, 92, 98–9, 139, 319, 321
  grand theory 41, 46, 308
  history and religion 298, 301, 303, 304,
    345
  'scale of forms' 7; cf. 301, 304
Collins, Elizabeth F. 307, 322
Colombick, Leigh 104
colonialism xxi, 9, 12, 15, 101, 113, 173, 186
  and anthropology 11, 15, 43, 49–50, 128,
    170–2, 271–2, 277–8, 285, 305
  and dance 77, 97
  and kinship 170–9
  and livelihood 214
  missionary conversions 131–3

modern forms 242, 244
  and violence 222, 271–5, 277–8, 282–6
  see also post-colonial world
colours 31, 58, 63–5, 77, 117
Comaroff, Jean 286, 324, 343
commodification xxii, 260–1
communication 45, 238–9, 257
  communicative action 14
  non-verbal *see* dance; gestures
  oral *see* speech
  travel as 244–6
Comoros 133
comparison of social forms as basic to
    anthropology 4, 11, 17, 41, 43, 48, 53, 301
  'butterfly collecting' criticised (Leach)
    46
  difficulty of finding terminology for
    comparison 123–4
competitive feasting *see* potlach
competitive reproduction 24
Congo 49, 62, 96, 132, 192, 214–15
Connerton, Paul 110, 286–7, 322, 343
consciousness 33, 131, 139, 194–5
  abnormal 195
  development of 29–30
  distinctive 194–5
  and history 36, 50
  see also birth; persons
consumption
  and class 261, 269
  commodified xxii
  conspicuous 239
  as ritual 257, 261
  see also market
conversation *see under* speech
Cooley, Timothy 94, 320
Coote, Jeremy 96, 320
Copperbelt (Zambia) 77–8
Cornwall, A. 332
corroboree 85, 121
cosmology 13, 58–61, 65–8, 106–8, 126–7,
    221
Cosslett, T. 334
Coudyzer, Ruphin 104
Coulanges, Fustel de 246, 339
Counihan, Carole 191, 332

cousins 158–9, 164–5, 169, 174
couvade 198–9
Cowan, Jane 79–80, 318
crafts 59, 167–8, 256
Crawford, Peter 320
creation myth 60
Crete 286
Cronin, Helena 310
cross-reference 58
Cubism 252
culture xix, 11, 299
  and cognition 29, 30, 56–8
  collectivity of 28–9
  commoditized 244–6
  cultural anthropology *see* social
    anthropology
  'culture' as too fixed a concept 5, 143
  profusion of local 16–17
  cultural difference over-emphasized 5,
    17, 48, 203
  genetics and capacity for 25–33
  high *see* art; drama; literature;
    museums; music
  and nature 216–17; separate 193–4
  popular 239–44, 256–7, 288–9
  psychologically embedded 38
  relativism 36–40, 143
  subjectivity 37
  text as 145–6
  as thing in itself 38–9
  see also ethnography
Cumbria 67 *see also* Lake District
Cunnison, Ian 327
Curry, Oliver 310
Cushing, Frank ii, 39
Cyrenaica 48
Czechoslovakia 242

Dalby, Andrew 142, 326
Dalby, David 141, 326
Daly, Martin 24, 310
dance as a human phenomenon xx, 5, 6,
  32, **74–99**, 302, 318–20
  and art 86–9, 95–9, 103
  'daughters of the dance' (music, gesture
    etc.) 74–99, 92, 139

  as image of social form 85–92
  as image of social practice (Bourdieu)
    84
  and kinship 159–60, 163
  as 'mother of all languages'
    (Collingwood) 86, 92
  and possession 117
  and social form; ethnographies 75–83;
    prototypes 84–92
  and sport 243–4
  see also music and choreography
Daniel, Valentine 291, 344
Darfur 294
Darwin, Charles/Darwinism 24, 31, 298
  see also evolution
Davin, Dan 40, 313
Davis, John H. R. 132, 147, 231, 286, 317,
  324, 336, 337, 343
Dawkins, Richard 20, 22, 300, 310, 345
Dawson, A. 313
days of week, villages named after 68
De Coppet, Daniel 321
De Coulanges, Fustel 246, 339
De Heusch, Luc 177, 274, 341
De la Pradelle, Michèle 337
De Lara, Philippe 307
De Vargas, Diego 253
De Waal, Alex 293–4, 344
deafness 140, 203
death 69
  always wins 87
  of child or foetus 200–1, 264
  and persons 184, 197–8, 200–1, 207
  rites 45, 197
decolonisation 15–16, 50, 97, 170, 278,
  285
deixis 148
demographic transition 238
Descartes, René 148, 194–5, 203
descent 102, 173–4
  see also genetics; matriliny; patriliny
Descola, P. 336
development/underdevelopment,
  economic and social 15, 34, 50, 291
dialectics of gender and generation *see*
  kinship and marriage

dialects 139, 142
Dinka (Sudan) 96, 126–7, 130, 132, 189, 195
'Dionysian' style 37
discourse 146, 168, 284
    see also speech
disease *see* illness/disease
display 8, 77–9, 260–1
diversity of language 141, 142
dividuals and dyads 166–7
DNA *see under* genetics
domestic life *see* kinship; livelihood
Donald, Merlin 28–30, 298, 311
donation *see* gift-giving
Donham, Don
    kinship and marriage 178–9, 330
    livelihood 230–1, 337
    peace and war 286, 289, 343
Donnan, Hastings 287–8, 343, 344
Douglas, Mary 36
    classifications 62, 312, 314, 316
    livelihood 214, 335, 337
    persons 189, 190, 191, 331–2
    religion and ritual 122, 132, 323, 324
Downing, John 291
drama/theatre 10–11, 37, 57, 257
    city devoted to *see* Santa Fe
    city layout as 246
    grand theory 22, 29–30, 32
    social form as 100–18, 136
    basic plots concept 272; *see also* social
        memory
    travel as 244–5
    see also acting, ceremonial
Dravidian-type kinship and marriage
    164–5
dreams and trances 10, 36, 120, 193, 270,
    279
Dresch, Paul 331
    kinship and marriage 170, 329
    livelihood 224, 337
    peace and war 286, 342, 343
    ritual 123, 323
Driessen, Henk 343
dualism 185
    binary contrasts in the analysis of myth
    45

open to criticism 7
exchange of sisters 177
friendship groups 165
gender bifurcation 164–5
God/humankind 123
good/evil 61–2
Inuit seasonal morphology 223–4
nature and culture 21–2, 193–4, 216–17
opposed sides in Puka Puka ('Akatawa')
    101–3
pairs of eggs in myth 60
pas de deux 88–9
primal social form 84–5
right/left 45, 61–2
sacred/profane 100, 121–2, 125
society/individual etc. 182, 185, 203
Yolngu paired dialects 139
see also moieties, structuralism, tetradic
    theory
Dumézil, Georges 121
Dumont, Louis 47, 131, 309, 314, 316
    livelihood 226, 337
    peace and war 277, 342
Dunbar, Robin 27, 30, 310, 311
Duranti, Alessandro 326
Durkheim, Émile/Durkheimianism
    xviii, xix, xx
    classifications 53–61, 69, 160, 313,
        315
    dance 85, 319
    grand theory 41, 42–5, 46, 309
    history and religion 298, 300
    kinship and marriage 172
    language 145, 326
    livelihood 226, 227–8, 337
    modern forms 246, 267
    persons 181–2, 185, 196
    ritual 100, 122, 130–1
    school of 42–5
    social facts 13–14, 42, 75
    totemism 121–2

Eade, John 134, 325
Eagleton, Terry 155, 238, 297, 299, 344
Early Humans 12, 26–8, 31–2
    see also Neanderthals

East Asia 97, 248, 305
  classifications and categories 53, 60–1
  history and religion 289
  livelihood 219, 225
  peace and war 273, 286, 287
  persons 191, 204
Eastern Europe 225, 242
ecology, ecological movement 15, 47, 213
  time 69–70
  see also environment, forests, nature
economics, economists 18, 35, 209, 258–62
economic anthropology 226ff
Ecuador 10, 198–9
Egypt 39, 125
Ehret, Christopher 326
élites 50, 239, 243, 244
Ellen, Roy 316, 335
emigration *see* migration
embodiment xx, xxii, 79–80, 90, 243
emotion *see* feeling
empire *see* colonialism
empiricism 43, 47
enactment and space 107–10
endogamy *see under* kinship
Engels, Friedrich 176, 330
English language 158, 305
Enlightenment 282, 306
environment 55, 108, 207–8, 213–18, 229
  see also ecology, forests, nature
Epstein, A. L. 339
equality
  in exchange 233–8
  and freedom 234–5
  modern idea of 187
ethics xxi, 35, 110, 200, 263, 270
Ethiopia xvii, xviii, 230
  classifications and categories 64–5, 68,
    70
  dance 82–3
  kinship and marriage 159, 171, 177–8
  peace and war 273, 275, 278, 286, 289–92
  ritual 115, 127, 128–9, 135
ethnicity 246, 283–5
  modern essentialization of 251, 304
  and music, 93–5
  today's profusion of 'ethnicities' 17

ethnography/fieldwork xix, 9–10, 13, 18,
    42–4, 302
  as art 7, 36–40, 46
  of disaster 291–2
  and evidence 18–19
  major areas of *see* Asia; Australia; Latin
    America; North America; Pacific
  major groups mentioned *see* Aborigines;
    Azande; Dinka; Inuit; Maale; Nuer;
    Trobriand; Uduk
  see also social anthropology
Europe, Western
  classifications and categories 65–7
  grand theory 18–19, 35, 49; culture 36,
    37, 39, 40; genetics 24–5, 31–2
  key questions 9, 10–11, 15–16
  livelihood: home 214, 215, 216–17, 225;
    work and exchange 228, 231, 234
  modern forms 237; market and person
    262, 265, 268; new spaces 240–3, 244,
    245–9, 257
  peace and war 271, 272, 273, 275, 277–8,
    282–6, 288
  persons 186, 187, 188, 191, 192, 195, 202
  ritual: drama 101, 112–13; religion 121,
    127, 131, 132
  speech 141, 142
  see also colonialism
Evans-Pritchard, Sir Edward E. ix, xvii,
    xviii, xxiii, 11
  classifications 69, 312, 313, 314, 317
  dance 76–7
  grand theory 19, 34, 41, 44, 46–9, 309
  history 298, 303, 306
  kinship and marriage 173, 330
  livelihood 224
  peace and war 277, 290, 342
  persons 192, 332
  religion and ritual 119, 123, 125–6, 130,
    322, 323, 324
  teaching of *The Ancient City* 246
Evans-Pritchard, Deirdre 251, 256, 339
evolution 19, 23–33 *passim*, 298
  evolutionary psychology 24–6, 30, 157
  of 'peoples of world' 12–14; *see also*
    genetics; Modern Humans

exchange 54, 168–9
  asymmetrical 161–2
  'exchangeism' criticised 169, 235
  generalized 161–2
  holding back on 168–9
  reciprocal in marriage 163, 166–7, 177–8
  and work 227–8, 231–6
  see also gift-giving
exogamy see under kinship
exorcism see under spirits
experience 9, 13, 131ff, 189–90, 194–6
  see also phenomenology, feelings
explanation in the human/social sciences
  xx, 4, 5–7, 18, 298
eyesight see sight

Fabian, Johannes 69, 317
fair exchange 233–8
Fairhead James 335
family see kinship and marriage
famine 234–5, 293–4
Fardon, Richard 235, 312–13, 316
  kinship and marriage 176, 177, 329, 330
  peace and war 284, 343
Faris, James 95, 96, 145, 320
feelings 88, 90, 94, 131, 193ff, 203, 306, 273
  Ilongot 205–7
  sociology of 44, 101
Feld, Steven 10, 217, 308, 336
feminism 16, 37–8, 157, 190 see also women
Ferguson, Brian 271, 341
festivals 69, 71, 80–1, 87, 150, 252
  anniversaries 71–2
  and history 297–306, 344–5
  Carnival 80, 257
  fiesta 250–6
feuds 280–1
fiction and ethnography 39, 102, 116
  see also writing; novels
Fields, Karen 13
fieldwork see ethnography
'fight or flight' 184
Fiji (Melanesia) 196
film 9, 96–7, 107, 271, 273
Fincher, Terry 244
Fingarette, Herbert 110–11, 322

Finley, Moses 234, 338, 340
Finnegan, Ruth 94, 149, 238, 320, 338
fire as focus of ritual 58, 112–14, 255
Firth, Raymond 313, 337
Fiumara, C. G. 148, 327
Florence 191
Foley, Robert 26–7, 32, 308, 311
Foley, William A. 326
'folklore', folktales 24, 121
Fonteyn, Margot 89, 90, 187
food 6, 190–1
  forbidden 62–3
  protein deficiency 271
  taro as symbolic 222
football 93, 243, 338
  hooligans 273
forests, trees 15, 214, 216–18
Forde, Daryll 176, 214, 323, 330, 335
Forge, Anthony 320
Fortes, Meyer 48, 175, 323, 330
Foucault, Michel xix, 146, 193, 327, 333
four categories of kin 173
  sections in 'dance of relatives' 84–5,
    159–60, 163
  see also tetradic theory
Fox, James J. 307
Fox, Robin 175, 310, 328, 330, 340
fragmentation of anthropology xxi
  see also anthropology
Frake, Charles O. 217, 316, 336
France 9, 15, 19, 177, 305
  colonialism 222
  French school and formation of British
    social anthropology 42–6
  see also in particular Durkheim
  livelihood 214, 233
  modern forms 239, 245–6, 257
  peace and war 282, 286, 289
  persons 187, 202
  Revolution 187, 225, 234, 282, 289
Franciscans 252–3
Frankenberg, Ronald 338
Franklin, Sarah 9, 308, 309
Frazer, Sir James 6, 111–12, 120–1, 147, 277,
  307
free market see market

freedom
and equality 234–5
illusions of 35, 213, 129
rights and fundamental liberties 202,
236, 262–3
sexual 191–2
and slavery 109, 234
Freeman, D. 332
Freud, Sigmund 19, 163, 298, 329
friendship 165–7
frontiers 225, 253
of empire 15, 271–2, 282
living on 287–9
Fuchs, R. G. 334
functionalism 15, 43, 106
see also Malinowski; Radcliffe-Brown
fundamentalism, see religion
future of anthropology 304

Gable, Clark 140
Gambetta, Diego 35, 312
Gamble, Clive 309
games 4, 112
as fundamental to human life and
culture 3, 87, 159
conversation 139, 148
self-referential 244
theory of games 34
over property and wealth 235
political, global 306
see also sport
Gamk (Sudan) 10
Gay, John 317
Geertz, Clifford xix, xxiii, 38, 132, 45, 312,
332
history and religion 297
livelihood 217
modern forms 249
peace and war 276, 341, 344
ritual 132–3, 324
Gell, Alfred 10, 308, 329
classifications 70–1, 73, 312, 317
dance 74, 78, 92, 97–9, 318, 321
history and religion 298
livelihood 217–18, 336
art and language 97–9, 145

Gellner, Ernest 146, 285, 327, 343
gender 10, 15, 16, 37–8, 50, 117–18
and dance 77–8, 79–80
dialectics of see kinship and marriage
and exchange 228
and hierarchy 226–7
and power 23–4, 115, 175, 178
and space 218–20
and violence 273–4, 292–3
and wealth 226–7, 230
see also men; sexuality; women
generation, dialectics of see kinship and
marriage
genetics 18, 20–33, 194
DNA 22–5, 26, 264
gene modification 21–2
and modern forms 263, 264
and rational choice 36
selfish gene concept 20–2, 33
sociality and culture, capacity for 25–33
Germany
colonialism 77
gestures 86
modern forms 262, 268
music 94
peace and war 282, 287
gesture 86–8, 184, 274, 280, 302
symbolic gestures in war and resistance
274, 279–80
'virtual' gesture in dance (Langer) 88–9
Ghosh, Amitav 39, 313
Giddens, Anthony 35, 304, 312, 345
gift-giving 19, 45, 166–7, 231, 262
as charity 232, 235–6
see also exchange
Gillies, Eva 339
Gilsenan, Michael 133, 287, 324, 342, 343
Girard, René 274, 341
Gisu (Uganda) 192, 273–4
Glick, Joseph A. 317
globalization, global movements 50, 237,
288–9
flows 238–9
politics, gestures of 257
see also universality
Gluckman, Max 49–50, 171, 281, 330, 342

God
  in Nuer ethnography 48, 126–7, 130
  as all-powerful male 122
  name of 126, 127
  see also religion
Godelier, Maurice 163–4, 309, 329
Goffman, Erving 246, 339
Goodall, Jane 25, 311
Goodman, Roger 287, 343
Goody, Jack 146, 310, 327
Gouk, Penelope 94, 320
Gould, Stephen Jay 310, 331
Gow, Peter 329, 332
grammar see language; langue
  'grammar' applied by analogy 45, 92,
    95, 145
grand theory 15, **18–50**, 298, 309–15
  and music 95
  see also anthropology; culture; genetics;
    social science; utilitarianism
Granet, Marcel 61, 316
Greece, ancient 305
  classifications and categories 53, 55, 64,
    283
  dance 79–80, 87
  language 53, 54, 148–9, 283
  'nature' 55
  persons 186
  ritual and myth 107, 119, 120–1, 133
  tragedy 37
Green, Maia 191, 332
Grillo, Ralph 342
Grimes, Ronald 251, 252, 255, 256, 339
Grimshaw, Anna 96–7, 320
Groce, Nora Ellen 325
Gubser, Nick 207, 335
Gumuz (Ethiopia) 162, 177–8
Gusii (Kenya) 201

Habishiya, Luliya 118
habitus 79, 110, 213, 215, 221, 261
  see also house/home
Hadza (Tanzania) 234
Halbwachs, Maurice 321
Halls, W. D. 331, 340
Hann, Chris M. 337

Hanna, Judith 74, 318
Hannerz, Ulf 246, 339
happiness, search for see utilitarianism
Hardin, C. L. 316
Harman Parkhurst, T. 250
Harris, Clare 97, 320
Harris, Marvin 271, 341
Harrison, Simon 202–3, 334
Hart, Angela 192, 332
Hart, Keith 345
Harvey, David 238, 298, 338
Harvey, P. 332
Hasani bin Ismail 320
Hastrup, Kirsten 10–11, 308, 327
  livelihood 215, 335
  play-acting 103, 321
Hatay (Turkey) 288–9
Hatch, Elvin 271, 341
Hawking, Stephen W. 315
Hazzard-Gordon, Katrina 80–2, 318
headhunters see Ilongot
Heald, Suzette 192, 273, 328, 332, 341
health see illness; medicine/healing
hearing 10, 148, 203
Heelas, Paul 195, 267, 333, 340
Heidegger, Martin 193
Heisey, Adriel ix, 60
Hendry, Joy 219, 327, 336
heritage see museums
Herskovits, Melville J. 36–7, 312
Hertz, Robert 45, 69, 316, 317, 333
Herzfeld, Michael 148–9, 286, 327, 343
Heusch, Luc de 177, 274, 341
Hewett, Edgar Lee 254
hierarchy 110, 226, 277
  see also caste; kings
high culture see art; drama; museums;
    music
Hinduism 61, 278, 279
  caste system 116, 168, 189, 226, 284
Hirsch, Eric 217, 336
history 4, 7
  anthropology and 46–8, 50, 297–306
  historical time 50, 69, 72, 185–6
  and language 142, 143–4, 155, 299, 302
  nostalgia 261

oral 177
past and present linked 109–10, 172,
    203–4, 215, 252–6, 302–5
political 172
and religion **297–306**, 344–5
integral to social phenomena 5, 7, 48, 83
see also evolution; memory; museums;
    time
Hobbes, Thomas 270, 280
Hobsbawm, Eric 286, 313, 343
Hocart, A. M. 277, 342
Hockey, J. 313
Hodder, Ian 219, 336
Hoffman, Susanna M. 313, 344
'Hofriyat' (Sudan) 114–17
holism 58–9, 277–8
home *see* house/home
Homo sapiens sapiens see Modern Humans
homosexuality/lesbianism 192, 267
Hoskins, W. G. 214
house/home 213–25
    destroyed and rebuilt 222–3
    local political space 224–5
    longhouse 218–19, 220–1
    Maori meeting 99
    relational view of 223–4
    and settlements 218–19
    as social form 220–3
    see also kinship
Howe, Leo 276–7, 341
Howell, Signe 269–70, 340, 341
Hsu, Elisabeth 191, 332
Huaorani (Ecuador) 10, 198–9
Hubert, Henri 45, 69, 122–3, 313, 314, 317,
    322
Hughes-Freeland, Felicia 320
Hugh-Jones, Stephen 220, 221, 336
Hughte, Phil ii, ix, 39
Huizinga, Johan 87, 90, 239, 319, 338
human nature 15, 23, 25, 33, 135, 236, 269ff,
    294
human rights 15, 50, 188
human sciences 7–8, 14, 134–6, 181, 183,
    185
    anthropology as a human science 17,
    134–5, **297–306**

Humphrey, Caroline 107–8, 124–5, 321, 323
hunters and gatherers 12, 13, 58, 67, 71, 167,
    229, 234
hunting skills 26, 30–1, 207–9, 214
Husserl, Edmund 193
Hutchinson, Sharon 314, 344
Hymes, Dell 326

Iceland 215
    Sign Language 141
iconicity, phonological 217
'idea signs' (Mauss) 184
identity
    distinctive of humanity 13, 181, 202
    profusion of local identities 17
    complexity of 82, 210, 265
    modern essentialization of 182, 304
    genetic 25
    and music/sport 93–5, 243
    politics 188
    sexual 192–3
    self and other 49, 210, 301
    see also persons; self; individual
ideology and language 146
ideophones 217
illegitimacy 201, 202, 264
illness/disease 117, 183, 189, 191–2, 196
    see also medicine/healing
Ilongot (Philippines) 204–6, 272
immigration *see* migration
immune system 184
implicit understanding 56
incest 163, 193
index, work of art as (Gell) 98, 99
India 4, 24
    classifications and categories 61
    dance 93, 97
    kinship and marriage 164–5, 168, 172
    livelihood 226
    modern forms 252
    peace and war 272, 278–9, 284, 285, 287,
    293–4
    persons 189
    polo 243
    ritual and religion 116, 123, 131; *see also*
        Hinduism

individual as an abstract concept xix,
  xxii, 4, 8, 17, 33, 41, 71, 125, 179, 181–2,
  187–8, 210, 262–3
  see also persons
Indo-European languages and ideology 4,
  61, 87, 118, 121, 143
Indonesia 132, 162, 167
industry, industrial society 238ff
inequality in exchange 168, 233–8
infanticide 200, 201
infertility, remedying *see* NRTs
Ingessana (Sudan) 10
Ingold, Tim 194, 313, 320, 333, 336
initiation rites 63, 221
injustice xxii, 15, 50, 236
intelligence 27, 28, 71
  Inuit ideas of 207–9
International African Institute 40
International Sign Language 141
introspection, religious 119–20
Inuit (Alaska)
  ideas of intelligence 189, 207–9
  livelihood 223–4
Iran 133, 136
Iraq 134
Ireland 94–5, 134, 201
  Sign Language 141
Isfahan 133
Islam/Muslims 9, 38, 82, 279, 299
  history and religion 301, 305
  and modern forms 235, 252, 259
  ritual 116–17, 123, 125, 128–35
  see also Middle East
Israel 267–8
Italy 2, 86, 191, 248, 275, 305

Jains 124
Jamaica 201
James, Allison 313
James, Wendy xvii–xxiii, 312, 315, 317, 319, 327
  kinship and marriage 330, 331, 333
  peace and war 341, 343
  ritual 322, 324, 325
Japan 97, 204, 305
  livelihood 219, 225
  peace and war 273, 286, 287

Jayeola (Yoruba ancestor) 151, 153
Jebel Miri (Sudan) 82
Jedrej, C. 333
Jenkins, Tim 225, 233, 337
Johnson, Douglas H. xviii, 303, 314,
  345
  peace and war 341, 344
  religion and ritual 127, 130, 324
joking relationships 159
Jones, Steve 310
Jones, William 203–4
Judaism 62, 268
  matriliny and NRTs 267–8
  persons 187, 200
  religion and ritual 119, 121–4, 131
  see also Bible
Julius Caesar 103, 104
jural rules (customary law and political
  forms) 16, 46, 171–6
Just, Roger 133, 324, 342

Kabre (Togo) 172
Kabyle (Algeria) 215, 218–19
Kahn, Joel 259, 340
Kahn, Susan M. 340
Kalasha (Hindu Kush) 93
Kaluli (New Guinea) 10
Kamin, L. J. 310
Kant, Immanuel 53, 71, 73
Karl, Rebecca E. 305, 345
Kay, Paul 63, 316
Kearney, Michael 343
Kédang (Indonesia) 162
Keen, David 293, 344
Kenya 170, 219, 245, 292
key questions 3–17, 307–9
  modern research 3, 9–12
  overview, need for new 14–17
  see also anthropology; evolution;
    language; patterns; social form;
    sociality
Khilnani, Sunil 342
King, Barbara 311
kings
  divine 178–9, 277–8, 290
  killing 110, 289

ritual: of passage 44; royal bath 108–9;
    shown to people 111–12
and violence 47, 110, 114, 174–5, 289
kinship and marriage 8, 13, 16, 30, 45, 58,
    156–80, 328–30
    African perspective 170–9
    bride's lament 150–1
    bridewealth 24, 132, 173, 310
    ceremonially structured 30
    endogamy 158, 167–70, 174, 177–8, 186,
        233
    exogamy 157, 159–67, 174, 220
    and names 148
    and religion 132
    and ritual 116
    roles 29–30
    terminologies 158–60, 163–5
    and violence 277
    see also children; house/home;
        livelihood
Kissidougou (Sahara) 216
Knight, Chris 30–1, 163, 311, 322
knowledge, basis and forms of 14, 38,
    54–5, 56–8, 108, 133, 189
    commoditized 303
    and dance 79
    encyclopaedic 4
    ethnographic xxi, 18
    explicit/implicit 56
    'distinctively human' ways of knowing
        (Durkheim) 13
    historically and socially placed 46
    indigenous 214
    truths absolute or provisional, 300,
        303
    regimes of truth 124
    see also cognition; relativism; writing
Kohn, Tamara 286
Konso (Ethiopia) 68
Koran 122
Kramer, Cheryce 94
Krapf-Askari, Eva 339
Kroeber, Alfred xvii, xxiii
kula exchange 232
Kuper, Adam 313
Kwakiutl (North America) 186, 188, 235

La Fontaine, Jean 193, 333, 339
La Rue, Hélène 93
labour *see* work
Lahore 252
Laidlaw, James 107–8, 124–5, 321, 323
Lake District (England) 216, 245
Lambek, Michael xvii–xxiii, 190, 332
    ritual 109–10, 119, 133, 321, 322, 324
Lamphere, Louise 157, 328
land/property 167–8, 225
Landau, Misia 22, 310
landscape 67, 213–19
    built *see* cities
    and language 217–18
Langer, Suzanne 87–9, 90, 91, 298, 319
language xx–xxi, 4, 5, 11, 14, 25, 29–30, 305
    academic models 145–6
    anthropology 64, 93, 253
    authority, within and against 154–5
    biblical 126
    body 84, 86, 88, 302
    and ceremonial action distinct 110–14
    classifications and categories 54, 57, 68
    and dance 82, 86–7, 90, 92, 243–4
    development/acquisition 27, 28, 29, 32,
        45; by children 30, 57
    dialects 139, 142
    diversity 141, 142
    and ethnicity 283
    as form of life 40–1
    and history 142, 143–4, 155, 299, 302
    and kinship 158, 163–4
    and landscape 217–18
    marginality of words 101–3
    and music 149–54
    non-verbal *see* dance; gestures
    oral *see* speech
    peace and war 283, 290
    and primates 25, 28
    proverbs and riddles 49, 158
    public, market as 259–60
    redundant 6
    and ritual and religion 121, 129, 299, 302
    sign (for deaf) 139–41, 325
    and social life (*oriki*) 149–54, 327
    unrecorded 9–10

language (*cont'd*)
  violence rationalized by 279–80
  within and against authority 154–5
  writing 11, 14, 30, 146
  see also logocentrism, signification;
    song; speech
langue, la 144, 315
Latin America (South and Central) 9–10,
    12, 61, 93
  kinship and marriage 160, 165, 167,
    169–70, 172
  livelihood 220–1, 235
  modern forms 248, 253, 261, 268
  peace and war 270–2
  persons 198–9, 201
Lave, Jean 209, 335
law/legality 281
  and ethics 263
  and kinship and marriage 171, 172
  and persons 186, 188
  traditional and customary law 171–2,
    192
Layard, John 98
Leach, Edmund E. 70, 217, 314
  grand theory 46, 309
  kinship and marriage 162, 328
  ritual 107, 122, 323
  speech 145, 326
Leach, Melissa 292, 335, 344
League of Nations 234
learning, cumulative 194
Leavis, F. R. 311
Lebanon 287
legality *see* law
Lele (Congo basin) 62, 132, 214–15
LeVine, R. A. 334
Lévi-Strauss, Claude 15, 320
  classifications and categories 61, 316
  grand theory 43, 45–6, 47
  history and religion 298
  kinship and marriage 162, 175, 177, 328,
    329, 330; 'atom of kinship' 160–1, 164,
    172; endogamy 167, 168
  livelihood 220, 221
  oral narrative of 326, 327
  persons 190, 332

ritual 21, 106
  speech 145, 148
Lévy-Bruhl, Lucien 44
Lewis, Ioan M. 128, 279, 322, 324
Lewontin, R. C. 310
Liberia 71
Libya 286
Lienhardt, Peter 93, 101, 133, 320, 321, 324
Lienhardt, R. Godfrey xvii, xxiii, 308, 314
  and persons 189, 195, 332, 333
  and religion 126–7, 130, 132
light
  as abstract notion 68–9
  colour conflated with 65
  and darkness 208; *see also* sight
liminal stage in rites of passage 245–6
Lindisfarne, Nancy 332
linguistics 11, 58, 142, 144
  see also language
listening 148, 203
  silent participation in music 92–3
  see also hearing
literature 29
  novels 24, 39–40, 103
  oral literature 49
  poetry 49, 106, 147, 217, 300; *see also*
    fiction and ethnography, myth, song,
    writing
Littlejohn, J. 218, 336
Littleton, C. Scott 322
Littlewood, Roland 195, 292, 333, 344
livelihood **213–36**, 335–8
  see also house/home; kinship; work
Llewellyn, Melisa 97
Lock, Andrew 195, 333
logic
  of practice, rather than the word or
    mathematics (Bourdieu) 84
  of kinship and marriage 157–8, 159ff, 164
  of symbolism 63, 117
logocentrism 95, 145–6
  see also language
London 96, 141, 257
longhouse 218–19, 220–1
Love-Brown, Susan 258–9, 339
Lowry, L. S. 240, 241

Lozi (Zambia) 281
Lukes, Steven 36
Luzon (Philippines) 203–7
Lycett, John 310, 311
Lydall, Jean 327
Lynd, R. S. and H. M. 339
Lyons, John 326
Lyotard, J.-F. **289**

Maale (Ethiopia) 178–9, 230–1, 278,
    289–90
MacClancy, Jeremy 9, 191, 243, 308, 338
MacCormack, Carol 328
Macdonald, Sharon 286, 308, 343
MacDougall, David 97, 320
MacIntyre, Alistair xxiii
McKie, R. 309
McKinney, M. L. 310
McLenann, John F. 163, 329
Macleod, Donald 338
McNeill, W. H. 318
Madagascar 56, 108–10, 176–7, 221–02
Maffi, Luisa 316
Mafia 35
magic 46–7, 111, 126, 130, 279
    magical power of art and design 99
Mahajanga 110
Maine, Sir Henry 172, 281, 330, 342
Makonde (Tanzania) 227
Malaysia 270
Malekula (New Hebrides) 98–9
Malinowski, Bronislaw 19, 42–3, 106, 166,
    309
    livelihood 231
    peace and war 285
    persons 191–2, 332
Malkki, Liisa H. 291, 344
Mallery, Colonel Garrick 325
'Man the Toolmaker' 33, 87, 297
    'the Speechmaker' 33, 297
    'the Player' 87
    'the Wise' 87
Mandari 189
Manus (New Guinea) 37, 192
Maori (New Zealand) 99, 235
Marakwet (Kenya) 219

Marcus, George E. 38, 39, 312, 313
Marett, R. R. 323
marginality of words 101–3
market 35, 233–6, 258–61
    days 68
    entrepreneur not orientated to 259
    'Free Market' 258–9
    and person concept 262–8
Marquesans 99
marriage 24
    bride's lament 150–1
    bridewealth 24, 132, 173, 310
    'marrying in' 116, 158, 167–70, 174, 177–8,
        186, 233
    'marrying out' 157, 159–67, 174, 220
    polyandry 267
    polygyny 24
    see also kinship and marriage
Martha's Vineyard 140–1
Martin, Emily 328
Martinez, Dolores 320
Marx, Karl/Marxism xix, 15, 42, 50, 131,
    190, 298, 313, 324
    history and religion 298
    ideology and language 146, 230–1
    kinship and marriage 178, 179
    livelihood 226, 230–1, 233, 236
    theory 258
    peace and war 278, 289, 290
Masai (East Africa) 97
masks 18
    Avatip 203
    Congolese 96
    and costumes in dance depersonalizing
        (Langer) 89
    Fonteyn with 187
    as persona 186, 203, 262
    prehistoric 32
mathematics in everyday life 209–10
matriliny 19, 20, 32, 102–3, 225
    kinship and marriage 174, 175, 176
    modern forms 267–8
    persons 191–2
    ritual and 102, 129
    seven daughters of Eve 22–3
Matisse, Henri 98

Mau Mau (Kenya) 170
Mauss, Marcel xviii–xix, xx, xxiii, 4, 307
    classifications 54, 55, 58, 69; on
        primitive forms 58–61, 315
    dance 90, 319
    grand theory 43, 45, 46, 47, 309, 313–14
    history and religion 298, 303
    kinship and marriage 166
    livelihood 223–4, 231–2, 233, 235, 335,
        336, 337
    modern forms 263, 340
    persons 199, 331; *see also* triangle *below*
    ritual 122–3, 323
    'totality', *l'homme total* 85, 110, 160,
        182–4, 244
    techniques of body 79, 85–6, 183, 215
    triangle (organic, psychological, social)
        182–96, 202–3, 262
    see also body, perceptions of; exchange;
        gift-giving
Mayer, Philip 339
Mayotte (Comoros) 133
Mead, Margaret 37, 192, 312, 332
media 9, 16, 40, 243, 257, 288–9, 291, 293
medicine/healing 11, 190–1
    and childbirth 116–17, 199–200
    death defeated by 197
    and music 94
    and persons 183, 189, 190–1, 210
Meillassoux, Claude 230, 233, 337
Melanesia 19, 107
    dance 97, 98–9
    kinship and marriage 166–7, 170, 172,
        174, 178
    livelihood 225, 231, 232, 235
    persons 190, 191–2, 196
memes 22
memory 8, 29, 36, 57, 109, 133, 185–6
    and conversation 147
    everyday 107–10
    violence rationalized by 279–80
    see also history; social memory
men: social shaping of life and character
    competitive 202–3
    and dance 77–8, 80
    dominance as 'natural' 23–4, 175

and family 228
homicidal 273–4
and house 219
male bias in ethnographic writing 49
masculinity 192; and war 292
more stimulating lives 205–7
as pure/good 61–2
sharing pregnancy and birth 198–202
see also gender; patriliny
Menelik II, Emperor of Ethiopia 275
mental processes *see* cognition
Merina (Madagascar) 108–9, 176, 222
Merleau-Ponty, Maurice 98, 189, 193, 332,
    333
metaphors
    body 43, 63, 158
    choreography xx, 84
    circle 161–2
    colour 64, 65
    dance as metaphor for community 79
    environment, human/animal 21, 217
    kingdom 252
    machine 43
    metaphor and reality 61
    music (Lévi-Strauss on myth) 45
    of sight 95
Mexico 253, 288
Middle East 12, 34, 62, 94, 101, 186
    kinship and marriage 169–70, 173, 174
    language 82, 129, 149
    livelihood 224–5
    modern forms 248, 267–8
    peace and war 286, 287, 288
    ritual 101, 123, 124, 131, 133–4, 136
    see also Islam/Muslims
migration 12, 67, 129, 223–4, 246
    see also refugees
military
    armies and dance 77–8
    élite 243
    training 274
    see also violence and order; war
Mill, J. S. 35, 42, 312
Miller, Daniel 125, 257, 261, 323, 339
Mills, David 317
Milton Keynes 94

mimesis, mimetic action 29–30
  see also drama
mind 28–9, 99, 207–10
  and (self-) consciousness 193–6
Miri (Sudan) 82
missionary conversions 131–2, 195, 205–7,
  215, 252, 289–90
Mitchell, Clyde 77, 94, 318, 339
Mithen, Steven 27–8, 30, 57, 308–9, 311
mob, rumour as voice of 101
Moch, L. P. 334
mode of production 230–1
modern activities 9–12
modern forms **237–68**, 338–40
  modern person 187–8, 263
  modern and primitive compared 44
  modernity xxi–ii, 73, 125, 224, 245, 256,
    303–4; supermodernity 245
  see also market; new spaces
Modern Humans (*homo sapiens sapiens*)
  12, 26–7, 30–2
moieties 93, 95, 101–39, 160, 177, 224
  see also dualism
Monk, R. 322
Montagu, Ashley 270, 340
Montgomery, Heather 192, 332
moon 30–1, 72
Moonies 10, 279
Moore, Henrietta L. 157, 219, 309, 328, 335,
  336
Moore, Sally 323, 334
Moraes Farias, P. F. de 150, 152
moral idea of time 71
Morgan, L. H. 163–4, 329
Mormons 267
Morocco 133, 288
morphology, as concept of social form
  (Mauss) 4, 47, 100, 224
Morphy, Howard 97, 320, 325, 335
movement, social implications of 238–9
multilingualism 141, 143
Murphy, Richard 252
Mursi (Ethiopia) 64, 70
museums and heritage industry 16, 36,
  42, 99, 118, 119–20, 245, 249, 254, 257,
  269

music 9, 45, 74, 88, 300, 302
  and class 93
  and drama 103, 105
  instruments 76–7, 81, 86
  international appeal 288–9
  and language 74–5, 149–54
  making time 70
  and myth 45, 95
  and nationalism 93–4
  and new spaces 238, 245, 256
  and religion 81
  rhythm 85–6
  ubiquitous 92–5
  see also dance; song
Muslims *see* Islam/Muslims
Myerhoff, Barbara G. 323
myth 31, 33, 45, 102, 103–7, 147
  creation 60
  and language 145, 326
  and music 95
  and religion 120–1
  structured plots of 106–7

names 148, 199, 262
narratives 101–2, 126, 147
nations/nationalism *see* states
Native Americans 37, 256
  dance 75, 79–83, 96
  kinship and marriage 168, 235
  livelihood 232, 235
  modern forms 249, 251, 252–3
  persons 186, 188, 200
  sign language 139–40
  'wild' and 'tame' 272
  see also Latin America
natural selection *see* evolution
nature and culture 215–17
  separate 193–4
Navajo (North America) 96, 254, 256
Nazi Germany 287
Ndembu (Central Africa) 63
Neanderthals 12, 23, 28, 31–2
Needham, Claudia 317
Needham, Joseph 199–200
Needham, Rodney 6, 44, 123, 307, 308, 323,
  334

Needham, Rodney (*cont'd*)
  classifications 70, 313, 317
  kinship and marriage 161, 329
  ritual 123, 323
Netherlands 87, 277
New Age religion 323
New Guinea 10, 78, 135
  grand theory 34, 35, 37
  kinship and marriage 165–6
  livelihood 217–18
  peace and war 279–80
  persons 192, 202–3
New Hebrides (Vanuatu) 98–9
New Mexico/American South-West ii, 37,
  59–60, 114, 235, 245–56
New Orleans 38, 81
new spaces 238–57
  scale and movement 238–9
  sport 239–44, 257, 338
  see also cities; travel
New Tribes Mission 204
New York 103, 246
New Zealand 99, 235
Ngundeng (Nuer prophet) 130
Nietzsche, Friedrich 37
Nigeria 149–54, 177, 248
Nile Basin *see* North-East Africa
Nipo Strongheart (Native American
  Chief) 140
non-space/non-place 245–6
non-verbal communication *see* dance;
  gestures
non-violent resistance 279
Norfolk (England) 217
North Africa
  grand theory 39, 48
  kinship and marriage 169–70
  livelihood 215, 216, 218–19
  peace and war 286, 288
  ritual 125, 133
  see also North-East Africa
North America (*mainly* United States)
  xvii, xxi, 304
  civil rights 16, 130
  classifications and categories 53, 59–60
  dance 75, 79–83, 96, 105

grand theory 24–5, 36–9 *passim*, 43, 49
  key questions 10–12, 15, 16
  kinship and marriage 168, 177, 235
  livelihood 217, 225, 231–5 *passim*
  modern forms; market and person
    258–60, 265, 266–7; new spaces 245,
    246, 249–56
  peace and war 284, 286–8, 290
  persons 188, 191, 192, 204
  ritual 103–5, 107
  speech 140–1, 142, 144
  see also Native Americans; Canada, New
    Mexico/American South-West
North-East Africa xvii–xviii, 107
  classifications and categories 64–5, 68,
    70
  dance 82–3, 95
  grand theory 34, 47–9
  kinship and marriage 159, 171, 172, 173,
    177–8
  language 145
  livelihood 224
  modern forms 242, 244, 264
  peace and war 272–5 *passim*, 278, 280,
    286, 289–94 *passim*
  persons 189, 195
  religion 120, 123, 125–9 *passim*, 132, 133,
    135; *zar* cult 114–17
  see also Ethiopia; Sudan
nostalgia 15, 261
  see also feelings; history; memory;
    museums
Notting Hill Festival 257
novels 24, 39–40, 103
NRTs (new reproductive technologies)
  179, 263–8
  AID and AIH 263, 264–5, 267
  cloning 264, 265, 266–7
  surrogacy 265
Nuba (Sudan) 82, 95, 145
nuclear family, criticised as basic unit of
  society 159, 161
Nuer (Sudan) 19, 303
  classifications and categories 57, 69
  dance 96
  kinship and marriage 34, 48, 173

language 126–7, 130
livelihood 224
peace and war 47–8, 272, 280, 290
religion and ritual 48–9, 123, 125, 126,
  127, 135, 303
Nunamiut (Alaska) 207–8
Nureyev, Rudolf 89
Nyerere, Julius 104

objectivity, objectivism xxiii, 41–2
tainted 119
see also positivism
Oceania 96, 97
O'Hanlon, Michael 217, 279–80, 309, 336, 342
Ojibwa (North America) 121
Okazaki, Akira 10, 308
Okely, Judith 308
Okuku (Nigeria) 149–54
Oliver-Smith, Anthony 313, 344
Olympic Games 244
Oñate, Juan de 252, 256
onomatopoeia 217
Opie, Iona and Peter 319
oral communication see language; song;
  speech
'Orientalism' 39, 119
oriki verses of Yoruba 149–54, 327
Orthodox Christianity 68, 290
Ortner, Sherry 157, 328
Orwell, George 196
Oxfam 293

Pacific 143
see also Melanesia; Oceania; Polynesia
Padel, Felix 274, 276, 341
paganism concept 19, 119, 120–1
pain-avoidance see utilitarianism
Pakistan 9, 34, 252, 279
Palsson, G. 336
Papua New Guinea see New Guinea
paradoxes, enactable 106–7
Paris 202, 245–6
Parker, Sue T. 310
Parkes, Peter 93, 338
Parkin, David xviii, 107, 287, 313, 321, 343
Parkin, Frank 40

Parkin, Robert 328
parole, la 144, 315
see also speech
Parry, Jonathan P. 70
pastoralism, herding 13, 34, 67, 96, 167, 229
participant observation 94
pas de deux 88–9
Pashtuns (Pakistan) 279
past see history; memory; nostalgia
Pathans (Pakistan) 34
patriliny 173, 174–5, 186
patrilocality 176
patronage 239
patterns 3, 43–4, 45, 62, 99
internalized 37–8, 41, 215
of movement 179–80, 204
of modern large-scale society 237ff
quest for see grand theory; key
  questions
peace and war xxi, 269–94, 340–4
peaceful societies 269–70
peace-making 280–1
see also states; violence and order
Peirce, Charles S. 98
performance 49, 74, 76–83, 92–5, 103–7,
  149–54, 190, 251
persons xix, 4, 10, 181–210, 331–5
beginnings and endings see birth; death
as free agents 34
and market 262–8
personality 54, 58
private see social shaping
selves as part of a 'world of persons'
  (Collingwood) 87
self-consciousness and language 143
triangle see under Mauss
phenomenology 9, 19, 72, 120, 189, 193–4,
  196, 217
philanthropy/charity 94, 232–3, 235–6
Philippines 186, 203–7, 272
philosophy xxii, 7–8, 35, 44, 53, 154, 193,
  281, 304–5
task of 55–6
see also Collingwood; Langer;
  Wittgenstein etc.
photography 9, 96–7, 203, 273

Picasso, Pablo 96; *see also* Cubism
Pickering, W. S. F. 323
picturesque, search for *see* travel
pilgrimage 107, 133, 134
Piot, Charles 172, 330
Pitt Rivers, General Augustus 269
places
  idea of 215–17
  names of 148
Plains Indians 37, 75
play
  -acting *see* drama
  culture as 87
  see also games; sport
pleasure-seeking *see* utilitarianism
plots, structured *see* social memory; myth
Pocock, David xvii, xxiii, 189, 332
poetry 44, 49, 106, 147, 151–3, 155, 217, 300
political/politics 34, 47–8, 63, 278
  and anthropology, 40, 47–50
  expression in dance 77, 80–3, 114
  and drama 103
  history 172
  and ritual 108
  and space, house/home 224–6
  see also peace and war
Polynesia 37, 101–3, 192
Pompeii 248
popular culture 239–44, 256–7, 288–9
population
  control by infanticide 200, 201
  growth and movement 238–9
  see also persons
Port Sudan 105
Portugal 271
positivism xix, 43, 46, 154
possession *see under* spirits
post-colonial world 15–16, 50, 128ff, 188, 230
post-structuralism 304
postmodernism 18, 155, 257, 262, 302, 304, 306
potlach 232, 235
  pseudo- 256
Pottier, Johann 191
poverty xxii, 9
  see also inequality; exchange; slavery
Power, C. 311

power
  and ceremony 274–8
  and gender 23–4, 115, 175, 178
  lack of 115, 178, 279
  political 226, 278
  see also class and status; colonialism;
    kings; peace and war
practice, social 84, 101–3, 183
  embodied 243 *see also* habitus
Prague school 144
present time
  consciousness of 72
  present-day *see* modern forms
Price, David 313
priests 118
  see also religion
'primal' nature of ritual 124–5
primates
  carnivals 74
  language and 25, 28
  male bonding 32
  memory 29
  rights 188
  stressed 185
'primitive' as concept 11, 15, 119, 195, 301
  classifications 58–61
  and modern compared 44
production *see* livelihood
prophets 127, 130, 303
prohibited partners 158, 163
prostitution 192–3
Protestants 81, 229, 235–6, 259
  ethic 71, 131, 228–9, 324
prototypes of dance 84–92
proverbs and riddles 49, 158
psychology 19, 33, 298
  cognitive 56–7, 194
  cultural 38
  evolutionary 24, 26, 30, 157
  Merlin's contribution 28–30, 298, 311
  psychological anthropology *see*
    cognitive anthropology
  universal human and ritual 108–9, 135
Pueblo settlements, peoples 59, 60, 186,
  252, 253, 254
  see also Acoma, Zuñi

Puerto Ricans 103
puja rite 124
Puka Puka (Polynesia) 101–3
purity, personal 116–17
Pym, Barbara 40, 313
Pyrenees 225

Quakers 128, 259

race *see* ethnicity
Radcliffe-Brown, A. R. xviii, 328, 330
  dance 75–6, 318
  grand theory 42–3, 46, 47, 313
  peace and war 278
Raelian cult 266
Ranger, Terence 77, 286, 318, 343
Rappaport, Roy 124, 323
Rapport, Nigel 195, 333
rational choice theory *see* utilitarianism
rationality xxi, 118–19, 155, 195
Raum, O. F. 334
reason xxi, 3, 8, 13, 19, 47, 114, 187, 195
reasonableness 171
reciprocity 8, 166–7, 226
  see also exchange; gift-giving
'recognition' of new child (Mauss) 199
reductionism criticised xx, 3, 8, 12
refugees xviii, 9, 83, 129, 237, 290
relational view/idea of relationship 54, 157
  of house/home 223–4
  of the qualities of social life 41, 46, 49, 148
  see also classifications; kinship;
    sexuality; sociality
relativism, cultural/linguistic xxi, xxiii,
    36–40, 41, 47, 56, 69–70, 143, 187, 203,
    271
relativity 55, 73
religion xviii, xix, 13, 48, 118–36, 322–3
  'animism' 120
  of anthropologist 128–9, 135–6
  Buddhism 135, 267
  buildings 65–7, 248–9, 252–3
  Christian *see* Bible; Christianity
  and classifications 62
  ethnography, translation and personal
    commitment 125–7

fundamentalism xviii, 9, 116, 125, 128,
    303, 306
'human science' questions 134–6
Indian *see* Hinduism, Jains
introspection 119–20
and music 81, 126
myth 120–1
New Age 323
and philanthropy 235–6
post-colonial changes 128–9
and reason 13
and reproduction 267–8
sacred (contrast with profane or secular)
    100, 121–2, 125
'totemism' 121–2
world religions 125, 130–6
see also God; Islam/Muslims; Judaism;
    ritual
Renouvier, Charles 53–4
representation 7, 96–8, 155
  collective 14, 32, 45, 56, 69
  crisis of 38–9, 304
  spread of religious 135
  of violence xxi
reproduction
  biological 20–5, 263–8
  of families and social groups 3, 9, 156–8,
    159ff, 167ff, 179
  'artificial' *see* NRTs
  competitive 24
  see also birth; kinship; sexuality
revolutions, wars and displacements 289–94
Reynolds, Vernon 25, 74, 318
Rhees, Rush 307
rhythm 85–6, 184
  and language 149–54
  in space and time 8, 73, 223–4
Richards, Audrey 175, 330, 343
Richards, Jeffrey 338
Richards, Paul 344
Riches, David 273, 341
Ridley, Matt 4, 26, 184–5, 307, 311, 331
right/left dualism 45, 61–2
rights 50
  over body 262–3
  freedom 262

rights (*cont'd*)
  and livelihood 234–5
  and persons 187, 188
  and ritual 130
  sovereign 283
  traditional 225
ritual xx, 6, 7, 31, 37, **100–36**, 321–5
  classifications and categories 62–3
  consumption as 257, 261
  drama, social form as 100–18; *see also* social memory
  grammar of sacrifice 45
  as key term 124–5
  language and 145
  and political power 31, 108–9
  rites of passage 44–5; birth 44; circumcision 109, 116, 129, 273; death 45, 197; initiation 63, 221; liminal stage 245–6; passing time 70
  transcendence 277–8
  see also ceremony; religion
Rival, Laura 10, 198, 218, 308, 333
Robarchek, Clayton 270, 341
Robey, David 326
rock paintings 32
Romans 305
  in Britain 7, 46, 248
  cities 247–9
  language 64
  livelihood 215, 231, 235
  in North Africa 271
  and ownership 262
  persons 186, 188, 262, 264
  roads 215
Romeo and Juliet 32, 103, 104, 105
Rosaldo, Michelle 203–7 *passim*, 272, 328, 334, 335
Rosaldo, Renato 203, 204–5, 207, 272, 334
Rose, S. 310
Rouch, Jean 96
Rousseau, Jean-Jacques 270, 280
Ruel, Malcolm 123, 323
Ruggles, C. 317
Runciman, W. G. 27, 311

rumour as political current 9, 101, 118
Russia *see* Soviet Union
Rwanda 273, 292

Sacks, Oliver 140–1, 325
sacred *see* religion
sacrifice 122–3, 135
  animal 57–8, 123
  and fire 112–14
  and peace and war 274, 276
  ritual grammar of 45
  voluntary 126
Sadah (religious élite in Yemen) 186
Sahlins, Marshall 71, 229, 230, 317, 337
Said, Edward 312
Sakalava (Madagascar) 109–10
Sallnow, Michael 134, 325
Salt Lake City 129
Samburu (Kenya) 78
Samoa (Polynesia) 37, 192
Sandawe (Tanzania) 32
Sangowemi (Yoruba *oriki* improviser) 151–2
Santa Fe (New Mexico) 245, 246, 249–56
  Zozobra burnt 114, 255
Sapir, Edward 143
Sardinia 191
Saussure, Ferdinand de 315
'scale of forms' *see under* Collingwood
Scandinavia 231, 268
Scheper-Hughes, N. 333
Schlanger, Nathan 183, 331
Schubert, F. 111–12
Schumaker, Lyn 94
Sciama, Lydia 338
Scotland 112, 142, 245, 249, 286
Scott, James 279, 342
scripts/schemata 56–7
seasons 47, 69–70, 72, 223–4
Seddon, David 191
Seeger, A. 93, 320
seeing art 95–9
segmentary politics 47–9, 224, 290
selection *see* evolution
self 187, 197, 202–3, 210
  see also persons

self-interest *see* altruism; utilitarianism
selfish gene concept 20–2, 33
self-referentiality
  games 244
  names 148
  of the scholar 7–8
self-knowledge, awareness, consciousness
  8, 14, 143, 193–5
self-reflection/reflexivity 5, 103, 119, 121,
  131, 148, 189–90, 297
self-sufficiency 169, 235
  in marriage *see* endogamy
Semai Senoi (Malaysia) 270
semantic grid *see* dance *under* language
semiotics *see* signification
sexuality 10
  abusive 193
  and dance 77, 78, 84
  grand theory 19, 30–1, 37
  homosexuality/lesbianism 192, 267
  incest 163, 193
  marriage as management of 163, 179–80
  and persons 183, 191–3
  prostitution 192–3
  reproduction separated from *see* NRTs
  as right 262
Shakespeare, William 11, 103–5, 107, 194
shape *see* classifications
Sharp, D. W. 317
Shaw, Rosalind 333
Shelton, Anthony 320
Shilluk (Sudan) 224, 277
shopping as religion 125
sight 95–9, 183, 207–8, 217–18
  see also colours
sign language 139–41, 325
sign (semiotics) *see* signification
signification and signs 45, 46
  and classifications and categories 315
  and dance 85–6
  elements of significant action 6, 85–6,
    184
  and language 154
  and modern forms 261–2
  and speech 140–1
Silber, Ilana 232, 337

Silicon Valley 246
Simpson, Bob 267, 340
slavery and slave trade 82, 109, 262, 233–4,
  235, 276–7
  in ancient world 187–8
  and dance 80–2, 279
  and kinship 171–2, 176, 235
  and livelihood 233–4, 235
Smart, J. C. C. 311
Smith, Adam 213, 226, 259, 335
Smith, W. Robertson 130, 323
Smith Bowen, Elenore 39, 313
Sneath, David 336
Sobo, E. J. 334
social anthropology xvii, xviii, 4, 12
  British xviii, 11, 15, 16, 39, 41, 42–6
    see Douglas; Evans-Pritchard, etc.
  cultural (in North America) 11, 15,
    19, 37 *see* Boas; Benedict; Mead;
    Geertz
  functionalist 15 *see* Malinowski;
    Radcliffe-Brown
  origins *see* Boas; Durkheim; Mauss;
    Tylor; Weber
  philosophical *see* Collingwood
  structuralist *see* Bourdieu; Leach; Lévi-
    Strauss; Needham, Rodney
'social brain' hypothesis 27
social class *see* class
social constructionism xix
social facts, objective existence of 42
social form, forms 3–5, 8, 17, 31, 33, 41
  and dance 8
  ethnographies 75–83
  prototypes 84–92
  house/home as 220–3
  shape and rhythm in 3, 8, **53–136**
  see also classifications; dance; ritual;
    social shaping; sociality; action
social memory, structured plots and
  102–18
  everyday memory 107–10
  myths, language 106–7, 147
  stage plays 103–5
  Sudanese *zar* 114–18
social process 46–50

social science, variants of 40–50
  French school *see under* France
  social process, history and humanities
    46–50
social shaping of private self 179–80,
    202–10
  Avatip (New Guinea) 202–3
  Ilongot (Luzon) 203–7
  Inuit ideas of intelligence 207–8
  in Mauss's essay on the person 187
sociality xix, xxi, 5, 14, 21, 46
  and dance 75–6
  choreographed quality 8
  genetics and capacity for 25–33
  historical formations of 305
  history and religion 297–8
  implications of scale and movement
    238–9
  innate 270
  key questions 13, 17, 301
  and language 148ff
  social beginnings and birth 183, 189,
    194, 198–202, 266, 297
  social category *see* persons
  see also kinship; social form
'society' as too fixed a concept 5, 79, 181,
    200
sociobiology 20, 24, 36
socio-geography 238, 298, 338
sociolects (dialects) 139, 142
sociology, comparative, anthropology as
    43
  see also comparison of social forms
Sohos (Greece) 69–80
Somali/Somalia 128, 292
song 74–7, 82, 85, 93–488, 147, 288–9
  and language 149–54
  speech distilled out of 75
sound
  perception of 10, 74
  phonological symbolism 217–18
  of speech 144–5, 153
  and time 70, 73
South Africa 104, 286, 304
South America *see* Latin America

South Asia 4, 9, 162, 170, 243, 267
  see also India; Pakistan
South-East Asia 132
  kinship and marriage 162, 167
  livelihood 217–18
  peace and war 270, 272, 276–7
  persons 186, 192, 204
  see also New Guinea
sovereignty *see* states
Soviet Union/Russia 283, 287, 289, 290
space 65–7
  category 53, 54
  and enactment 107–10
  'formatted' 8, 67, 298
  giving shape to 8, 65–7, 218–19, 223–6,
    251
  orientation and 59
  see also new spaces
Spain 132
  modern forms 243; Spanish in Santa Fe
    252, 253, 256
  peace and war 273, 288
  persons 192, 195
species *see* classifications
speech xx–xxi, 7, **139–55**, 315, 325–8
  conversation 147, 148
  dialects 139, 142
  distilled out of song 75
  double-talk 49
  ethnographic history model 142
  logocentricity 95, 145–6
  multilingualism and bilingualism 139,
    141, 143
  myth, oral 146, 326
  narratives 147, 200
  oral histories 177
  oral narrative 326, 327
  oral text (*oriki*) 149–54, 327
  rumour 101
  speaker and listener 148–9
  thought-frameworks 142–4
  transition to 32
  universals, quest for 144–5
  see also language
Spencer, Herbert 269

Spencer, Paul 78, 318
Sperber, Dan 135, 325
spirits 120
    possession (and exorcism) 114–18, 120,
        133
sport 93, 102, 239–44
    gymnastics 84, 242
    modern forms 244, 257, 338
    symbolism of 239–40, 243
    violence in 273
Sri Lanka 267
stage plays 103–5
    see also drama
states, nations and nationalism 269, 278,
        282–94, 304
    and classical music 93–4
    new states 283
    revolutions, wars and displacements
        289–94
    unnecessary 19
    see also frontiers
status see class; class and status
Steiner, Franz 62, 316
Steiner, George 87, 147
stereotyping 270–1, 272
    see also ethnicity
Stocking, George 308
Stokes, Martin 93–4, 95, 288–9, 320, 338, 344
stone circles 65–7
Stonehenge 66–7
Strathern, Andrew 190, 332
Strathern, Marilyn 235, 333, 338
    kinship and marriage 157, 166, 328, 329
Strecker, Ivo 327
stress, body's reaction to 184–5
Stringer, Chris 309
structural linguistics 45, 58, 144
structuralism 15, 44, 47, 145, 169–70
    see also under social anthropology
structure and agency 35–6
Stuart, O. 338
subjectivity 16, 37, 189, 196
    in the anthropology of religion 48
    inter-subjectivity 10, 14, 196
    see also social shaping of private self

subsistence mode 215–16, 229–30
    see also agriculture; hunters and
        gatherers; pastoralism
Sudan xvii, xviii, 19, 303
    classifications and categories 64–5
    dance 82–3, 95
    grand theory 34, 47–9
    Khartoum University xvii, 128–30
    kinship and marriage 116–18, 159, 173
    language 145
    livelihood 224
    modern forms 242, 244, 264
    peace and war 129, 272, 280, 290–1,
        293–4
    persons 189, 195
    religion 120, 123, 125–9 passim, 132, 133,
        135; zar cult 114–17
Suya (Amazon) 93
Swahili (East Africa) 93
Swat Pathans (Pakistan) 34
Sykes, Bryan 22–3, 310
symbolism 7
    dance 77–8
    house 219–23
    sound 217–18
    sport 239–40, 243
syntax see langue
Syria 94, 288

Taiytu, Empress of Ethiopia 275
Tangu (New Guinea) 165–6
Tano language (North America) 253
Tanzania 32, 191, 200–1, 234
Taussig, Michael 309
Taylor, Lawrence 133–4, 325
technology 238–9, 257
    clocks 71–3
    military 269
    reproductive see NRTs
television 97, 114, 141, 243, 249, 270
Temne (West Africa) 218
tetradic theory 58–9, 159, 165, 172
    four sections in 'dance of relatives'
        84–5, 159–60, 163
    see also dualism

Tewa language (North America) 253
text, culture as 145–6
　see also language; signification
Thailand 192
theatre see ceremony; drama
thinking see cognition
Thomas, Nicholas 329
thought-frameworks 142–4, 146
Tibet, Tibetan diaspora 97
Tierney, Patrick 341
Tiger, Lionel 310, 340
time
　category 53, 54, 62
　giving shape to 68–73
　lunar cycle 30–1, 69, 108
　persons and concepts of 185–6
　and ritual 44
　seasons 47, 69–70, 72, 223–4
　and sound 70, 73
　see also history; present time
Togo 172
Tonkin, Elizabeth 327
tool-making 28, 33
Toren, Christina 181, 196, 331, 333
Toronto 117–18
'totality' see under Mauss
totemism 121–2, 126
tourism see under travel
trade 167–8, 171–2
　see also slavery
tradition/traditional, a concept to be
　　handled with care xxi, 9, 15, 16, 72,
　　116, 118, 121, 192, 202, 213, 215
　kingdoms 249, 276–7
　manipulated 102–3, 225, 229, 286–7
　rights 225
transformation 56–8
translation 13, 45, 48–9, 54, 100, 106–7,
　　126–7, 129–30, 141, 218, 230–1
　'translation of culture' 48
　essentially translatable kinds of cultural
　　expression 301
travel and tourism 9
　like theatre-going 244–6
　see also Santa Fe
trees see under forests

Trobriand Islanders (Melanesia) 19, 191–2,
　231, 232, 305
trust 35, 123
truths see under knowledge; relativism
Tshidi (South Africa) 286
Tswana (Botswana) 104
Tukanoans (Amazon) 220–1
Turkey 93–4, 243, 288–9, 338
Turner, Victor W. 44
　classifications 63, 64, 316
　history and religion 298
　modern forms 251, 339
　peace and war 291
　persons 189–90, 331, 332
Turton, David 64, 70, 316, 317, 320
Tylor, Edward B. 36, 119–20, 163, 312, 329

Uduk (Sudan/Ethiopia) xvii, xviii, 64–5,
　82, 128–9, 159, 326
Uganda 192, 273–4
Umeda (New Guinea) 10, 78, 217–18
unfair exchange 233–8
United Kingdom see Britain
United Nations 234, 293
United States see North America
universality
　of human condition, and anthropology
　　xxii
　linguistic 144–5
　rites of passage 44
　difficulty of finding universal rules 3
　time 73
　see also globalization
urban society, urbanization 94, 192, 224,
　237ff
　Lowry portraits of 240, 241
　see also cities
Urry, James 308
utilitarianism xix, xxii, 18–19, 26, 33–5, 42,
　155, 226, 229, 233–6, 300
　the 'old enemy' of anthropology 36

Valentine Daniel, E. 344
Van Gennep, Arnold 44, 107, 197, 313, 333
Vansina, Jan 147, 327
Vaughan, Megan 335

Veblen, T. 239
Venezuela 270–1, 272
Vidal de la Blache, Paul 214, 335
violence and order, theatres of xxi,
    269–81
  forgotten 253
  and gender 273–4, 292–3
  and human nature 269–72
  Ilongot as exemplars 204–6, 272
  kings, religious holism and ritual
    transcendence 277–8
  language and memory rationalizing
    279–80
  non-violent resistance 279
  in ritual and ceremony 111–12, 114–16,
    274–7
  and states xxii
  Yanomamo as exemplars 270–1, 273
  see also peace and war
visual anthropology 95–9
Volosinov, Valentin see under better known
    name Bakhtin
Vom Bruck, G. 331

Wahgi (New Guinea) 279–80
Waldren, Jacqueline 338
Wales 141, 249
Wallman, Sandra 33, 228
war xviii, 15, 75, 82, 120, 128, 204, 222, 253,
    272–3, 290–3, 305
  civil xviii, 82, 129, 289–92
  see also Cold War; military; violence
    and order; World Wars
Warmington, W. A. 334
Warnock, Mary 73, 266, 311–12, 317, 340
Waterhouse, J. 317
Watson, C. W. 327
Watson, Elizabeth 317
Watson, James L. 337
Watts, Ian 311
wealth and work 226–31
Weber, Max 42, 50, 313, 317
  livelihood 228–9, 235–6, 337
  ritual 131, 324
Welsch, Robert 309
Werbner, Pnina 338

Werbner, Richard 134, 291, 325, 344
West Africa 201, 248
  kinship and marriage 175, 176, 177
  speech 149–54
West Indies 256–7
West Side Story 103, 105
Westermarck, E. 200, 334
Wheatley, Paul 248–9, 339
Whitehead, H. 328
Whitehead, Neil 271, 341
Whitehouse, Harvey 135, 325, 333
Whorf, Benjamin 143
Wild, Larry 104
Williams, B. 311
Williams, Drid 74, 318
Willis, Roy 269–70, 340, 341
Wilson, Bryan 309
Wilson, Chris 253, 339
Wilson, Edmund O. 310
Wilson, Margo 24, 310
Wilson, Thomas 287–8, 343, 344
Winch, Peter 40–1, 42, 46, 313
witchcraft 5, 46–7, 201
Wittgenstein, Ludwig xix, xx, xxiii, 6–7,
    31, 298, 307
  'forms of life' 6, 40
  distinction between language and
    ceremonial action 110–14
  'forms of agreement' 92
  ritual 110–14, 322
women: social shaping of life and
    character 37, 61–2, 157, 185
  circumcision 116, 129
  and dance 79–80
  and ethnography 190
  in film 97
  houses and land 218–19, 225
  menstrual-lunar cycle
  power lacking 115, 178, 279
  reproductive life 30–1, 198–202
  rights/independence lacking 188
  and speech (oriki) 149–54
  spirit possession 114–18
  suttee 276
  violent 273, 292–3
  witchcraft accusations 47

women (*cont'd*)
  see also birth; feminism; kinship and
    marriage; matriliny
Woodburn, James 234, 338
Wordsworth, William 120, 147
work 94, 226–36, 297, 299
  and exchange 227–8, 231–6
  and wealth 226–31
World Wars
  First 42, 185
  Second 125, 204, 282, 291, 292–3
wrestling 243, 338
writing, textuality 14, 18, 30, 38–40, 57,
    129–30, 146, 302
  see also logocentrism
Yakö (West Africa) 176
Yanomamo (Venezuela) 270–1, 272

Yemen 123, 170, 186, 224–5, 286
Yolngu (Australia) 139
Yoruba (Nigeria) 149–54, 248
  oriki verses 149–54, 324, 327
Yurgaitis, Danial 104

Zafimaniry (Madagascar) 176–7, 221–2
Zambia 77–8, 216, 281
Zande people (central Africa) *see under*
    Azande
zar cult 114–17
Zeitlyn, David 148, 327
Zimbabwe 243
Zozobra burnt 114, 255
Zuni people, Pueblo (North America;
    older spelling Zuñi) ii, 37, 39, 75, 256
  classifications and categories 53, 59–60